D0709521

Hamlet's Castle

THE STUDY OF LITERATURE AS

A SOCIAL EXPERIENCE

The Dan Danciger Publication Series

Hamlet's Castle

THE STUDY OF LITERATURE AS

A SOCIAL EXPERIENCE

BY GORDON MILLS

UNIVERSITY OF TEXAS PRESS, AUSTIN & LONDON

Grateful acknowledgment is made for permission to quote from the following:
"Between Walls," from William Carlos Williams, *Collected Earlier Poems*.
Copyright © 1938 by New Directions Publishing Corp. Reprinted by permission of New Directions Publishing Corp.
"Daisy Fraser," from *Spoon River Anthology*, by Edgar Lee Masters, the Macmillan Co. Copyright © 1968. By permission of Mrs. Edgar Lee Masters.
"The Dry Salvages," from *Collected Poems 1909–1962*, by T. S. Eliot. Copyright © 1963. Reprinted by permission of Faber & Faber Ltd. Reprinted from *Four Quartets*, by permission of Harcourt Brace Jovanovich, Inc. Copyright © 1943.
"Existences" (p. 32), from *Someday, Maybe*, by William Stafford. Copyright © 1973 by William Stafford. By permission of Harper & Row, Publishers.
"The Jewel Stairs' Grievance," by Rihaku. From Ezra Pound, *Personae*. Copyright © 1926 by Ezra Pound. Reprinted by permission of New Directions Publishing Corp. Reprinted by permission of Faber & Faber Ltd. from *Collected Shorter Poems*, by Ezra Pound. Copyright © 1952.
"Lethe" and "Oread," from H.D. (Hilda Doolittle), *Collected Poems*. Copyright © 1925, 1953 by Norman Holmes Pearson. Reprinted by permission of New Directions Publishing Corp. for Norman Holmes Pearson.
"Logical Gap and Paradox," by Gordon Mills, of which Chapter 8 is a revision, from *The Southern Review* 3, no. 2, n.s. (April [Spring] 1967): 479–495. Copyright © 1967.
"Magi," from *Crossing the Water*, by Sylvia Plath. Copyright © 1971 by Ted Hughes. Reprinted by permission of Faber & Faber Ltd. and Harper & Row, Publishers.
"The Man in the Dead Machine," by Donald Hall, reprinted by permission of Curtis Brown, Ltd., 60 E. 56th St., New York, N.Y. 10022. Copyright © 1966 by Donald Hall (originally appeared in the *New Yorker* magazine).
"On a Marsh Road: Winter Nightfall," from *Collected Poems*, by Ford Madox Ford, by permission of Martin Secker & Warburg Ltd. Copyright © 1916.
"Perception of an Object," from *The Complete Poems of Emily Dickinson*, ed. Thomas H. Johnson, by permission of Little, Brown & Co. Copyright © 1914, 1942 by Martha Dickinson Bianchi.
"Provide, Provide" and "Stopping by Woods on a Snowy Evening," from *The Poetry of Robert Frost*, ed. Edward Connery Lathem. Copyright © 1923, 1969 by Holt, Rinehart & Winston. Copyright © 1936, 1951 by Robert Frost. Copyright © 1964 by Lesley Frost Ballantine. Reprinted by permission of Holt, Rinehart & Winston, Publishers, and the Estate of Robert Frost.
"Reason," from *New Poems*, by Pablo Neruda. Reprinted by permission of Grove Press, Inc. Copyright © 1972 by Grove Press, Inc.; English texts copyright © 1972 by Ben Belitt. Reprinted by permission of Carmen Balcells, Agencia Literaria, in representation of the Heirs of Pablo Neruda. Copyright © 1969 by Pablo Neruda.
"A Refusal to Mourn the Death, by Fire, of a Child in London," from *The Poems of Dylan Thomas*. Copyright © 1946 by New Directions Publishing Corp. Reprinted by permission of New Directions Publishing Corp. and by permission of J. M. Dent & Sons, Ltd., and the Trustees for the Copyrights of the late Dylan Thomas.
"The Sun Romps in the Morning," by Genevieve Anderson. By permission of Genevieve Anderson.

Library of Congress Cataloging in Publication Data

Mills, Gordon H   1914–
  Hamlet's castle.
  (The Dan Danciger publication series)
  Includes bibliographical references and index.
  1. Criticism. 2. Books and reading. 3. Literature
and society. I. Title.
PN81.M53   809   76-8020
ISBN 0-292-73005-5

In the spring of the year 1924 the young German physicist Werner Heisenberg went on a walking tour with the great Niels Bohr in Denmark, Bohr's homeland. The following is Heisenberg's account of what Bohr said when they came to Kronberg Castle.

> Isn't it strange how this castle changes as soon as one imagines that Hamlet lived here? As scientists we believe that a castle consists only of stones, and admire the way the architect put them together. The stones, the green roof with its patina, the wood carvings in the church, constitute the whole castle. None of this should be changed by the fact that Hamlet lived here, and yet it is changed completely. Suddenly the walls and the ramparts speak a different language. The courtyard becomes an entire world, a dark corner reminds us of the darkness in the human soul, we hear Hamlet's "To be or not to be." Yet all we really know about Hamlet is that his name appears in a thirteenth-century chronicle. No one can prove that he really lived here. But everyone knows the questions Shakespeare had him ask, the human depths he was made to reveal, and so he too had to be found a place on earth, here in Kronberg.
>
> —Werner Heisenberg,
> *Physics and Beyond*, p. 51

CONTENTS

ACKNOWLEDGMENTS

Many people have assisted me generously in my work on this book and I want to thank them here. For time free from teaching duties I am indebted to Dean Stanley Werbow, to W. Rea Keast, chairman of the Department of English, and to the members of the Executive Committee of the Department of English of the University of Texas at Austin. I acknowledge this support with a very special sense of gratitude because it was given voluntarily.

The manuscript was read in its entirety by the following people: Alan W. Friedman, to whom I am particularly indebted for repeated advice and assistance; Austin Gleeson, who was very helpful in his review of what I have ventured to say about physics; Anthony Hilfer, whose informed perception of theoretical issues led to a good deal of needed revision; Neill Megaw, who revealed new perspectives in problems of mutual interest; W. O. S. Sutherland, Jr., who is the real author of many insights claimed in these pages; and John A. Walter, on whose advice I have often relied, here as in the past. C. L. Cline read a portion of the manuscript and provided encouragement which was as important to this work as to much other work I have done. I shrink from the thought of how much better this book might have been had I known how to take full advantage of all the help I've been given.

I want to express an especial indebtedness to the memory of Dr. C. J. Lapp, who long ago opened a door for me through which I have here tried to take a step.

On the testimony of the editors, the typing of the manuscript by Mary and Roy Holley was done with that technical knowledge and skill which make editorial life easier.

Obligations for materials used, and for help with some specific problems, are noted below and in the text.

Finally, everyone will concur in my saying that by far my greatest single indebtedness is to Vody Mills, whose counsel and assistance with this book have been invaluable.

INTRODUCTION

Perhaps literature is created almost as much to be talked about as to please the solitary reader. A reader's discovery that someone else's response to a text has differed from his own can be dismaying, but often it is an occasion of pleasure and new understanding. In fact such experience is eagerly sought for its own sake—in reviews, critical studies, classrooms, and personal conversations. The character of such experience is the subject of this book.

The most obvious setting in which to observe how readers relate to one another while sharing the experience of a text is of course a classroom, and in much of what I have to say there will be either an implied or an explicit reference to a classroom. The meaning of "classroom," however, requires some thought. The word has a bad flavor. In one of his "metalogues" Gregory Bateson, as Daddy, tells Daughter that schoolteachers filled one-quarter of his brain with fog. And none of us has escaped; I am myself a schoolteacher and have participated in the process from both sides. Yet the passivity of the individual whose brain is being filled by somebody else is not limited to classrooms. What is the difference between hearing a lecture given to a large class in a university and reading a review of a book? I can think of some differences but I don't know how important they are. Gregory Bateson says another quarter of his brain was fogged by reading newspapers. The meaning of "classroom" changes considerably, however, when instead of designating a large lecture section the word is used to designate a group small enough to share in a discussion.

The classroom I have in mind in this book will be occupied by such a small group. Still, the important criterion is not the size of the group or the place in which it meets, but rather the idea of a reciprocal relationship; no one involved is merely passive. Yet I am not quite sure how passivity should be defined. Sometimes greatly gifted lecturers or reviewers or writers—like Gregory Bateson—so involve the hearer or reader that the experience of sitting silently and listening or reading scarcely seems passive at all. Nevertheless, my characteristic reference will be to a real room and a small group of people.

One of my concerns throughout this book will be the mood of uncertainty about their professional objectives which is just now so pervasive among teachers of literature. Many seem to feel

that their critical methodology is bankrupt and that they are
losing their integrity. In my opinion this anxiety is, in our present circumstances, natural but unnecessary. All any teacher
need do to restore his sense of purpose is observe what is right
in front of him and attend to the actual, vital interests of the
people he talks with and to. There is plenty of excitement about
literature. Our problem is merely to address this excitement in
terms that relate sensibly to it. And what more fascinating problem could anyone desire? A second problem often encountered
by teachers is, of course, what to say when talking with people
forced to confront literature without having any desire to do so.
As a problem to be pondered, this one is no less interesting than
the first. It must, however, be approached with a different set of
terms. As I hope will become convincingly evident, both these
problems—how to talk with people who are interested in literature and how to talk with those who are not—are representative of factors which play an important part in our culture as a
whole, not just in our academic life.

Despite the fact that the interests I have been describing are
centered in the classroom, this is not a book about teaching.
Apart from occasional suggestions in passing, nothing will be
found here concerning the best way to conduct a class. I do not
feel qualified to deal with a pedagogical subject. Instead, my
discussion will be centered on the experience of an individual
with a text and on the relationships of individuals to one another within what might be called the environment of a text.
These interests can be reduced to the abstract problem of relationships among individuals and perceptions, and sometimes we
will find it worthwhile to consider such a reduction, but for the
most part our subject will be real people and real books.

The subject matter of this book is in fact centered around
three fundamental issues: the relationship between a reader and
the illusional quality of literature, the relationship between a
reader and the meaning of a text, and the concept of social experience within the environment of a text. The first two of these
issues are both contributory to the third. To see, in principle,
what the concept of social experience within the environment
of a text means and how the other two issues noted are contributory to this concept, we might ponder some examples.

As the first, let us consider how the illusional quality of lit-

erature becomes involved in social experience. That is, how does
one individual's experience with the illusion created by literature affect another individual's experience with this illusion?
The instance that comes to my mind is an excerpt from a diary
written in the mid-nineteenth century by a young American
girl. I've forgotten where I saw this excerpt but it might have
been in Herbert Ross Brown's *The Sentimental Novel in America.* The girl wrote in her diary a description of an evening on
which her father read aloud from a novel—a sentimental
novel—to the other members of the large family group. After a
time he came to a very sad episode, and presently one of the
family, overcome by tears, rose and left the room. Soon another
was similarly overcome, and followed. And then others. Finally
only the one girl and the stern old father were left. In her diary
the girl recorded her embarrassment and distress over the fact
that she had been unable to cry.

Any experienced teacher has seen episodes of this type in the
classroom. Today the cause of the individual's embarrassment
and anxiety is not likely to be an inability to cry; incidents of
anxiety over feeling *different* are common, however.

The episode described in the girl's diary is at first glance no
more than an example of the fact that responses to the illusion
of literature do have a social dimension and that a reader may
indeed be dismayed by a difference between his own response
to a text and somebody else's. Yet on second thought there is an
additional element to consider. Apparently most of the family
members shared, or at least did succeed in sharing, the response
revealed by the first person to leave the room. There was, that
is to say, a communal response. On the other hand, it is conceivable that the real trouble of the girl who wrote the diary
was not that she couldn't cry but that she had a keener perception than the others did of what was actually in the novel. Perhaps she wasn't so easily dominated by the illusion of a merely
sentimental grief. Thus, inevitably, the question of meaning
returns. We might therefore now consider some instances of
how one individual's interpretation of meaning may affect another's.

There is good reason to believe that although the interpretation of the meaning of a text or other data is not determined by
cultural or social influences alone, these influences nevertheless

have an important role. Robert Merton has revealed particularly impressive evidence on this point with reference to the formation of opinion and even of creative thought in science, that seemingly least social of the scholarly disciplines. Surprisingly, he has shown that more often than not scientific discoveries are made independently by two or more individuals at the same time, frequently with resulting disputes over priority.[1] This simultaneity discounts the legend of the solitary thinker, though of course it does not reduce the importance of the thinking done by individuals. Further evidence of the social character of science is found in Thomas Kuhn's analysis of the way in which a theory achieves a dominant position through confirmation by consensus, sometimes even despite empirical evidence casting doubt upon the validity of the theory. Kuhn points out, for example, that when Lavoisier's theory of oxygen was first winning acceptance it could not explain the combustion of hydrogen as well as could the rival phlogiston theory.[2] Like the history of science, the history of literature reveals that commanding movements or developments emerge from an intense interaction among groups of people. A recent and still developing instance is the appearance of structuralism as a force in literary studies. It is through confirmation by such groups that a given idea, or a given way of interpreting either a set of physical phenomena or a text, achieves a dominant position. In Part Three, this idea will be discussed under the heading of the discrimination pool.

But what practical significance do these instances of the influence of one individual upon another have with respect to illusion and meaning? What actually happens in the reading of a literary work? Although a reader's relationship to a text, like a scientist's relationship to a theory, can be altered by encountering ways of viewing the text different from his own, literary studies don't usually pay much attention to this fact. Our primary interest is normally, and naturally, in the effect the author or the text has upon the reader, even though in what we *do* we are constantly trying to influence one another's relationship to a text. Henry James is an example, with his saying that the author creates the reader—or our contemporary Roland Barthes, who attributes changes in the reader directly to the text, regarding the author only as a kind of conduit through which language flows. The reader, for his part, is referred to as a "space" in which the writing is inscribed. It is within this space, Barthes says, rather than within the author's mind, that the elements of the work take on coherence. Yet the reader, Barthes concludes, is devoid of history or biography or psychology.[3] Apparently the reader is, as reader, only the coherent content of the writing.

To anyone pondering the practical influence of one reader upon another, Barthes's shift from author to text may not at first seem to change things very much. Reading a literary work from his point of view is nevertheless not the same kind of experience as reading it from James's. There is, for example, a different feeling about time, exactly as Barthes predicts. Obliged to disregard the author, the reader is more likely to see the writing as a timeless, continuing act than as an embodiment of an experience out of the past. It may take the reader a while to realize that the change he has undergone in his relationship to the text was caused not by either the author or the text itself but by that other reader, Roland Barthes. Apparently, then, readers are created by authors, texts, and other readers. Still, "created" appears too strong a word. The process of becoming a reader is so prolonged and complex that words like "modification" and "influence" seem more appropriate.

But now we come to another fundamental issue. Is the meaning of a text nothing more than what a group of people influence one another into accepting? Or do literary texts—at least the great ones—each have a single meaning which can be determined according to a set of rules? Since our subject is the relationships among readers and a text, this ancient puzzle cannot be ignored. Today this puzzle is often referred to, a bit curiously, as the problem of the validation of a text; discussion of the problem of proof or validation will be found in Part Two under the heading of the logical gap and in Part Three under the heading of validation.

Recently, however, Stanley Fish has suggested that this problem of the relative objectivity versus subjectivity involved in the interpretation of a text might be solved by the concept of an ideal reader. Such a reader would by definition be both sensitive enough and knowledgeable enough to respond appropriately to anything a text contained. At the same time, this ideal reader would be able to suppress by an act of will any potential response that was merely personal or idiosyncratic. He could therefore not be manipulated unawares by either the text or the author, and he would in addition even be free from the possibility of having his judgment warped by his own prejudices. A response to a text by a truly ideal reader would be adequate from every point of view. But there is this difficulty: in the real world there are no ideal readers. Anybody who tries to play the role of ideal reader is in danger of trusting his subjective judgment too far and making great blunders. Fish is well aware of this hazard. He replies that it is better to take as a model the notion of an ideal reader, subjective though such a model must be, than to pretend there is some way of attaining an absolute objectivity in the interpretation of a text. To abandon a subjective model, he argues, would make sense only if a better procedure were available.[4]

I see no way of avoiding the dilemma Fish has pointed out in regard to a choice between the subjective and the objective. Or, rather, I see but one way to avoid it. That way is to stop short of attempting an ultimate theoretical solution and to consider what happens in the real world. Two sentences will indicate the outer limits concerning what can be said on this issue of the subjective versus the objective. The first is that there is very little interest any more in claiming that the knowledge human beings possess can properly be described as absolute knowledge. The second is that with achievements of such magnitude as we see all around us, no one will argue that human knowledge is not, in some meaningful sense, real knowledge. Our problem in interpreting texts is to find some point of balance between the limits suggested by the two sentences above. What we seek is a way of making statements which are useful without being foolishly positive. It is my impression that all scholarly disciplines are now struggling toward this same point of balance between the subjective and the objective. I further suspect that the nature of this point of balance will increasingly be expressed in some version of the theory of probability. If you know something but have reservations about saying you know it absolutely, then you may wish to say you know it as a strong probability. For the interpretation of literary texts E. D. Hirsch's reasoning concerning determination of an author's most probable intention is particularly useful. This general problem will be discussed in Part Two.

Nevertheless, the unique cultural or social contribution of the literary classroom—as distinguished from such merely personal contributions as the heightening of pleasure in reading—does not lie in the interpretation of the abstract meaning of texts. Everybody seems to agree on this point. There are no abstract meanings in literary texts which cannot also be found in other kinds of texts. Consequently, the primary cultural value of literature must somehow be involved with the illusion of life that literature creates; and this principle, as will become apparent, holds even more strongly for the cultural value of the literary classroom as a social institution than it does for a literary work in the hands of a solitary reader. For example, there is no doubt that in the earlier part of its history the novel itself served as a source of information about social customs for readers who desired to improve their social status. Yet there is general agreement that the role of the literary classroom should not include making this sort of information available for its own sake. Admittedly, this agreement is often honored more in theory than in practice, but I wouldn't know where to turn for a modern defense of using the literary classroom to provide information— for its own sake—about social customs or about any other non-literary subject. What, then, are the special cultural values the literary classroom provides? What cultural functions justify the classroom's existence?

One answer to these questions appears to be found in classroom confrontations over the import of a text. In the first place, as we will see, a direct part of such confrontations is often the question of the reader's response to the illusional aspect of a work. Second, in such confrontations it becomes apparent that problems in human relationships may be related to a structural limitation. In the literary classroom the structural limitation immediately concerned is that of the work being studied, but the principle involved applies to social structures as well.

All works of art are limited. No work of art can be all works of art or embody all of human experience. To speak of the limitations in the structure of a great work of art is therefore not to deprecate the work but to define it. Disputes over the import or value of a work of art often arise, however, out of a failure to recognize the inherent limitations in the structure of the work. An example is seen in the intense differences of opinion encountered by the brilliant outburst of writing in English which followed the First World War. Works which are now regarded as monuments to man's search for understanding and compassion were denounced as sensational and devoid of taste. Evidently the new works suffered from the limitation that they could not simultaneously be what they were and articulate these ancient values of understanding and compassion in a form easily recognized by persons accustomed to older structures. The same sort of response occurred at the beginning of the Romantic movement. I will not comment on contemporary art, which so many of us realize is sensational and devoid of taste.

Like works of art, social structures have inherent limitations. No society, for example, can be both democratic and feudal at the same time. Each of these very different social structures offers certain opportunities and pleasures which are denied in the other. When a group of people choose one of these forms of society in preference to the other, they inevitably condemn themselves to certain denials and thus to certain tensions. It is generally acknowledged, to take an example, that the opportunity for upward mobility in a democratic society is not present in a feudal society. A limitation in the structure of feudal society is that it does not provide this opportunity. On the other hand, the tension created in a democratic society by the opportunity for upward mobility is not found in the feudal society either. The structure of democratic society is limited in that, unlike feudal society, it cannot provide the kind of stability which inhibits the appearance of this particular tension. The competition between two members of a democratic society over a given chance to move upward would evaporate were these two people suddenly transported into a feudal society. Once there, however, they would discover limitations in the feudal structure which could again precipitate them into conflict. To the best of my knowledge, no social structure has ever been devised which is free of tension, although some create more tension than others. Absence of structure also creates tension, as can be seen in the account Claude Lévi-Strauss gives of the Nambikwara.[5]

An inference concerning the cultural role of the literary classroom can thus be drawn from the fact that the limitations of both literary and social structures generate tensions. The classroom provides an environment in which a confrontation arising out of a structural problem can occur in a "distanced" mode. Participants in the confrontation directly experience the fact that disagreement may originate not only in personal incompatibility but also in the limitations of structure. They discover that structure can separate individuals from one another, as well as unite them. They also discover that an understanding of structure can in some degree free the individual from its power. And yet the classroom confrontation in which this experience occurs, while real, is not vital. It is a genuine social experience, but because it is centered within the environment of literature it is without material consequences. Its effects are intellectual and psychological.

In these considerations, therefore, we can discern a primary social contribution of the literary classroom. Without questioning the fact that other contributions are also made by the classroom, we can probably agree that the kind of confrontation described is one of the defining characteristics of a class regarded as an interacting group rather than as a passive audience. It is because the subject of this book is so much concerned with interactions among readers that the idea of confrontation has been given special emphasis. No suggestion of harshness or abrasiveness is intended in this term, only the common experience of differing responses to a given text. Nor should any inference be drawn to the effect that only confrontations are of interest; cooperative exploration of ideas is an important element in any well-functioning group. Nevertheless, in my own experience the greatest illuminations are achieved not through an uninterrupted flow of agreement but through unanticipated encounters with different ways of looking at a text.

Of course many confrontations arise out of differences between temperaments or personal philosophies rather than problems concerning the structure of a literary work. It is unlikely, for example, that a Marxist and a member of the John Birch Society would respond in the same way to a novel by Ayn Rand, even though they agreed on the meaning of the novel. In such cases, if communication is to continue and an understanding is to be reached, we are forced into consideration of what the reader is bringing to the work. Agreeing upon the meaning, we examine the differences between the readers. In regard to differences concerning the illusional aspect of the work this problem leads to the concept of fusion—that is, to the way in which a reader's prior experience fuses with the experience he undergoes while reading. In regard to abstract meaning, this problem leads to the concept of significance. The idea of fusion will be discussed in Part One and the idea of significance in Part Two.

Finally, it should be emphasized that the literary classroom is not an encounter group. The confrontations being discussed here are challenges directed not at the character of an individual but instead at the interpretation of a text. For such an exchange of opinion as this, a classroom offers certain advantages not present in other media or on other occasions. These opportunities arise from the fact that the classroom is both more and less structured than other possibilities. On the one hand, it is given structure by its recognized educational objectives and by the nature of the text being discussed. On the other, it provides the freedom of an immediate challenge to any opinion presented. The classroom thus encourages a very special kind of confrontation.

The foregoing description of the cultural role of the literary classroom is somewhat unusual, but the practice described is itself common. I think this practice has not been conceptualized heretofore because we have been predisposed to perceive the function of the classroom in a different way. We need only observe the confrontations constantly taking place to understand the practice.

In my opinion, it is in such terms as the preceding that the excitement literature continues to inspire can be sensibly addressed in the classroom. It is surely a mistake for teachers of literature to doubt the value of their professional purpose.

One limitation in the scope of what has been said must be mentioned. My comments have been directed chiefly to that kind of literature which creates an illusion of life, yet it is obvious that not all literature is devoted to such a purpose. In Part One, I will therefore make a distinction between that kind of literature which seeks to create an illusion and that which does not, and I will try to assess the significance of such a distinction.

In summary, my objective is a practical book about a rather theoretical subject. My subject is the nature of literary experience in the context of a group discussion. Although occasional references will be made to arts other than literature, these references will be only incidental—partly because of my lack of competence in other arts and partly to keep the scope of my subject within reasonable limits. The reader I have in mind is anyone interested in thinking about what happens when people compare their responses to a literary work.

To carry out the purposes which have been indicated, this book is divided into three principal parts. Part One is devoted to the illusional aspect of literature. Part Two, entitled "Abstractions," is concerned with how literature is structured by meaning. The final part, "Validation," relates the ideas developed in the preceding sections on illusion and meaning to the problem of judging the quality of a work and to the cultural role of the classroom. Throughout, an effort is made to approach problems in a way which would seem practical within that classroom discussion which has been taken as the reference point for the entire book. Despite this concern for practicality, I will try to keep in mind François Bordes's wise saying, in *A Tale of Two Caves*, that to do something seriously it is not necessary to do it gloomily.

Part One.

Semblance

In the most general sense, a semblance is an illusion. For example, when we go to a theater to see a play we understand all along that what we are about to perceive is an illusion, not actual life. "Semblance" is simply a name for this kind of illusion.

Semblance is the life of the dominant types of literature: fiction, drama, and much of poetry. Bereft of the power to present illusion, these types of literature would be reduced to tedious and largely pointless tracts. Conversely, bereft of the power to create and perceive semblance, the human mind would probably be incapable of anything more than a rudimentary culture; some say it would even cease to be mind. Regarded objectively as a capacity of the human intellect, semblance is a means, an instrument, for examining aspects of human experience not available for inspection in any other way. A literary classroom in which the power and importance of semblance were not recognized would be comparable to a course on radio circuitry in which no reference was made to electricity.

Many other terms besides semblance have been applied to the general experience with which we are concerned. Probably the most common has been "aesthetic emotion." Roger Fry calls it "alert passiveness" and "disinterested intensity of contemplation," Eliseo Vivas "intransitive rapt attention," John Dewey "aesthetic emotion" and "aesthetic quality," Morse Peckham "psychic insulation." Edward Bullough says the experience occurs when the work of art creates a "psychical distance" between the audience and the practical world, Michael Polanyi that the experience takes place in a "transnatural domain." Sartre refers to "analogue," Heidegger to "irrealization." In a great deal of American literary criticism the experience has been loosely implied by the word "concrete," usually in contradistinction to "abstract." Ezra Pound was fond of this distinction; Ernest Hemingway employed it in a famous passage in *A Farewell to Arms*. Of course the terms that have been mentioned are by no means all synonymous but the people represented would all agree they have a subject in common.

One important differentiation will be made among these terms later. Meanwhile, a natural ambiguity in the word "semblance" has already become apparent. Sometimes this word is used to refer to a subjective experience, sometimes to the source of the subjective experience. As with the word "illusion," semblance sometimes means what is perceived and sometimes the state of perceiving it. In certain aesthetic theories this distinction is important, but for our purposes it is only occasionally of consequence and I will usually not discriminate between the two meanings.

A crucial element in the concept of a semblance is the fact that a semblance is not merely a visual image. The concept always implies potentially the illusion of human experience in its totality. For example, when we read a novel we do not feel ourselves limited to visual observations of the protagonist; we experience the illusion that we are participating in his life.

Although the concept of semblance as the illusion perceived while watching a play or reading a story is thus reasonably clear, the question of the range of application of the idea is troublesome. Potentially, the range would seem to be bounded at one extreme by a child's open-mouthed absorption in a story and at the other by an adult's immersion in a complex abstract problem. Aestheticians disagree, however, as to whether the idea of semblance is meaningful throughout this range. The illusion associated with dramas and stories is presumably a fundamental mode of experience, but it is not clear in how wide a variety of other situations the same kind of illusion can be found. My purpose here will be to examine a few of the segments within the potential range of application of the idea of semblance and to consider ways in which the idea can be of practical value in the literary classroom.

The discussion will be organized around three principal topics. The first will be the composition of a semblance: what it is made of and how its parts relate to one another. The second will be a consideration of how the concept of a controlling purpose on the part of the author is related to the idea of semblance. The third will be an examination of evidences as to how a reader's relative maturity affects his perception of a semblance. Finally, three special problems of particular importance in the literary classroom will be discussed briefly.

How can the human imagination become deeply engrossed by, and care about, events it knows all the while are unreal? The only true answer to this question is, simply, by being intelligent and imaginative. It is just something human beings do, and no one knows why or how. Kant provided a helpful way of thinking about this human experience, however, in his twin concepts of free beauty and adherent beauty. Frank Lloyd Wright's familiar catchphrase, form follows function, is approximately an expression of what Kant meant by adherent beauty. That is, we judge a thing to be beautiful when its form perfectly embodies its purpose. As examples of adherent beauty, Kant mentions a church, and a horse. Possibly a more dramatic example for our own time would be an airplane. I'm sure Kant would say that in judging the beauty of an airplane we ask ourselves how well the form of the airplane serves the purpose of flight. But he also raises the question of how we judge the beauty of something having no apparent purpose at all. How, he asks, do you judge the decorative border on wallpaper? Or how do you judge the beauty of a flower? These are examples of free beauties. For our purposes, the question to ask is how you judge the beauty of the "unreal" events of a poem or story. These are all "beauties in themselves." To use Vivas's phrase in thinking about Kant's ideas we would say that people who are neither botanists nor florists look upon flowers with intransitive rapt attention. In contrast, if you are about to make a flight in an unfamiliar kind of airplane on a stormy day you may take a speculative transitive look at the thing. Kant believed only free beauty provides pure aesthetic pleasure—that is, pleasure unaffected by questions concerning the purpose of the object.

Later, Hegel presented a similar idea, but in the form of terminology we can use directly: material and semblance. Hegel pointed out three different ways of viewing an object. The first two ways both regard the object as simply material. One of these, the practical, thinks of how to use the object in the interest of practical desires, as a florist might regard a flower in terms of what he could sell it for. The second, the scientific, transmutes the object into universal scientific laws. Both of these first two ways may be said, in effect, to destroy the object in their use of it. That is, neither is interested in the object itself, but rather in some advantage to be derived from it. The third way of viewing an object or material is the aesthetic. Here, the object is accepted as it is. Its sensuous presence is valued just for itself and is exalted into a semblance. Hegel wrote:

> . . . in the sensuous aspect of a work of art, the mind seeks neither the concrete framework of matter, that empirically thorough completeness and development of the organism which desire demands, nor the universal and merely ideal thought. What it requires is sensuous presence, which, while not ceasing to be sensuous, is to be liberated from the apparatus of its merely material nature. And thus the sensuous in works of art is exalted to the rank of a mere *semblance* in comparison with the immediate existence of things in nature. [Italics in original.][1]

I will use the words "material" and "semblance" as Hegel uses them here, with one exception. As implied by the word "exalted," Hegel believed that the transformation of material into a semblance in art involves not only the creation of an illusion but also the spiritualization of the illusion or semblance. I will not enter into consideration of this latter idea.

In the passage quoted, Hegel provides us with two basic concepts. The first is that art is a semblance, or illusion. The second is that a semblance is created out of material nature, or matter. The idea of material in this context is difficult to define precisely. It is easy to think of physical objects as material, but a great deal of a novelist's subject matter seems quite immaterial. The motivations of an individual character, for example, hardly appear to have the same materiality as a house. Nevertheless, novelists probably spend more time writing about motives than about houses. This kind of problem is a familiar one in philosophy as well as literature, and philosophers have a comfortable tradition which can serve our purpose too. In philosophy, material is what there is to think about, as distinguished from the form taken by the thought. Comparably, we can say that in literature material is the stuff writers think about, even if it is as intangible as an idea or a feeling.

The practical literary significance of the concepts of semblance and material can be seen at once by putting them into the form of a different version of the simple question asked earlier. How can a person enjoy the semblance of a literary work without becoming absorbed in the materialistic aspect of it? Suppose, for example, a writer has produced a historical novel containing a dramatic account of the publication of the tenth *Federalist* essay. In other words, as material for his novel the writer has used, in a version of his own making, the real history of this event. A politically minded reader of the novel might find his attention strongly attracted to the relationship between the tenth *Federalist* and the one-man-one-vote issue recently in the news. Conceivably the reader could allow his interest in this relationship to overwhelm his interest in the novel itself. Should this happen, Hegel would say the reader is viewing the historical event as material, as a scientist would, oblivious to the "sensuous presence" of the event. The reader trying to find in this material a universal principle to use in analyzing the political problems of his own time is failing to perceive the material as a semblance. Kant would say he is failing to perceive the material as free beauty. Such failure would destroy the possibility of reading the novel as a literary work.

Nevertheless, the relationship of the tenth *Federalist* to the one-man-one-vote issue *is* interesting; whether or not to spend time on such matters in a group discussion of a literary work is often a puzzling question. People disagree about it. I myself feel that such background discussion, within certain limits, actually contributes to the perception of a semblance. In Part Two I will explain why I think so.

Our principal concern at the moment is the implication of Hegel's observation that a semblance is derived from material. Or—to turn the idea around—that an artist must have material out of which to create an illusion. Paintings can't be made without colors and a surface to put them on; novels can't be made without events and words to describe them with; dances can't be danced without bodies, motion, and sufficient space. Our consideration of the composition of a semblance begins with the raw material out of which it is made.

One additional term is helpful in a discussion of semblance: "element." An element is simply part of a semblance. A semblance is composed of elements. There is a convenience in having a special term for such a part, but it is merely a convenience. Susanne Langer, in whose work the terms semblance, element, and material take on a technical meaning, says, "Paints are materials, and so are the colors [the paints] have in the tube or on the palette; but the colors in a picture are elements."[2] The process of transforming material into an element in a semblance is easily demonstrated with a jigsaw puzzle. Suppose we have a puzzle depicting a landscape. It has been completely assembled except for the last piece, which happens to be a uniform blue. This piece will form part of the sky. If this piece is carried into another room and shown to someone who has not seen the assembled puzzle, it can represent nothing to him except material. He might guess it was to serve as part of anything from a lake to a portion of a woman's dress. When placed in the assembled puzzle, however, the piece is immediately transformed into an element in the semblance of a landscape. The transformation is created by the relationship of the piece to the other elements in the semblance.

The same kind of transformation can be observed with language. Consider, for example, the following sentence.

> The water was very cold.

Since we are concerned with a matter of feeling it is impossible to be sure, but probably most people would regard the sentence above as linguistic "material" in the simplest sense. In other words, it represents the linguistic equivalent of the piece of blue sky from the jigsaw puzzle. As with the puzzle, when the sentence is placed in the proper context it becomes an element in a semblance. This particular sentence was taken from the episode in *A Farewell to Arms* in which Lt. Frederic Henry plunges into the river to escape from the battle police.

> There were shots when I ran and shots when I came up the first time. I heard them when I was almost above water. There were no shots now. The piece of timber swung in the current and I held it with one hand. I looked at the bank. It seemed to be going by very fast. There was much wood in the stream. The water was very cold. We passed the brush of an island above the water.[3]

Inspection of this passage reveals that almost every sentence in it, when isolated, has the same flat, neutral quality of simple material as the one sentence singled out for special attention. The conversion of these materials into elements must therefore be effected by the character of their relationship to one another and to some controlling purpose, just as the piece of blue sky from the puzzle is transformed into an element only by its relationship to other elements in the finished picture.

Hemingway's style is a very special one, however. In the fiction of other writers the transformation of materials into elements is by no means always so evidently a direct function of the relationship of the sentences to one another. The problem this difference raises can again be expressed with reference to a picture. Suppose, instead of removing a piece of blue sky from a puzzle, we cut out of an oil painting a bit of canvas on which a human face appears. The face must have served as an element in the painting from which it was removed; and yet, if we isolate one of the many faces in, say, Raphael's *The School of Athens*, we see it has an intensity of its own, quite unlike the inertness of the patch of blue mentioned earlier. Similarly, it isn't difficult to find elements in the language of fiction that are not reduced to inert material by removal from their context. Here, for example, is a passage from Camus's *The Fall*. The narrator is just about to describe the laughter which affected him so strangely.

> You see, *cher monsieur*, it was a fine autumn evening, still warm in town and already damp over the Seine. Night was falling; the sky, still bright in the west, was darkening; the street lamps were glowing dimly. I was walking up the quays of the Left Bank toward the Ponts des Arts. The river was gleaming between the stalls of the secondhand booksellers. There were but a few people on the quays; Paris was already at dinner.[4]

Here, unlike the Hemingway passage, there are several phrases that isolation from the context does not altogether reduce to the inertness of simple material. In such lines as "the street lamps were glowing dimly" and "The river was gleaming," we sense a desire to communicate not only a material fact but also a feeling associated with the fact. Hemingway might have achieved somewhat the same effect, had he wanted to, by writing something like "The water was deathly cold." Or he might even have anticipated the more appropriate phrase used by Camus's narrator later on, when the narrator is brooding about the evening on which a young woman threw herself into the Seine: "the bitter water of my baptism."

We have now observed that some elements, like most of those in the Hemingway passage, are reduced to inert material by removal from their context, but that some others remain quite lively. A natural question, then, is whether these lively ones can be regarded as semblances in their own right. Suppose we return to Raphael's *The School of Athens* and this time snip out an entire human figure. We cannot deny that the figure is only one of the many elements in this painting, yet surely it deserves to be called a semblance in its own right. When isolated from the rest of the picture it creates an illusion of life. Next, let us detach the head and examine it in isolation from the rest of the figure. Same result. But the head was an element in the semblance constituted by the figure as a whole, which in turn was only an element in the complete painting. We are clearly entangled in a regression which can terminate only in absurdity, perhaps with a microscopic speck of paint.

Fortunately, this regression never forces itself upon us: we use the concepts of semblance and element as we need them. There is no harm in referring to one of the figures in *The School of Athens* as a semblance even though that figure is an element in the picture as a whole. We therefore conclude that a lively element such as one of these figures may indeed constitute a semblance, and that whether we want to think of it as a semblance rather than an element simply depends upon circumstances.

In spite of this relativism, there is one arbitrary definition which affords a helpful insight here—a definition of the smallest conceivable semblance. Let us say that the smallest possible semblance is one in which there is a barely discernible pattern or order created by the relationships among the elements. The advantage of this arbitrary definition is that it permits a distinction between mere vividness or intensity, such as a single color or a single note struck on a piano, and a significant relationship among elements created out of such materials. Looked at from the point of view of this arbitrary definition, a phrase like

Thomas Wolfe's "supper-silent highway," from *Of Time and the River*, is simply vivid material. In context, it becomes an element in a semblance. Frank Kermode is making essentially the same point when he describes the song "Some of These Days" as "a minimal work of art, the tiniest conceivable check to contingency."[5] By "check to contingency" he means the power of art to create order and meaning. In the three minutes of its duration, he says, the song creates a pattern.

The aptness of Kermode's particular choice of song underscores the risk of assuming that any given semblance is indivisible, that a part of the whole cannot stand as a semblance in its own right. "Some of These Days" belongs to a class of popular songs which are thirty-two bars in length, divided into four parts of eight bars each. Typically, three of these four parts simply repeat the same melody; the one part having a different melody is the third. The melody in the four parts can thus be represented as A, A, B, A. The third part, not unnaturally, is called the release. The atypical structure of "Some of These Days," however, is A^1, A^2, A^3, A^4. Had Kermode selected a song with a conventional structure, like Duke Ellington's "Solitude," we might have wondered whether one of the relatively undifferentiated A parts could not conceivably stand as a semblance in its own right, as a barely discernible pattern.

In the *Poetics* Aristotle makes the same point Kermode does, only from the opposite view. Aristotle declares that a very tiny creature cannot be beautiful because it is impossible to perceive the relationship of its parts to one another; there can be no perception of the order constituted by its body. Aristotle's principle, like Kermode's, appears to exclude from the province of beauty, and from the power of evoking a semblance, the brief, lively phrases quoted above.

The vividness of these phrases nevertheless calls attention to the intensity of the language of poetry and to the question of whether the mere intensity of the phrases comprising a brief poem might be sufficient to create a semblance. Narrative or anecdotal poetry such as *The Odyssey* and *Spoon River Anthology* affords a semblance, an illusion, like that of fiction and hence presents no special problem. It does, of course, offer kinds of pleasure not characteristic of prose, such as rhyme and meter, but these qualities need not alter the reader's perception of it as

essentially illusional. Lyric and meditative poetry, on the other
hand, is sometimes almost totally devoid of the capacity to create any experience that could reasonably be called an illusion.
Here is an example from Emily Dickinson.

> Perception of an Object costs
> Precise the Object's loss—
> Perception in itself a Gain
> Replying to its Price—
>
> The Object Absolute, is nought—
> Perception sets it fair
> And then upbraids a Perfectness
> That situates so far—[6]

Is it poetry at all?

With this question we come to the anticipated need for a differentiation among the terms initially associated with the concept of semblance. So far, we have been thinking of semblance
as an illusion that the real-life activities of living people are
being presented for our observation—an illusion given its clearest form in realistic dramas and films. But of course many other
illusional situations are actually found in both literature and
films. A writer may present the illusion of a landscape, as
Hardy does so powerfully in *The Return of the Native*; or a
writer may present the illusion of the feelings aroused in a character who is looking at a landscape; or he may present the illusion of the consciousness of a character who is engaged in solitary
abstract thought. Or, like Emily Dickinson, he may present the
abstract thought directly. But by the time we reach this last situation the idea of illusion or semblance is beginning to lose its
appropriateness. A kinship does exist between Hardy's landscape
and Dickinson's playful thinking; everyone is content to call
them both literature. In Dickinson's poem, however, it is difficult to find anything that could be called illusion or semblance,
as we have been using these terms. To name the kind of experience her poem evokes, a different term is needed. Vivas's
phrase "intransitive rapt attention" is strikingly appropriate
for just this experience, although this use of the phrase is
narrower than he intended.

We thus have an implicit polarity. At one extreme is the sem-

blance of the direct observation of the activity of conscious beings, as in a drama. At the other extreme is the related but different experience of becoming enraptured by the free beauty of
a verbal structure which implies very little about a concrete
physical world, the consciousness of a character, or the imagination of a specific author. The elements of the latter are created
in the same manner as the elements of a semblance.

Such a polarized way of thinking is helpful in understanding
the experience of literature, but unless its limitations are kept
in mind it can be a source of confusion too, like most polarities.
The chief hazard is the possibility of overlooking aspects of the
experience of literature that do not naturally show up along the
spectrum between the two poles. For example, which creates the
more intense illusion for a mature, intelligent reader—one of
the scenes of violence in Mickey Spillane's *Mike Hammer* or
the scene of the sermon on the green in George Eliot's *Adam
Bede*? It isn't an easy question to answer although most thoughtful readers apparently find Spillane's treatment of violence
somewhat repulsive. Any speculation about which scene creates
the more intense semblance brings up issues concerning the
reader's attitudes and perceptions. And these issues cannot be
understood in terms of the polarities of semblance and intransitive rapt attention. It is quite possible to be intensely gripped by
a scene which is at the same time repulsive. Socrates tells a story
of a man who, while walking outside the city, came upon a
corpse. He averted his eyes, but felt a strong desire to look. Finally he said to himself, "Very well, eyes, take thy fill of the
horrid sight!"

Our subject at the moment, however, is not the psychology of
responses to literature but the basic concept of a semblance and
how it is created. For this purpose the distinction between semblance and intransitive rapt attention is useful. If poetry must
create a semblance in the sense of an illusion of the observation
of either a real or a fantasy world, then Dickinson's poem is not
poetry. But if poetry may be known by its power to create intransitive rapt attention her poem is indeed poetry. In content
a common perceptual theory, in form this poem is language at
play. We are enraptured by the play of the words; we enjoy the
luxury of an intransitive gambol with language. Dickinson has
transformed the material of language into the elements of a very

special kind of pleasure. It is possible for such poetry to present ideas that are new and interesting, but more often than not the ideas are not new and we read for the pleasure of the language play only.

Still, a great deal of caution is needed in the use of such a phrase as "language play." When seemingly most playful, language can suddenly bite. Language, unlike mathematics, is never about nothing. Human experience is always in some sense involved. Familiar as the ideas in Dickinson's poem may be, her articulation may present them with a new force.

Such poetry as "Perception of an Object" shares with *The Odyssey* the language play, but it does not share the illusion. Most lyric poetry probably falls somewhere between these two extremes. An interesting example is Frost's "Stopping by Woods on a Snowy Evening," where the language is so simple that in spite of rhyme and meter the poem's power seems to reside in the reader's illusion, in his virtual experience of sharing with the poet the time and the place. But then in the famous last two lines there is the sudden intense language play, in the form of a repetition ("And miles to go before I sleep, / And miles to go before I sleep."[7]). The poem delights us by combining with an effective semblance these lines in which language is reveling in its power. Many combats have been, and are being, waged over the question of whether poetry must be fundamentally illusional or may be fundamentally only language play. I suppose everyone must have something to fight about.

Although the distinction between semblance and intransitive rapt attention required by this brief look at poetry proves helpful in a number of ways, it will have to be thought about again and finally modified. Now, however, I would like to turn to a last example of the general concept of materials, elements, and semblance; I would like to consider an instance in which there is a failure. What has gone wrong when materials refuse to be transformed into elements? I have chosen the simplest example I could think of—a passage from Horatio Alger's *The Young Acrobat*.

In this novel, a teen-age boy named Kit Watson has been driven out of his rightful home and is supporting himself as an acrobat in a small circus. He meets a girl named Evelyn, daughter of the mayor of a town the circus visits, and Kit and Evelyn have the following conversation. (Mr. Barlow is the owner and manager of the circus.)

> "What a nice old gentleman Mr. Barlow is," said Evelyn, in a low voice.
> "I have found him an excellent friend. He won't allow any of us to drink or gamble while we are in his employ."
> "I hope you wouldn't want to do either, Mr. Watson."
> "I have no disposition to do so. But, Miss Evelyn, I want to ask you a favor."
> "What is it? If it isn't anything very great, I may grant it."
> "Don't call me Mr. Watson."
> "What shall I call you, then?"
> "My friends call me Kit."
> "That's a nice name. Yes, I'll call you Kit."
> It will be seen that the two young people were getting on famously.[8]

No part of this passage is brilliant, but the author's concluding generalization—"It will be seen that the two young people were getting on famously"—undershines all the rest. This generalization seems so utterly unsuccessful that I dare to hope everyone will agree that here is a material which never made the leap into the form of an element. Everyone, that is, with the exception of those thousands of readers who enjoyed this novel. But as we look at the passage now, why does it seem so bad? Perhaps because it does not seem a valid statement in relationship to any conceivable significant purpose controlling the composition of the scene. This reasoning can be given perspective by assuming, for the moment, that Alger's purpose was different from what we know it to have been. If we look at the passage with the assumption that Alger was a subtle, sophisticated writer like Nathanael West and that *The Young Acrobat* was intended to be a parody of the same sort as West's *A Cool Million*, then we may feel that the concluding sentence in the passage quoted is effective. Its ironic import, in this case, would be that we *haven't* seen two young people getting along famously and, in fact, that we haven't even seen two young people but only two figures of straw. This purpose we could happily accept.

I have so far commented on the kind of element brought into being solely by the context in which it appears, on the kind that possesses an intensity of its own, on the shifting relationship between element and semblance, on a distinction between semblance and intransitive rapt attention, and on a failure to transform material into the elements of a semblance. One additional factor in the concept of an element should be mentioned here, perhaps the most important one of all from a practical point of view. This factor is the value of such a concept in clarifying the place of abstract ideas in a literary prose work and in providing a way of distinguishing between prose that is fiction and prose that is not.

Our first problem is to find an example of abstract thought which has been effectively transformed from material into an element in a semblance. The following passage from Bellow's *Mr. Sammler's Planet* will serve as a beginning.

> And the charm, the ebullient glamour, the almost unbearable agitation that came from being able to describe oneself as a twentieth-century American was available to all. To everyone who had eyes to read the papers or watch the television, to everyone who shared the collective ecstasies of news, crisis, power. To each according to his excitability. But perhaps it was an even deeper thing. Humankind watched and described itself in the very turns of its own destiny.[9]

There is much to think about in these words, and no doubt there is a good deal of room for disagreement. Take as just one possibility the sentence, "And the charm . . . was available to all." Many would disagree; I would disagree. Has Bellow then shattered the semblance of this portion of his novel? I don't think so. These words, from halfway through Chapter 2, actually represent an interior monolog, thoughts flowing through the mind of Mr. Sammler. Within the paragraph containing the sentences quoted above, Bellow three times forcibly directs the reader's attention to Mr. Sammler's consciousness: "This sort of experience, in Mr. Sammler's judgment. . . . He didn't even think that he himself qualified. . . . Daily at five or six a.m. Mr. Sammler woke up in Manhattan and tried to get a handle on the situation." In addition, there are other less explicit instances of such direction of the reader's attention within the paragraph.

What Bellow is offering in the passage quoted are not direct propositions but a characterization. Mr. Sammler's opinions may not be acceptable to everyone, but they are interesting because he is interesting and because his consciousness is the center of the illusion of life the novel constitutes. Granted a competent reader, the semblance need not be harmed by Mr. Sammler's abstractions. The real problem—granted the competent reader—is how much of this sort of thing can be sustained. Bellow lavishes care upon this problem, repeatedly calling the reader's attention to Mr. Sammler the person and thus continuously relating the import of the thought to the personality of the man. On the whole, my opinion is that the numerous passages of abstract thought in this novel successfully take their place as elements in the story.

Reasoning from this example, we may draw an obvious but useful distinction between prose that is fiction and prose that is not. Fiction is prose in which every part, including any passages of abstract thought, has been transformed into an element in a semblance.[10] This is a useful statement provided one caution is kept in mind. The sentence looks like, but is not, a definition of fiction. It is not enough to say fiction is prose which sustains a semblance, unless the concept of a semblance is qualified in ways not yet considered. And a further reservation to be noted, paradoxical though it may appear at the moment, is that the transformation of an abstraction into an element does not apparently preclude the reader's taking an interest in the soundness of the abstraction.

Let us now look at an example of an abstraction which is less clearly an intrusion by the author than in the passage from Alger, but more certainly the author's own voice than in the passage by Bellow. The passage below, from James's *The Wings of the Dove*, is taken from the scene in which Milly Theale, heiress to an immense fortune, is talking with Lord Mark at Mrs. Lowder's dinner party. Milly is seriously ill and does in fact die not many months later. Most of those present, like Lord Mark, are strangers to Milly, and she is just beginning to perceive something of the complex relationships among these people. In the following words, James is suggesting a connection be-

tween the swiftness of Milly's perceptions and the possibility
that she has not long to live.

> Nothing was so odd as that she should have to recognize
> so quickly in each of these glimpses of an instant the
> various signs of a relation; and this anomaly itself, had
> she had more time to give to it, might well, might al-
> most terribly have suggested to her that her doom was
> to live fast. It was queerly a question of the short run
> and the consciousness proportionately crowded.[11]

The abstraction most clearly evident is the concluding sentence:
"It was . . . a question of the short run . . ." James is referring to
the possibility of Milly's premature death. Technically his assertion is a proposition: what he says is either true or false. The
anomaly—that is, the swiftness of Milly's perceptions—is either
a function of the possibility of her early death or it is not.

Once we have it out of context we eye this proposition sus-
piciously. How do you know that what you say is true, Mr.
James? What is so anomalous about making quick surmises concerning the relationships among a group of people who are
strangers to you? Perhaps what you should have written, Mr.
James, is only that Milly was excited by the party and for this
reason seemed to experience unusually swift and intense
perceptions.

Had James's sentence actually provoked such extreme doubts
on first reading, the semblance would have been damaged. The
reader would have been dropped back with a thud into the
"real" world of painfully necessary decisions, as James himself
complained happened sometimes in Hawthorne's fiction. I felt
no such doubts myself, however; I noticed James's abstraction
only when I went hunting for it. In my opinion, he was successful in transforming this abstraction into an element.

On the other hand, it is conceivable that James was successful—for me—because the sentence actually presents itself as a
thought in Milly's mind more nearly than as a direct assertion
by James. If it is only Milly's thought, we should feel no concern about its objective truth; as with Mr. Sammler, we should
accept it as part of the total set of attributes which make up the
character of Milly, who may hold many opinions with which
neither James nor the reader would agree. There would then be

no threat to the semblance. But the possibility that the sentence is only Milly's thought does not hold up well under examination. James says it *might* have been her thought if only "she had more time to give to it." Since she did not have time, James must be advancing the thought as his own. A curious, indirect bit of evidence seems to give additional support to this conclusion. A few sentences earlier James permits himself the rare and, in *The Wings of the Dove*, probably unique intrusion of his own voice in the form of the first person singular: ". . . the fear in her that I speak of." Possibly he was emotionally involved in this scene to an unusual degree.

But if James's direct, abstract proposition is indeed a successful element, as I claimed it to be, how was the transformation from the raw material achieved? Why does James's abstraction fare better than Horatio Alger's generalization about the two young people, which is similarly a direct proposition by the author? Comparing the content of these two propositions doesn't help much. The language play in James's sentence is more vivid than in Alger's, and possibly this gives James an advantage. But some people are not at all pleased by James's mannered way of playing with language; and, anyhow, the issue we are considering is not the evocation through brilliant language of an intransitive rapt attention but the sustaining of an illusion of life. The context in which James's sentence appears is simply more effective than Alger's in creating such an illusion—granted a competent reader. At least I think I am safe in making this assumption. It is the idea of a context that needs to be thought about, then. But a fictional context is, generally speaking, constituted by the relationships among the elements in a semblance. The explanation of the effectiveness of James's sentence may therefore somehow be found in the relationship to one another of these two terms, element and semblance. Examination of this possibility leads to recognition that a semblance is created by an author's purpose and that the relationships among the elements making up the semblance are controlled by the author's purpose.

The notion of purpose in this sense is fundamentally simple. With reference to a limited scene in a novel, we can often describe the author's purpose by saying he wished to create an illusion of sadness, or excitement, or intense concentration on an abstract problem, or spiritual exaltation. With larger units such descriptive terms become inadequate. Nevertheless, even if we cannot articulate the purpose we sense in the entirety of a major work of art we can discriminate between the purpose of one work and that of another. To attribute the same purpose to *Madame Bovary* as to *Paradise Lost* is unimaginable.

It must be emphasized that the purpose we are concerned with here is the author's purpose of creating a particular illusion. This emphasis is necessary because an author can also have a different kind of purpose in mind. He can intend to impart a meaning. As a matter of fact, references in literary criticism to an author's intention are usually directed much more to the question of interpreting the meaning of a text than to the character of its semblance. At a more appropriate time I will illustrate the practical value of maintaining a distinction between purpose (concerned principally with semblance) and intention (concerned principally with meaning). Despite the practical value of the distinction, it probably represents only a provisional, useful insight, not an ultimate principle. (For further discussion see Part Two, pp. 135–136.) In what follows during the present discussion I may occasionally be a little careless and use purpose to refer to both purpose and intention, but the principal subject will be semblance, and purpose as related to semblance.

The usefulness of the concept of purpose can be seen by reversing our former point of view about the relationship between elements and semblance. After exploring this idea I will return to the passage from James. Previously, we looked at semblances as they became smaller and smaller: we divided a semblance into its elements and then noted that each element in turn might be perceived as a semblance in its own right, and so on down through the steps of a prolonged regression to a final absurdity. Suppose we now look in the other direction, so to speak, and watch individual semblances taking their place as elements in ever larger and larger semblances. In the process, we will discover the function of purpose.

We might, for example, imagine that we rejoin the head and the body of the figure cut out of *The School of Athens*. The head, a semblance when perceived by itself, now serves as an element in the semblance constituted by the figure as a whole. When restored to the entire painting, the figure in turn becomes an element in the semblance constituted by the entire painting. It is conceivable, moreover, that the entire painting could be used as an element in some still larger work. What would be the necessary end point in this imaginary progression?

There must be some limit in a sheer physical sense to a progressive transformation of semblances into the elements of a larger semblance. When Aristotle remarks that an animal can be too small to be beautiful, he goes on to say that one can also be too large. He invites the reader to consider the difficulty of apprehending the beauty of an animal or of an object so large the eye cannot take it all in at once. ". . . the unity and sense of the whole is lost," he says. He concludes these remarks by shifting his attention to literature, observing that the plot of a tragic drama must never be longer than memory can retain. This is a sensible way to establish a sort of physical limit for a tragedy, one which will presently prove to have an unexpected usefulness.

There is, however, more to think about than the physical limits of size in a sequence of ever-larger semblances. An obvious fact is that such a progression is brought to a very quick termination indeed in any brief work of art or in any unit of a longer work. What brings the progression to a conclusion? In a literary work, the terminating point of the progression, the "semblance" that transforms all the parts of the work into a single, unified whole, is established by the emergence of purpose. When the dominant purpose becomes clear the parts fall into place, either within a single episode or within a work as a whole. On the scale of a single episode, this fact may be observed in the dinner-party scene in *The Wings of the Dove*.

James's purpose in this scene is clearly to draw the reader into the experience of a young woman, who is full of vitality and interest in life even while knowing she may be mortally ill. The abstract proposition he intrudes into his presentation of her experience at the dinner party is, again, the idea that the threat of her illness enhances the swiftness of her perceptions. Looked at objectively it is an intrusion, and yet I find this intrusion not at all disturbing. What robs James's proposition of its offensiveness is, I believe, the fact that it is so thoroughly subordinated to his objective of creating an intense illusion for us, of helping us participate in the acuity of the young woman's perceptions while recognizing how relatively viscous and obtuse are the perceptions of the worldly Lord Mark.

I concede that another reader might be disturbed by the intrusion. I must also concede that people often dispute about a writer's purpose. For example, in *A Portrait of the Artist as a Young Man* is it Joyce's purpose to treat Stephen ironically or straightforwardly? Opinions differ.[12] Nevertheless, both sides agree the question of purpose is crucial—which is the point we are concerned with just now.

The fact that James's proposition appears early in the novel, only about one-fifth of the way through, is a little awkward, however; there's still a long way to go before the terminal point in the progression of elements in this novel as a whole is reached. If the apprehension of purpose is truly the terminal point of such a progression, it is not clear how the purpose controlling the novel as a whole could have become apparent only one-fifth of the way through. How, then, is the overall controlling purpose related to the dinner-party scene? I will return to this difficulty later in this discussion (p. 46) and again in Part Two, where it will be considered in relationship to the idea of an intrinsic genre. But for the present I would like to assume that the concept of purpose is the answer to the question of how James transformed his material into an element. More generally, I would also like to assume that the force and clarity of his purpose transformed and illuminated all the materials in *The Wings of the Dove*. Horatio Alger had a clear and forceful purpose too. It was to create the semblance of a very simple world, so simple that no mature imagination can dwell there.

work, whether literary or other, is something somebody has made, and has made on purpose. When we examine a work of any sort we have an eye for the purpose that brought it into being. A multitude of stones left in a field by a retreating glacier are purposeless; formed into a wall, or a bridge, or a building they are eloquent of purpose. Each stone has its own part to play in a unified whole, and the character of the whole is dependent on the designer's purpose. The key to understanding the concept of purpose as we are thinking of it now is the fact that different relationships can be established among the same collection of materials. Just as a mason can use a given collection of stones to create either a wall or a bridge, a novelist can use a given collection of materials to create different kinds of fictional structures. Materials commonly used in eighteenth- and nineteenth-century sentimental novels, for example, included a seduction, a good woman who administered to the needs of others, a great many tears, a little child who brought sunshine into the lives of adults, and a good death scene. Very different kinds of relationships among these basic materials were created by Susanna Rowson in *Charlotte Temple*, Nathaniel Hawthorne in *The Scarlet Letter*, and J .W. De Forest in *Miss Ravenel's Conversion.*

A semblance is brought into being by a creative, purposive act; it is the force of intuited purposiveness which, for the reader, transforms materials into elements. This idea can also be expressed in other ways. For instance, it can be expressed as a function of design, as implied by the jigsaw puzzle considered earlier. When a viewer grasps the overall design of a painting, he perceives how each part is transformed into an element in the illusion created by the whole. It is from this point of view that the Russian formalist critics approached their subject. The idea of purposiveness can also be expressed in terms of the structure of literature. We can say it is through a reader's grasp of the structure of a literary work that he perceives how each part is transformed into an element. This structuralist way of expressing the concept of purpose is somewhat self-contradictory, however, in that it dehumanizes the willed human act of creation. We'll return to this problem later.

Probably as we begin reading any serious literary work we yearn vaguely but positively for evidence of a purpose so profound and comprehensive as to lead to, or toward, some ultimate order within which our self may be perceived as an element. Scientific study, I believe, can induce much the same feeling, although it does not always do so. The incredibly complex, orderly, and purposive sequence of events in the movement of a signal along the nerves from a hand to a head, for example, may be perceived as evidence of a sacramental secret that just possibly might soon be revealed. Abstract or nonrepresentational art, along with its various offspring such as found art, is an attempt to identify the human imagination with the same unthought and unwilled order and purposiveness as this progression of electrical and chemical events. The abstract artist Robert Motherwell was expressing such a point of view when he remarked that "art is just one's effort to wed one-self to the universe."[13]

Recognizing that a creative purpose brings a semblance into being doesn't help much in understanding *how* this happens, but here we come close to the limits of what can be discussed with any sort of objectivity. Subjectively, we effortlessly know the difference between a powerful literary illusion and an immediate practical problem; we recognize as a semblance Shylock's calculations about money, but we are under no illusion as to the stark necessity of our calculations about our own money. Objectively, we can do little more than provide names for these different mental states, since not much more is known about them than how they subjectively feel.

Moreover, to say that purpose determines which mental state will be experienced is obviously true, within reasonable limits, but at the same time puzzling. "Invitation" is in some ways a more helpful word than purpose. Shakespeare invites us to slip into that mode of apprehension we call semblance or illusion. His invitation comes in the form of the architecture of the stage, of printed announcements, of the mannerisms of the actors, of adherence to the conventions of a familiar genre. But Shakespeare's purpose is not limited to an invitation, and purpose remains the better word. Shakespeare's purpose is not only to enable his audience to enjoy an illusion but to control the character of the particular illusion they perceive. His control is of course totally dependent on the capability of his audience. Are there people who cannot perceive *The Merchant of Venice* as a semblance? Probably. I reiterate this idea because semblance, which is created by the writer's purpose, is the life of the dominant literary forms, and if people leave a literary classroom without having enhanced their readiness for experiencing a semblance in a mature way the classroom has failed. If people do not also carry with them from the literary classroom a capacity for using semblance as an instrument in examining many of the problems of their real world, then—in my opinion—the classroom has failed again. I do not mean to suggest that the literary classroom might prove the source of any panacea. Regarded as an instrument, semblance can serve either virtue or villainy; but we shall think about this idea in Part Three.

The idea that purpose plays a crucial role in the creation of the illusion characteristic of literature has been widely accepted. John Dewey, for example, writes,

> No matter how imaginative the material *for* a work of art, it issues from the state of reverie to become the matter *of* a work of art only when it is ordered and organized, and this effect is produced only when *purpose* controls selection and development of material. [Italics in original.][14]

Susanne Langer writes, "The illusion, which constitutes the work of art, is not a mere arrangement of given materials in an aesthetically pleasing pattern; it is what results from the arrangement, and is literally something the artist makes."[15] Similarly, the Russian formalists believed that a literary work "was defined not as a cluster of devices, but as a complex, multidimensional structure integrated by the unity of esthetic purpose."[16] Some structuralists deny the concept of purpose, but others grant it a carefully qualified place. Representative of the latter is Claudio Guillén's remark that "the informing energy involved in the poetic function of language so orders the linear and temporal succession of verbal events as to endow these events . . . with the value of 'necessity.' "[17]

Two problems involved in these ideas deserve mention. The first is the possibility, pointed out by Fredric Jameson, that the formalists' concept of purpose is actually an inversion of the Aristotelian concept. Jameson argues that in the Aristotelian view all the elements in a literary work exist for the sake of some "ultimate purpose"—this purpose being the special pleasure the work is supposed to provide. An example of such a special pleasure would be the emotions of pity and fear. For the formalists, on the other hand, "everything in the work exists in order to permit the work to come into being in the first place";[18] what this means is that purpose is devoted only to achieving coherence among the elements in the semblance, indifferent to the emotions the work may produce in the reader. Jameson compares this inversion to Saussure's disconnection of the referential and to Husserl's bracketing in phenomenology. What is the practical import of such an inversion?

As Jameson's argument indicates, the formalist position does have some advantages over the Aristotelian (as he conceives it) in analyzing the process of creating a semblance.[19] The formalist position is less dependent on the unpredictable response of a reader. Nevertheless, the formalist position cannot evade the fact that literary works do exist to be read and that whatever the author's purpose may be, it must encounter the reader's response. The issue Jameson presents is therefore, in terms of his distinction between Aristotelians and formalists, really a choice between emphases rather than between alternatives. One way of looking at the function of purpose stresses the relationship of purpose to the work's effect on the reader, but also insists that purpose creates coherence among the elements of the work; the other way stresses the role of purpose in creating coherence but must concede that the purpose does affect the reader. In either case, the importance of the concept of purpose is apparent.[20]

A second problem also appears in the group of quotations about the idea of purpose with which this discussion was begun. This problem concerns not the form in which purpose appears but the question of whether purpose should be related to an individual author. The issue becomes evident in Guillén's phrase "informing energy involved in the poetic function of language." The phrase "informing energy" is a cautious substitute for a reference to the author's purpose. Roland Barthes, whose objection to granting the author a privileged position was noted earlier (p. 4), believes that the writing of a novel is essentially the activation of a great many "codes" or "structures" which have evolved within the culture. From this point of view, to assert that the most recent novel published was "written" by its author is as pointless as to say that the most recent model of car produced by the Ford Motor Company was invented by Henry Ford II. The principles of steering wheel, hydraulic brakes, pneumatic tires, spark ignition, and a multitude of other elements were no doubt thoughtlessly assumed "conventions" in the process of design. Similarly, the novelist was not put to the trouble of thinking up the conventions of control of point of view, or a recognition scene, or monogamy. And was he even aware that the writing of fiction is itself a convention—as is analyzed so well in Thomas Roberts's *When Is Something Fiction?* Viewed in this way, the structuralists' wariness of the idea that a novel is created by an individual author is understandable. What structuralism has so far failed to establish is that such a process is entirely independent of conscious individual control (for further comment see note 59, Pt. Two).

Related to the second problem just mentioned is the fact that when employed by structuralists, the idea of purpose often implies the creation of meaning rather than, or in addition to, the creation of a semblance. Yet it is possible to conceive of the purpose of creating a semblance without at the same time intending a meaning. A simple illustration of this idea is a movie made by directing a camera at a set resembling a street corner, with actors coming and going aimlessly. Here we would have the illusion of human life but no discernible meaning. To help maintain the distinction between semblance and meaning I will therefore relate the word "purpose" to semblance and the word "intention" to meaning. In practice, semblances which are devoid of meaning are not often found. Nevertheless, the distinction between purpose and intention is useful. When readers grasp an author's intention but fail to enjoy a semblance or intransitive rapt attention and are simply bored, the concepts of purpose and semblance may become the principal means of communication available for classroom discussion of their difficulty. These ideas will be further developed in Chapters 9 and 12.

Although the concept that semblance is brought into being through purpose is widely shared by theorists, some artists—particularly abstract or nonrepresentational artists—deny allowing purpose to enter into their art at all. In contrast, however, it is so common for readers to report a continuous sense of the presence of an artist's intelligence and imagination as part of their experience of his work that the idea of purposeless literature becomes difficult to accept. I will discuss these two contrasting aspects of the concept of purpose and will then return to the conundrum of how purpose can be recognized before the reading of a novel or poem has been completed.

An interesting example of the rejection of purpose in art is found in the work and thought of the composer John Cage. Asked how he could make a musical "continuity" without intending to do so, Cage answered, ". . . by not giving it a thought." Asked what is the purpose of experimental music, he responded, "No purposes. Sounds." Asked if his music is athematic, he answered, "Who said anything about themes? It is not a question of having something to say." Asked whether, if music is nothing but sounds, one person could not compose it just as well as another, he responded only with a joke.[21] He asserts that he composes by chance operations, sometimes from observation of imperfections in the paper he is writing on. And —in *Silence*—he includes a brilliant lecture on the question of whether it is possible to compose a musical piece which is "indeterminate with respect to the performer"—that is, which would impose no constraints on the freedom of the performer. This subject is interesting to Cage because of its bearing upon his hope that each of us will "give up the desire to control sound, clear his mind of music [i.e., tradition], and set about discovering ways to let sounds be themselves rather than vehicles for man-made theories or expressions of human sentiments."[22] But when are sounds only sounds and not art at all—and not even of any special interest?

A central problem in abstract or nonobjective art of every kind is to decide at what point evidences of purpose have become so slight that the work can no longer be recognized as art. Would a row of bales of hay along the edge of a field be recognized by an art lover as art? Such a work, entitled *Joint*, by Carl Andre, was exhibited in 1968. Of course the act of bestowing the title was a gentle plea for certification that the artist had been wedded to the universe. The same need is seen in artist Stephen Kaltenbach's statement during an interview that he wished to specify certain work he was doing as an art activity.[23] All these instances exemplify the central epistemological dilemma of our time. If the design of a work is arbitrarily willed the work cannot embody truth because the human mind has no access to ultimate or divine knowledge; but if the human will is withdrawn from the work the result is bereft of significance. The bearing of this dilemma upon the literary classroom will be considered in Part Two, together with its most extreme manifestation—works of art intended to attack the concept of art itself.

Whatever may be the case in the graphic and plastic arts, only a very special kind of literature could conceivably be described as not having something to say. A reader's relationship to a literary work is much like a musician's to a musical score. The fewer evidences there are of purpose in the score, the more the musician, or reader, is required to depend upon his own imagination, if he is to perform at all. Cage discusses Earle Brown's *4 Systems*, a musical composition in the form of rectangles of various sizes which the performer is invited to view rightside up, upside down, or sideways. Cage remarks that the few relationships thus suggested among the rectangles constitute the raw material out of which the musician is to make his performance. It is helpful to examine such a literary work as Burroughs's seemingly chaotic *Naked Lunch* from this point of view. Burroughs's "novel," which like Brown's composition is not conventionally organized, offers the reader the raw material constituted by the relationships among events thrown together helter-skelter. Yet there are probably more cohesive and purposive relationships within *Naked Lunch* than within *4 Systems*. Structure in the former is derived from thematic elements, from the character of the rhetoric, and from both straightforward and ironic statements of purpose. Structure in the latter is dependent on nothing more than geometric relationships. Poetry can more easily than fiction tolerate a minimal evidence of purpose. But people are generally delighted when someone publishes a successful analysis of the purpose of an obscure poem. Now I am getting into deep water, however, because "purpose" is beginning to take on a stronger connotation of "meaning" than I intended.

To consider the contrasting view of the idea of purpose—the possibility that the author's imagination is sensed as present throughout his work—let us return to James one more time and to the question of whether such a presence is felt in *The Wings of the Dove*. In the preface to the New York edition of this novel James says something which possibly throws light on the quotation considered earlier. He writes:

> I can scarce remember the time when the situation on which this long-drawn fiction mainly rests was not vividly present to me. The idea, reduced to its essence, is that of a young person conscious of a great capacity for life, but early stricken and doomed, condemned to die under short respite, while also enamoured of the world.[24]

Here James is expressing essentially the same idea he presented in the passage from the novel concerning Mrs. Lowder's dinner party. Here, however, he stresses the vividness the situation had long had in his own imagination. Later in the preface he returns to the same episode and again the power of the situation to grip his imagination can be felt in his language: ". . . the long passage that forms here before us the opening of Book Fourth, where all the offered life centres, to intensity, in the disclosure of Milly's single throbbing consciousness."[25] Now, do these passages from the preface differ significantly in their effect from the passage in the novel itself? Is the presence of that mind known as Henry James noticeably less apparent in the fiction than in the preface where it addresses the reader directly? This is a very subjective question, and it is a little unfair as well since the passage I chose from the novel is one in which the author is possibly uncommonly close to the surface. Nevertheless, most people would probably agree that the felt presence of James's imagination is an important part of the reader's experience of the novel.[26] I am reminded of Patrick McCaughey's comment on the painter Thomas Eakins: "With Eakins we are always aware of his presence in the painting. . . . the fundamental force of the work is Eakins' power of seeing."[27] Similarly, Maurice Natanson has written about Camus: "It is Camus himself that attracts us. At the end of the absurd world he describes, we find him waiting for us."[28]

The idea of a sense of the artist's presence as part of the experience of his work becomes most difficult and probably must be abandoned when we encounter works written deliberately to focus attention upon the writing itself rather than upon anything the works are "about." Consider, for example, Jonathan Culler's comment on Robbe-Grillet:

> In Robbe-Grillet's *La Jalousie* . . . descriptions are not conducted according to what a reader would notice or might conclude if he were present, and consequently it becomes impossible to organize the text as communication between an implied "I" and an implied "you."[29]

The "I" referred to is of course a narrator, not the author, but the difficulty Culler refers to in organizing the text stands as a barrier between reader and author. To illustrate the principle he had in mind, Culler had earlier pointed to the opening paragraph of Robbe-Grillet's *In the Labyrinth*, where successive sentences assert "Outside it is raining" and "Outside the sun is shining." "We are forced to realize," Culler declares, "that the only reality in question is that of writing itself which, as Jean Ricardou says, uses the concept of a world in order to display its own laws."[30]

Given a writer whose purpose is only to display the laws of writing, we have little from which to infer anything more than abstract intellectual activity, as distinguished from the full range of activity of a mind. We are confronted with works more interested in creating an intransitive rapt attention than a semblance. Indeed, structuralists make a parallel distinction between "unreadable" and "readable" texts.[31] Unreadable texts are those which deliberately try to block an interest in anything except the act of writing itself.

If it is true that in readable works a sense of the presence of the author's mind is important, the concept of purpose in general becomes both clearer and more complex—even for a writer like Burroughs. It becomes more complex because to the idea of a formal, relational, aesthetic purpose is added the pervasive presence of the author's intuited imagination or consciousness. It is clearer because, as Georges Poulet insists, the virtual life of the work is felt to arise in part from the artist's consciousness and not merely from a formal design. Purpose becomes humanized. Looked at from this point of view, terms like virtual life, semblance, and illusion reveal a second ambiguity. Illusion, semblance, is experienced as, and recognized as, the response of a real and purposive mind to the real world. Whether mirror-

like or lamplike, the creative purposiveness of the artist has
usually been consciously valued for the insights it yields into
this world. Purpose in art is generally felt as more than just a
structure: it is felt as mind.

The concept of mind, it is true, is itself the troubled subject of
endless debate. Indeed, exactly as structuralism insists, what a
reader perceives as an author's mind may often be not much
more than a collection of attitudes the author has inherited from
a particular social class. In group discussions of literature, on
the other hand, we must not allow theories about the concept of
mind, or about the implied author, to obscure direct observation
of how people respond to what they read. There seems no reason
to question the persistence of readers' experiencing literary
works as purposive communications from other human beings.
Ideas about what a human being is will change, as will ideas
about ethics, motivation, and structure in both art and conduct.
It is most unlikely, however, that these changes will cause
readers to relate to literary works as if they were those tribal,
oral myths Lévi-Strauss describes as seeming to come out of
nowhere. The kind of art we normally have in mind when we
refer to literature—poetry, fiction, and drama—will surely continue to be perceived as the work of individual human beings.
This kind of perception will no doubt persist, too, regardless of
how we come to think about the nature of a human being or of
the mind. The practical force of these thoughts is exemplified
in a review of Frederick Buechner's recent novel *Open Heart*.
Although this review displays no interest in the kind of speculation I've just been pursuing, one short paragraph in it happens
to be directly relevant.

> Through it all, Antonio [the hero] remains essentially
> an equivocal but clever device to help the author work
> things out in his head. Given this undisguised sketchi-
> ness in a central character, it is something of a mystery
> how Buechner has produced a live, warm, wise comic
> novel. And yet that is exactly what . . . he has done.[32]

In the words "undisguised sketchiness," the reviewer is asserting
that the central character was never wholly transformed into an
element; in the words "live . . . novel," he is asserting that he
experienced the novel as a semblance. It must be inferred that

the author's purpose did not become apparent simply through the conversion of materials into elements, but was in some degree perceived directly by the reader, and that, further, this direct perception was capable in some degree of evoking a semblance. Such a line of thought seems to lead to the concept of a literary charisma, where the virtual life of a work springs straight from the charismatic force of the implied author.[33]

A hazard in such speculation, however, and a conclusion and counterpoint to the example from James, may be seen in a fascinating comment by Virginia Woolf on Charlotte Brontë's *Jane Eyre*. The import of Woolf's comment is that Brontë used this fictional work to communicate her own personal discontentment to the reader. In *A Room of One's Own*, Woolf quotes a passage in which Jane is looking out over the countryside and brooding about how people blame her for dreaming of a life of greater scope and interest. The passage quoted by Woolf begins with Jane's saying, "Who blames me? Many no doubt." It concludes with Jane's remark, "When thus alone I not infrequently heard Grace Poole's laugh." Jane is speaking in the first person, to the reader. According to the principle of my own earlier comments there should be no threat to the semblance in what she says. The words are hers, not directly the author's. Nevertheless, Woolf describes these words as an "awkward break."

> It is upsetting to come upon Grace Poole all of a sudden. The continuity is disturbed. One might say . . . the woman who wrote those pages had more genius in her than Jane Austen; but if one reads them over and marks that jerk in them, that indignation, one sees that she will never get her genius expressed whole and entire. Her books will be deformed and twisted. She will write in a rage where she should write calmly.[34]

Whether or not Woolf's criticism is justified, there is no doubt about her distress. Her complaint is that the author has objectionably intruded.

And yet the intrusion Woolf senses here occurs within the speech of a character; there is no ostensible interference on the part of the author at all. In short, I myself condoned a manifest intrusion by James, but Woolf denounces a subtly sensed intrusion by Brontë. This contrast suggests that the kind of intrusion

really damaging to a semblance is one in which the reader feels
the author to be using the occasion principally to indulge his
ego—begging for sympathy or admiration or venting his anger.
An open intrusion may scarcely be noticed if it is felt to be truly
subordinate to a less self-serving purpose. Really great literature
seems to be dependent upon a writer's conceiving of semblance
as an instrument for exploring human experience rather than
as a direct outlet for personal feeling. It is as if the writer must
perceive himself as an element in a semblance he is creating out
of some larger purpose if he is to make effective use of his personal feeling in the process. The embarrassing self-dramatizing
that mars the semblance in Jack London's *Martin Eden* is an
illustration of what happens when such a perception is not
achieved. In summary, the sensed presence of an author's mind
is apparently felt as creative purpose only when the author is
not manifestly attempting to use the reader's attention for merely personal ends. What the writer may be up to covertly, perhaps without fully realizing it, is a very different matter, as
Kenneth Burke has made clear in numerous brilliant analyses.

A last necessary qualification concerning the possibility that
the presence of the author's imagination is sensed throughout
his work brings us back to the concept of intransitive rapt attention. It has often been remarked that a brief lyric may afford
very little evidence from which to infer the personality of its
author. As noted earlier, when we move away from literary
forms evoking a semblance toward those evoking only an intransitive rapt attention we tend to lose a sense of the presence
of the author's imagination. Emily Dickinson's "Perception of
an Object" is really pretty impersonal. Immature people are, I
think, often made ill-at-ease by the absence of the warmth of an
implied personality—a probable factor in the rather general
preference for fiction over poetry.

Earlier, I mentioned the difficulty about determining at what
point an author's purpose becomes clear. In principle, as I remarked, purpose can emerge clearly only at the end of a work,
whereas in fact James's purpose is evident in *The Wings of the
Dove* long before that time. I shall bring to an end these comments on the idea of purpose with a brief consideration of this
difficulty and with a tentative suggestion about disputes over
the purpose of a particular work.

In his comments on size and beauty Aristotle's switch from the perception of an object to the memory of a plot affords a good perspective on the two literary problems just mentioned. He says, quite reasonably, that we can perceive the beauty of an object only if it is not too large to see all at once; if it is too large to see all at once we lose the sense of its unity and wholeness. He does not accept the possibility that memory might serve our purpose, that we might walk around or along a very large object and finally apprehend its unity and its beauty in our memory, in our mind's eye. Yet no tragedy can be seen all at once except in memory, as he himself points out. Of course the same is true of any literary work except the briefest poetry. Our theoretical dilemma is therefore that we cannot begin to enjoy a literary work until we have reached the end of it, when at last we are enabled in memory to apprehend its unity and to observe its transformation into a semblance by the emergence of its purpose.

Susanne Langer offers the boldest sort of solution to this dilemma. She declares that in the first few lines of a literary work the reader intuits the overall purpose or "vital import."[35] John Dewey says much the same thing: "Even at the outset, the total and massive quality [semblance] has its uniqueness."[36] When I first encountered such opinions I thought them very ingenious but quite incredible. Now I am not so sure they really are incredible. Analogies to other disciplines are thought-provoking. Logicians, for example, point out that new meanings do not burst upon a reader at the end of every sentence—and only then. Similarly, meaning does not suddenly emerge only at the end of a book. William James remarked that a reader can give appropriate emphasis to words in an unfamiliar text he is reading aloud. As he proceeds, a reader must anticipate or intuit meaning which has not yet been expressed. Noam Chomsky and his followers have attached great importance to the same principle in their linguistic theory, and recent accounts of experimentation with reading give support to this principle.[37] Yet how can a reader intuit what is coming in a part of a sentence he hasn't read? Opinions differ. Inherent ability, conditioning, and combinations of these two factors all have their advocates.[38]

Nevertheless, there is clearly the possibility that a reader's first intuition of meaning, or of a semblance, might be in error.

Suppose, for example, the reader intuits a purpose which transforms the materials of the first part of a novel into exciting elements, only to discover later that his intuition had been wrong. Are the elements of the first part of the novel dissolved back into materials? Something like this actually happened to me during my first reading of *A Farewell to Arms*. The trouble occurred in Chapter 29, which is concerned with the great retreat of the Italian army in World War I. Lt. Frederic Henry, the protagonist, is trying to free a truck stuck in the mud and orders a couple of passing Italian soldiers to help. They refuse and walk away. He repeats his order but they do not stop. Then, in accordance with the rules governing the rights of officers, he shoots one and tries to shoot the other but misses. It is simple, brutal murder. Dead, the soldiers could be no help. As it turns out, the truck was hopelessly stuck anyhow. And Lieutenant Henry was not warding off a general mutiny: one of his own men enthusiastically assisted in the killing.

This Frederic Henry did not seem to me at all the same tough but good-humored and tolerant man who earlier had befriended the priest others in the officers' mess were tormenting and who had tried to help a man scheming to avoid front-line service. My memory of my reading is that I felt lost, uncertain of my own perceptions; the illusion of life was diminished. Soon afterward, however, all was made clear—or so I came to believe. In the very next chapter Lieutenant Henry himself is about to be shot because of some pointless rule in the minds of the battle police who have seized him. Confronted with this situation, his feelings about war and the rules of war undergo a great change. To be fair to Hemingway I should add that he had actually been preparing for this change for some time. When it thus became apparent to me during my reading that Hemingway's dominant purpose was to present the experience of undergoing exactly this change, I realized he wanted to be sure the reader saw clearly what attitude was being given up by Lieutenant Henry as well as what new attitude was being adopted. The attitude being given up was presented in extreme form in Lieutenant Henry's killing of the soldier. I finished the novel with pleasure, but not with as much pleasure as I'd felt prior to the killing scene.

This experience seems a good example of what happens when

an initial intuition runs into difficulties, but as an example it does, in my opinion, have the defect that the difficulty was created by the author himself. So let's consider a second example. Why did *The Sound and the Fury* at first outrage so many people (the word "garbage" was used at least once), only to be generally accepted later as a masterpiece? One reason is that it must be very difficult on a first reading to apprehend its purpose, in the complex sense, without the assistance of one of the various guides now available and without even having been informed by the news media that Faulkner was a genius and a compassionate man. On the other hand, some early readers did intuit something in the novel that caused them to continue struggling with it. I believe the breakthrough came in the fall of 1948 when Lawrence Bowling published an essay on *The Sound and the Fury* in the *Kenyon Review*—nineteen years after the appearance of the novel.

These examples merely confirm the everyday observation that serious errors in the apprehension of the overall purpose of a fine novel may occur not only at the beginning but well along into the book or even after the reading has been concluded. And, as in the case of *The Sound and the Fury*, the error may be great enough to inhibit the experiencing of a semblance. Many intelligent readers must have looked at this work in the first ten years of its life without enough of that initial experience Dewey calls raptness or seizure to lure them into a really comprehensive reading. Still, a few people were seized. Why? How could they feel interested in the book before they had really apprehended it?

This question, which is simply our basic problem as first presented with reference to Aristotle's *Poetics*, can be approached in two different ways. One way is by analogy, the other by analysis. The analogical way is the more reassuring and, ultimately, probably the truer. The analytical way is the more useful. I will consider each in turn. Elsewhere, I will return to the same question in connection with the concept of intrinsic genre (see Pt. Three, p. 264).

A particularly interesting analogy can be drawn between the initial perception of a semblance and the initial perception of the personality of a new acquaintance. The initial perception of a personality is so complex that any attempt to enumerate all its parts would seem ridiculous. Also, initial perceptions of personality are often proved mistaken by experience. And yet, even if we have made an admitted mistake about someone's personality, we don't therefore lose the ability to recognize that personality. Similarly, I believe it is safe to say that someone who has read and thoroughly misunderstood both *The Adventures of Joseph Andrews* and *Pamela* would nevertheless be able to discriminate between the semblances of the two. I say I *believe* this is true; I don't know how it could ever be demonstrated. Remembering the contour of a head or a face is not the same as remembering a personality, and remembering the content of a page of text is not the same as remembering a semblance. Such scholars as Georges Poulet and J. Hillis Miller have done thought-provoking work in relating the "being" of a writer to his texts, however, and my belief that the analogy of a semblance to a personality is too impressionistic to be very useful for our purposes might be checked against what they have to say.

Before entering into an analytical approach to our problem, it is helpful to consider for a moment the inherent weaknesses of such an approach. The problem is, again, that materials can be transformed into the elements of a semblance only when the purpose of a work has been apprehended, but the purpose cannot be fully apprehended until the work has been finished. In principle, this difficulty is what is known in the theory of interpretation of texts as the "hermeneutic circle."

The weakness in the analytical approach is that although terms like semblance and purpose must be used, the human imagination is not contained in boxes with such labels. The classical example of this kind of logical difficulty is Zeno's paradox about Achilles and the tortoise, as we are reminded by such different writers as Geoffrey Hartman and Walter Slatoff.

Achilles and the tortoise ran a race. Because Achilles could run twice as fast as the tortoise, it was given a head start of a hundred feet. But, Zeno pointed out, when Achilles had run this hundred feet the tortoise had run fifty; when Achilles had run the fifty feet the tortoise had run twenty-five. If Achilles ran twelve inches the tortoise ran six. Achilles could never catch up. The error in such reasoning is that the relative velocities of Achilles and the tortoise cannot be expressed in static units of distance. Given the relative *motion* (feet per second) of Achilles and the tortoise, we discover the paradox has vanished. A mathematician would say that a more direct response to Zeno's paradox in its own terms is found in the concept of a convergent series, a concept unknown to Zeno.

The paradox I constructed about semblance and purpose is not exactly the same as Zeno's paradox, and I am not suggesting we embark on a search for a "motion" language for our problem. The comparison to Zeno's paradox is intended only to help indicate the "static" character, or tendency, of the terms semblance and purpose. Once we are aware of their limitations, we can see better how to use them.

John Dewey offers the term "fusion" for the analysis of our problem. Perceptions from the reader's past experience, he declares, are fused with perceptions acquired as he reads. Similarly, then, perceptions from earlier stages in the reading are fused with perceptions from later stages. Perceptions from a first reading of a work are fused with those of a second reading.

Dewey means "fuse" quite literally. During the act of reading, when two perceptions have been fused a single perception results. For example, a reader's perception of the description of a river is fused with his earlier experience of rivers; he perceives only a single river as he reads, but this perception is always affected by, is fused with, the perceptions constituting his experience prior to the reading. Similarly, a reader's single perception of the conclusion of a literary work is affected by, is fused with, the perceptions that preceded it in the reading. "Fused with" expresses Dewey's meaning more precisely than "affected by."

Dewey's line of thought may only seem to reassert the paradox that a semblance can't be experienced until a reading has been completed, but he would emphatically reject such a possibility. He insists that every work of art possesses, or presents, a unique quality (i.e., semblance).[39] He believes the reader intuits this unique quality at the very outset, if only vaguely, and the process of fusion unites the initial perception with the conclusion. Exactly how the vagueness of the initial perception of a unique quality is fused with the presumably sharper final perception without being rendered false Dewey does not say, but he takes note of the problem. He remarks that the elements of a work of art "fuse in a way which physical things cannot emulate,"[40] which is another way of saying that our tendency to put our thoughts into boxes with labels like element and semblance inevitably distorts experience. He simply and sensibly attributes the fusing of elements to the imagination, which is somewhat like putting the concept of velocity into Zeno's paradox. "Imaginative vision," Dewey declares, "is the power that unifies all the constituents of the matter of a work of art, making a whole out of them in all their variety."[41]

The distinguished philosopher Stephen Pepper further developed Dewey's concept of fusion and speculated interestingly on the possibility of ever-changing "specific qualities" within a stable overall "controlling quality."[42] Pepper's ideas may be seen as an attempt to approach a "motion" language for the clarification of this particular problem. As a type of thought, they bear some resemblance to John Crowe Ransom's structure and texture and to ideas in theoretical physics about the substitution of a spectrum of alternatives for the Aristotelian concept of dichotomy.[43]

A somewhat similar approach to the role of imagination in reading literature is found in phenomenological theory. Wolfgang Iser points out that what he calls "indeterminacy" or "gaps" in a text are necessary if a reader is to use his imagination. He means a text cannot, and in fact should not, contain every detail of what is being described. He explains his idea by referring to the difference between reading *Tom Jones* and seeing a filmed version of the novel. While reading, he declares, we can visualize Tom almost as we please; part of our experience in the reading is our sense of the great range of possibilities regarding Tom's appearance. But the moment we see Tom in a filmed version our imagination is put out of action. We are confined to physical perception, and we may even feel annoyed at finding Tom different from what we had expected. And yet, despite our annoyance, we may never have had a really sharp visual image of Tom before seeing the film. An instance of what Iser seems to have in mind is F. Scott Fitzgerald's remark that during the writing of *The Great Gatsby* he never did see Gatsby clearly. Iser's ideas resemble Dewey's concept of the role of the imagination, but Iser does go farther in thinking carefully about what really happens. In particular, his ideas raise a doubt concerning Dewey's belief that a fusion results in a single perception. Probably most readers would agree that their mental image of Tom is likely to be rather changeable and uncertain compared to what they see in a movie. If so, perhaps there is in the reader's mind no single perception of Tom's appearance but rather what Iser refers to as a "vital richness of potential" for the imagination, a richness that is present during reading but not during a film.[44] In any case, Dewey's analytical concept of fusion, when treated with the restraint he himself displayed, provides a useful way of thinking about purpose and semblance.[45]

A practical value in Dewey's concept is that it provides an insight into one of the important functions of the literary classroom—the furnishing of information needed for the appreciation of a literary work. It does this by making possible a distinction: some background information will fuse with initial perceptions in the reading to help create a semblance, some will not. A rather paradoxical example that occurs to me is my possession of a newspaper photograph of Chester Gillette, the original of Clyde Griffiths in *An American Tragedy*. I have determined—not with verifiable certainty but to my own satisfaction—that an opportunity to see an actual photograph of Chester Gillette does more to help young people perceive *An American Tragedy* as a semblance than does a lecture on naturalism. Anyone who has tried to entice a group of young people into reading *An American Tragedy* in its entirety will recognize the significance of this finding. Ultimately limited though it is, an analytical approach to the relationship between purpose and semblance is useful in answering such questions as what to say to someone about to begin *The Sound and the Fury*.

In sober fact it must be conceded that not much of a semblance at all may be experienced in the first reading of some works, particularly difficult poetry. Even with relatively straightforward texts and situations the unexpected happens and the semblance fails. This point is seen vividly in a story Susanne Langer tells about the shock she felt as a child at a performance by Maude Adams of *Peter Pan*.

> It was my first visit to the theater, and the illusion was absolute and overwhelming, like something supernatural. At the highest point of the action (Tinkerbell had

drunk Peter's poisoned medicine to save him from doing
so, and was dying) Peter turned to the spectators and
asked them to attest their belief in fairies. Instantly the
illusion was gone; there were hundreds of children, sitting in rows, clapping and even calling, and Miss Adams,
dressed up as Peter Pan, spoke to us like a teacher coach-
ing us in a play in which she herself was taking the title
role. I did not understand, of course, what had happened;
but an acute misery obliterated the rest of the scene.[46]

I myself recall with a real pang what happened the first time I
had occasion to discuss Conrad's *Heart of Darkness* in a large,
required college course. After spending a good while explaining
what I regarded as the fine points, so everyone could more fully
enjoy this truly magnificent work of art, I discovered to my as-
tonishment that many of the people in the class thought it a dull
book. No doubt I was foolish, but the possibility that anyone
could fail to enjoy *Heart of Darkness* had never entered my
mind. When I asked why the book seemed dull, one young man
said there was too much description in it. I can only presume
that for him, and for all the others who agreed with him, Conrad had failed to transform a lot of his materials into elements
—and I had failed to provide the kind of information and insight which could fuse with parts or aspects of the book to produce a semblance.
    When two readers disagree about Joyce's purpose in *A Por-
trait of the Artist as a Young Man*, then, the question of where
each stands within the whole process just reviewed might at the
outset be even more significant than the question of which one
is correct. To say this is not to deny the primacy of the literary
classroom's twin goals of correctness of interpretation and an
intense semblance, although the meaning of correctness will
have to be considered further later on; it is only to recognize
that the fusions individual readers have experienced while going
through a work may have varied a great deal. C. P. Snow's *Two
Cultures* is a prolonged testimonial to the necessity of our living
with this fact. Looked at from the point of view of variations
among initial, individual readings of a work, literary study in
general and the literary classroom in particular can find a real
value in the analytical concept of fusion. It provides a means of

conceptualizing the fact that initial interpretations of a work often depend as much on the skills and personal experience brought to the reading as on the content of the work itself. It provides a way of thinking about differing interpretations that is both gentler and closer to the reality of experience than is a single-minded drive for correctness. Correctness, as will be explained later, remains one of the two primary objectives in the treatment of a text.

4. SEMBLANCE &

THE READER'S MATURITY

The character of the semblances enjoyed by a given individual is in some measure dependent on his maturity. The fact that for a given individual *The Young Acrobat* might create an entrancing illusion whereas *Heart of Darkness* might not, or vice versa, is a matter of crucial importance in the classroom. Of course many factors besides maturity are involved. I am reminded of a comment by William Sheldon in his *Varieties of Temperament*. He said he had encountered numbers of people who had virtually no capacity for introspection. He added that when one of these people fell into the hands of a psychiatrist he sometimes proved a gold mine, because if he could be taught to introspect he took such pleasure in it he kept coming back for more lessons. Sheldon's comment no doubt occurred to me here because of the fairly obvious possibility that the nature of an individual's response to literature is related to his ability to introspect; but I must add at once I am not sure this supposition is valid. A similar question arises concerning a possible relationship between an individual's tendency to dream while sleeping and the character and intensity of his response to literature. The psychologist Frank Barron, well known for his studies of dreaming, told me in conversation that when he asked engineers how often they were aware of having dreamed, the answer was, typically, two or three times a month. On the other hand, when the question was put to creative writers the typical answer was several times each night. Again, little is known about what precise relationships may exist between these differences and responses to literature, and my purpose in mentioning the differences at all is simply to emphasize how complex the idea of semblance becomes when its implications are explored.

However, I would like to take a little time for what is probably the most important of all individual differences with respect to the idea of semblance—the relative maturity or immaturity of the individual to whom the semblance is presented. Some possible effects of immaturity have been implied in incidents already mentioned. A closer examination into dissimilarities between mature and immature responses to literature suggests a surprisingly large and interesting number of questions concerning both literary theory and classroom practice. I will review several such questions.

The following highly personal account by the well-known

historian J. H. Plumb clearly describes what many people would probably feel to be the single most important change in an individual's experience with literature as he matures.

> As a child I could be spoken to, yet not hear; I could be physically moved and not know it. Once my head was in a book, the world was lost and a vicarious life opened for me—wonderful, beautiful, sometimes horrifying, but entirely mine. This habit persisted through adolescence to early manhood. Proust and Dostoevsky were like a drug. Only time spent in their worlds was real; my grinding academic chores were an illusion.
>
> Then, slowly, the magic of books began to fade. Not that I read less, but my reading changed: I sought literature to feed my mind instead of my emotions. Novels and poetry gave way to history, biography, and social criticism, books that often excite the intellect but rarely banish the realities we have to live with. It is probably a decade now since any book has seized me entirely. The two I remember were curiously idiosyncratic: Denton Welch's *Journal* and Raleigh Trevelyan's *A Hermit Disclosed*. These must have struck some strange inner chord. I wonder how many readers' experiences are like mine. Are there some who are luckier and carry into middle age and beyond that wonderful childhood capacity for total absorption?[47]

The striking similarity between the account of childhood experience here and Susanne Langer's account of *Peter Pan* leads at once to a question. Is semblance, as Langer conceives it, essentially a phenomenon of childhood or, rather, of immaturity? It seems impossible to answer either yes or no. To say yes would be to deny the intensity of experience many mature adults report in the reading of a novel or the viewing of a drama. As John Keats said, "The excellence of every Art is its intensity." To say no, on the other hand, would be to ignore the apparent fact that almost no adults are utterly absorbed by a book or a drama in the way children often are. Indeed, when people speak disparagingly of using literature as nothing more than a source of vicarious experience what they usually have in mind is something like the thoughtless semblance of childhood—as suggested by Ian Watt's comment, in his study of eighteenth-century literature, on "the public's uncritical demand for easy vicarious indulgence in sentiment and romance."[48]

The puzzling difference between childhood and maturity is probably of great importance in the classroom. I have so often been asked if scholarly study of literature did not spoil the literature that I am convinced anyone who talks with "immature" people about literature should never even for a moment lose sight of the problem. All too often the vital experience of a great work of literature is put entirely out of reach and the reading of it reduced to a grinding academic chore, to use Plumb's words. I don't know whether Plumb meant to include literary works in his comment, but I do know Paul Goodman said that at age twelve he read *Macbeth* with excitement while browsing in the library but in class couldn't understand a word of *Julius Caesar* and hated it. At one time I came to believe that assigning a literary work to a class invariably spoiled it for them, and so I began to talk to my classes about the problem. I soon decided my belief was wrong; many people asserted that their enjoyment was enhanced by the context of the "classwork." Whether some of those who enjoy the classroom context are also those for whom literature creates a childlike semblance I do not know.

The problem of vicarious experience brings up the related question of how emotion enters into a semblance. Obviously, literature is somehow emotional—and yet the emotions a mature reader is aware of as he reads a story aren't usually exactly the same as those of real life. A mature reader may experience satisfaction in seeing a hero of a story beat off a vicious dog that is trying to bite him, but the reader's state of excitement is normally not much like what it would be if he himself were about to be bitten. Marcus Hester says what the reader experiences is not genuine emotion but the image of an emotion. Langer says it's the idea of an emotion, and this seems to me a particularly good way to put it. We know the hero's anger, but we do not possess it. The anger remains within the realm of illusion. These comments are by no means an explanation of the role of emotion in a semblance, only a recognition of what happens; this problem will have to be given further consideration later. Moreover, even as a recognition, these comments are inadequate. For example, descriptions of sexual acts are known to be capable of

creating real sexual desire. It is probable that descriptions of
food can similarly arouse hunger, and descriptions of various
dangers, anxiety. Perhaps all that can be said with confidence
is that virtually all mature—and sane—adults and most children have some innate means of avoiding confusion between the
illusional world of literature and the real world of their daily
lives. They can also distinguish between memories and present
reality[49] and between imagined future experiences and present
reality.

Nevertheless, as Plumb's remarks indicate, a mature reader
keeps his grip on the real world more firmly than does a child,
and this fact introduces another problem. It is easy to accept the
idea of the transformation of materials into elements within the
magic spell of childhood's reading, but what about the transformation within the reading of an adult, where the magic is less
potent? If, in contrast to the child, an adult does not lose his
awareness of the world around him, how can the transformation
ever be complete? As long as awareness of the immediate environment remains, it would seem, the reader would also be continuously aware of the whole process of the writer's selecting
materials and laboriously turning them into elements.

This problem has some fascinating and puzzling implications.
A sophisticated reader can hardly become aware, for example,
of a writer's working at creating a formal series of some sort
without wondering if the series will be successfully integrated
into the conclusion of the story. For the duration of his act of
wondering, with its implication of distrust, the reader must be
contemplating the materials and the elements of the story in a
very complex way. He must be noting that certain materials
have been successfully transformed into elements and at the
same time be wondering whether the author will make it to the
end of the book without getting into trouble. A simple illustration is seen in a reader's relationship to the series formed by the
carefully planned appearances of the word "innocent" in James's
Daisy Miller or by the image of the centipede in Robbe-Grillet's
Jealousy. Tell a group of readers to make a note of each appearance of "innocent," and some will object that you're ruining
any chance of their enjoying the reading. Avoid telling them
to make such notes, however, and many will fail to perceive the
formal structure. In the group there may be some whose state

of mind while reading is similar to the state J. H. Plumb remembered from his childhood, and others whose state of mind is
similar to the state he reported in his maturity. There may be
some who seldom dream and some who never introspect, although as noted earlier the significance of these possibilities in
the study of literary experience is uncertain. There are also other
differences, to be pondered elsewhere. In any case, our practical
problem can be represented by the question of whether a class
should be instructed to make notes about each appearance of
"innocent" in *Daisy Miller*.

On the other hand, our theoretical problem is that if we think
about the writer's use of materials we can't simultaneously experience the materials as elements, but if we don't think about
the writer's use of materials we are behaving in an immature
manner and our intuition of the semblance may be in error.

Historically, the theoretical problem is a version of a fundamental paradox encountered in the New Criticism and formalist criticism. In formalist terms, a poem is autonomous and non-
referential—that is, it is not a statement *about* human experience; it is not a generalization; it is not abstract thought; it is
not sociology. This seems to be roughly the equivalent of saying that a poem is childhood's semblance. The other side of the
paradox is that most good poetry represents the disciplined, controlled intellectual activity of the poet. The formalist critic Kester Svendsen, for example, citing Langer as his authority, declares the duty of the classroom is to help people see a poem or
play as a "made thing." That is, again, the teacher's effort
should be to help the class perceive the work as a nonreferen-
tial semblance created by the artist's transformation of materials into elements. But Svendsen further says that the proper
method of such teaching is to analyze the structure of the work.
He thus completes the outline of the paradox just noted. The
abstract analysis of structure inevitably reduces the elements
in the semblance to the materials out of which they were created. One of the objectives of such analysis is precisely to note
the transformation of materials into elements through their relationship to the structure of the work as a whole. But, according to formalist doctrine, what is perceived as a mere material
cannot be perceived as an element in a semblance. Consequently

the semblance, the presumed object of study, disappears as soon as an examination of structure is begun.[50]

New ways of thinking about the formalist paradox have been emerging, resting upon a challenge to an assumption. To understand this challenge let us once again rehearse the fact that from the formalist point of view if we think about the writer's use of materials we can't simultaneously experience them as elements; in formalist terms, a poem can't simultaneously be autonomous and referential. It has seemed obvious, in other words, that a reader couldn't, at one and the same time, analyze the logic of the "innocent" series in *Daisy Miller* and submit himself unrestrainedly to the "concrete" delight of being carried along by the story.[51] But suppose we ask why not? Is it possible that what seemed too obvious a fact to be worth thinking about is actually only a mistaken assumption? I believe the answer to this question is yes, although it proves to be a qualified yes. But let's look at some evidence.

Langer's childhood experience is not representative of that of all theatergoers or, I should imagine, of her own adult experience. A few years ago the drama critic Walter Kerr wrote a column on the subject of illusion on the stage in which he described an interesting incident from a production of Lillian Hellman's *The Little Foxes*. In this production, the part of the villainous and, as Kerr says, "morally horrifying" character Ben Hubbard was played by the gifted actor George C. Scott. The incident Kerr described was that as Scott made an exit after an especially nasty speech the audience broke into wild applause. The illusion of the story must have been broken, Kerr says; the audience was certainly applauding the actor Scott, not the villainous Hubbard. But, he continues, a moment later the audience appeared to be again utterly engrossed in the story of the Hubbard family. Was the illusion really broken, Kerr asks, or do theatergoers have a kind of double, or multiple, vision? Is it possible for an individual to be simultaneously making judgments about the quality of an actor's performance (i.e., the actor's success in turning materials into elements) and engrossed in the story (in the semblance)? People do it all the time, Kerr declares; the only way to explain such commonplace occurrences as a burst of applause for an actor in a play clearly gripping the imagination of the audience is to assume that the people in the audience do have some sort of multiple vision.[52] I don't believe, however, that children spontaneously applaud an actor for his performance.

Comparable things are reported concerning a solitary reading of a literary work. Walter J. Slatoff, for example, describes his intense feeling during the reading of a certain novel, while at the same time he was carefully attending to the structure of the story.[53] Lévi-Strauss asserts bluntly that "theoretical knowledge is not incompatible with sentiment and . . . knowledge can be both objective and subjective at the same time."[54] To back up his contention he quotes the following passage from a book written by the director of the zoo at Zurich:

> "Flippy [a dolphin] was no fish, and when he looked at you from a distance of less than two feet, you had to stifle the question as to whether it was in fact an animal. So new, strange and extremely weird was this creature, that one was tempted to consider it as some kind of be-witched being. But the zoologist's brain kept on associat-ing it with the cold fact, painful in this connection, that it was known to science by the dull name _Tursiops truncatus_."[55]

In the simpler and more innocent pre-Jamesian world, au-thors seemed to be curiously unconcerned about the dangers of shattering the semblance they were creating. Everyone remem-bers Fielding's lectures in _Tom Jones_, Scott's discussion at the beginning of _Waverley_ of the problem of choosing a name for his hero, Hawthorne's moralizing in _The Scarlet Letter_. Mel-ville, as he begins to describe Claggart, in _Billy Budd_, says bluntly, "His portrait I essay, but shall never hit it." In the light of modern sophisticated craftsmanship the undesirability of such unselfconscious authorial intrusions seems clear, although de-liberate toying with the semblance is now common—as with Stencil, in _V_, who dreamed once a week it had all been a dream. Our interest at the moment, however, is not in theories of crafts-manship but, again, in the question of the capacity of the read-er's imagination to accept an author's direct comment without a painful shattering of the semblance. As I suggested earlier, I suspect that our anxiety about the delicateness of a semblance is more nearly a learned response than a spontaneous one. My recollections of my own experience, in any case, are that I first became concerned about violations of the semblance through reading works on the art of the novel. As I discovered from such studies the very real pleasure of maintaining a deliberate analytical awareness of the craftsmanship in novels I was reading, I began to dislike authorial intrusions in fiction which I had until that time enjoyed. For this admittedly subjective reason I am inclined to feel, like Slatoff, that a variety of extraneous matter can be absorbed by the reader's imagination without destroying the semblance. The testimony of psychologists provides somewhat more objective evidence. Andrew Weil, for example, asserts that a person who is in a light trance may have a sense of dual reality. As an instance, he cites "the simultaneous experience of reliving the tenth-birthday party while sitting with the hypnotist." He later uses the phrase "light trance" to describe the mental state of a person watching a movie.[56] I don't know how careful he was being with his terminology here. Natalie Sproul reports that children can attend closely to a television program while talking with each other.[57] Rollo May describes a psychotherapist colleague who says of himself that he "alternates as in a tennis game between seeing the patient as an object—when he thinks of patterns, dynamics, reality testing . . . —and as subject, when he empathizes with the patient's suffering and sees the world through the patient's eyes."[58] Coleridge declared that during the trance in which "Kubla Khan" came to him he experienced simultaneous perceptions. Referring to himself as "the author," he wrote, ". . . the images rose up before him as *things*, with a parallel production of the correspondent expressions."[59] Ernst Kris has commented on the historical coexistence of two different ways of perceiving religious images, like the colossal lions guarding the entrances of Assyrian palaces. Were the lions thought of as "real" or as mere representations of an impersonal power? Probably both, simultaneously, he concludes.[60] Of course there must be limits to a reader's ability to experience a semblance while also noting aspects of the structure of a work. The psychologist Jerome Singer, for instance, describing his studies of daydreaming, asserts that people frequently conduct fantasies while performing daily tasks, provided that the tasks are not too demanding. The day-dreamer, he says, can alternate rapidly between inner and outer "channels."[61] If it is not unreasonable to assume a rather intimate relationship between fantasy and semblance, Singer's findings imply the possibility of similar alternations between inner and outer channels during the reading of a novel as long as the outer or "analytical" channel is not too demanding.

What these observations lead to, it seems to me, is a familiar idea which if applied in a reasonable way can have liberating effects on the literary classroom. This idea is that we must not casually draw conclusions as to how the mind works from evidence as to how language works. Because words like "materials" and "elements," or "abstract" and "concrete," stand in a mutually exclusive relationship, many people have somehow assumed that if the mind were experiencing materials it could not at the same time notice elements. Or the mind could not simultaneously be aware of, or notice, abstraction and concreteness. Without too much exaggeration, it can be said that the whole of formalist literary theory is based on assumptions about the mind's not noticing. But the mind does notice. Within reasonable limits, a mature mind does simultaneously comprehend materials and elements. After all, as far as anyone knows, the most complex thing in the universe is a human being. And the relationship between mind and language is itself so complex that there has not yet been the slightest indication it will yield to analysis—as is revealed in the linguists' courageous but so far ineffectual struggle with the concept of the vaguely preverbal deep structures of language. The human mind is not the prisoner of its language; it creates language—slowly, it is true, but powerfully. Or where did language come from?

Presumably, throughout the history of art as we know it, mature minds have been able to entertain simultaneously a semblance and an interest in the way the semblance was created; they have also noted the relationship of the semblance to their "real" environment. As Ernst Kris says, "a firm belief in the 'reality of play' can coexist with a certainty that it is play only."[62]

With these thoughts in mind let us return to our starting point—the distinction between a mature and an immature response to literature. We can now observe that while the sem-

blance perceived by one person in a group may have approxi-
mated childhood's almost magic absorption in what was happening in the story, the semblance perceived by another may
have been much more characteristic of maturity. The more mature response may have involved a complex mixture of absorption and awareness of the referential or material aspects of the
work being read. If the latter individual is an experienced reader
he may also have had considerable awareness of how the semblance he was experiencing was being created. Such differences
actually do occur among people of college age, at least to a considerable degree, as can be determined simply by listening to
what they say. A very different case is that of the individual
who declares he got nothing at all out of a book his peers enjoy.
His difficulty is probably not one of immaturity as we've been
thinking of it, and he can be put off until we get to Part Three.

Should immature people be required to make notes about
each appearance of "innocent" in *Daisy Miller*? My own opinion is that although this question does indeed represent a practical problem, the solution to the problem doesn't lie in an answer to this particular question. I think the solution lies rather
in the possibility of learning to take pleasure in a mature approach to literature. The search for maturity is a pretty natural
process. Perhaps it's worth recalling that although childhood's
pleasures are intense, so are its terrors. In a wonderful philosophical essay entitled "Never Nothing," George P. Elliott
makes this point in a story about a childhood semblance. Like
Langer's, his story concerns his first attendance at a dramatic
performance except that in his case the drama was a Christmas
nativity play in a Quaker church. Elliott was four or five years
old. His father sang the part of Herod. His father's robe and
crown and make-up made him seem tall and cruel. At a certain
point in the play his father shouted that all the first-born men-
children in his kingdom must be killed.

> I was sheltered by my mother's arm, the room was full
> of tranquil-seeming people, that very afternoon [my
> father] had kissed my elbow where I'd fallen on the ice
> and bumped it. But for these, I would surely have given
> way to the hysteria that swelled to bursting in me, for

all that my emotion knew at that moment was that he wanted to kill me. For an hour that night he sat by my bed holding my hand till I dared to go to sleep.[63]

I don't know; sweet as some remembered childhood semblances are, I don't believe I'd want to go back. Mark Twain is better than Wordsworth at helping a person see the whole truth about all that. And maturity has its own pleasures. It seems to me no one could read Elliott's essay without feeling these things to be true and without feeling also that one of the intense pleasures of maturity is the flow of understanding, of wisdom, from mind to mind. The latter experience need not be separated from the experience of a semblance; in fact, in certain ways, the semblance is no doubt an essential part of it. I differ somewhat from Plumb on this point.

Perhaps it makes better sense to try to help an immature person comprehend what attracts a mature mind to a work of art than to tell him, in principle, that what he is supposed to do is count the appearances of "innocent." Sometimes the counting may help, sometimes not; of course the greater the complexity of the text the more likely it is to become necessary. But the development from an immature to a mature perception of the illusion of literature is probably desired as much as it is resisted. I believe most mature people, looking back over their own personal experience, would agree. This idea is given force when put into the impersonal language of psychology—as in another story about a child's first attendance at a drama, told by the psychoanalytic critic Ernst Kris. In Kris's story the child's grandfather, a famous actor, had the role of a tyrant who, during the acting, is killed; and when the murder had been enacted on the stage the child cried out in horror, "Grandpa is dead!" Kris's sober comment is that "under the impact of rising fear and aggression, the function of reality testing breaks down; stage and reality are being confused."[64] Most adults can probably recall instances of childish terror arising from confusion and of the relief that came when "reality" was discerned and when, like Elliott, they dared to sleep.

I have often encountered among young people in their first or second year in college what appears to be, in principle, a late and complex version of the childish experience just described.

When given a novel narrated in the first person (e.g., *Huckle-berry Finn*), these young people have not infrequently expressed irritation over what they identify as the author saying "I" all the time. Apparently an immature person may find in the first-person narrative convention something so threatening to his ego that, like the children at the dramatic performances (excepting Langer), he is unable to experience the convention as an element in a semblance. Sometimes the irritation may be partly relieved, in any event, by some examination of the principles and history of a novelist's management of point of view. In these cases, semblance seems not only to tolerate a simultaneous analytical attitude but to depend upon it. A somewhat similar experience may occur, I have noticed, with novels or dramas having a "tragic" ending, although these experiences are still more complex. But even here consideration of the structure, and of the convention, may somewhat alleviate an individual's emotional discomfort over the tragic ending. Kris discusses this kind of problem very interestingly from a Freudian point of view;[65] possibly his explanations are correct.

In summary, it seems reasonable to believe that with the development of intellectual and emotional maturity there is increasingly a natural desire to grasp as a comprehensive whole the relationships among self, semblance, elements, structure, materials, and environment. I have of course been using the word "maturity" as a name for the ability and desire to succeed, in some measure, in achieving just such a comprehensive grasp. Maturity in this sense has some relationship to a person's chronological age, but chronological age is not a sufficient condition for maturity. A primary purpose of the literary classroom is, I presume, to facilitate development of the kind of maturity we have been thinking about.

5. THREE SPECIAL PROBLEMS

In addition to the general considerations which have been discussed, there are three special problems about the idea of semblance that are important in the literary classroom. These are the implications of "simultaneous" in the statement that a semblance can be experienced simultaneously with analytical thinking, the question of whether a semblance can be evoked by any means other than art, and, lastly, a new kind of problem involved in the idea of purpose.

Simultaneity and Analytical Thinking

Bertrand Russell's autobiography contains a passage about an occasion on which, as a young man, he was riding in a carriage and watching the shadows of the leaves of trees moving in erratic patterns on the carriage top. He remarks that as he watched he became aware that he was thinking analytically about the patterns formed, rather than enjoying the play of light and shadow for itself as he might have done not so very long before. Russell's account indicates he felt it to be an either/ or situation. Either he took a sensuous pleasure in what he saw or he analyzed it intellectually. This account suggests a need for a good deal of wariness about the idea that a reader can enjoy the illusion of a story and at the same time think analytically about the content or structure of the story.

It does not suggest that what was previously said about the simultaneity of these experiences is in error, only that it needs to be somewhat refined. Kerr's account of the behavior of theatergoers, for example, is as meaningful as Russell's observations. We are simply forced to the conclusion that not every occasion affording opportunity for enjoyment of sensuous beauty is, or can be, "used" for that purpose; not every analytical exercise in the presence of a beautiful object is or can be associated with a semblance. Edward Bullough has a couple of terms which are helpful here. As mentioned earlier, Bullough's phrase "psychical distance" expresses much the same idea as semblance. He also uses the terms "underdistance" and "overdistance." With reference to drama, underdistance is a failure on the part of the theatergoer to maintain sufficient separation between the drama and reality. Like the children who were frightened, he lets himself be drawn into the action as if it were real. Overdistance is of course just the opposite, an inability to identify sufficiently with the drama to "feel" it. These two terms fail to take into account all the dimensions of the experience Bullough was thinking about, but they are useful in the present context.[66] Suppose, for example, we say to a ten-year-old boy that if he can correctly report the number of times the word "innocent" is uttered in a stage production of *Daisy Miller* we'll give him a new trail bike. Under these conditions, how could the poor child possibly perceive the play as a semblance? He is overdistanced. Or suppose we tell a young man that if he writes certain books and articles about the structure of Shakespeare's plays we will make him a professor in a university? An interesting question.

Overdistancing may arise from many different causes, just one of which is an intense motivation to analyze some aspect of the structure of the work of art. Whatever the cause in a particular case, it seems obvious that a display of knowledge about the structure of a literary work is no guarantee the reader has seen the work as a semblance. I suspect, as a matter of fact, that some people do reasonably well in all the courses in literature required of them throughout their schooling without ever once becoming engaged in the illusion constituted by a great literary work. Admittedly, this is a risky statement; semblance being a matter of degree, it is hard to imagine a human being who could read many great literary works without once being touched even lightly by the illusion of a story. I believe I'll stand my ground, though. I think again of what Paul Goodman said about reading *Julius Caesar*.

It is becoming evident that the circumstances in which illusion, or semblance, and analysis can coexist are more complex than it is worthwhile to try to unravel here. However, a further discussion of this subject is found in Walter Slatoff's *With Respect to Readers*. I will bring my own comments on this matter to a close by noting two points Slatoff makes, in each case hoping not only to round out my own discussion but also to provide a brief introduction to his much fuller treatment of some of the complexities involved in the idea of the coexistence of illusion and analysis.[67]

Before presenting the two points from Slatoff's book, perhaps

I should review briefly some distinctions which have emerged during the course of the preceding discussion. A "material" is something an artist takes from the environment for use in his work. It may be, for example, blue pigment or a philosophical proposition. When abstract reasoning becomes an integral part of a story, the reader's attention is focused primarily not on the validity of the reasoning but instead on the part played in the story by the act of reasoning. An example is Huckleberry Finn's reasoning that if he turns Jim in he'll have to go to hell. Most readers no doubt reject the validity of the theological proposition Huck is making, but their grasp of the story as a whole enables them to perceive this material as an ironic element. A distinction must therefore be kept in mind between a reader's analytical reasoning about the structure of a story and a character's analytical reasoning about some problem he is facing within the story. In a successful story, the character's reasoning appears as an element in the structure. A mature reader, however, may simultaneously experience the character's reasoning as an element and form an opinion as to whether the character's reasoning makes sense in the "real" world. In other words, such a reader may enjoy the episode in which Huck decides he'll go to hell, and at the same time think to himself that Huck is confused.

Slatoff's treatment of the subject of the coexistence of semblance and analysis is set up in the form of a criticism of the traditional but rather thoughtless distinction between a reader's involvement in a story and his detachment from it. Slatoff argues that the terms "involvement" and "detachment" are actually misleading. Careful examination reveals, he says, that a reader can in fact be involved and detached simultaneously and that the terms therefore tend to obscure the true character of the experience of literature. We may, he says, be moved to tears and at the same time be coolly fighting them off. Or, again, it is when we contemplate an object (e.g., a tree) aesthetically that we are most keenly aware of our relationship to it, rather than when we think of it as a source of lumber. Put into the terms I've been using, I believe Slatoff's point is not only that a reader can be simultaneously aware—in a broad sense—of semblance and structure, but also that he can be detachedly aware of how his own feelings have become elements in the semblance.

The force of the idea he is developing is captured in the following paragraph.

> If what I am saying is true, if the fullest being-within, for author and reader alike, requires a simultaneous being-without, the distinctions between empathy and sympathy, and even between sympathy and judgment, become less pronounced. Not only can they occur simultaneously but harmoniously as well. Shakespeare can be Lear and at the same time pity and judge him, and so can the reader.[68]

In a general way, what Slatoff has in mind appears to be what philosophers of history call Verstehen—the achievement by a historian of a personal, emotional identification with a historical personage he is studying, without being at all blinded as a historian by such an identification. It is also intimately related to Dewey's concept of fusion.

In the terms I've been using, the possibility offered by Slatoff's idea is that, somehow, a portion of the elements making up a semblance is created directly out of the materials constituted by the reader's own feelings, and that the reader is aware of this fact.[69] Part of the experience of looking at a tree, for example, consists of the heightening of our awareness of ourselves induced by the contemplation; part of our experience of a drama is awareness of the tightening of our muscles as the tension rises. Dewey believes that when two perceptions are fused a single perception results; Slatoff believes that two perceptions can occur simultaneously. Slatoff might prefer, however, that I say two points of view can be held simultaneously. The terminology is tricky, especially when the possibility we are considering is extended to include abstract ideas, as it is in Slatoff's discussion.[70] Dewey would say we alternate between perception and analysis.[71]

An example which occurs to me of the contribution made by personal feeling to a literary semblance is a discussion I once had with a young veteran of the navy about *Billy Budd*. He was fascinated by Melville's story, and I could see that in many ways he felt it to be *his* story—a formulation of tensions he had himself been subjected to. He appeared to find in the story a new and "distanced" way of looking at feelings which were still vitally a part of himself. As I think it over now, it seems to me that here was an instance in which a relatively mature mind succeeded pretty well in grasping as a perceptual whole the entire range from self through semblance, elements, structure, and materials to environment. In this instance, there did appear to be a genuine simultaneity of detachment and involvement, as Slatoff insists there can be.

With such evidence in mind, we can hardly question the importance in the classroom of doing everything possible to help people respond in a mature way to literature as a semblance, not just as a sort of mechanical structure to be outlined in preparation for a test. And that is the second point I wanted to cite from among those made by Slatoff. He says we should be concerned with the question of "how much of the reader's being was involved and how significantly" and adds that we should observe "the extent to which the reader would properly be described as having had an experience as opposed to a mere passing encounter or exercise."[72] He also notes the lack of any formal way of determining whether a reader has had a genuine experience—a deficiency which has undoubtedly had a pervasive and bad effect on the literary classroom. It is because of the lack of easily gradable ways of determining whether a reader has had an experience as opposed to a mere exercise that examinations tend to be concerned with "facts" and formal lectures with "structure."

The problem of testing the character of a reader's encounter with a particular work does seem to be insoluble in any formal way or in terms of any procedure, as Slatoff suggests. Fortunately, a great difference occurs when this problem is moved out of the context of formal theory and into the context with which we are primarily concerned here: the discussion of literature by a small group. In a small group, the answer to the question of who has had a significant encounter with a book is usually fairly clear. Within reasonable limits everybody just knows. The insoluble problem proves here to be not much of a problem at all.

To avoid misunderstanding, I think I should add one more comment concerning Slatoff's fine discussion. The first point I cited, how an aesthetic experience may heighten an individ-

ual's self-awareness, requires some qualification. As a matter of
fact, there are a great many testimonials that art often has just
the opposite effect, encouraging not a heightening of self-
awareness but a transcending of the ego: "Not shut up here,
but every Where," as Traherne says in his poem "My Spirit."
R. A. Durr has collected a wide variety of evidences on this subject.[73] Among the many writers he quotes are Whitman, Thoreau, and Emerson, thus involving American transcendental-
ism in general, to take just one intellectual tradition. If we join
together the contrasting and seemingly authentic evidences offered by Slatoff and Durr, respectively, we are presented with
the remarkable possibility that as a reader's sense of self is
heightened by an aesthetic experience, he achieves a dissolu-
tion of his individuality. Logic is benumbed by the discovery
that something resembling this paradoxical circumstance was
actually reported by Tennyson.[74]

What this all adds up to is obviously an epistemologist's
nightmare. Within the confines of our own more modest subject, however, it is less daunting. Reasonably mature readers, at
least within my own observation, are not usually overpowered
by personal involvement in literature they read; they find it
possible to keep in mind the fact that they are dealing with an
illusion. On the other hand, if they do achieve a sense of release from their material self it is not so great that they lose
sight altogether of their mortal ties. Nevertheless, any teacher
can cite numerous instances of practical difficulties in both these
directions. An example of too strong a personal awareness
which I recall from one of my own classes is that of the thirty-
year-old man who asked me not to insist he complete his reading of Charles Brockden Brown's *Ormond* because of an intense
distaste for it. Later, he added that Constantia, the strong-willed
heroine of this story, reminded him of his wife. Another example, representing not too much self-awareness but perhaps too
little, is that of a brilliant but rather eccentric young woman
whose response to literature seemed to be almost hallucinatory.
She virtually lived the things she read. At the same time, she
so resolutely refused to "think" about literature that the only
kind of discussion about books I was ever able to carry on with
her was a series of appreciative comments. This was a long time

ago and the image remaining in my mind is one of a very lonely person. I don't really know whether I should describe her response to literature as showing too little self-awareness, but it was unquestionably sadly limited.

It is these issues of the wholeness of a reader's response that are of primary concern in the classroom, rather than conjecture about the mechanics of the involvement of the self with the work. Again, I don't mean in any way to belittle conjecture or theory; I presume these words are only names for efforts by our imagination to help us see, as exemplified in our next topic.

Semblance in Fields outside of Art

A second special problem is the relationship of the two concepts of semblance and intransitive rapt attention to fields outside of art. This problem can be broken down into three topics as follows. First, it raises a fundamental question about the relationship of art—and of the literary classroom—to other areas of experience. Second, it suggests some curious ideas about the distinction between creative and appreciative activity. And, third, it indicates a need for a modification of our previous distinction between semblance and intransitive rapt attention.

For consideration of the relationship of art to other fields I will choose mathematics and theoretical physics. It is not at all uncommon to find mathematicians and physicists talking about their work in terms that, surprisingly, would seem more natural among artists. The phrase "intransitive rapt attention" proves to be especially appropriate for their experience.

The great nineteenth-century mathematician Henri Poincaré, for example, wrote eloquently about his conviction that creative ability in mathematics was fundamentally dependent upon an aesthetic sensitivity. He declared that the beauty and elegance of mathematics evoked a "kind of aesthetic emotion" in the true mathematician. He believed that to do creative work it was necessary for a mathematician to be able to discriminate aesthetically between mathematical combinations which were beautiful and those which were not. Recently the same idea has been explored in great depth for science in general by Michael Polanyi, who says: "A scientific theory which calls attention to its own beauty, and partly relies on it for claiming to represent empirical reality, is akin to a work of art which calls attention to its own beauty as a token of artistic reality."[75]

The role of sensuous imagery in the aesthetic aspect of scientific thought is suggested by Polanyi's review of an incident in the history of Einstein's discovery of relativity. The point Polanyi is especially concerned with is the surprising fact that the origin of the theory of relativity might be said to lie in a paradox Einstein hit upon at the age of sixteen. The teen-age Einstein asked himself what he would observe if he were able to fly through space behind a beam of light, at the light's own speed, and watch it. Would the beam of light appear to be at rest, somewhat as today a space vehicle appears to be at rest when viewed on TV from another space vehicle following it at the same speed? Einstein's own words, quoted by Polanyi, are that he wondered if the beam of light would appear "as a spatially oscillatory electromagnetic field at rest." His intuition that it would not appear to be at rest led ten years later to the theory of relativity, as he explained in his autobiography and further confirmed in response to a query from Polanyi.[76] It is impossible not to wonder what went on in the mind of the sixteen-year-old Einstein. Did he see in his mind's eye a physical image of the beam of light? Did he feel himself to be witnessing a drama with intransitive rapt attention?

The sensuous, imagistic content of scientific thought has recently been discussed by the nuclear physicist Martin Deutsch, who asserts that the creative imagination can "function only by evoking potential or imagined sense impressions." Deutsch adds, "I have never met a physicist, at least not an experimental physicist, who does not think of the hydrogen atom by evoking a visual image of what he would see if the particular atomic model with which he is working existed literally on a scale [large enough to be] accessible to sense impressions."[77] Similarly the theoretical physicist Theodore Taylor has remarked, "I have thought of billiard balls as the examples in physics as long as I can remember—as examples of types of collisions from Newton's mechanics to atomic particles."[78] No doubt Taylor is a David Hume buff. Of course there are numerous phenomena in physics that do not yield in any helpful way to imagery, a common example being transient currents in electrical-power transmission lines; these currents can be effectively conceptualized only mathematically. But this is not to question the profound importance of sensuous imagery to the scientific imagination, of which there are countless evidences.

A particularly complex and moving example of the aesthetic dimension of creative work in science is found in a few sentences the physicist Werner Heisenberg has written about a night of work which led to an important discovery. In the early morning hours, he wrote,

> I could no longer doubt the mathematical consistency and coherence of the kind of quantum mechanics to which my calculations pointed. At first, I was deeply alarmed. I had the feeling that, through the surface of atomic phenomena, I was looking at a strangely beautiful interior, and felt almost giddy that I now had to probe this wealth of mathematical structures nature had so generously spread out before me.[79]

One of the more remarkable evidences I have come across of the power of mathematics to evoke the kind of delight Heisenberg expresses is the simple coincidence of a word choice by Thomas Jefferson and Bertrand Russell. To describe their feeling about mathematics, both chose the word "delicious." (I have heard the same word applied to the language of a poem.) Similarly, Einstein remarked that if Euclid "failed to kindle your youthful enthusiasm, then you were not born to be a scientific thinker." The physicist Wolfgang Pauli, after reading a paper on quantum mechanics by Heisenberg, said the paper had restored his joy in life.

To conclude these observations on the aesthetic quality of scientific thought, however, I would like to quote at length from an astonishing prose ode to science recently published not by a physicist or a mathematician but by a medical man. The author of the following passage is Lewis Thomas, Dean of Medicine, Yale University.

> The most mysterious aspect of difficult science is the way it is done. Not the routine, not just the fitting together of things that no one had guessed at fitting, not the making of connections; these are merely the work-

aday details, the methods of operating. They are interesting, but not as fascinating as the central mystery, which is that we do it at all, and that we do it under such compulsion.

I don't know of any other human preoccupation, even including what I have seen of art, in which the people engaged in it are so caught up, so totally preoccupied, so driven beyond their strength and resources.

Scientists at work have the look of creatures following genetic instructions; they seem to be under the influence of a deeply placed human instinct. They are, despite their efforts at dignity, rather like young animals engaged in savage play. When they are near an answer their hair stands on end, they sweat, they are awash in their own adrenalin. To grab the answer, and grab it first, is for them a more powerful drive than feeding or breeding or protecting themselves against the elements.

It sometimes looks like a solitary activity, but it is as much the opposite of solitary as human behavior can be. There is nothing so social, so communal, so interdependent. An active field of science is like an immense intellectual anthill; the individual almost vanishes into the mass of minds tumbling over each other, carrying information from place to place, passing it around at the speed of light. . . .

There is nothing to touch the spectacle. In the midst of what seems to be a collective derangement of minds, with bits of information being scattered about, torn to shreds, disintegrated, reconstituted, engulfed in an activity that seems as random and agitated as that of bees in a disturbed part of the hive, there suddenly emerges, with the purity of a slow phrase of music, a single new piece of truth about nature.[80]

In view of the emotional, sensuous, and dramatic character of the thought of these scientists and mathematicians, it cannot be doubted that the term intransitive rapt attention is appropriate to their experience.[81] The term refers as aptly to Poincaré's experience with mathematical symbols as to Emily Dickinson's with the verbal symbols of her poem "Perception of an

Object." Intransitive rapt attention would, in fact, appear to be an appropriate descriptive phrase for the experience of virtually all creative thought in science and mathematics.

A reciprocal question is whether the same descriptive phrase could be extended very much beyond Dickinson's poem into the field of literature. This question is both unanswerable and of considerable practical importance in the literary classroom. Not only is there a fair amount of literature, mostly poetry, of the type represented by Dickinson's poem, there is also the possibility that some people are temperamentally predisposed toward an interest in the structure and abstract concepts involved in literary works rather than primarily in the illusion of life the works may offer. And there is the further possibility that what is done in a literary classroom may actually enhance analytical ability at the cost of a diminished response to the semblance.[82] Having so little knowledge concerning these possibilities, we can only ponder—and observe. In any event, there must be some literary experience for which the phrase intransitive rapt attention is more appropriate than the term semblance. One of the most puzzling, and even disturbing, possibilities suggested by these considerations is that an apparently identical enthusiasm shown by two people for a given work might originate from quite different kinds of interests.

A second topic concerning the problem of relating semblance and intransitive rapt attention to fields outside of art involves some rather curious ideas about a distinction between creative and appreciative activity. This distinction centers on the word "intransitive." It has been assumed all along that the word "intransitive" was a way of expressing the same idea Kant intended in his word "free" in the phrase "free beauty." That is, when the beauty of an object is entirely unrelated to any practical value the object might have, then its beauty is free beauty, and attention given to it is intransitive. Alas, such an easy assumption proves unacceptable.

As accounts of the experience of creative minds in both art and science make clear, creativity is sometimes coupled with a highly competitive or even belligerent attitude. In literature, Hemingway and Zola come at once to mind. In science, James Watson and Ernest Rutherford. The question of whether such men contemplate their creative ideas intransitively is of course extremely subjective; perhaps even they could not say with assurance. Only a tentative and cautionary observation can be ventured, therefore, which is that creative activity may well be less intransitive than appreciative activity. My personal opinion is that our terminology is too imprecise, and our knowledge too limited, to attempt a confident description of what actually happens. We may nevertheless draw one modest and useful inference. People are often stimulated by a literary work into an intense creativity concerning its interpretation. During this phase of their activity, which presumably follows the initial seizure (to use Dewey's term), it is therefore a wise bystander who remembers the potential coupling of creativity and belligerence.

Finally, we need to make a slight modification of the initial distinction between intransitive rapt attention and semblance. We can begin with the question of whether the term semblance is ever appropriate to an experience in science or mathematics. According to the understanding that semblance must involve the illusion of human life, the answer is plainly no. There is a teasing ambiguity left over, however. Exactly what is it that so excites the imagination of the scientist or mathematician? The mathematician responds readily with the words beauty, elegance; and in fact the physicist usually does the same. Although a love of beauty is not likely the entire explanation of a laborious lifetime in the study of physics or mathematics, it is obvious this passion can be a powerfully motivating force. We are confronted with the ancient conundrum: what is beauty?

Rather than closing the door on this conundrum, I am going to speculate for a moment. My subject will be the idea that beauty—however many meanings the word may have—is intimately related to life itself, that is, to the concept of life in its most fundamental sense. The terms beauty and semblance are commonly applied indiscriminately to such very different works as *King Lear* and an unadorned vase. It is said that in the vase there is a semblance of life, a virtual embodiment of a purposeful imagination, as there is in the play—and my own introspection agrees that this is true. If there is virtual life in a vase, or in the beautiful structure of sounds comprising a symphony, why not in a structure of mathematical symbols? With such thoughts in mind I myself would enlarge the sentence quoted earlier from Motherwell. I would say that in art and in science and mathematics alike we seek to wed ourselves to the indefinable but often intensely felt life we call, vaguely, universe. By whatever means they have, human beings strive to define themselves and to locate themselves in the all-encompassing ocean of space-time-life. As Ruth Nanda Anshen has written, ". . . underlying the new ideas, including those of modern physics, is a unifying order, but it is not causality; it is purpose, and not the purpose of the universe and man but the purpose *in* the universe and *in* man."[83] At the core of such hope as these words express must lie a conviction that eventually there will emerge a new and more fruitful concept of what unity and order mean and that it will prove possible for the conscious purpose of an individual mind to wed itself to this new meaning. In such a fruition, and even in the mere hope that it will occur, the distance between semblance and intransitive rapt attention is somewhat lessened. Both are in the end concerned with life.

Given our modest preoccupation with what happens day by day in a literary classroom, however, the distinction between these two terms remains steadily useful. Verstehen should be our final goal, embracing both correctness of understanding and semblance, and a difficult goal it is. Nevertheless it would be a meager classroom which did not occasionally remark that its own version of quantum mechanics was not the only version capable of adding, or even restoring, joy to life.

Semblance, Purpose, and Behaviorism

A third and last special problem to consider in respect to the meaning of semblance is, once more, the concept that semblance depends on a purposive act by the artist—but looked at now with reference to a special challenge. This challenge is found in the idea that a work of art—or, more precisely, an art object —is actually not dependent on purpose at all but is simply anything before which an individual adopts the aesthetic attitude. If it affects you as art, the reasoning goes, then why not call it art? In such a view of the matter, a pebble picked up at random on a beach might properly be regarded as art by anyone who believed himself affected by it in an artlike way. The idea is nicely expressed by Morse Peckham, in behavioristic terms: "A work of art is any perceptual field which an individual uses as an occasion for performing the role of art perceiver."[84] Put simply, the issue is this: can an art object be identified as an art object by inspection? For those who believe it can, the identification is made through evidences of the artist's creative purpose. His creativity is demonstrated by his success in transforming materials into elements. For those who believe art objects cannot be identified as art by inspection, interest is of course centered not upon the art object itself but upon the behavior of the perceiver, as seen in Peckham's statement. We need not be concerned with the whole scope of this difficult problem, only with those aspects of it that affect the literary classroom.

First of all, we should ponder a strange fact. However antithetical they may be in theory, both these opposing views concerning the nature of art are of practical value in the classroom. Indeed, they effectively complement one another.

Classroom discussion often begins with an unspoken assumption that an art object can be identified as art by inspection. "What purpose does this episode serve in the novel?" we ask. In other words, how does this material function as an element in the semblance? We assume that the work is art and that anyone who inspects it will recognize it as art and perceive it as a semblance. In asking what purpose a given episode serves we are seeking the source of the cohesiveness creating the semblance that we have assumed everyone will experience. But possession of cohesiveness or structure does not ensure that a given work will create a semblance for everyone who reads it; and this appears to be true even if we limit the readers to intelligent and reasonably mature people. It is quite possible to demonstrate to a reader's entire satisfaction that a certain work is beautifully structured only to have him say he finds it dull.

When a demonstration has failed in this way, we naturally turn to the opposite point of view. Our question now is, what is inhibiting the reader from accepting the role of art perceiver? What is preventing his acceptance of the transformation of the materials into a semblance? Granted, again, the necessary aptitudes and reasonable maturity, a reader's inability to respond to a work being enjoyed by his peers must originate in some attitude or expectancy he brings to the reading or viewing, as was noted earlier.[85] Many times, for example, I have heard literary scholars say of some widely admired author, "I simply can't read him." I used to think it an affectation, as I'm sure it sometimes is, but I've become convinced it is often something more significant than that. My most vivid memory of a rejection of the role of art perceiver, however, is not related to a colleague but to a young woman in one of my classes. One day I had been talking, not without pride and enthusiasm, about a few structural components I had figured out in Djuna Barnes's difficult novel *Nightwood*, and after class this young woman stopped to say she had found the discussion quite interesting but the fact was the book made her sick to her stomach. Both Kenneth Burke and T. S. Eliot have expressed admiration for *Nightwood*. Eliot wrote a foreword for it. I myself find it fascinating. The young woman was highly intelligent, and reasonable. What went wrong? I don't know, but I suppose her inference as to the author's purpose in some of the admittedly unpleasant episodes in the novel was different from that of readers who were not made sick to their stomach. And why such a difference? I can only speculate that it originated in some deeply held values or attitudes on the part of the young woman. Certainly my efforts to demonstrate the cohesiveness of the novel, to trace the transformation of material into semblance, did not greatly help her. She did not succeed in playing the art perceiver's role. I believe now I could have been more helpful had I begun, when I first assigned the novel, by discussing not its structure but the ideas and attitudes which are given symbolic expression in it, and the relationship of these ideas and attitudes to the environment out of which the novel came. Perhaps with some background preparation, the novel could have been perceived at once as a semblance, and the discussion of its structure could then have had significance from the outset.

These comments may seem to attach more importance to the idea of the art perceiver's role than I really intended. Possibly I can in some measure offset any such lack of balance by recalling Henry James's memorable assertion that the novelist creates his reader—an observation to which I would certainly add, as my own testimony, that a great literary work can grip a reader with a force which is genuinely astonishing. Sometimes the perceptual field takes the perceiver by the throat in spite of all he can do. Sometimes, though, it doesn't, and then it is comforting to have more than one way to think about the endlessly fascinating and baffling subject of the relationship between reader and work.

6. SUMMARY OF PART ONE

A semblance is the illusion created by literature, or by any art, and possibly by imaginative thought or attention in other areas as well. Its character is determined by the printed text, or the art object, and by the capabilities of the reader or audience. In the literary classroom both these determinants are contemplated, each serving as a means of contemplating the other. In comparing one another's responses to a text, people acquire some insight into themselves and into one another; at the same time, they learn something about printed texts. Although the concept of semblance is both broad and complex, it is probably derived from a fundamental mode of experience. In Part Two I will try to relate the concept of semblance to the role of abstract thought in the literary classroom.

I am reminded, however, of a remarkable sentence by Lucien Goldmann, which will serve to conclude this discussion of semblance:

> . . . the human being is one who places his stakes on the possibility of giving meaning to a word which will eventually, at some point, resist this meaning.[86]

Part Two.

Abstractions

W hen a person looks at six horses, does he see six things or seven? Horse sense says six; some philosophers say seven. The seventh is a universal, the class of things to which all horses belong. It is with this ghostly seventh horse our subject begins.

The problem is, six real horses are six unique individuals. How, then, does the mind bring them together, their individual uniqueness unimpaired, into a single class called "horse"? Opinions differ. Some say through perception of the seventh thing, the universal. Such a universal is called "real." Others favor merely nominal universals.[1] The word "horse," in any case, is a universal or abstraction. Conversely, an individual horse is what in literary studies is usually referred to as a concrete particular, according to the Hegelian distinction between the abstract and the concrete.

Jean Piaget's studies of children throw light upon an elemental form of the problem of universals. Typically, if a four-year-old child is shown five black beads and two white ones and asked whether there are more black beads or white beads, he will reply correctly that there are more black ones. But if he is asked whether there are more *black beads* or more *beads*, he will still reply that there are more black beads—because there are only two white ones. Most four-year-olds are incapable of a simultaneous awareness of a class (all the beads) and a subclass (the five black ones). Consequently, the child is unable to compare the five black beads with all seven beads. Of course an adult mind handles these distinctions with ease—but how much farther can the adult mind go in simultaneous awareness of universals and particulars in the complex environment of literature?

Many people have believed that literature's concern should be with concrete particulars and not with universals, or abstractions, at all. The point of view sustaining this belief appears in an engaging story Sir Arthur Eddington tells about an elephant. One morning somebody discovered an elephant standing precariously on a grassy hillside. The hill was steep; the grass was slippery with dew; the elephant was ponderous. An outcry was raised and a group of scientists and engineers were hurried to the scene to figure out how to get the elephant safely down off the hill. One of these men promptly started to measure the angle of slope of the hill. Another studied the coefficient of friction of the dewy grass. A third determined the mass of the elephant. A fourth studied wind velocity. I may have embroidered this story a little around the edges.

Eddington believes that what the scientists did was all very well; he himself does not want to dispense with abstractions. But he asks a question: what has become of the elephant? In place of a sweet and grassy hill we have an angle and a coefficient of friction. In place of the fresh wind, a velocity. In place of the elephant, a number representing its mass. Nothing but abstractions.[2]

The literary critic Cleanth Brooks has taken a position resembling Eddington's but somewhat more extreme. In an essay entitled "The Uses of Literature," Brooks recently observed: "A formula can be learned and applied, but the full, concrete, appropriate response to a situation can only be experienced. Literature is thus incurably concrete—not abstract."[3] Long ago, he asserted that poems never contain abstract statements and that "a genuine poem does not confront us as abstraction—that is, as one man's generalization from the relevant particulars."[4]

This abstract-vs.-concrete kind of problem is not merely theoretical. In group discussions of literature it appears in a most blunt and demanding way. I recall an occasion on which I discussed *Brave New World* with a class of freshmen. Not knowing any better, the first thing I said was, "Well, how did you like *Brave New World*?" To this mistake, after a moment of silence, I added another. I called on a certain young man by name. He sat in the left front corner seat. He was shy, had fair skin, gold spectacles. After a stunned moment, turning a bright pink, he burst out, "It sounds wonderful to me!" This was before the beginning of the ecology movement.

This young man must have had some sort of concrete experience with *Brave New World* that he wasn't supposed to have had. Or was Huxley himself carried away in depicting those gorgeous, willing girls? One thing does seem certain: the young man had not felt the bite of the abstract meaning in Huxley's satire.

The problem represented by this experience is purely practical. It does not arise out of any theoretical approach to literature but out of the nature of literary experience itself. Not only *Brave New World* but many other fine literary works can be enjoyed without perceiving the author's true or full intention. Does an explanation of the full abstract meaning in such works reduce the reader's pleasure? On the other hand, are there works which are devoid of abstract meaning? These are practical problems for the classroom.

In our most familiar critical terminology these problems appear as an opposition between the abstract and the concrete. Other pairs of terms have been used to express essentially the same opposition, however. One traditional pair is reason and passion; another is sense and sensibility, although sensibility is a slippery word. Aestheticians are fond of contrasting cognitive and emotive. John Crowe Ransom chose structure and texture; Marshall McLuhan refers to linear and simultaneous. Both the latter two sets of terms are regarded by Northrop Frye as partial recognitions of fundamentally different types of mental operations; he refers to these operations as critical and precritical. Georg Lukács speaks of universal and individual. An especially interesting and complex pair is Roman Jakobson's metaphoric and metonymic. Among these pairs of terms and others which could be added to them, there is a considerable range of meaning. Nevertheless, with the exception of Jakobson's terms all share the kind of concern we have in mind when asking someone for a concrete example of what he meant by an abstract statement he made.

Jakobson shifts the center of interest to the kind of relationships included within each term. Relationships included under metaphoric he identifies as based on similarity; those under metonymic he identifies as based on contiguity. The latter are more abstract, involving such relationships as cause and effect. We will not need to employ Jakobson's terminology to benefit from his insights.

In addition to abstract or abstraction, I will use the terms universal, generalization, and meaning. It might appear simplest to use meaning alone, but in our context there is a fundamental ambiguity in this word, to say nothing of the heavy load of connotations created by all the writing that has been done about it. In our context, meaning sometimes means an abstract statement (e.g., all men are mortal) and sometimes the full import, both intellectual and emotional, of a complex work of art. I will restrict meaning to abstractions except on a few occasions specifically noted. It will become necessary to use "meaning" when we discuss the abstract meaning of a text, since it is hardly acceptable to talk about the abstractions of a text.

A universal is an entire class of things, or a proposition about an entire class. A generalization is a somewhat looser version of a universal, often more limited in meaning. That is, a generalization may not refer to an entire class. I will comment further on the meaning of all these terms as they appear in the course of the discussion.

Despite the disappearing elephant and the young man's misapprehension about *Brave New World*, it would probably be safer to say that literature is incurably abstract than that it is incurably concrete. With the passing of time it has become evident that neither proposition is very attractive, however. Usually literature is concrete. As far as I can see it is always, in some sense, abstract. Rather than trying to determine precisely which of these polarities is more nearly correct, I would like to think about how each enters into literature and how each can most helpfully be talked about in a classroom. To the degree to which the concrete can be defined as semblance it has, to the best of my ability, been discussed in the preceding part of this book. The objective of the present part is to undertake a comparable review of abstractions. This review will be organized around six principal topics: the historical context of our problem, briefly considered; meaning, significance, and the author's intention; series and probability; limited generalizations; the advantages of explicit generalizations; and the nonrational.

8. HISTORICAL CONTEXT:

THE LOGICAL GAP & ABSTRACTIONS

The terminology of the abstract and the concrete, as distinguished from the real problems to which these terms refer, was given a special prominence in critical vocabulary because of a series of historical events. Twenty years ago Meyer Abrams concluded his great book *The Mirror and the Lamp* with a sentence that summarized these events.

> It was only in the early Victorian period, when all discourse was explicitly or tacitly thrown into the two exhaustive modes of imaginative and rational, expressive and assertive, that religion fell together with poetry into opposition to science, and that religion, as a consequence, was converted into poetry, and poetry into a kind of religion.[5]

Abrams's "imaginative" and "rational" are roughly the equivalent of Cleanth Brooks's "concrete" and "abstract." Abstraction became a kind of epithet; a complex of anxieties and hostilities were embodied in the word. When this complex was added to such fundamental practical problems of meaning and feeling as the one I described earlier (p. 88), serious difficulties were created in the literary classroom.

Although Abrams's sentence is still entirely true today, it now calls for a supplement. The supplement needed concerns the changing role of science in our time and consequently the changing relationship between the imaginative and rational modes of discourse. If the concept of science now held by thoughtful people were substituted for the meaning actually carried by the word "science" in Abrams's sentence, the sentence would lose its coherence. The reason is simply that science looks more like poetry than it did twenty years ago, to say nothing of what it looked like in the Victorian era about which Abrams was writing.

Some evidences of changing attitudes among scientists have already been seen in Part One, and others will be considered in the latter part of the present discussion. Meanwhile, our general subject of abstractions can be initially clarified by reviewing what it was that not only divided discourse into the two modes Abrams identified but also aroused such intense distaste among some people for the one mode. This mode, the abstract, is still—more than a century later—often denounced. Why? Upon reflection, it seems a curious antipathy.

Part of the explanation lies in the historic pressure of an increasingly powerful science on ideas about meaning and truth. Another part of the explanation lies in the concept of abstraction itself, which upon examination breaks up into a number of different concepts. I will take up these two topics in turn: the historical context, as viewed from the perspective of the logical gap, and the meaning of abstraction.

The Logical Gap

An insight into why the pressure of science on ideas about truth created antagonism toward abstractions is found in a most unlikely place: a handbook of logic. It must be emphasized that what is found here is indeed only an insight, not an explanation. Nevertheless, it points the way toward explanations. The material of special interest in a handbook of logic is primarily the treatment of the process of induction.

Induction is customarily represented as made up of the following elements, except that I have modified and pieced them out a little:

particulars—logical gap—generalization—finality

From left to right, the first three terms are the ones ordinarily used, with the single difference that "intuitive leap" or "inductive leap" is usually preferred to "logical gap." Although the latter term is not found very often it can be seen, for example, in Michael Polanyi's *Personal Knowledge*, where it is used as equivalent to intuitive leap. The term logical gap has the advantage of calling attention not only to the act, the leap, but to the gap that is leaped over. It is the gap, rather than the leap, that is most significant for our immediate purpose.

Historically, this idea of the gap between the particular and the general or the universal is probably most familiar in the form of David Hume's questioning of induction and of cause and effect. If, several times in a row, one billiard ball striking a second billiard ball "causes" the second ball to roll away, can it be proved that the same result will be seen on the next try?

No, said Hume. Or if, several tries in a row, we time a freely falling stone, can we leap to the generalization that $S = \frac{1}{2}at^2$? In Hume's opinion, it would be a leap indeed. Of course the whole question is extremely complex; I will make only a few simple observations about it.

The picture before us is of a human mind (whatever that is) making a hazardous leap from a collection of particulars to a generalization; once established on the generalization, the mind peers back down into the dizzying infinity of the logical gap and wonders how it can ever establish a safe and comfortable bridge between the generalization and a particular. How can the mind ever acquire enough confidence to assert that if a particular object motionless in space is acted upon by the earth's gravity, what *will happen* is that the object will move the distance S in time t? In other words, what does the scientist have to put across the logical gap that will "verify" his generalization? The answer is, both obviously and curiously, the prediction itself. He predicts that his generalization will hold true, and after a few successful tries everybody is reasonably well satisfied that it will, and his generalization is established. He cannot, however, explain why his prediction holds true, nor can he guarantee that his prediction will hold true on the next try. Actually scientists usually prefer to say they verify their laws through testing rather than through predicting. The concept of verification has itself been questioned, but this is a subtlety having no direct bearing upon our subject.

I haven't yet mentioned the fourth term, finality, which is an addition of my own to the materials found in a handbook of logic. There may well be better terms to use, in spite of the vaguely Aristotelian quality of finality. Perhaps "full disclosure" would be better. I was seeking a term which would reflect the dream of the perfection of knowledge, or of total comprehension. The notion of anything even approaching finality is not in very good standing any more, but such notions used to be alluded to often enough. Albert Einstein, for example, could say, "The supreme task of the physicist is to arrive at those universal elementary laws from which the cosmos can be built up by pure deduction."[6]

There are two reasons for adding finality to the usual three terms in which the process of induction is stated. Both have to do only with our limited, immediate objective. The first is that the inductive method is preeminently the method through which science pursues the mythical goal of total comprehension. Henry Adams wittily pointed this out when he remarked that the scientific era began with Bacon's advice to his contemporaries. Bacon's advice, said Adams, was to stop trying to derive the universe from an idea and to start trying to derive an idea from the universe. Although accepted scientific laws are applied deductively, as Einstein indicated, the process of the discovery of new laws is characteristically inductive (or abductive, but that's another subject). Bacon was urging the use of induction.

The second reason for adding the fourth term has to do with the problem of proving the truth of general statements. And here we come upon one of the strangest chapters in all the history of thought about literature. An insight into this bit of history begins with another glance at the two fundamental logical processes of deduction and induction.

In outline, there are two ways of objectively demonstrating the truth of a general statement. One is by deducing the statement from a truth which has already been established. The other is by testing. As already noted, testing is the bridge used to get across the logical gap in the process of induction. Testing is what follows when observation of several concrete particulars has led to a guess that a certain generalization will hold true. The strange thing that has taken place is that again and again modern literary theorists have passionately committed themselves to "particulars," as if they were engaged in the process of induction, while at the same time rejecting the inference of general, abstract ideas from these particulars. And yet without some generalizations to which they can be related, the particulars lose their significance; mind itself vanishes.

It is true that Lévi-Strauss attributes a "science of the concrete" to primitive peoples, but he nevertheless observes that in the final analysis a concrete particular by itself reduces to unintelligibility.[7] A science of the concrete, as he describes it, is a network of relationships based upon direct sense perceptions rather than upon such abstract qualities as mass or duration. Like any science, a science of the concrete is dependent on the recognition of relationships among the particulars perceived.

And modern psychology asserts, of course, that without some kind of generalizing framework of relationships even our perceptions would be reduced, in William James's famous phrase, to a buzzing blooming confusion.

On the other hand, Lévi-Strauss also believes that a structure deliberately and consciously designed into a work of art has less authority than one emerging spontaneously from the artist's unconscious. At the beginning of a discussion of abstractions in literature, this opinion deserves thoughtful consideration. It's impossible to be sure Lévi-Strauss is right, and yet there probably is something in what he says. I am inclined to agree with him. In Chapter 13, under the general heading of the nonrational, I will return to this subject. Meanwhile, our objective will be to determine the role played by abstractions in literature rather than to determine whether they originate in the author's conscious or unconscious mind.

I must confess I have a good deal of sympathy for those theorists who adopted the strange position described above. In fact, I believe what happened was virtually inevitable—as will become apparent upon our looking a little further into the history of the matter. Another curiosity in the situation, however, is that the distinguished writers and scholars who led the attack on abstractions and the movement in support of the concrete generally took occasion to recognize the importance of the abstract, as will also become apparent.[8] And in day-by-day literary work everybody made incessant use of abstract reason in a great variety of ways, despite all the denunciations of abstractions.

The first justification for adding finality to the usual three terms of the inductive process is to recognize the belief of earlier scientists in the possibility of attaining a full understanding of the physical universe through the use of the inductive method. The second justification is to provide a way of relating people's ideas about truth to their behavior concerning the logical gap. A glance at history will help explain the behavior of the literary theorists just noted.

Historically, people who had a serene faith in a source of absolute truth were not greatly troubled about the logical gap. I suppose only people who do not think at all are not troubled at all about such a problem. Nevertheless, if we compare modern

Americans to the early Christians or to the people of twelfth-
century Europe, there is an obvious change concerning their belief in the possibilities of absolute truth, or of finality. And this
change involves not only the degree of their faith in absolute
truth, it also involves the kind of faith they hold.

The concepts of the logical gap and finality could, I suppose,
be used as the basis for an extended analysis of the shift away
from religious faith toward faith in science and (in Abrams's
sense) in art, and finally toward the present relativism. Our
purposes can best be served, however, by applying these concepts
to only a few carefully selected figures, with special emphasis on
a sequence running from Henry Adams and the so-called scientific historians through Charles Beard and Gertrude Stein to
Ernest Hemingway. To provide reference points, I will first
refer briefly to Saint Paul, Emerson, and Einstein.

Although in no simplistic sense, Saint Paul represents an essentially deductive habit of mind. His thought moves from the
finality of God's will to generalizations received from God and
across the logical gap to judgment in particular cases. "But unto
the married I give charge, yea not I, but the Lord, that the wife
depart not from her husband" (1 Cor. 7:10). He admonished
individuals for particular acts violating such generalizations.
His generalizations were verified by their source in the finality
of God. There might be some question about the appropriateness of the concept of the logical gap in this context, where the
general law is known and the only problem is the application
of the law to a particular case. Many an honest man has had a
fall into the logical gap while trying to work his syllogisms,
however, a fact well known among logicians. And of course
Saint Paul himself recognized the hazard, in his own terms, as
shown in his beautiful line contrasting mortal to divine wisdom: "Now we see in a glass darkly, but then face to face" (1
Cor. 13:12).

Like Saint Paul, Ralph Waldo Emerson received messages
from God, but in the form of private intuitions rather than com-
mandments. Emerson was not a lawgiver. Rather than a nearly
anthropomorphic God, Emerson's finality was an Oversoul.
Saint Paul's mind appears to move from right to left, deductively, across our four terms, but it is hard to say how Emerson's
mind moves. He does not speak of instructions received but of

intuitions experienced. Still, his faith in the finality of the Oversoul relieves him to a considerable degree from concern about
the logical gap. He believes truth is available without testing.
When he says "Trust thyself!" what he means is trust your ability to commune directly with the Oversoul, intuitively.

In relationship to our set of terms, Einstein represents a point
somewhere between Emerson and Adams. He resembles Emerson in his faith in a pantheistic God (Emerson's Oversoul), a
faith he held with deep feeling. He also resembles Emerson in
his belief in the importance of intuition. He differs from Emerson, however, in the nature of his concept of intuition. Einstein's
intuition is not one that, like Emerson's, yields Truth; Einstein's is closer to what is called insight. It is formed by practice and must usually be verified by testing. His attitude is indicated in the following words: ". . . only intuition, resting on
sympathetic understanding of experience, can reach [new
physical laws]."[9] Einstein does not share Emerson's lack of concern about the logical gap, either in science or philosophy. Exactly what Emerson's position was in respect to the scientific
method is unclear, although he was apparently more cautious
there about intuitions than in the areas of ethics and religion.

Einstein's confidence in the possibility of crossing the logical
gap, on the other hand, was derived from his conviction that the
universe is orderly and meaningful. This belief was at the heart
of his long argument with his friend Niels Bohr. As we'll see
later, Bohr's universe is in the end enigmatic. The logical gap
ultimately becomes an unbridgeable chasm. Einstein, in contrast, continued to believe the logical gap could be crossed by
intuiting the laws governing the universe and verifying them
through prediction or testing.[10]

Compared to the figures we have looked at so far, the significance of Henry Adams in regard to the problem of the logical gap lies in the extremity of the view he held for a time. A
leading member of the short-lived but influential school of
American scientific historians, he staked his success on particulars. In effect he undertook to confine his work to the left-hand
side of the logical gap. This, of course, requires shifting the
concept of finality also over to the left-hand side of the gap and
locating it among the particulars.

Like others in the scientific school of historians, Adams rea-

soned that he might be able to create an absolutely true piece
of historical writing if he simply put down one fact after another in his text. Since each fact would be unassailably true, his
text would be true. He describes the idea in these words:

> He [i.e., Adams himself] had even published a dozen
> volumes of American history for no other purpose than
> to satisfy himself whether, by the severest process of stat-
> ing, with the least possible comment, such facts as
> seemed sure, in such order as seemed rigorously conse-
> quent, he could fix for a familiar moment a necessary
> sequence of human movement.[11]

There are three fundamental ideas in this passage: facts, order,
and comment. First, as to facts. Adams gave little attention to
the problem of what constitutes a fact, although later historians
have thought a great deal about this subject. For the moment,
we can assume that everybody knows what a fact is. Next, the
idea of order in Adams's statement has to do with sequence.
Changing the sequence or order in which facts appear affects
their meaning, as in the following statements: (*a*) He ran; he
saw a bear. (*b*) He saw a bear; he ran. Adams hoped to present
facts in what might be called their natural sequence, so as not
to distort their meaning. This purpose is expressed in his words
"such order as seemed rigorously consequent" and "necessary
sequence of human movement." Finally, by "comment" Adams
meant what we would call interpretation. He believed, or
hoped, that if facts were clearly presented in a natural sequence
their general meaning would be self-evident. No comment or
generalization would be necessary.[12]

   He and the others of his school thus offer a nearly perfect example of the next-to-the-last extremity in attempts to solve the
problem of the logical gap. The problem is to be solved by not
attempting to cross the gap at all. Only particulars will be confronted; possible generalizations will not be articulated. Finality is located in the particulars themselves; it is moved over to
the left-hand side of the set of terms representing the process of
induction. Adams did not at first grasp the significance of his
reader's inability to test any generalization inferred from the
unexplained facts in the text .The one position that could be

more extreme in regard to the problem of the logical gap is outright nonrationality.

Of course Adams's theory of how to avoid generalizations and write an absolutely true history proved a failure, as he himself admitted. There are fundamentally three reasons for this failure, all of which in our own time seem obvious: it is extremely difficult to define the concept of fact; the selection of facts to include in a text is itself an organizing, generalizing act of mind; and—like selection—the determination of the order in which the facts are presented is a generalizing act. Nevertheless, Adams's attempt to put his theory into practice resulted in brilliant work. It is commonly agreed that his history of the administrations of Jefferson and Madison is an outstanding contribution to American historical writing.

Having glanced at these various strategies for solving the problem of the logical gap, we can approach our subject of abstractions in literature through consideration of the historian Charles Beard and, then, Ernest Hemingway, with a glance aside at Gertrude Stein. Beard's ideas and his vocabulary provide a transition from scientific history to fiction as conceived in the Hemingway milieu and in a major phase of the New Criticism. In principle, no new ideas are involved here, only the transposition of ideas from history to fiction. I should make it clear at once, however, that I don't believe there was any conscious borrowing by literary people from historians. I believe the two disciplines shared a common source, but that is a subject we needn't get into here.

Adams developed and attempted to put into practice his theory of scientific history in the closing years of the nineteenth century. Beard's well-known *An Economic Interpretation of the Constitution of the United States* appeared in 1913. In the opening pages of this work Beard explains and defines his theory of historical writing. His position is basically the same as Adams's. For example, he quotes another historian's statement about the "ever-advancing standard of justice" in law and then scoffs, "In other words, law is made out of some abstract stuff known as justice." Although at this time Beard shared Adams's dedication to concrete facts, he differed from Adams by condoning abstractions at one point in a text. After presenting his concrete facts, Beard felt, the historian should summarize and explain them. He later compared this obligation of the historian to Darwin's method in natural science.[13]

In 1913, however, Beard seems not to have been much aware of the hazard of the logical gap in disciplines which, like historical writing, do not permit the verification of generalizations through testing. Twenty-one years later he had become very much aware of the hazard. In *The Nature of the Social Sciences* (1934) he observed that all the essential ideas of the scientific historians had been challenged, and he explicitly rejected the idea of anything like a "raw fact."[14] Of even greater interest for our purpose, he now undertook a classification of kinds of historical writing. Two of his categories are particularly relevant: "history as knowledge" and "history as thought."

Beard's category of history as knowledge is to provide for texts made up of nothing but "facts." In other words, what Beard has in mind is the equivalent of Adams's theory, although Beard may not have been making this particular association. To illustrate the idea of history as knowledge, Beard offers the following example: "George Washington was the first President of the United States under the Constitution; John Adams succeeded him; and Thomas Jefferson was inaugurated in 1801."[15] Needless to say, this is a type of history Beard himself did not write. As mentioned earlier, in *An Economic Interpretation* he had in principle rejected it because of its failure to provide a synthesis of the facts. Now, in 1934, he is questioning the concept of fact itself. Nevertheless, he points out that in the simple illustration above we seem to have an entirely true statement. Each of the propositions is true, and the order in which the propositions are stated does not affect their truth. The trouble is that any history actually written in this way would be unbearably simple and tedious.

While on this subject, I should mention Allen Tate's famous concept of literature as knowledge, which he presented in an essay published seven years after Beard's *The Nature of the Social Sciences*. As far as I know there was no conscious borrowing on Tate's part. Moreover, the two concepts differ in important ways. On the other hand there can be little doubt that Beard's interest in the concept of history as knowledge, like Adams's similar interest, sprang from the same cultural source as Tate's theory of literature as knowledge. Both were attempts to deal with the problem of the logical gap.

What Beard meant by history as thought, the second of the two categories I mentioned, is essentially what he had in mind at the time of *An Economic Interpretation*: facts accompanied by generalizations or abstractions. I am introducing this category principally to contrast it with ideas shared by Gertrude Stein and Ernest Hemingway. For example, in a book published in 1936, two years after Beard's *The Nature of the Social Sciences*, Gertrude Stein declared, "In a masterpiece there is no thought."[16]

Stein and Hemingway are closer to Adams than to Beard. There is no need to get into the subject of Stein's ideas here, except to recall that during Hemingway's formative years as a writer he had many discussions with her concerning literary technique. That he himself sought to write masterpieces without thought has been widely recognized. Like Adams, he failed —and in the process produced distinguished work. I will conclude these remarks on the logical gap with a brief consideration of Hemingway's position.

The passage in Chapter 27 of Hemingway's *A Farewell to Arms* in which he attacks abstractions and defends the concrete is so well known that I will not take time to quote it. An even more pertinent statement, however, appears in *Death in the Afternoon*:

> . . . the greatest difficulty, aside from knowing what you really felt, rather than what you were supposed to feel, and had been taught to feel, was to put down what really happened in action: what the actual things were which produced the emotion you experienced . . . the real thing, the sequence of motion and fact which made the emotion.[17]

If this statement is added to Hemingway's attack on abstraction, in *A Farewell to Arms*, the sum total is exactly the same three elements observed in what Adams had to say: facts, the right sequence, and the least possible comment (or abstraction).

Hemingway's greatest effort to adhere to these principles occurred early in his career. The following is an example from the story "Big Two-Hearted River":

> He came down a hillside covered with stumps into a
> meadow. At the edge of the meadow flowed the river.
> Nick was glad to get to the river. He walked upstream
> through the meadow. His trousers were soaked with the
> dew as he walked. After the hot day the dew had come
> quickly and heavily. The river made no sound.[18]

Like the illustration made by Beard, the sentences in this passage are simple propositions. If only there were no need for
concern about what a fact is or about the selection and ordering
of facts as an abstract, organizing mental activity, we could feel
that here indeed was a means of solving the problem of the logical gap. Perhaps, at that, this fine story will not "go bad afterward." I hope not.

Of course the concept of fact is not the same in fiction as in
historical writing, so great caution is necessary in comparing
Hemingway to Adams. The point at which the comparison is
most certain and meaningful for our purpose lies in the desire
of both these writers to avoid abstractions. Neither succeeded
in this virtually impossible attempt. Whether Hemingway ever
grasped the difficulties that Adams finally acknowledged, I do
not know.

In concluding, we might consider one fairly representative
example of critical opinion about Hemingway's early stories.
The following comment is from Philip Young's book, *Ernest
Hemingway*:

> The qualities of these early stories which attracted most
> attention to Hemingway, and which seemed to mark his
> work as his own and no other's, were the rigorous objec-
> tivity with which they were told, their complete lack of
> "thinking," and the unbelievably sharp and simple
> prose.[19]

Had Young referred only to the lack of thinking and not to "rigorous objectivity" as well, it might be supposed he had nothing
more in mind than Hemingway's care not to destroy the semblance by moralizing. The addition of the idea of rigorous objectivity, with its overtones of the scientific method, casts doubt
on such a conclusion. Young seems to be saying that Hemingway succeeded in presenting such facts as seemed sure, in such

order as seemed rigorously consequent, and thus in solving the problem of the logical gap.

In summary, two simple but useful conclusions emerge from these evidences of how people responded to the problem of the logical gap. The first is that as awareness of the problem increased, along with the growing prestige of science, there appeared in literature a strong antipathy toward abstractions—or universals, or generalizations. The second conclusion is that efforts were made in literature to avoid having to cross the logical gap at all and instead to find some way of dealing only with concrete particulars. These efforts were unsuccessful, but they resulted in some excellent writing.

Finally, I want to repeat what I said at the outset concerning the limitations of the concept of the logical gap. It is only a clue, a perspective, it is not an explanation; it will serve its purpose if the historical phenomenon of hostility to abstractions appears more understandable and inevitable than might otherwise be the case.

Abstractions

It is time now to make some distinctions in the meaning of "abstraction." In a literary context, abstraction may convey any one of several different ideas. These include material not transformed into the elements of a semblance or intransitive rapt attention, the thought processes of characters in a drama, the thought processes of an author while composing his work, generalizations or universals, limited generalizations, and—in a technical sense—perceptions and images. Later, the word "meaning" will have to be added to this list.

Material Not Transformed into Elements. The use of the word abstraction to refer to material not transformed into elements is illustrated in the lines below, together with the comment by Ezra Pound that follows. These lines are from the beginning of Ford Madox Hueffer's "On a Marsh Road: Winter Nightfall."

> A bluff of cliff, purple against the south,
> And nigh one shoulder-top an orange pane.

> This wet, clean road; clear twilight held in the pools,
> And ragged thorns, ghost reeds and dim, dead willows.
> Past all the windings of these grey, forgotten valleys,
> To west, past clouds that close on one dim rift—
> The golden plains; the infinite, glimpsing distances,
> The eternal silences; dim lands of peace. . . .[20]

Ezra Pound had this to say, in *Poetry* (March 1913): "Don't use such an expression as 'dim lands of *peace*.' It dulls the image. It mixes an abstraction with the concrete."[21] Surely Pound is right; these words have not been transformed into elements. They remain an abstraction, or mere material.

Thought Processes of Characters. Abstract thinking is found inside a work—for example, by the characters in a drama—and, also, so to speak, outside the work, as the author deliberately plans his themes and effects. T. S. Eliot recognized the natural tendency to refer to the content of a work, the "inside," as thinking, but he objected to it. He wrote, for example,

> It is the general notion of "thinking" that I would challenge. . . . The poet who "thinks" is merely the poet who can express the emotional equivalent of thought. But he is not necessarily interested in the thought itself. . . . Did Shakespeare think anything at all? He was occupied with turning human actions into poetry.[22]

But how can you turn human actions into poetry without thinking about what you are doing? You can't, unless you work in a wholly nonrational way—a possibility that will constitute the last subject in our discussion. Eliot's point is that Shakespeare is primarily concerned with the drama of Hamlet's situation, rather than with the philosophical soundness of Hamlet's opinions. In other words, what Eliot has in mind is the problem of semblance. For example, Hamlet thinks about the relationship between suicide and immortality. But, if Hamlet's thinking about this subject has truly been transformed into poetry, it forms part of the semblance. Its intrinsic soundness is not an issue. A little later in the same essay Eliot raises a similar question with respect to belief. What about the beliefs expressed in a poem? The answer is the same. A poet does not have to have complete confidence in a belief before he can articulate its force as an element in a semblance. I shouldn't think, however, that anyone would want to express in his own voice, as in a lyric, a belief he didn't really hold.

Thought Processes of the Author. A third kind of abstraction, then, is found in the thinking a writer does *about* his work. Eliot will again provide an example. In his introduction to St. John Perse's *Anabasis* he compares the process of selecting and arranging the images in the poem to the process of arranging an argument.

> The reader has to allow the images to fall into his memory successively without questioning the reasonableness of each at the moment; so that, at the end, a total effect is produced.
>
> Such *selection* of a *sequence* of images and ideas has nothing chaotic about it. There is a logic of the imagination as well as a logic of concepts. People who do not appreciate poetry always find it difficult to distinguish between order and chaos in the arrangement of images; and even those who are capable of appreciating poetry cannot depend upon first impressions. I was not convinced of Mr. Perse's imaginative order until I had read the poem five or six times. And if, as I suggest, such an arrangement of imagery requires just as much '*fundamental brain-work*' *as the arrangement of an argument*, it is to be expected that the reader of a poem should take at least as much trouble as a barrister reading an important decision on a complicated case.[23] [Italics are mine.]

Having copied this passage out, I suddenly realize that the word "thinking" does not appear in it at all. I hope "brainwork" and "selection" can be accepted as equivalents. At any rate, Eliot clearly asserts that the images in an imagistic poem have to be thoughtfully selected and have to be organized into some kind of orderly sequence. It is worth remembering that Pound spent months working on his tiny imagistic poem, "In a Station of the Metro." What Eliot has in mind here we'll consider shortly.

The idea of such abstract thinking in the making of literature is, however, a delicate subject. On the one hand, many writers feel that to stress their conscious craftsmanship is to be

false to the almost overwhelming experience they sometimes
have of being in the grip of a creative force they could hardly
control if they wanted to. On the other hand, to stress the un-
controlled spontaneity of such experience would be false to the
painstaking and exhausting "fundamental brain-work" they
expend in their efforts. On this subject of spontaneity versus
craftsmanship, William Carlos Williams is a sheer delight.
With the force of a mighty temperament he simply overrides
the logical disaster of what he has to say. Listen to him:

> . . . it is absolutely essential to the writing of anything
> worth while that the mind be fluid and release itself to
> the task.
>   Forget all rules . . . every form of resistance to a com-
> plete release should be abandoned.[24]

> When a man makes a poem, makes it, mind you, he takes
> words as he finds them interrelated about him and com-
> poses them—without distortion which would mar their
> exact significances—into an intense expression of his
> perceptions and ardors that they may constitute a reve-
> lation in the speech that he uses.[25]

The importance Williams attaches to the craftsmanship of the
poet is further suggested in a definition he once gave of a poem
as "a small (or large) machine made of words."[26]
    Less ardent temperaments can hardly ignore the incompati-
bility between Williams's assertion of the deliberate making
(mind you) of a poem and the poet's abandonment to "complete release." It's as if he were telling us that after all there is
no difference between the abstractions so feared by Pound,
Hemingway, and Brooks and the concreteness of a spontaneous
or unanticipated experience. And yet who could doubt that Williams is honestly trying to describe his own experience as a
writer? What shall we say, moreover, about people who, unlike
Williams, do not even concede there is any need for making but
who will say only, "The lines just came into my head"? This is
the kind of account we have of "Kubla Khan." I would like to
put off such problems and return to the subject of the various
meanings of abstraction.
    Generalizations and Universals. For our purpose, no distinc-

tion is necessary between the general and the universal (either real or nominal); both are thought of as abstract. Perhaps the identity of usage between these concepts in literary studies is self-evident, but here is a representative instance:

> The poet can legitimately step out into the universal only by first going through the narrow door of the particular. The poet does not select an abstract theme and then embellish it with concrete details. On the contrary, he must establish the details, must abide by the details, and through his realization of the details attain to whatever general meaning he can attain.[27]

With the possible exception of material not transformed into elements, and of perceptions, all the meanings of abstraction being considered could be called either generalizations or universals.

Limited Generalizations. In this fifth meaning associated with abstraction I am taking a liberty by changing a traditional term. According to formal logic, the subject we are concerned with here is called the quantity of a proposition. Quantitatively, a proposition can be either universal or particular. A universal proposition refers to an entire class, a particular proposition to only part of a class. The following statement is an example of a particular universal: "Quarter horses tend to be faster than thoroughbreds over a short distance." The proposition is about classes of horses but does not assert that all members of one class are faster than all members of the other. For the term "particular universal" I am substituting "limited generalization." My reason is that in discussions of literature the words "particular" and "universal" are commonly regarded as polar opposites. The term limited generalization, which we will need to use again later, will avoid the possible confusion of seeming to unite these polar opposites.

Perceptions and Images. A sixth meaning relates the concept of abstraction to the concept of perception and raises the possibility that abstractions merge into concreteness along a spectrum, so to speak. This meaning must be called only a ghost meaning, since I have never seen abstraction used in quite the way I am suggesting. The existence of such a meaning is only implied by the terms and ideas we are examining.

In the directive-state theory of perception, it is held that an individual's perception of the environment actually amounts to an interpretation of it. What an optical physicist sees in a sunrise is different from what a meteorologist sees. This is a familiar and appealing theory.

In discussions of literature not much is said about perceptions but a great deal is said about images. Images are spoken of as concrete. How is an image related to a perception? I am thinking here of visual images, not of that use of the word "image" that blends into the concept of a symbol. A simple visual image can properly be regarded as identical to a perception. If an image of a human face were flashed briefly on a movie screen, the image and the perception could be regarded as identical. When we imagine the face of an absent friend, however, we are confronted with a much more complex problem. We have seen this face many times, from many different angles. After some introspection, we may agree that the image in our mind's eye is one we have assembled for ourselves from a great many isolated perceptions. And then—is it a kind face? A rugged face? A beautiful face? Probably we relate our mental image to some such abstract category. In view of all these considerations—and many more—it can be argued that to some degree a visual image, like any perception, begins life as a generalization and becomes progressively even more general or abstract as we relate it to broader and broader categories of interpretation.[28] The very idea of a perception as a simple, sensuous experience is cast into doubt.

It might seem to follow from the character of these relationships among the concepts of abstraction, perception, and image that it is a mistake to refer to literature as concrete, but I think such a conclusion would be wrong. For one thing, the directive-state theory of perception is only a theory; it has been challenged in various ways. Jacques Derrida denies the concept of perception itself.[29] For another, it is a fact of experience that literature often has a felt impact that surely deserves to be called concrete. The practical value of attention in the classroom to such ideas as the directive-state theory of perception is simply that they encourage a healthy caution in forming opinions about the nature of literature. It is true that literature is concrete, but it is at least equally true that it is abstract; and the two terms constantly threaten to merge with one another along a broad spectrum of possible meanings.

To my mind, the boundaries suggested for the idea of the concrete and the abstract aspects of literature, respectively, are most easily comprehended in the form of insights rather than elaborate analyses. I believe one such insight into the concreteness of literature emerged in a conversation I once had with a friend concerning Saul Bellow's *Herzog*. In this novel, Bellow tells a story about a savage who, for the first time, saw a piano and heard it played. The astonished savage exclaimed, "You fight 'im, 'e cry!" I described this incident to my friend, who hadn't read the book. He said this must be a true story. Nobody, he said, could possibly have thought that up by himself. This is concreteness: a sudden complete trust that you are confronting reality itself.[30] But Alfred North Whitehead presents a somewhat contradictory insight. He says we really trust abstract relationships more than we do our own perceptions. We trust our arithmetic to tell us, for example, how far we can drive our car on a tankful of gasoline, but we may be unsure whether a sensation experienced on our skin was caused by heat or cold or even merely imagined.

Both these two somewhat incompatible insights, our trust in the concrete and our trust in the abstract, seem to me to be true. I presume the principles involved in both are incessantly at work in the literature we read and in our response to it. The incompatibility between the principles in these insights is probably only a reflection of the mystery of our situation in the universe. It would be a very different universe if we could trust either all our perceptions or all our abstract relationships.

This is a good point at which to review the half-dozen meanings and implications of abstraction that have been mentioned and to look forward to what uses can be made of them. The first two—the failure to transform materials into elements and the thought processes of characters in a drama (or beliefs in a poem)—are only restatements of the subject of materials and elements considered in Part One. The last—perceptions—probably has no more relevance to literature than to any other subject in the curriculum. Some knowledge of theories of perception seems to me basic to almost any subject. That leaves three others: abstractions in the form of an author's thinking about his composition, in the form of generalizations within the composition, and in the form of limited generalizations within the composition.

A reader must relate appropriately to all of these last three varieties of abstraction if he is to comprehend literary works. To understand how a reader may relate to these three varieties of abstraction, however, we need to think about a special characteristic of any abstraction. A single abstraction may present two quite different aspects to a reader at the same time. One of these aspects is the public meaning; it is that meaning which, ideally, everybody agrees on. The other aspect is strictly personal. It has to do with the way the public meaning of the abstraction affects the reader or with the reader's personal relationship to it. This latter aspect, which can be called the *significance* of the abstraction, will be one of the principal topics of the next chapter. The subject of significance is as important in the literary classroom as is the subject of the public meaning of abstractions to philosophers.

9. MEANING, SIGNIFICANCE, & THE AUTHOR'S INTENTION

Abstractions are contained in, or represented by, texts, and to consider a reader's relationship to abstractions we must talk about texts. For this reason, I will now begin to use the word "meaning" rather than "abstraction." As I remarked earlier, it is better to speak of the meaning of a text than of the abstraction of a text—although in what follows either word would signify the same thing (with exceptions to be noted). My subject will be meaning and significance, and subsequently, as aspects of this subject, the concepts of the author's intention and of the authorless text.

Meaning and Significance

Some of the complexities in the idea of meaning can be appropriately acknowledged by quoting from E. D. Hirsch's *Validity in Interpretation*, to which I am greatly indebted. Hirsch says verbal meaning is "whatever someone has willed to convey by a particular sequence of linguistic signs and which can be conveyed (shared) by means of those linguistic signs."[31] Later he adds, "Now verbal meaning can be defined more particularly as a *willed type* which an author expresses by linguistic symbols and which can be understood by another through those symbols."[32] Elsewhere he refers to meaning as "the determinate representation of a text for an interpreter."[33]

We won't actually have occasion to employ these definitions, but in saying this I mean no criticism of Hirsch. His definitions serve his purposes, as they would ours also if we undertook to make use of them. The difficulties in defining meaning are like those in defining consciousness. In the traditional formula for definition (i.e., term, linking verb, etc.), there is no effective genus to which to assign these terms. But, as Hirsch says, meaning is surely intimately involved with the idea of using language to represent something. I especially like Michael Polanyi's descriptive way of putting the matter. He points out that when you look at a text in a foreign language you do not understand, all you see is words. But as you learn this foreign language you begin to look *from* the words *at* what the words mean.[34] As images and symbols take on meaning, the same thing happens, although to a lesser degree.

Significance, our second word, is a relationship between a meaning and something else.[35] The phrase "something else" harbors all sorts of possible complexities, but the key word is "relationship." We need consider only three common relationships: (1) between a reader (or hearer) and a text or utterance, (2) between a reader and an author's intended meaning, and (3) between an author and his own intended meaning. I will begin by outlining the essential idea of significance and then give some attention to each of the three versions just identified.

In the first place, the idea of significance requires a reader's awareness of two things simultaneously. One is what a text means, the other is what the reader feels or thinks about the meaning. In other words, a reader becomes aware of a meaning, and he also becomes aware of the significance the meaning has for him. For example, when the weatherman says, "There's a 50 percent chance of showers this afternoon," his meaning is clear. But the significance of this meaning is quite different for a city dweller who reflects he'll not bother to water the lawn and a farmer who has mown hay he decides he'd better get baled during the morning.

Let's consider another example. On a cold and rainy night we watch a dog curl up before a fire in the fireplace. He circles a couple of times, settles down nose to tail, sighs, and shuts his eyes. What does he mean by the sigh? There may be some disagreement about it. As the linguist Yuen Ren Chao points out, you can't say a sneeze; that is, a sneeze is not a linguistic symbol. Can you say a sigh? Shakespeare seems to imply that Hamlet did and that Hamlet meant something by it. I don't know about Bowser. He has so little to mean with. Yet I am concerned about his well-being, and at least it makes sense to ask what his sigh means *to me*. To me, the meaning of his sigh is that he is at last comfortable and sleepy. My relationship to this meaning—the significance it has for me—is one of pleasure. My relationship to Hamlet's sighing is one of dramatic tension.

In literature, we find the clearest evidences of the concept of significance in a reader's change of attitude toward a text. Bernard De Voto, for instance, warmly praised Sinclair Lewis's *Arrowsmith* when that novel was first published, but years later he denounced it as trivial. The text had not changed with the passing of time. What had changed was De Voto's relationship to the text, its significance for him.

In group discussions of literary works, the concept of significance seems to me particularly valuable in two ways, each of which deserves some thought.

First, it dignifies an individual's natural impulse to compare his feeling about a work with other people's. The uniqueness of every individual human being guarantees that no two will ever relate in precisely the same way to any work of art. And surely the uniqueness of every individual is entitled to respect. When discussion of a literary work is focused solely on the idea of establishing a single correct interpretation, to the exclusion of what I am calling significance, part of the individual's self may be denied. As will appear later, sometimes an author ponders his relationship to his own meaning. In brief, the concept of significance provides a quasi-theoretical basis on which to temper the excessively legalistic tone that may become evident in a discussion directed solely to a search for the right interpretation. It provides a little room for being merely human.

But where there is freedom there should also be responsibility, which is the second point. The idea of significance is also valuable in the classroom because it clarifies an individual responsibility as well as an individual need. This responsibility is to avoid, as far as possible, permitting the thoughtlessly accepted significance of some aspect of a literary work to determine the meaning attributed to the work. This second point needs explanation.

Theoretically, it is impossible for significance to determine meaning. Meaning is grounded in the work, significance in the reader's relationship to the meaning. But what actually happens?

I once was present at—in fact presided over—a heated discussion of Robert Frost's poem "Provide, Provide." I believe what happened on that occasion will serve as an example. This poem reads as follows.

PROVIDE, PROVIDE

The witch that came (the withered hag)
To wash the steps with pail and rag
Was once the beauty Abishag,

The picture pride of Hollywood.
Too many fall from great and good
For you to doubt the likelihood.

Die early and avoid the fate.
Or if predestined to die late,
Make up your mind to die in state.

Make the whole stock exchange your own!
If need be occupy a throne,
Where nobody can call *you* crone.

Some have relied on what they knew,
Others on being simply true.
What worked for them might work for you.

No memory of having starred
Atones for later disregard
Or keeps the end from being hard.

Better to go down dignified
With boughten friendship at your side
Than none at all. Provide, provide![36]

The discussion of this poem, as I recall it, gradually focused on
the almost passionate insistence of one man that the point of the
poem was the wisdom of acquiring a lot of money. He had both
supporters and opponents. Challenged to defend his view, he
pointed to the last stanza. Told by an opponent that the real
meaning of that stanza was different from the apparent meaning, he demanded evidence. Where, he asked, does the poem
say it's *not* better to go down with boughten friends than none
at all? His opponents stressed the importance of the fifth stanza.
He replied that what worked for them might work for you but
apparently it might not, too. I asked him if he thought anything
in life was more important than money. He replied that, generally speaking, there were certainly other things that were just
as important as money but nothing that was more important
than money.

It occurred to me it might be interesting to speculate about
where the thinking of the two parties to the debate began, so to
speak. Was there a particular point in the poem at which each
interpretation originated? The outspoken young man seemed

always concentrated on the last stanza, his opponents on the fifth stanza. His opponents insisted the poem meant you should provide for yourself by acquiring friends and by living a friendly life. There appeared to be no disagreement between the two parties about what the sentences they referred to meant, only about what the poem meant.

It appeared to me, in the end, that what had happened was this. The young man had found a sentence containing a special significance for him. Starting from this sentence, he had construed the rest of the sentences in the poem in a way that caused them to conform to this significance. And in doing so he had not distorted the literal meaning of any of the sentences. His opponents, inclined toward a different life style, had done exactly the same thing, with a totally different conclusion. As the session broke up, the contending parties were proposing to one another that perhaps they were looking at the same thing in different ways. I don't see how such a description of their positions could be true, but as they left the room they were talking about the relative values of friendship and money. Since these concepts were the aspects of the poem that clearly had the greatest significance for the two sides, respectively, I inferred that some recognition had been achieved of the relationship between meaning and individual response.

Hirsch treats this kind of problem in interpretation under the heading of "the self-confirmability of interpretations."[37] That is, when some aspect of a work has particularly caught a reader's attention and has led to a hypothesis about the meaning of the work, he then tends to perceive all the evidence in the light of his hypothesis. To some degree, his hypothesis tends to constitute the evidence. This is an idea which can be most helpful in a classroom. Given this orientation, an observer of a debate in a classroom may find his attention initially caught not so much by the question of who is correct but of what the sources of the difference of opinion are. The significance that some detail has had for a given reader may afford a clue. Finally, of course, the observer-as-instructor may want to point out any elements of the whole to which the parts under contention have not clearly been related.

Without guaranteeing the correctness of my view, perhaps I should express my own opinion about Frost's poem, just to ter-

minate this account. I believe the young man had missed the
derision of such a line as "Make the whole stock exchange your
own!" On the other hand, I think his opponents had missed the
Yankee common sense in the idea that boughten friendship is
indeed better than none at all. I conclude that Frost in this
poem recommended the pursuit of wisdom and brotherhood
and depicted wealth as an inferior but real value. Most abstractly, then, the poem laughs at any single, simple concept of the
good provider.[38] A reader who misses the irony in this poem on
his first reading but perceives it on the second must have a very
different experience the second time. A great part of the interest
in the second experience must lie in his contemplation of the
enhancement of his own perceptions.

As a way of summarizing what has been said so far, an
analogy will prove useful. We might pretend, for a moment,
that meaning in a literary work is as easily perceived, as definite, and as unvarying as a rock. We observe, however, that
people respond differently to the rock: some admire it and
others find it uninteresting. And some take note of this difference by saying that the significance of the rock is not the same
for everybody. On the other hand, no disagreement is found
about what the rock is. It's just "there," plain for all to see. This
concept of meaning and of significance is seen in the example
of the weather report.

If meaning is assumed to be as easily perceived, as definite,
and as unvarying as a rock, and two people nevertheless disagree about a meaning, what then? At least one of them must
be confused. Perhaps one of them, or both, are not making the
necessary distinction between significance and meaning. If so,
the solution is easy. Because the meaning is easily perceived,
they can be shown what the meaning is and then shown the
difference between the meaning and the significance the meaning has for them. This is pretty much how the debate about
"Provide, Provide" actually worked itself out.

Literary compositions are not often so simple as a one-sen-
tence weather report, however. Sometimes more than one meaning seems genuinely plausible. When this is true, the distinction
between meaning and significance can become rather arbitrary.
One reader's meaning may be another reader's significance.
This arbitrariness does not necessarily destroy the practical

value of the distinction; in a group discussion, consideration of the difference between meaning and significance may help individuals to realize that their interpretation is derived from their special relationship to the meaning rather than from the inherent plausibility of the interpretation they have chosen. The following poem by Hilda Doolittle, a member of the imagist group, will serve as an example.

OREAD

Whirl up, sea—
whirl your pointed pines,
splash your great pines
on our rocks,
hurl your green over us,
cover us with your pools of fir.[39]

The poem is addressed to the sea—or to the wilderness; it is apparently uttered by a mountain maiden, as indicated by the mythological reference of the title. What is the point of the maiden's exhortation? Three possibilities might be considered. One is that the sea is being given an exuberant challenge. Another is that the speaker is begging for refuge and concealment within the sea, or forest. This second possibility is reminiscent of a recurrent phrase in such primitivistic fiction as Cooper's Leatherstocking stories and Simms's *The Yemassee*: "They plunged into the depths of the forest." A third possibility is that the speaker is addressing the sea, or forest, as a source of sensuous pleasure.

The character of these three possibilities indicates at once that the idea of a literal meaning, as exemplified by the weather report, has become less certain. The figurative nature of the language in the poem nudges the idea of meaning away from the words themselves toward the intention underlying the words. Viewed as an intention of challenge, the poem means something different from what it does when viewed as a plea for refuge. As I continue to use the word "meaning," therefore, this word will have mixed into it a connotation of intention that was lacking from its earlier use in regard to the weather report. In a few moments I will take up the element of intention directly, but meanwhile I will complete examination of the possible meanings of "Oread" and of some of their implications.

As a challenge, the poem expresses a feeling familiar to small-boat sailors who like to venture out when the water is rough or to people who just like to watch big waves roll in and pound the shore. The speaker challenges the wave to go ahead and break over his own body: "See if I care!"

When the poem is considered as a plea for refuge and concealment, on the other hand, attention is called especially to the last line: "cover us with your pools of fir." Perhaps the covering envisioned here is to be permanent, a final refuge, like Quentin's suicidal drowning in *The Sound and the Fury*.

The third possible meaning derives from the image of whirling and splashing and green pools: a grand whirlpool bath with sexual overtones.

Still other possible meanings could be identified, but we should return to our primary subject, which is significance. Suppose we somehow have authority to say that the true meaning of the poem is the idea of the challenge, as we might actually have said if we knew it had been written in the spirit of Henley's "Invictus." Understanding and accepting this meaning, a reader might nevertheless respond, "Although I don't deny the correctness of the meaning you identify, the appeal the poem has for me—in contrast to its meaning—lies in its depiction of an ultimate refuge, after the storm has been borne by the speaker until he, or she, has become exhausted." The *significance* found in the meaning this reader has accepted is therefore simply the second of the possible *meanings* I ventured to suggest. It is easy to see how one reader's significance can be another reader's meaning.

This ambivalence is complicated by the introduction of emotion. So far, I have referred to significance only in the context of abstract intellectuality but, as implied by the example just considered, the concept of significance may involve emotion too. The relationship of significance to emotion will become clearer if we review the basic propositions that have just been made. We began by thinking of meaning and significance as both strictly intellectual. A meaning was assumed to be as clear and definite as a rock, to be just there. The significance such a meaning has for an observer may be as clear and intellectual as the meaning itself. The weather report was our example. We next assumed the existence of a literary work with two (or more) equally plausible meanings, and we regarded these meanings at first as clear and intellectual. But a choice among equally plausible meanings inevitably raises questions about a reader's emotional relationship to the meaning he chooses. And at once we must confront not only the idea of meaning but the idea of significance as well. By definition, a reader's relationship to a meaning *is* significance. Could a choice between equally plausible meanings remain purely intellectual, free of emotional bias? I believe psychologists would agree it could not. In fact, I believe they'd say it's not a good question in the first place, because such a concept as pure intellectuality is indefinable. At least it is surely indefinable in the context of the interpretation of a literary work. Like analogies in general, my comparison of meaning to a rock was not "true" but only useful. When a person has to choose between equally plausible meanings, his emotions are almost certain to become involved.

It might be objected that the chance of encountering literary works having two or more equally plausible meanings is remote. This objection may be warranted, but when looked at from the point of view of the classroom the probability of finding two strongly held but different interpretations of a literary work is high. An almost daily experience is to observe debates in which neither side will believe for a moment that its opinion is less plausible than the other's. It is this practical dilemma that encourages some scholars to endorse such a view of the matter as the following, which was expressed by the psychoanalytic writer Norman Holland: ". . . meaning is not simply 'there' in the text; rather it is something we construct for the text within the limits of the text."[40]

In thinking further about the relationship of significance to emotion, it is helpful for our purposes to make a distinction between the interests of the critic, or the literary theorist, and the interests of the classroom. In one way or another, the theorist is almost incessantly concerned with defining his subject matter— as he should be. An indispensable part of his business is to have good ideas about the concept of literature, for the simple reason that literature is always threatening to transform itself into some other discipline such as anthropology. But most people do not read literary works for the purpose of learning to define literature. They read for the experience the literature affords them, and they are interested in discussing their experience from as many points of view as possible. Consequently, the moderator of a group discussion is continuously required to recognize and somehow deal with significance in its emotional as well as its intellectual form. A theorist may be impatient with a colleague who dislikes Pound's *Cantos* because of their political content; it can be argued with some reason that such a dislike has nothing to do with the literary quality of the work, that it arises only from a thoughtless significance. However that may be, impatience with the same dislike in the classroom would surely be a mistake. What is called for is precisely a very patient unraveling of the tangled web of meaning and, likely enough, idealistic feeling on the part of the unhappy reader. Further consideration of this problem, in another context, will be found in Chapter 19.

But, finally, can the web of meaning and feeling ever really be unraveled? Are the concepts of meaning and significance ultimately mutually exclusive? I doubt that they are. Meanings aren't rocks. Even perceptions of rocks aren't rocks. If even the perception of a rock comes to us partly preformed by our personal history of perceptions, as I suppose it does, what hope can there be of our perceiving the meaning of a sentence with true objectivity, to say nothing of an entire work of art? The best we can do is to compare our observations with those of other people calmly and thoughtfully, remembering meanwhile the human tendency to confuse the feelings inside us with the "facts" outside us. In this endeavor, the concept of significance can provide a great deal of help even though it cannot be expected to lead to the final determination of the true meaning of a work of art.

What H.D.'s real intention was in "Oread" remains a puzzle. All the meanings I suggested seem to have some plausibility. I reason, therefore, that if H.D. wanted to present us with a poem carefully designed not to present a single meaning, then we might as well enjoy it in any way the text will permit. Perhaps the poem wasn't intended to mean anything more than Bowser's sigh was. Nevertheless, there is one additional avenue to explore. What could we determine about H.D.'s intentions by looking elsewhere?

In the old anthology where I found the poem it is followed

by another of H.D.'s poems, entitled "Lethe." I'll not quote the entire poem, but the last of the three stanzas reads as follows:

> Nor word nor touch nor sight
>   Of lover, you
> Shall long through the night but for this:
> The roll of the full tide to cover you
>   Without question,
>   Without kiss.[41]

Is it H.D.'s habit of mind to associate the sea with easeful death, or with oblivion, as she apparently does in "Lethe"? No H.D. scholar, I can't answer the question. If it were proved that this is indeed her habit, then the *probability* that in "Oread" it was her intention to assert a longing for oblivion becomes high enough to be taken seriously.

This sort of reference to the author's intention as a means of determining the correct interpretation of a literary work is, in my opinion, almost a necessity in the classroom. Nevertheless, it presents both practical and theoretical problems. Practically, it invites the dilemma of taking up a work for discussion and then setting the work aside, the discussion only begun, to study some other work in order to understand the first work. It needn't be all that bad, but it can be. Theoretically, the idea of going outside the work for help may violate a principle that, although not in any simple or absolute form, was a tenaciously held part of the New Criticism. On the other hand, the concept of the author's intention is attractive as a way out of the kind of problem represented by "Oread," where it is uncertain whether a given interpretation represents only significance or meaning itself.

The next section will be concerned with these problems of the relationships among meaning, significance, and the author's intention.

The Author's Intention

There are two ways in which to formulate the concept of the author's intention. One is the natural, spontaneous way, the

other might be called technical. I will be concerned principally
with the former.

An example of the spontaneous way of thinking about the
author's intention appeared in a review of Mona Van Duyn's
book of poetry, *Merciful Disguises*: "The poems, nearly all of
them, are interesting to read because of [Mona Van Duyn's]
company, her persona. . . . [T]his book is a good one, a pleasure to have and to move around in, for the pleasure of the company."[42] Not long before coming upon this review, while reading C. M. Bowra's discussion of Aeschylus's *Prometheus Bound*,
I found the following sentence concerning Prometheus's compassion for mankind: "Aeschylus surely means us to feel this."
These comments reflect the sort of spontaneous response everyone has experienced with regard to the author of an admired
work. Shadowy though he may be to the eye of the mind, the
author becomes a felt presence, an intention.

When we wish to see how much we can discover about the
precise character of an author's intention we turn analytical.
We become technical. I am thinking now of the situation in
which we go beyond a mere awareness of the author's general
intention to a deliberate analysis. A wide array of possibilities
for such analysis is spread before us: straightforward biographical investigation, studies of imagery, psychoanalytic studies,
formalist analysis, Marxist analysis, structural analysis, analysis of the kind Kenneth Burke developed, and others.

Among the analytical methods mentioned above, the amount
of interest taken in the author as a person varies from biographical study at one extreme to certain versions of structuralism at
the other. As noted earlier, structuralists such as Roland Barthes
reject the concept of the author as a privileged consciousness,
substituting the concept of language that writes itself. Barthes's
notion is put into a revealing perspective when related to a comment by Lévi-Strauss during a colloquium. At the moment, the
subject being discussed was possible similarities between the
structure of DNA and language—DNA being the biological
language containing the information necessary for development
of an organism. In DNA, Lévi-Strauss remarked, we see a biological structure resembling language which has neither consciousness nor a subject.[43] Barthes's concept of literature stops
far short of the icy depersonalization of such an idea as a lan-

guage without consciousness or a subject, but his concept nevertheless bears a discernible relationship to Lévi-Strauss's thought.
Here we glimpse one of the sources of structuralism's appeal:
the drive to reduce a subject to its ultimate components. In our
own subject, however, one of the important, if not ultimate,
components is a reader's natural, spontaneous response to a literary work as a communication from another mind. To neglect
this fact of experience is almost as impoverishing as to pretend
that an exchange of opinion between people in a classroom is
merely an encounter between verbal structures, with no minds
or feelings involved.

An evaluation of the various kinds of technical analyses just
mentioned lies beyond the scope of the present discussion. Instead of attempting to compare ways of analyzing intention, we
need to concern ourselves with the more fundamental problem
of the advantages and disadvantages of giving any classroom
time at all to analyses of intention, particularly to those going
beyond the text itself. When time is given for this purpose, circumstances will determine what methods are used—such circumstances as the instructor's own special interests, the current
state of the art of criticism, and the nature of the text being studied. Having considered the role of the author's intention as a
concept in class discussion, we can then turn to the subject of
significance as a relationship between a reader and the author's
intention.

A reader's sense of the author's intention is so pervasive, however, so much a part of the natural reading situation, that it may
help bring the concept of the author's intention into focus if we
first contemplate a text which has no author at all. But finding
such a text calls for some thought.

One possibility sometimes mentioned is a text composed by
a computer or by a random selection of words. Unfortunately,
texts of this sort that I have seen were not exactly meaningful.
They had an eerie quality of being almost meaningful. Another possibility sometimes mentioned is a text in which an effective element was created by a printer's error. The difficulty here
is that the effectiveness of such an element, in those instances I
know of, is dependent on the element's place in a context created by intention. Still another possibility sometimes mentioned
is the anonymous text—*Beowulf*, for example. Specialists in the

theory of the interpretation of texts, however, debate the meaning—in our present context—of anonymous. They point to the many internal evidences tending to attribute the text to a certain time and place and even, in a rhetorical sense, to an implied author.

Nevertheless, there is one way in which to obtain a genuine authorless text. We can simply make a rule that a given text has no author. Such rules have been made, here and there. One of the most interesting is the rule in jurisprudence that what a legal contract means is not what was intended but what was said. As Justice Oliver Wendell Holmes explains, the rationale for the exclusion is that in the creation of a contract there are always at least two parties, or "authors," and their intentions tend to be at cross purposes.[44] When a question of interpretation arises concerning a contract already drawn up and signed, consideration of the idea of intention would invite chaos. If intention were admitted, each party would claim that his intention, and therefore the meaning of the contract, was whatever would be to his own advantage. Of course all this is merely theoretical; in fact people constantly fail to grasp the significance, and even the meaning, of contracts, and there is much arguing about intentions. Holmes's discussion of this subject was meant to serve as a help in the solution of such conflicts. Nevertheless, the concept of a contract as an authorless text, or a text in which the author's intention is irrelevant, plays an important role in jurisprudence.

As far as the literary classroom is concerned, a serious weakness in the concept of the authorless text is, surprisingly, its tendency to obscure the distinction between meaning and significance. This is a difficulty that deserves some thoughtful attention. Instead of taking as one of their primary objectives the problem of learning to think about their own relationship to the literary work and to discern differences between their emotional response and the meaning confronting them, participants in a legalistic discussion are likely to learn only to think harder about meaning. As with a contract at the focal point of a legal discussion, an authorless text at the focal point of an exchange of opinion in the classroom imposes constraints. It exerts a force tending to transform questions about significance into questions about meaning.[45] An example of this tendency developed once in a sophomore class I had asked to read Wordsworth's poem, "A Slumber Did My Spirit Seal." We were using an anthology. What we were supposed to be learning in all the many sections of this sophomore course was not so much the poetry of Wordsworth, or of any other particular author, as how to read poetry. The idea of the author's intention was thus weakened at the outset. I discussed the poem without any special reference to Wordsworth, in accordance with the assumption that we were just practicing reading a few poems.

Before continuing, I had better provide the text of the poem, for easy reference. This is one of Wordsworth's "Lucy" poems.

> A slumber did my spirit seal;
>   I had no human fears:
> She seemed a thing that could not feel
>   The touch of earthly years.
>
> No motion has she now, no force;
>   She neither hears nor sees;
> Rolled round in earth's diurnal course,
>   With rocks, and stones, and trees.[46]

This poem has been the subject of a great deal of controversy.[47] Among the issues involved, one of the most troublesome has been the question of whether the poem expresses consolation in the idea that Lucy is now part of nature or only a bleak sense of loss. How, for example, should the last line be interpreted? Lucy is here associated with rocks and stones and trees. Is Wordsworth thinking that all nature is alive? That rocks and stones are as alive as trees and that Lucy shares in all this life of nature? Or is he thinking that trees are as inert as rocks and stones and that Lucy is as lifeless as all three?

What happened in my class was that after I pointed out the possibility of the life-in-nature idea I got an objection. One of the men in the class said he had recently lost a brother in an automobile accident and he didn't see how a tree was going to make him feel any better. It seemed a delicate moment. After offering my sympathy, I ventured to remark that of course, as far as the poem was concerned, what we had been talking about was the feeling the poem itself contained. That is, I was trying to say to him that perhaps he could respect the feeling in the poem even if it was different from his own. The young man did not appear emotionally upset, but still he objected. Finally, after class, I made a suggestion. Maybe, I said, if he acquainted himself with Wordsworth's mind in some depth he would find it possible to understand how—for Wordsworth—solace for grief could be found in rocks and stones and trees. As a matter of fact he accepted the suggestion and wrote a good paper on the subject. It now strikes me as highly paradoxical and instructive that his interest in Wordsworth the man was stimulated by my reluctance—and inability in the time we had—to go beyond the constraints imposed by "the poem itself." Through the writing of his paper, this man ultimately profited from the experience of our class discussion, but the others in the class did not profit from it in the same way, as far as I could tell.

My practical problem was to define rocks and stones and trees in a way that would permit this man, and everyone else, to apprehend and assent to the pantheistic meaning, or significance, that natural objects are said to have had for Wordsworth (in 1799). I had explained this meaning, in terms I believe Wordsworth scholars would have thought not too bad. But it was an abstract meaning I was trying to explain—mistakenly, I now think. To the man who objected, a love of nature meant hunting and fishing and a religious feeling meant a fundamentalist Protestantism. Nothing that I could think to derive from the language of the poem, or finally even from generalizations about what Wordsworth believed, satisfied him. Understandably, he could not at first see beyond the inertness trees signified for him to the possibility that a pantheistic interpretation might make sense. In such circumstances, a weakness in the concept of the authorless text emerged, and it seemed only natural to seek evidence beyond the poem concerning what was in the author's mind. In the case described, additional reading enabled the man to apprehend and assent to Wordsworth's pantheism; it also enabled him to discriminate between the meaning in the poem and the significance he himself found in the meaning. To tell the truth, he did not acquire a very high opinion of either Wordsworth or his poetry, but I do believe he acquired an insight into his own relationship to another man's view of life.

A second disadvantage for the classroom in the concept of an authorless text can be dealt with more briefly: treating a text like an object may conceivably lead to treating the author like an object too. This is a speculative point, and I mention it only tentatively. When we view a text as an object, however, it is easy to forget how much hard work and uncertainty may have gone into its production. Examination of the original manuscript—or manuscripts—of a work is often a revealing experience on this point. It was precisely a desire for the appearance of an objectlike certainty, it is now known, that led Isaac Newton to fudge some of the data in his *Principia.* Of course it is very bad if an author's purpose obviously wavers in the creation of a semblance, but our subject just now is meaning and significance, not semblance. An example can be found on page 131 below of what may happen to meaning when an authorless text is transformed into an "authored" text.

Of course there are advantages as well as disadvantages in the concept of an authorless text. The first is the idea, made familiar by the New Criticism, that concentration on the text helps avoid turning the study of literature into the study of something else. The fact that this idea was for a long time somewhat overemphasized should not be allowed to obscure the common-sense value in it.[48]

A second advantage is a corollary of the first: there emerges a tendency to intensify examination of the text itself. As with a legal contract, relationships among the people in a classroom accepting the idea of the authorless text become lawyerlike, at least in my experience. A competitive excitement is created. Instead of facing a demand for an erudite understanding of the cultural and biographical backgrounds of a text, the readers are challenged to untangle what lies directly before them. The rules resemble those of puzzle solving. The social context, in a reasonably happy classroom, resembles that of a participant sport. There are real values inherent in such an approach, as well as those hazards already noted, and it seems to me it impoverishes a classroom never to attempt it.

A third and last advantage of the authorless text is its help in guarding against mistaken assumptions about an author's intention derived from works other than the one under discussion. Writers do change their minds, and there can be no guarantee that a given work will reveal the same intention found in the author's other works.

We come now to the idea of the author's intention. The question to be considered is how a reader relates to a meaning conceived of as the author's intention in place of a meaning found in an authorless text. As used at first, meaning will refer to abstractions. Later, some ambiguities in thinking of an author's intention as abstract will be noted, and the idea of intention will be related to the idea of the author's purpose in creating a semblance. Another necessary qualification is that in thinking about intention we will have little interest in what an author might say about it, outside his text. Authors are not very trustworthy on this point. Our principal concern will be with what can be inferred from the literary work itself and with relatively "objective" biographical and cultural considerations. Still another distinction is needed between how an author intends a meaning and what meaning he intends. Basically, the problem here is that a text may contain a meaning originating in three different sources. One source is the author's conscious, deliberate will. A second is the conventions, the codes and structures, of his culture; these conventions are so familiar that an author may employ them without fully realizing he is doing so. A third source of meaning is the author's unconscious (this third possibility will be explored in the chapter on the nonrational). In the present discussion, intention will refer to meanings originating in any one of these three sources; *how* an author happened to intend a meaning will not at this point be an issue. The fact is, obviously, that authors often can't say how a meaning originated. The line between arriving at an idea by a process of logic and having an idea appear out of nowhere or even discovering that an idea has been employed unawares cannot be sharply drawn. This ambivalence is clearly illustrated in a comment by the painter Robert Motherwell on how he works, as quoted in C. H. Waddington's *Behind Appearance*:

> I begin somewhat by chance but then work by logical sequence—by inter-relations, in the Hegelian sense—according to strictly held values. . . . A picture is a collaboration between artist and canvas. "Bad" painting is when an artist enforces his will without regard for the sensibilities of the canvas.[49]

The idea of sequence, already familiar from our earlier discussion, becomes highly ambivalent when the base of the sequence is related to the idea of values. Nevertheless, it is evident Motherwell feels that his involvement with both logical sequence and values is interpenetrated by his intention—but that his intention itself originates in chance. It is also true that authors endorse meanings in their texts they had been unaware of until someone else pointed them out.

As noted earlier, the question of what meaning an author intended may call for use of the entire array of possible techniques of interpretation, including a study of both internal and external evidence, but evaluation of the relative merits of these techniques lies beyond the scope of this discussion. Our concern is the more basic one of how a reader relates to the author's intention. One word of caution is appropriate here, however. Since no human being can ever see fully into another human being's mind, nobody can ever be entirely certain about someone else's intention. The art of the interpretation of texts is an art of probabilities. E. D. Hirsch is surely correct in saying that "only one interpretive problem can be answered with objectivity: 'What, in all probability, did the author mean to convey?' "[50] I'll return to this point later.

Compared to the authorless text, there are fundamentally three advantages for the classroom in the idea of the author's intention: the first is psychological, the second involves the problem of the ambiguous work, and the last is related to the concept of genre. In addition, I'll comment on how the idea of intention is related to rhetoric and on how a comparison of poetry to music clarifies the idea of intention.

Psychologically, the idea of the author's intention seems to fulfill a felt need. Not without reason, we perceive language as an indication of the presence of another mind. It is as natural to speak of reading Shakespeare as of reading *King Lear*. The concept of the author's intention relates to a natural interest in the basically human quality of the literary work of art.

The second advantage has already been illustrated in the problem of interpreting "Oread." If a work is ambiguous, the probability of determining a correct interpretation may be increased by inquiring into the author's habit of mind in other works.

The third advantage depends upon relating the meaning of

intention to the concept of genre, and beyond that to what for
the present I'll call personal orientation. The idea of orientation will be explored more fully under the heading of intrinsic
genre in Part Three, as will the concept of genre itself. The relationship of intention to the concept of genre is readily apparent when thought about in the following way.

Let us create in our minds a purely imaginary reader with
these unusual characteristics: although he is literate in English
he does not enjoy reading; he rarely reads even a newspaper
and scoffs at people who do; his interests are in machinery, mechanical things; he lives in a village on an island in some remote corner of the Atlantic ocean; and by a strange chance this
man has never seen or even heard of a poem or anything even
approaching a poem. To this man we present the following two
stanzas from a poem by Christina Rossetti.

UPHILL

Does the road wind uphill all the way?
    Yes, to the very end.
Will the day's journey take the whole long day?
    From morn to night, my friend.

But is there for the night a resting place?
    A roof for when the slow dark hours begin.
May not the darkness hide it from my face?
    You cannot miss that inn.[51]

Wayne Shumaker, who quotes these stanzas to make essentially
the same point I am making, says the journey is life, the night
is death, and the inn is a tomb, and surely he is right. Would
our imaginary reader grasp this meaning? I am most dubious,
and I believe Shumaker would be too.[52] People who are accustomed to reading poetry have no difficulty with this poem, but
our imaginary reader must begin with the great task of comprehending that such a class of things as poems exists. He must
discover that it is possible for someone to have the intention of
writing a poem. The existence of the intention and the existence
of the genre present themselves to him as a single new perception. Our imaginary reader must also go on to learn something
else about the class of things called poems and about the author's

intention before he will understand this poem. He must learn about indirectness.

This example is so far-fetched it can have little practical value with reference to the ideas of significance and intention. We can come closer to the real world by considering a second example, for which the first has helped prepare. The second example is by William Carlos Williams.

BETWEEN WALLS

the back wings
of the

hospital where
nothing

will grow lie
cinders

in which shine
the broken

pieces of a green
bottle[53]

J. Hillis Miller says that, "like radium, the broken pieces of green glass in 'Between Walls' shine with the light of universal beauty."[54] I believe I can say they shine for me as they do for Miller, but I have found others for whom they do not shine. Out of curiosity I once selected several of my colleagues who, I was pretty sure, did not take an interest in modern poetry and asked them, individually, what they thought the point of the poem was. All of them—there were four—thought it was meant to depict the gritty, grimy atmosphere around a big hospital. On another occasion I asked a group of about thirty people in a graduate course what they thought. This course had nothing to do with poetry; we had not been talking about Williams. Reactions were mixed. Some took the gritty view, some the shining beauty view, a fair number sat on their hands.

There was a time when I would have sat on my own hands. Just as the imaginary reader had to learn about the class of things (or genre) "poetry" to understand "Uphill," I myself once had to learn about the subclass of things "poems by Wil-

liams" to understand "Between Walls." I had to discover what
his orientation was. Earlier, of course, I had had to learn about
the class "poetry." Once a reader has become accustomed to
Williams's habit of mind, to his characteristic intention, "Between Walls" is only another example of a familiar type. Similarly, wide reading in the work of such a poet as William Blake,
with the help of a volume like Foster Damon's *Blake Dictionary*, gives a clarity to an individual poem it might not otherwise have.

In short, author's intention, as I have been using this term,
actually includes several elements. It refers to the specific meaning in the author's mind (either conscious or unconscious) as
he writes, to his choice of a particular genre, and ultimately to
that particular view of life he absorbs almost unawares from
his culture and transmits in his work.[55] A reader's relationship
to a given work may involve any or all of these elements of the
author's intention. In the case of "Between Walls" there is, as
far as I can see, no possible way in which a single sure meaning
can be determined by examination of the language of the poem
alone. Thus the question of the author's intention becomes con-
cretely involved in the interpretation of the poem. Of course if a
reader feels no interest in the author's intention he may merely
conclude that the poem is ambiguous. By itself, it is. Or so it
seems to me. But this poem does not exist by itself at all; it exists in a world of poetry. And I would certainly agree with J.
Hillis Miller that a reader who believes "Between Walls" is
about the unpleasantness of the cinders around the hospital is
confused. I would say that such a reader has mistaken significance for meaning and that he made this mistake because of an
inadequate relationship to the author's intention or personal
orientation.

There are occasions in the classroom in which it is unforgiv-
able to ignore the problem of the author's intention. Consider,
for example, Faulkner's *Sartoris*. In this novel Byron Snopes
emerges as a detestable character, virtually a villain. In an early
manuscript version of the novel entitled *Flags in the Dust*, published for the first time in 1973, the depiction of Byron Snopes
is markedly different: he is treated compassionately. Particularly in his last appearance, the inner drives that have led to

his offensive behavior are stressed, and the reader shares the torment his emotional problems have created for him. This intention on Faulkner's part was obscured, and Byron Snopes became a villain, when the earlier version was cut to satisfy the publisher's demand for a shorter manuscript. The cutting was principally done not by Faulkner but by his literary agent. Not to explain these facts to people who are reading *Sartoris* is in effect to endorse a false conclusion about the fictional world Faulkner had set out to create in this novel. Faulkner's moral responsibility for the version actually published as *Sartoris* is an interesting question.

I would like to insert a one-paragraph digression here concerning a crucial distinction between the demands of a theory of literature and the needs of the classroom. The theorist's primary concern is to identify general principles or laws, and the laws he seeks must include all instances. When he discovers an exception to his theory he is distraught. This concern about exceptions is an element in the theoretical debate over the concept of the author's intention. Just because an author has revealed the same intention in ten of his works, it doesn't necessarily follow that in the eleventh his intention won't be different. It is a bit of a jolt to read Emerson's "Experience" right after "Nature" and "Self-Reliance." Consequently, like Beardsley, a theorist may insist that establishing an author's characteristic intention is no guarantee of an acceptable interpretation of any individual work. The study of literature in the classroom presents a different problem, however. There, the objective is usually not to test a theory through analysis of possible exceptions but to find clarifying relationships. A college freshman who is puzzled by Blake's "The Chimney Sweeper" in *Songs of Innocence* is advised to read the poem of the same title in *Songs of Experience*—and many more of Blake's poems as well. The purpose of this good advice is to acquaint him with Blake's habit of mind, since this knowledge will help him understand individual poems. There is no reason, however, that along with this good advice he shouldn't be warned that authors sometimes change their minds. The idea isn't all that astonishing.

As indicated earlier, two other topics should at least be mentioned with reference to significance and the author's intention: the rhetorical aspects of intention, and a particular kind of comparison between poetry and music.

Intention becomes a complex rhetorical problem in works that are essentially dramatic: dramas, many novels and short stories, and some poems. Analysis of the possible distance between the implied author and the characters becomes an important part of the interpretation. And this analysis, of course, centers on the search for evidence regarding the author's intention. Wayne Booth devotes Chapters 11 and 12 to this subject in *The Rhetoric of Fiction*. Moreover, an author may intend a distance between himself and the entire genre in which he is working, as Donald Barthelme sometimes does. I am only mentioning this interesting subject, rather than trying to explore it, because it does not add anything new in principle to the concepts of significance and the author's intention. The rhetorical analysis of intention is primarily concerned with how intention is embodied in a work. The present discussion has been concerned with the reader's relationship to intention, regardless of the particular way it is embodied in the work.

A brief comparison of poetry and music is of interest at this point because it permits bringing together the two ideas of intention and purpose, thinking now of purpose as this term was used during the discussion of semblance in Part One. In the context of a comparison of poetry and music, attention is drawn to the fact that the creation of either a poem or a musical composition requires a deliberate choice of the kind of act to be performed. And this choice involves the concepts of intention and purpose.

Let us first consider the kind of decision represented in determining to write a poem. Writing a poem is a verbal act, but it is only one among a great many kinds; the concept of verbal acts includes commands, invitations, prayers, poems, and many others. A speaker can try to get the same result, for instance, by issuing either a command or an invitation. Yet the speaker's choice of verbal act will make a good deal of difference in the kind of relationship established between himself and his hearer, even if the action the hearer takes is the same in either case. Since poetry is not usually written to result in action of the kind sought in a command or an invitation, it cannot be thought about in quite the same way. Nevertheless, just as a person who issues a command or an invitation is normally concerned with something more than establishing a certain relationship between himself and his hearer, so is a person who issues a poem.

For example, a military officer who commands a squad of soldiers to stand at attention is concerned with maintaining his relationship of authority over them. For this reason, he does not merely invite them to stand at attention. But he is also concerned with the practical results of his verbal act: he wants the squad actually to stand at attention. Similarily, a poet desires a certain relationship between himself and his reader. This desire is most apparent if we observe poets in the act of reading their poetry aloud to an audience. But, like the officer, the poet is concerned with something more than this relationship. He too wants a practical result. His additional concern is to create a semblance (or intransitive rapt attention) and impart his intention. If I may put the idea rather whimsically, in a literary work the writer's purpose is to express his intention in the form of a semblance.[56] His intention is what he means.

As remarked earlier, there is actually a certain advantage in using both these terms, purpose and intention, as will become evident in relating them now to music. Like a poet, a musician —either a composer or a performer—engages in an act with a publicly recognized form. His purpose is to create a semblance in the form of music. But at this point the difference between poetry and music emerges. Given the form he has chosen, the musician cannot intend a meaning; he can only have the purpose of creating a semblance.

It is true that some people have regarded poetry as a kind of music. An example is Henri Bremond, who was convinced that poetry and music are the same thing and that it is unnecessary to grasp the meaning-content of a poem to appreciate the poem properly.[57] Such an eccentric view need not concern us here, however. Edgar Allan Poe, who was also fascinated by the musical quality of language, took a more cautious view. In his "Letter to B———" Poe wrote, "Music, when combined with a pleasurable idea, is poetry; music without the idea is simply music."[58]

The distinction between purpose and intention is thus illuminated by recognition of a fundamental difference between music and poetry, uncertain and shifting though the precise boundary between them may be. Both music and poetry embody purpose, but only poetry embodies intention. The closest approach in literature to works containing no intention is found in imagistic and surrealistic poetry. But when we come to Chapter 12, "Drama and Intention," we will observe how even in imagistic works a semblance is usually built up out of bits of meaning. Surrealistic poetry, which presents a different problem, will be discussed in Chapter 13.

Despite the usefulness of differentiating between purpose and intention, it seems to me the ultimate relationship between these two ideas, as between semblance and meaning or concrete and abstract, is a mystery. Such a term as concrete universal is not a help, only a restatement of the problem. Is not the final mystery here the question of how life enters into the inanimate, of how feeling and thought are born?

In any event, the distinction between purpose and intention can be made on a practical level, and it is a distinction which is extremely useful in the classroom, as I hope has been made clear throughout this discussion of significance, intention, and the authorless text.[59]

This is a good point, nevertheless, at which to emphasize the fact that both the idea of an authorless text and the idea of an author's intention are only aids to interpretation of meaning. They are not guarantees that a true interpretation will be achieved. Any complex text is a container that is open at both ends, and any hope of an absolutely true interpretation constantly dribbles away out of both ends. The reader's end of the container is the language he sees confronting him. The other end is the writer's intention. At the reader's end, we ponder the fact that apparently unresolvable disagreements about the interpretation of literary texts are common. The same fact is observed with legal documents; settlement by a court decree of a sincere disagreement about the interpretation of a legal text is often an act of force rather than an intellectual solution of a textual problem. For the classroom, the important point is that even one genuinely insoluble disagreement by competent scholars about the public semantic properties of a text is fatal to the theory of the authorless text. As long as one insoluble case exists, we cannot claim to have a proven theory of interpretation

without reference to the author's intention. At the other end of
the container stands the author. But how can we ever be certain
of what an author intended? Actually we cannot. Unless we
wish to rule on the meaning of a text as if we were a court of
law the best we can do is determine the author's most probable
intention. Not only is the semantic problem, in all its synchron-
ic and diachronic dimensions, a barrier to certainty, but the
author may be unsure of his own intention. The unconscious
plays an intricate role in creativity. The intention that produces
a literary work may be ambiguous in many ways. It is occasionally a temptation to plunge without reservation into that
atomization of consciousness represented by some structuralist
thought, but there is no finality in this direction either.

For our purposes these are unnecessary complexities. The
limitation involved in the concept of the author's most probable
intention is by no means devastating or crippling; it is only a
recognition that authors and readers alike are merely human.
Indeed the last topic to be considered in this review of significance and intention takes us the final step in recognition of human limitations. This step is an examination of the possibility
of an author's having reservations about his own meaning. The
meaning an author intends may have a significance for him
which causes him to feel a distaste for his own intention.

A striking example appears in Joyce Carol Oates's recent
book, *New Heaven, New Earth*. Because of its relevance to the
whole subject of significance, I would like to quote at some
length from her discussion of Sylvia Plath. The passage below
is taken from a section in which Oates has been discussing the
poem "Magi," from *Crossing the Water*. She has pointed out
that in this poem Sylvia Plath is contemplating her six-month-
old daughter and is imagining the Magi of Abstraction—that
is, abstract philosophical concepts—hovering like "dull angels"
over the child.

> [Sylvia Plath's] attitude is one of absolute contentment
> with the physical, charming simplicities of her infant
> daughter; she seems to want none of that "multiplica-
> tion table" of intellect. If this poem had not been writ-
> ten by Sylvia Plath, who drew such attention to her
> poetry by suicide, one would read it and immediately

agree with its familiar assumptions—how many times we've read this poem, by so many different poets! But Miss Plath's significance now forces us to examine her work very carefully, and in this case the poem reveals itself as a vision as tragic as her more famous, more obviously troubled poems.

It is, in effect, a death sentence passed by Plath on her own use of language, on the "abstractions" of culture or the literary as opposed to the physical immediacy of a baby's existence. The world of language is condemned as only "ethereal" and "blank"—obviously inferior to the world of brute, undeveloped nature.[60]

Two ideas in this passage are of special interest. The first is that Sylvia Plath's suicide changed our relationship to her poetry. The second has to do with Plath's relationship to her own meaning.

I don't believe Oates's use of "significance" is exactly the same as mine, but the word is in my own sense nevertheless appropriate. She is saying that our consciousness of Plath's intention in her poetry has been heightened by her suicide. Presumably any reader would agree. At any rate, in this observation by Oates we have a dramatic affirmation of the concept of significance in the form of a relationship between the reader and the author's intention. The psychological dimensions in the idea of significance that were considered earlier are again suggested when Oates further remarks, "The experience of reading [Sylvia Plath's] poetry deeply is a frightening one."[61] For the classroom, the practical problem contained in this observation is made vividly clear in an account by Barrett John Mandel of what happened when he assigned some of Plath's poetry to a class at Douglass College.

Mandel's class of eighteen highly capable, tense, freshman women had two sorts of trouble with the poetry. One was simply the difficulty of comprehending it. "I don't understand a word of this!" one young woman wrote. As to the other problem:

Worse yet: some of the girls actually caught glimpses of what Sylvia *means* in the welter of words; they heard, for a moment, her feet, flintlike, strike a racket of echoes. These students, perhaps the more sensitive ones, were frankly terrified into defensive postures. Rather than confront the dismal horror of her bleak vision, which would require internalization, momentary suspension of their own sanity, tentative examination of the world through Sylvia's eyes and ears, the girls chose to retreat back to the level of voiceless, dense misunderstanding. It was far less painful to appear stupid than to allow Sylvia to tap their own vulnerability with the urgency of her hysterical suffering. Their outrage was as intense as anything I've seen in ten years of teaching.[62]

The word "terrified" seems pretty strong. Nevertheless, a great value in Mandel's account is its clear depiction of what happens in a classroom when a negative significance overpowers the possibility of assent. What teacher has not had the experience of seeing a wall go up when he tried to discuss a certain book? Mature, sophisticated people are capable of submitting themselves with rapt attention to Plath's poetry and of assenting to it without being engulfed in it. Apparently the women in Mandel's class were not capable of either the first or both of these commitments. Mandel's own conclusion is that he erred in selecting the Plath text, that the encounter with despair in Plath's poetry was too much for women already under the pressures of an intense new experience.

A second idea suggested by the passage quoted from Oates is that Plath found in her own meaning a negative significance. The notion that an author might have a negative relationship to a meaning he himself has expressed takes a moment of getting used to, perhaps, but it's really an old and familiar idea. Someone asks us, "What do you intend to say in your letter?" We answer, "That the trip will have to be canceled." That is our intention, our meaning, but its significance is distasteful. We had looked forward to the trip. Life is full of such tensions between intention and significance.

What can be said about Sylvia Plath's intention in "Magi"? I would choose three things to consider. First, that she dreamed of escape from life's problems into simple nature. Second, that the meaningful act of denouncing the intellectual life was complementary to this dream. Third, that she was continuing to find the emotional and intellectual experience of poetry a source of rapt interest, that a fundamental element in her intention was to perform a verbal act of the class "poetry." This element in her intention is not apparent in the semantic content of the poem. Indeed, the semantic meaning of the poem is seemingly at odds with the author's intention to write a poem. And this oddity becomes evident only when we ask ourselves what her intention was in writing the poem at all.

Before going farther I will copy the poem out, so its contents can be examined.

MAGI

The abstracts hover like dull angels:
Nothing so vulgar as a nose or an eye
Bossing the ethereal blanks of their face-ovals.

Their whiteness bears no relation to laundry,
Snow, chalk or suchlike. They're
The real thing, all right: the Good, the True—

Salutary and pure as boiled water,
Loveless as the multiplication table.
While the child smiles into thin air.

Six months in the world, and she is able
To rock on all fours like a padded hammock.
For her, the heavy notion of Evil

Attending her cot is less than a bellyache,
And Love the mother of milk, no theory.
They mistake their star, these papery godfolk.

They want the crib of some lamp-headed Plato.
Let them astound his heart with their merit.
What girl ever flourished in such company?[63]

As Oates says, it is indeed common to find poets denouncing abstractions. "Magi" is not unusual in that respect. But in the usual instance the abstractions denounced are contrasted with the concreteness of literature. In "Magi," abstractions are contrasted only with what Oates calls brute, undeveloped nature. In which category did Plath mean to place poetry—the world of abstractions or the world of undeveloped nature? My guess is that she would have said poetry has its own place, different from either. I do not feel, however, that Oates is therefore wrong in her conclusion that "Magi" is a rejection of language and culture. Plath's suicide doesn't seem to tell us what she meant in the poem: her suicide was a rejection of the world of physical nature as well as of language and culture. But her suicide does assure us of the intensity of her concern about her subject matter. Given her tremendous sensitivity to language, she must have pondered the chance that the lack of any hint in the poem of a difference between papery godfolk and the value of the concreteness of art would lead to exactly such conjectures as Oates presents. She must have realized that the love of poetry demonstrated in the act of writing the poem was at least to some degree at odds with the meaning she intended the poem to convey. In other words, there is reason to suspect that the significance her intention had for her was not a wholly comfortable one.[64] Many intellectual people who have written antiintellectual works must have experienced such ambivalent feelings.

The point is clarified by contrast to a genuine, unqualified antiintellectualism. I once encountered what seemed to me a nearly perfect example of antiintellectualism, because it was entirely good-humored. A man showed up in one of my classes who was, any way you looked at him, a genius. I even went to the trouble of looking up his score on an IQ test he had taken and found he had scored far up into the "genius" range. In my class, when he did any work it was invariably brilliant. But he seldom did any work. One day I talked with him about it. He said he just wasn't interested in all this. He'd been a truck driver before coming to the university, he explained, and he'd recently decided to go back to truck driving. He'd owned his own truck. It was a pretty good life.

There was nothing doctrinaire about his devotion to a nonintellectual life; it was long before the days of the "student movement." So I presented an argument. I pointed out that he could hardly avoid thinking about things. I said I wondered what, with a mind like his, he would find to think about as a truck driver that could keep him interested. "Well," he said, grinning, "if I don't think about it it won't bother me."

As far as our subject of meaning and significance is concerned, at any rate, the example of Plath indicates that the textual container may in some sense be open at both ends for the author as well as for the reader. The inescapable conclusion is that a full formalization of the rules governing the interpretation of a literary text is unattainable. To a considerable degree, interpretation must always be intuitive. A less formidable but perhaps more important conclusion is that it would surely be wrong not to help readers explore the full intention represented by, as well as contained in, such a poem as "Magi."

As I approach the end of these remarks about the subject of meaning and significance I am reminded of the driving-school paradox. In all the states of the union it is a law that a car on the driver's right has the right of way. The driving-school paradox is represented by the diagram below.

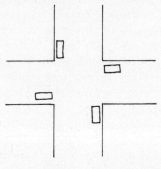

All four cars have reached the corner at precisely the same moment and stopped. There is no signal light, no stop sign. Which car has the right of way? None. Or all. The law is utterly exhausted by this situation. The drivers are reduced to reliance on such primitive signals as gestures and grins. And yet four reasonable and courteous drivers will solve this problem with no real trouble at all. Similarly, I observe that in spite of the lack of an airtight theoretical basis for the interpretation of literary texts, reasonable and courteous people seem to have a fairly successful and happy experience not only with their reading but with exchanges of opinion about their reading.

In this discussion our primary concern has been significance, with its necessary companion, meaning. Significance, as I have used the term, is a relationship between a reader and a meaning. A general problem, therefore, is to locate the meaning to which the reader can relate. One possibility is found in the authorless text; a second in the meaning the author intended in the act of writing; a third in the genre the writer selected; a fourth, which was not explored, in the cultural context in which the author was working. Both the concept of the authorless text and the concept of the author's intention have advantages and disadvantages for the classroom. The idea of finding a theoretical basis for a universally sound method of interpretation is hopeless because the semantic properties of texts are often controversial and the author's intention is ultimately not verifiable. In view of this inherent limitation in the possibilities of finding true interpretations, it is important to encourage people to become aware of everyone's tendency to confuse significance and meaning. A powerful semblance can help a reader avoid this confusion and help win his assent to a meaning he cannot himself endorse.

10. SERIES & PROBABILITY

In the chapter just concluded concerning the relationship of a reader to meaning, the presence in literature of meaning, or abstractions, was assumed. Now we should consider how meaning gets into literature. Obviously, this problem is vast in scope, and my discussion of it must be severely limited. The principle of the necessary limitation will again be practicality—what might seem helpful in the day-to-day classroom. Even from a somewhat more general point of view than the demands of the classroom, however, the primary need in determining the role of abstractions in literature is not so much to struggle with complex issues as to play with simple ones. I will approach the subject through consideration of the idea of a series and of probability.

The concepts of series and probability are themselves complex, but they can be usefully applied in simple ways. Actually, both are relied upon everywhere in the analysis of literature —and that is why they are appropriate here. As Paul Goodman remarked, "The formal analysis of a poem is largely the demonstration of a probability through all the parts."[65] Or as Hugh Kenner says, in analyzing a poem by Pound, ". . . now that three instances rule out accident."[66]

A simple illustration of probability theory is found in the tossing of a coin. Common sense says that in one toss the probability that a coin will come up heads is 1 to 1. The same idea can be expressed more elaborately by saying that the probability is 1 to $2^n - 1$, where n is the number of tosses. What, then, is the probability that heads will come up, say, three times in a row, by mere chance? The answer is 1 to 7. That is, it's 1 to $2^3 - 1$.

These numbers are not important for our purposes except in calling attention to the hard fact that the more often a given structural element appears in a literary work the less likelihood there is it can be accounted for by mere chance.[67] Just as we can ask what the probability is of encountering a series of three heads in a row when tossing a coin, we can ask what the probability is of encountering a series like that formed by the word "innocent" in *Daisy Miller*. In other words, could the sequence of "innocents" have occurred by mere accident? The latter question is many times more difficult than the question about the coin and involves a somewhat different logic, but at bottom it too is a problem of probability.

The idea of probability is associated with a series in a literary work in two ways. First, as just indicated, there is the question of whether a given series could have come into existence by pure chance. Very often, as with *Daisy Miller*, the answer is obvious as soon as the question is raised. Chance could not possibly account for such a series. For this reason, an instructor can make effective use of works containing a strongly marked series to provide novice readers an insight into how literary works are organized. Usually the tracing out of a clearly formed series, with emphasis on the question of probability, will persuade the most skeptical reader that the author really did mean all that. Second, there is a question of probability when one or two of the items in a clearly marked series deviate in some way from the rest. But what is a series?

A series is a row of things which are related to one another. A recent issue of *Time* magazine remarks casually that for Hemingway "reality emerges from careful, linear detail."[68] Somewhat more soberly considered, however, the principle to think about is not mere linearity. A series is not merely a group of things arranged in a line; it is a line in which each item is related to the preceding item by some law. There is a great deal of difference between simple linearity and that "necessary sequence" of which Adams and Stein and Hemingway dreamed. As already seen, in terms of structure rather than style the idea of a series is familiar in literature through the concept of a recurrent motif.

The laws governing the formation of a series can be either simple or complex. The simplest sort of series is one in which every item is exactly like every other: for example, a row of buttons down the front of a man's shirt. If we should notice that in a row of five such buttons the middle button was red but the others were white we would wonder how come. We would assume the deviation had not occurred by chance. Another example of a simple series is the numbers from 1 to 10. We'll return to this example in a moment. An instance of a series formed according to a more complex rule is 1.41421 . . . , which is the square root of two, or which is formed according to the law of how to find the square root of two.

Among all the patterns of structure found in literary works, probably none is easier to perceive than a simple series. In a merely mechanical sense, of course, all the structural elements in literature appear in the form of a series simply because of the linearity of the text. In my paperback copy of Pynchon's *Gravity's Rainbow*, there is somewhere around a mile and a half of text, allowing 25 percent for space breaks, if the text were printed linearly on a ribbon of paper.

Some of the patterns found in literature are extremely complex, however, as any reader of *Gravity's Rainbow* will agree. While traveling his mile and a half through this text the reader encounters many images of the V-2 rocket. It is not yet clear to me whether this sequence of images can properly be called a series. However that may be, in the limitless space of the reader's mind these images are gathered together into both linear and nonlinear patterns so intricate they could be duplicated only in other minds. They could not be copied in diagrams on paper or in models. The verbal text out of which they come is only an analog. Such complexities, however, are implied by, and indeed often arise out of, the simple series with which we will be concerned. In thinking about the nature of the simplest sort of series we will see why literature could hardly exist without abstractions and why abstractions in fact contribute to the health and strength of literature.

It will be helpful to begin by thinking about some numbers. The sequence of numbers from 1 to 10, for example, is a series which obeys the law that each number represents one more item than the preceding number, beginning with one item for number 1.

Knowing this simple law, if we find such a series from which some number has been omitted we can supply the missing number. This is only the arithmetic of our childhood, but let me go on with it for a moment. If the items we are numbering are x's, we see at once that three x's, or the number 3, has been omitted from the following:

$$x \quad\quad = 1$$
$$xx \quad\quad = 2$$

$$xxxx \quad = 4$$
$$xxxxx = 5$$

Similarly, if such a series of numbers stops with 9, we know the next number should be 10.

Still concerned with the same kind of reasoning, however, we come upon two circumstances which particularly suggest the usefulness of the idea of a series in exploring abstractions in literature. The first circumstance has to do with symbols arbitrarily but logically inserted into a familiar series, like the numerals from 1 to 10; the second has to do with a symbol inserted into such a series for emotional rather than logical reasons.

The first circumstance is illustrated by the arbitrary insertion of two symbols into the following series:

$$1\ 2\ 3\ 4\ 5\ 6\ 7\ 8\ 9\ \lambda\ \delta\ 10\ 11\ 12\ 13\ 14\ 15\ 16\ 17\ 18\ 19\ 1\lambda\ 1\delta\ 20$$

The logic of the two symbols (λ, δ) arbitrarily inserted into this familiar series becomes clear when we try some additions based on the series.

$$2 + 2 = 4$$
$$4 + 4 = 8$$
$$8 + 8 = 14$$

The fact that 8 plus 8 actually does equal 14 is readily seen in this way:

$$\frac{1\ 2\ 3\ 4\ 5\ 6\ 7\ 8}{8} + \frac{9\ \lambda\ \delta\ 10\ 11\ 12\ 13\ 14}{8} = 14 \quad 15\ 16\ 17\ 18\ 19\ 1\lambda\ 1\delta\ 20$$

Pondering this situation, we conclude that Humpty Dumpty had a point. A numerical symbol means whatever we want it to mean.

$$10 \text{ may mean } xxxxxxxxx$$
$$\text{or } 10 \text{ may mean } xxxxxxxxxxx$$

We can further conclude that this is an example of what happens when one or two items in a series deviate from the rest.

In the example shown, what the series maker wanted the inserted symbols to mean was only numeration, exactly the same kind of meaning contained in all the other symbols in the series. His purpose in introducing new symbols was simply to change the base from 10 to what we conventionally call 12.

Nevertheless, encountering an unfamiliar symbol in a familiar series is always a bit of a shock. It warns us that somebody has been tinkering or that there's been an accident. Of course poets count heavily on this shock, a fact to be examined in a moment. Meanwhile, let us move slightly in the direction of literature: we will insert an arbitrary symbol that goes just a step beyond pure numeration toward what might be called verbal meaning. In this second circumstance the motive appears to be feeling rather than logic.

1 2 3 4 5 6 7 8 9 10 11 12

This series is probably the most minimal literary work I have ever come across. The surprise comes with the discovery of the French (or, more generally, European) crossed seven introduced into a series in an English text. Again, the probability that it appeared there by pure chance is extremely small. I wonder if there is a French seven in the Rand Corporation's thick volume of random numbers? As to the possible meaning of this mini-work, I can only say I have noticed that not infrequently young people return to this country from a visit to Paris with the habit of writing a French seven, and I suppose they are poetizing. A visit to Paris is truly a thing to be proud of.

But the French seven might have been written by a visitor from Paris to the United States. Just for fun, here is another version of the same series: a sketch of a watch on a postcard with the numeral seven transformed into a French seven.

Why no hands on the watch? I don't know. It is all in the spirit of a charming young woman who recently wrote to my wife that she had enjoyed the Gila cliff dwellings more than other cliff dwellings because she had had more opportunity for fantasizing there. More context is found in the example of the watch than in the previous one, but not enough to determine a single meaning. The problem is similar to what we encountered in "Oread" and "Between Walls." The message might be anything from "Buy French watches, it is later than you think," to a note from a visiting Frenchwoman meaning, "Meet me at seven but keep your hands off." There is unquestionable evidence of mind play here. Chance cannot account for what we see. But the intended meaning of the message is obscure. Poets often work the same strategy, inviting the reader to the delights of fantasizing.

In the first example we looked at, that of pure numeration, there was no discernible context or background. We had a natural series, the accumulation of items one by one, to which an arbitrary but conventional succession of symbols had been assigned (i.e., 1, 2, 3, etc.). The existence of this succession of arbitrary symbols is itself evidence of the activity of mind, but it is an activity conventionalized by centuries of use. The discovery of the intrusion of two unexpected symbols (λ and δ) into the familiar array is evidence of an immediate and innovative presence of mind and intention. Because there is no discernible context or background for this intrusion, however, the intention underlying it is a mystery. We can only wonder what improvement in arithmetic anyone had hoped to obtain.

In the second and third examples, on the other hand, the series is charged with feeling, even though the charge is tiny. The unexpected crossed seven, while a logical part of the series, is not a familiar part in our conventional succession of number symbols but is a familiar part of somebody else's conventional succession of number symbols. With the introduction of a French seven into an English text we move outside the world of numbers and into the conventionalizing world. We move into that world in which people say to each other, "My conventions are better than your conventions are." Here we see the faintest possible beginnings of drama, of semblance.

To create our minidrama, or minipoem, two things were needed: a series both writer and reader could recognize and an intrusion both could recognize as charged with feeling. Without the recognition of the abstract relationships (either real or nominal) represented by the series, no drama; also no drama without recognition of the feeling created by the inserted symbol.

Could there be, however, a natural series made up of nothing but concrete feelings in which the relationships among the items in the series are only felt rather than recognized as abstractions? This is a hard question; the best answer is probably a cautious yes. We seem to have such an experience in listening to music or watching those kinds of dancing which, unlike most classical ballet, are not intended to imply a story. Something vaguely comparable may occur in imagistic or surrealistic writing. These literary possibilities can be examined later.

We have so far thought about the concepts of probability and a series, about symbols arbitrarily but logically introduced into a numerative series, and about a numerative series faintly touched by poetry or drama. The hint of poetry or drama was created by the deliberate introduction of a logical but atypical symbol demanding attention to questions of motive. It is now time to think about a series made not out of numbers but out of words.

We can begin with a situation roughly resembling the first numerative series looked at. What is wanted is a series in which emotion is not an issue and in which symbols (in this case words) are introduced that are surprising but nevertheless logical. Casting about for an example, I recalled a passage in an old history of a region of northwestern Maryland in the Appalachian Mountains.

> In the latter part of the nineteenth century when the town of Deer Park, Maryland, had become probably the most famous of the mountain resorts serving the Washington area, the Deer Park Hotel maintained a herd of deer in a nearby meadow as a novel and pleasant spectacle for its distinguished patrons. To care for these deer, the hotel employed a man to serve as deerherd. Although his name has not been recorded by history, he is reputed to have been sober and trustworthy. This deerherd soon learned that some of the deer were gentle and kindly but others were ill tempered and malicious. Deer of the first kind the deerherd called dear deer; apparently he had a

designating term for the others as well, but this other term has somehow been deleted from the records.

Among the dear deer, some had been born in captivity, others had been captured in the forest and sold to the Deer Park Hotel by woodsmen. These latter deer were of course expensive, and the deerherd always spoke of them as the dear dear deer. Among the dear dear deer, however, was one who never became reconciled to captivity. It dreamed always of the great world beyond the meadow. One day, seeing the sadness in its eyes, the deerherd determined to let it go so it could return to the freedom of the forest, and he called his wife to help him.

"When I tell you," he said, "you open the gate and let it go."

His wife, who was apprehensive about all this, replied hesitantly, "Well, I will on your say so do so so that that dear dear deer can go free."

Whereupon the deerherd said gently to his beloved wife, "Dear dear dear deer should always be treated with the utmost consideration."

Although a necessary sequence is involved in this series, the fundamental relationships among the items are phonic and punning. The meaning depends heavily on the context. Taken out of context, the words "dear dear dear deer" or "say so do so so that that" constitute just about as much of a puzzle as would "9 λ δ 10." Both sets of symbols are given certainty of meaning and relationship to one another by placing them in a context or entire network of relationships. The effectiveness of such a network is evident in the fact that when first reading the entire passage about the deer a reader could both supply and understand the missing words if the last sentence were printed as follows: "Dear ——— ——— deer should always be treated with the utmost consideration."

I've been using the word "context" without having explained what I mean by it. It's a loose term, bounded at one extreme by the concept of the cultural background of a text and at the other by the elements within a meaning itself. The concept of genre stands roughly at a halfway point between these extremes. I am using "context" to suggest those aids to understanding which lie outside what might vaguely be called the primary text. Sometimes context may refer to elements lying completely outside a text—as with the culture implied by the French seven. When attention is concentrated on a given passage, other parts of the same text may constitute a context. In the first example above, that of simple numeration, there was no context except in the most general cultural sense. In the example of the crossed seven the context was an assumed awareness of differences between two cultures—French and English (and American). Through the choice of a French symbol in an English text the person who wrote down the series could assert his familiarity with French culture. In the example of the deerherd the context escapes easy identification. The context is a narrative, a succession of events and situations that are part of the text itself.

For the needs of the classroom, the best place to go for consideration of the idea of a context is not to the theory of the interpretation of texts but to historiography. Like the instructor in a literary classroom, the historian is prone to think of that sort of context lying outside the text itself as background and to relate it to problems of narration. He may also, however, speak of context within the text as background. Here are a couple of representative comments by historians:

> [A classical European novel] is by no means a "linear series," but something much more complex. Its author must also refer to an "essential background" which cannot itself be "formulated in terms of narrative."

> The claim that intelligible narrative requires knowledge of a background, whether actually sketched or only assumed, is quite compatible with there being good histories containing long stretches of straight narration.[69]

We should next consider a verbal series in which the motive for introducing a symbol is feeling. This example should be a verbal equivalent of the numerical series in which the French seven was found. As a possibility, here is a poem by Edgar Lee Masters.

DAISY FRASER

Did you ever hear of Editor Whedon
Giving to the public treasury any of the money received

For supporting candidates for office?
Or for writing up the canning factory
To get people to invest?
Or for suppressing the facts about the bank,
When it was rotten and ready to break?
Did you ever hear of the Circuit Judge
Helping anyone except the "Q" railroad,
Or the bankers? Or did Rev. Peet or Rev. Sibley
Give any part of their salary, earned by keeping still,
Or speaking out as the leaders wished them to do,
To the building of the water works?
But I—Daisy Fraser who always passed
Along the streets through rows of nods and smiles
And coughs and words such as "there she goes,"
Never was taken before Justice Arnett
Without contributing ten dollars and costs
To the school fund of Spoon River![70]

The base of the series is charitable acts. The items in the series
are "giving," "helping," "give," and "contributing." The key
item is "contributing." As in the example of the French seven,
the key item forms a logical element in the series. But, as in the
other example, it also brings into the field of view what might
be called two different cultures: that of the hypocrites—editor,
judge, banker, and preachers—and that of the openly acknowledged prostitute. Had editor, judge, banker, and preachers been
either more honest or more open about the kind of men they
really were, the ironic force of Daisy Fraser's saying "contributing" rather than "being fined" would have been lost. As with
the simpler instances previously looked at, the idea of probability—or improbability—leads to the conclusion that the termination of the series of charitable acts by the slight deviation of
the irony in "contributing" was a deliberate choice. (We
haven't yet considered, however, what "deliberate" means. The
concept of will leads into some strange places.)

I will conclude these examples of the application of the concepts of series and probability to literature with brief references
to longer works. Shelley's "Ode to the West Wind" will serve
as an instance from poetry.[71] In this poem, which is divided
into five sections, the first three sections are concerned respec-

tively with the action of the wind upon leaves, clouds, and
waves. The base of the series is the effect of the wind. In the
fourth section Shelley twice recapitulates the series. In lines 43–
45 he writes:

> If I were a dead leaf thou mightest bear;
> If I were a swift cloud to fly with thee;
> A wave to pant beneath thy power . . .

And in line 53:

> Oh! Lift me as a wave, a leaf, a cloud!

The context of this series is of course complex, involving ideas
about the brotherhood of man, the responsibilities of the poet,
the innocence of childhood as an ideal, and other things. I'll not
try to discuss this context.

As a last example we might take the rather amusing case of
The Catcher in the Rye. This novel, which hit college campuses
like a tidal wave when it first appeared, contains a series based
on the word "fall." This word is used to pun on a physical fall
and on the myth of the fall from innocence. The amusing part
of the history of this novel is that the "fall" series, which was
evidently intended to culminate in the protagonist's major recognition scene,[72] went virtually unnoticed when the novel was
enjoying its first popularity—as did the recognition scene itself.
A survey of the initial reviews makes this conclusion perfectly
clear. What people liked in the novel was what appeared to be
an uninhibited attack on phoniness, rather than the compassionate understanding of phoniness finally achieved by Holden
Caulfield, the teen-age narrator. In other words, they carried
away from their reading a kind of pleasure it turns out they
were supposed to have discovered was bad for them.

The series begins, unless I missed something, with a boy's
falling—actually, jumping—to his death to escape abuse in his
dormitory room at school. The boy is described as innocent, ineffectual, and brave. Within two pages but in another setting,
Holden is saying that what he'd like to be, if he had his choice,
is the catcher in the rye. He fantasizes about children playing
in a rye field at the edge of a cliff, with himself standing guard
to catch any who are about to fall off. Later he talks with a former teacher who warns Holden that unless he acquires self-

discipline he himself is heading for a fall—a kind of fall in which the victim just keeps falling and falling without ever hitting bottom. It was this teacher who had cared for the body of the boy killed in the fall from the dormitory window. Soon afterward Holden is so emotionally disturbed that he can't step down from a curb without fearing he will begin an interminable fall. Finally, he watches his little sister riding on a merry-go-round and is filled with anxiety lest she fall off. But now, at the end of the novel, he tells himself he mustn't intervene: "The thing with kids is, if they want to grab for the gold ring, you have to let them do it, and not say anything to them. If they fall off, they fall off, but it's bad if you say anything to them."[73] Holden has had his recognition scene: he has realized that the myth of the fall from innocence is reenacted in every individual's life as he learns about phoniness, or evil. In the last paragraph of the book Holden paraphrases something his teacher had told him earlier—that through the creation of art men become humble and compassionate rather than filled with hatred for phoniness.

Holden's initial concern with the innocence of childhood is like Shelley's, as seen in lines 47–50 of "Ode to the West Wind":

> If even
> I were as in my boyhood, and could be
>
> The comrade of thy wanderings over Heaven,
> As then . . .

But what would Salinger say to Shelley about the famous line 54?

> I fall upon the thorns of life! I bleed!

In any case, the popular response to *The Catcher in the Rye* was more in the spirit of Shelley's line 54 than of the compassionate maturity recommended at the end of the novel or—I should add in fairness—of the compassionate maturity recommended in Shelley's later work *Prometheus Unbound*.

The popular response to *The Catcher in the Rye* seems to indicate that the context simply overpowered the "fall" series it was ostensibly designed to serve. That is, the assault on phoniness from the perspective of childhood's innocence created a powerful illusion of life, whereas the "fall" series was only mea-

gerly related to an illusion of life. Readers scarcely felt it or
didn't notice it at all. The term "phony" itself also constitutes a
series, of course; it is richly developed. In view of this fact, a
strong argument could be made that the book would be better
without the "fall" series. A reader might assent to the virtual
world that would be left—that of a teen-ager in a serious emotional crisis. As it is, the "fall" series is so underdeveloped as to
be hardly an integral part of a reader's experience.

So far, the only kind of series considered has been made up of
simple terms or concepts. Another kind which obviously needs
attention is one made up of images. What is an image? Pound
said it is "that which presents an intellectual and emotional
complex in an instant of time." He also said, "Go in fear of abstractions."[74] In a way Pound's definition of an image is good,
and in a way it isn't. Anyhow, to simplify the following discussion, I will have reference principally to visual images—which
I find easier to comprehend than complexes. Of course there
are several other kinds of images: auditory, kinetic, and so on.

Northrop Frye says, "The meaning of a poem, its structure
of imagery, is a static pattern."[75] No doubt it is a static pattern
—on the page, that is—but Frye's equation of meaning with
imagery sets up an old and familiar problem. How do images
mean? The answer is that they mean in the same way other
symbols mean: by taking their place in a set of relationships.
It's just as easy to make a series of images as a series of numbers
or concepts. The following is the simplest example I could think
of:

The physical relationship of these images to one another on the page suggests that a meaning was intended. And probably everyone would agree that the meaning intended is something like, "If you drink, don't drive." It couldn't be proved that this is the meaning of the images, however. For instance, they might mean that the person shown is fortifying himself with liquor before visiting the grave of someone he had loved. As in earlier illustrations, the lack of context makes the meaning uncertain. Enriching the context could specify the meaning. Nevertheless, because of their lack of syntax, such images can never communicate specific complex meanings as effectively as language does. Indeed, the only "grammar" binding these three images together is their linear relationship on the page and their reflection of a context of familiar situations or attitudes. All "imagistic" logic works in this way, of course. A famous example is Picasso's *Guernica*. Josephine Miles asserts that in modern poetry context is especially important because the vocabulary found there tends to be comprised of natural objects or images—"wing, shadow, rain, stone, hill, grass"—and these natural objects in the poetry tend to be "unattached," except through context. An image is an invitation to the reader or observer to try out all the interpretations he can think of; it is not normally an articulation of a single idea. Pound spoke of an image as something "from which, and through which, and into which ideas are con‑stantly rushing."[76]

Here is another example of a series of visual images, this time in verbal form. The point of this example is, again, that a series of images—either graphic or verbal—can convey an abstract meaning.

> An enormous number of dolphins crowding
> Just below a still surface
> Their jostling pushes one dolphin
> Above the surface, then another
> And another, so rapidly
> And so closely
> It might be a single dolphin
> Flashing across the water

There seem to be three images in this series: the dolphins crowding below the still surface, the jostling of the dolphins, and the summing image of the single dolphin flashing across the water. What does the series mean? Nothing, as far as I can tell, except "I saw this and it delighted me." It is little more than the verbal equivalent of presenting a reader the symbols 9 λ δ 10 with no other context whatsoever.

Actually, given some context this example proves to be what a historian would call a narrative series and a poet a metaphor: and I must confess to a trick. These lines were taken from a discussion of the wave form of subatomic particles. The subject being considered is essentially the famous paradox that light is both a motion of particles and a wave motion. The argument being presented is that a subatomic particle can be conceptualized as a packet. This packet, it is argued, moves through space as an entity, a particle; but its interior, so to speak, is actually a seething wave motion. The passage out of which I extracted and rearranged the lines above reads as follows:

> The movement of a wave packet is . . . like an enormous number of dolphins crowding just below a still surface. Their jostling pushes one dolphin above the surface, then another and another, so rapidly and so closely that it might be a single dolphin flashing across the water, according to the laws of classical particle physics. Similarly the wave maxima . . . are "pushed" into being by a swarm of continuous wave disturbances, and each maximum is just a little farther along in the direction in which the whole school moves. This is a crude picture; but so, when it comes to that, are all the wave-diagrams. These illustrations are ladders we shall certainly throw away once they are climbed.[77]

The series of images thus leads to an abstract concept which can be presented in wave-form diagrams. I was wrong, however, in comparing the series of images to 9 λ δ 10. A dolphin flashing across the water is an image of energy and delight. It is presaged—in the faintest possible degree—by the French seven rather than the inert λ δ.

As a third and last example of a series of images I have selected a recently published poem by William Stafford. The images here are not all visual, and the series formed is intricate, perhaps too intricate.

EXISTENCES

Half-wild, I hear a wolf,
half-tame, I bark. Then
in the dark I feel my master's
hand, and lick, then bite.

I envy leaves, their touch: miles
by the million, tongues everywhere
saying yea, for the forest,
and in the night, for us.

At caves in the desert, close
to rocks, I wait. I live
by grace of shadows. In moonlight
I hear a room open behind me.

At the last when you come
I am a track in the dust.[78]

What does it mean? I don't know. In specificity, it seems to
stand about midway between "Oread" and, say, "Provide, Provide." I enjoy the poem; the kind of feeling I have is one that
comes where there is intention. On first reading, the poem created a meaning that was itself only an image at the far edge of
my mind. I have tried to tease this image out where I can see
it better.

The title seems to establish the base of a series: existences.
Such an inference could hardly be drawn from the title alone,
but only a glance is needed to see that in some sense the poem
is concerned with a variety of existences. In the first stanza the
"I" wavers between wildness and domestication, wolf and dog.
What does "I" represent, then? Probably the poet's imagination, taking on alternately the role of wolf and dog. Presumably
"hear a wolf" means something like "feel a kinship with the
wolf." In the second stanza the poet appears to address the
reader directly. The invitation to enter in imagination into the
experience of a leaf is centered in the word "envy"; the poet
wishes he could touch as leaves touch and perhaps speak as they
do. Perhaps the poet's imagination does not feel it can enter into
the world of a leaf in the same way it entered into the world of
a wolf and a dog. If "I" at the beginning of this stanza is indeed
the poet, then "us" at the end is probably people, anyone (or

perhaps any creature) who hears the leaves in the forest at night.

The third stanza shifts to existences in the desert. Here the poet's imagination assumes the form of desert creatures and again speaks to us through the creatures it has become. "I live by grace of shadows," for example, is apparently the voice of a desert creature sheltering from the sun in the shadow of a rock. The next line, however, seems to reintroduce the voice of the poet himself. The word "room" as a place which can be "opened" is related to the human world, not to the world of nature.

The reference to a room is a pleasurable deviation in the series that has been developing. All the prior existences are focused on the natural world, whether they are speaking as part of the natural world or in the poet's own voice. As soon as the reader grasps the fact that such a series is emerging, it threatens to become tedious. We begin to think of all the natural existences through which we could speak or which we could envy: murmuring brooks, roaring winds, majestic clouds, leaves of grass. The shift to "room" is a dramatic relief from a series that might continue interminably.

The "I" in the last stanza might be the principle of existence which has assumed various forms in the natural world, or the poet himself. These possibilities are justified by what has come before. But who is "you"? There must be possibilities here to match the meaning of "I."

If "I" is any one of a myriad of forms of existence, "you" may be the poet, or the reader, or anybody at all who has had a particular existence. Namely, everybody. In this case, the poem seems to be asking a question. How close can you come to existence, whether wolf, or dog, or leaf, or forest creature, or desert creature, or human creature? Isn't true existence always just a step ahead, a track in the dust? As the narrator in Beckett's appropriately entitled work *The Unnamable* says, "Where now? Who now? When now?" Jacques Derrida has meditated brilliantly upon this question as an aspect of language itself. No sooner is a meaning formed into language, he suggests, than a remoteness is felt between the meaning and what was actually said.

On the other hand, if the meaning assigned to "I" in the last stanza is the poet's own voice, then who is "you"? One possibility is the commonplace idea that two individuals can never truly know each other, but this idea has not appeared earlier in the poem and it seems unlikely such a new idea would be introduced in the last stanza. I can't imagine Stafford's putting the idea in this egoistic way, anyhow. He'd more likely choose the gentler form, "When I come, you are a track in the dust." This seems gentler because it would indicate the speaker's desire to make an effort at communication, then his own sense of failure, rather than attributing the failure to the other person. Nevertheless, it seems unlikely Stafford meant to introduce this new idea, in either form, into the last stanza. Probability points instead toward taking "I" as the principle of existence rather than as the poet himself.

A third possibility, pointed out to me by a friend, is that "you" means death. This is a particularly interesting idea. Perhaps, then, "room" suggests a tomb, or even the unknown. This interpretation is given dramatic force if related to the preceding lines, "I live / by grace of shadows. In moonlight / I hear a room open behind me." For the desert creature to venture from the safety of shadows into the moonlight is to encounter death. Yet we cannot be certain that the third stanza should be coupled to the last two lines of the poem in this way. Such a coupling excludes the leaves of the second stanza from participation in the conclusion of the poem; leaves do not live by grace of shadows. And the title, "Existences," appears to dedicate the poem impartially to all forms of life. An additional difficulty is that if "you" is death but the last two lines of the poem are not coupled to the third stanza, the significance of "room" is lost.

The series in the poem as a whole thus establishes the limits of interpretation but terminates in a closure which falls short of an open specificity; and we are required or permitted to engage in the pleasures of fantasizing.

Many poems constructed around a series do not have even a hint of a generalization at the end, however (e.g., see p. 181 below). In such a poem, has the author expressed a generalized meaning or has he not? This is a natural question to raise, but in the classroom I think it is not a very important one. The question is likely to present itself in a different form. Instead

of "Has the author generalized?" the question will be "What is
the author's intention?" Given this latter question, it matters
very little whether the answer is found in a forthright generalization by the author or in a series clear enough that everybody
could agree on a generalized meaning derived from it. Moreover, we see here at least a partial solution to the old conundrum about whether a poem should mean or simply be. It often
seems impossible to say what the meaning of a literary work is.
What does Donne's "The Canonization" mean, or Hemingway's
"Fifty Grand"? Confronted with this question about literary
works, I myself usually feel a kind of mental paralysis setting
in. I don't know how to answer. But when this question about
meaning is transformed into a question about the author's intention, the answer is much less difficult—as will be evident
when we come later on to an examination of the works just
mentioned.

Perhaps I should repeat that the ideas about the role of series
and probability in literature which have just been considered
are not intended to suggest that all literature can be "cognitive-
ly" understood by hunting for evidences of a series. Obviously,
a series is only one of many patterns to be found in literature.
Examples of other kinds of patterns aren't hard to locate. Kenneth Burke has analyzed the symbol of the leaf in *Leaves of
Grass* as what he calls an associative cluster rather than as a
series. Caroline Spurgeon and Edward Armstrong have analyzed
intricate clusters of images in Shakespeare's work. An analysis
of the patterns of sound in Yeats's "Her Triumph" cannot be
contained in a series. Patterns of similarity and contrast often
cannot be reduced to a series: for example, the stories of Caddy
and her daughter Quentin in *The Sound and the Fury*. As a way
of indicating more clearly what is involved in these examples
we might substitute the word "systems" for "patterns." Concerning William Carlos Williams's "Young Sycamore," Hugh
Kenner says, "The poem's system is that of a short story."[79] But
what is a literary system? The structuralists are trying very
hard to find an answer to this question. With reference to poetry, Jonathan Culler has made the following suggestion:

> The most basic models would seem to be the binary op-
> position, the dialectical resolution of a binary opposi-

tion, the displacement of an unresolved opposition by a
third term, the four-term homology, the series united by
a common denominator, and the series with a transcend-
ent or summarizing final term.[80]

As Culler's suggestion indicates, what has been said in the
present discussion about the concept of a series itself is far from
exhausting the subject. For example, we have not considered
the important idea of emphasis. Both Monroe Beardsley and
E. D. Hirsch note the role of emphasis in Wordsworth's "A
Slumber Did My Spirit Seal." The series, "rocks and stones and
trees" would create a different effect if the final emphatic position were given to stones instead of trees. In the discussion of
"Between Walls" in my class, mentioned earlier, an ingenious
young woman called attention to the possibility that Williams
could have clarified his presumed intention by giving "shine"
the position of the last word in the poem. We could also follow
the concept of series into historiography, where one theory holds
that a linear narrative series can function as an explanation.
What we most need to consider in concluding this examination
of the idea of a series, however, is a special kind of semantic relationship which is frequently found in a literary series.

Fundamentally, this special semantic relationship can be described as metaphoric or as what the anthropologist Kenelm
Burridge calls the "fruitful literary device of anomalous juxtaposition."[81] We are concerned with an import which is different from, and greater than the sum of, the import of the individual terms out of which it arises. Strictly speaking, a metaphor contains only two terms, but actually, as we will see, a
series of several terms can function metaphorically.

The simplest sort of metaphor is exemplified in such a state-
ment as "My love is a rose." A couple of lines of Marvell's "To
His Coy Mistress" present an instance of greater complexity.
Marvell exhorts his mistress. Let us, he says,

> . . . tear our Pleasures with rough strife,
> Thorough the Iron gates of Life.[82]

The relationship of "gates" to "life" seems different from the
relationship of "love" to "rose." Everyone agrees, however, that
both of these two pairs of terms are metaphors. In his fine study

of metaphor and meaning, Marcus Hester suggests at the outset four possible kinds of relationship between the parts of a
metaphor—analogical, ornate, interactive, and tensional.[83]
Were we to explore the concept of metaphor we would clearly
need to examine some such set of possibilities. But for our more
limited purpose the classification of kinds of relationships among
the parts is not of much interest. The important point here is
the fact that although meaning may be introduced into a literary work through a series or other pattern, the relationships
among the parts of the series are sometimes (but by no means
always) different from the relationships among the items in
such an "abstract" series as the numerals from 1 to 10.

A single example of this difference will suffice. In *Wuthering
Heights*, one of the narrators is Nelly Dean, a woman who properly describes herself as "a steady, reasonable sort of body."
But as Clifford Collins has said, Nelly Dean's reasonableness
"is also her limitation, and as intensity increases she tends to
become less adequate as a commentator."[84] What we are looking for is, of course, exactly an instance of a meaning which
somehow escapes a literal-minded reasonableness; we are seeking a meaning which has been generated metaphorically. Such
a meaning need not be unreasonable, but only not literal-
minded. Finally, we would like to find a metaphorically generated meaning contained in a series. These requirements are
satisfied by the series of names Catherine Earnshaw, Catherine
Heathcliff, Catherine Linton.

Near the beginning of *Wuthering Heights* the principal narrator, Lockwood, spends a night in a gloomy, cluttered room at
the Heights where he finds these three names scratched on the
paint of a ledge piled with books. Catherine Earnshaw, who
grew to womanhood in this house, loved a man named Heathcliff and married a man named Linton. The daughter of this
marriage, also called Catherine, married the son of Heathcliff
and his wife Isabella, who was the sister of Linton.

The sequence of the three names on the ledge at Wuthering
Heights is odd, anomalous. Catherine Earnshaw's name reasonably comes first, but why Catherine Heathcliff next? The answer to this question requires a look at the context in which the
series of names appears.

Both Catherine Earnshaw and her daughter Catherine Linton had, as maidens, dreamed of acquiring the name of Heathcliff. Catherine Linton did acquire it—but, obviously, not before she was Catherine Linton. The intensity Nelly Dean misses is suggested by the first Catherine's passionate assertion to Nelly, "I am Heathcliff." Nelly failed to understand, deeming Catherine's remark only foolishness. What Nelly Dean failed to comprehend, it has been plausibly argued, is clarified through the context provided the series of Catherine names by other patterns in the novel. One of these patterns is the interaction between Wuthering Heights—a wild, grim, free place—and Thrushcross Grange, the cultured, domesticated home of the Lintons. Another is the relationship of the senior Heathcliff to both these houses. A gypsy foundling, he is alien to both Thrushcross Grange and Wuthering Heights, even though reared at the latter. Thus when Catherine Earnshaw of Wuthering Heights, just before her marriage to a Linton of Thrushcross Grange, says to Nelly Dean "I am Heathcliff," a powerful cluster of both personal and social forces is metaphorically released. And in the patterns involving Thrushcross Grange, Wuthering Heights, and Heathcliff it becomes evident that a metaphoric function is not limited to tightly knit sequences like the Catherine series but may be found in the relationships among such widely separated elements as Thrushcross Grange and Wuthering Heights.

On a first reading the Catherine series is only a puzzle, but on a second reading or in retrospect the presence of the name Heathcliff in the middle of the series is therefore filled with a metaphoric power never found in such a juxtaposition as that of the numeral 9 to the numeral 10. A metaphoric force is nevertheless faintly but discernibly present in the juxtaposition of 7 to 6 and 8 in an English text.

Michael Polanyi compares our apprehension of the meaning of a metaphor to our apprehension of the meaning of the information brought to our eyes by light.[85] Our eyes scan our physical environment and from all the thousands of bits of data thus obtained we glean a comprehension which is in large part derived from relationships among the data. Similarly, Polanyi declares, we scan the parts of a metaphor and achieve a comprehension which is derived only from the juxtaposition of the parts, not from the sum of the parts independently regarded.

Max Black and Paul Ricoeur, among others, have both presented slightly different versions of this same fundamental concept of the nature of metaphor.

In short, we can say that the presence of a series or a pattern in a text indicates meaning but that a thorough understanding of how such devices may function would require exploration of complexities so intricate they have never been fully understood. The principle of the juxtaposition of anomalous elements, I should add, was carried to its ultimate limits by the surrealists, whose ideas will be considered in Chapter 13.

As remarked earlier the reason for discussing series and probability has been to illustrate, in the simplest way possible, the principle that abstractions are a natural part of literature. The probability of almost any meaningful pattern in literature coming into existence by mere chance is so slight that we can usually assume the pattern has been deliberately willed into existence by the author. But we haven't yet discussed will.

The rationale for this discussion of series and probability, in summary, has been the following.

1. Of all the patterns or systems of organization found in literature, probably none is simpler than a series.

2. It is easy to find examples of series in literary works.

3. The probability that a meaningful series would appear in a literary work by pure chance is extremely small.

4. Virtually all literature is abstract in either or both of the following two ways.

(*a*) The concrete elements in the work are organized into willed, meaningful patterns. The author hopes the reader's perception of the meaning of these patterns will be as much a part of his experience in the reading as will his perception of individual concrete images. (When pushed to an extreme, the idea of concreteness is quite puzzling, but for the practical purposes of the classroom it is useful. The problems involved in the term "willed" can be taken up later, in the chapter on the nonrational.)

(*b*) An author sometimes generalizes explicitly, as Hawthorne does in *The Scarlet Letter*. Although such generalizations are historically common, I have not commented on them because of their obviousness.

11. LIMITED GENERALIZATIONS

Before discussing series and probability I noted some relationships among the terms "universal," "generalization," and "abstraction" and pointed out that I would substitute "limited generalization" for the more conventional "particular universal" (see p. 107). In the discussion of the subject of series and probability, however, no reference to this substitution was necessary, inasmuch as we were concerned only with the presence of meaning and not with a distinction between restricted and unrestricted meanings. We will now take up the subject of restricted or limited generalizations and of their role in literature.

Technically, a limited generalization, as I am using the term, is one that applies to only part of a class rather than to the entire class. The example I gave was "Quarter horses tend to be faster than thoroughbreds over a short distance." This mere technicality is reflected in one of the dominant characteristics of literature—the fact that most generalizations found in literary works are limited rather than unrestricted. It is true that unrestricted universals aren't hard to find. Writers do make unqualified judgments about human experience. For example, in his poem "A Refusal to Mourn the Death, by Fire, of a Child in London," Dylan Thomas writes as his closing line: "After the first death, there is no other."[86] Of course it is not a simple line, even though on its surface it appears to be only a truism; in context, it comes weighted with the grief and horror of the "majesty and burning of the child's death," as Thomas writes in his third stanza.

Still, this closing line of the poem, like any universal or abstraction, is capable of evoking that skeptical demand for proof so fatal to semblance or intransitive rapt attention. *Is* there no other death than the first? Shakespeare suggests in *Julius Caesar* that cowards die many times before their death; Hemingway, in *A Farewell to Arms*, deliberately echoes Shakespeare in his remark that the brave die many deaths in their imagination. In "The Hill Wife," which is about a lonely woman who loses her sanity, Robert Frost speaks of "finalities besides the grave." For any reader in whose mind Thomas's closing line provokes such thoughts, the effectiveness of the poem is likely to be weakened. If not withheld, intellectual assent may be at least suspended.

Characteristically, literature seeks to win assent not so much through a train of logic culminating in unrestricted universals as through an appeal to experience and intuition set within the boundaries of limited generalizations. I have witnessed more than one debate in a classroom which would never have begun had both parties recognized how eager the author of the debated point had been to limit his argument. And it must be reemphasized that writers are not alone in their wariness about unrestricted universals. An instance of a similar wariness on the part of scientists is seen in the following statement from one of the leading physics textbooks currently on the market: "Physical laws are constructions of the human mind, subject to all the limitations of human understanding. They are not necessarily fixed, immutable, or good for all time, and Nature is not compelled to obey them."[87]

The concept of limited generalizations in literary works is most easily thought about in terms of specific examples. Among the great variety of possibilities, I have arbitrarily selected the following areas for comment: style, irony, self-limiting generalizations, and a limitation derived from a series.[88]

Style

The subject of style will serve as a way of easing ourselves into consideration of some limited generalizations. A literary style both is and is not a generalization. The idea of style as meaning lies in the outer limits of the whole concept of meaning. Style is related to explicit meaning somewhat as the cultural background of a novel is related to a theme in the novel. It is a stance, an attitude toward things, as perhaps human personality is. Yet the idea of style associates itself with deliberate choice. Geoffrey Hartman remarks, for example, "It can be argued . . . that the style of [Lowell's] *For the Union Dead* reveals a genuine spiritual change, a revision of thought on the deepest and most internal level."[89] The full implication of such a comment can be felt by imagining that Mark Twain, after publishing *Huckleberry Finn*, had written his next work in the manner of James's *The Golden Bowl*.

Part of the illusion of life in art is no doubt derived from style. Style seems to be an embodiment of temperament in art. As Zola said, "Art is a corner of nature seen through a temperament."[90] The sense of felt life created by style is, or can be, a steadying counterbalance to any tendency of the abstract aspects of a work to overpower the semblance. Style thus can serve as a means of restraining the effect of generalizations asserted in or implied by a literary work.[91] I recall an instance in which Hemingway's style seemed to have the effect of counterbalancing a well-meant but possibly overstrained generalization implied in one of his books.

There was in one of my classes a man who wanted to become a professional racing driver. He was a fine athlete and had already acquired some experience in racing. He was studying mechanical engineering. One day he came to my office to talk about the current assignment, which was Hemingway's *The Sun Also Rises*. Basically, he had two things to say. One was that he didn't like the book. The other was that he felt a great deal of admiration and respect for Hemingway the man. Actually, as I learned during the conversation, he didn't know very much about Hemingway, just what he had picked up from the news and from a brief biographical sketch I had given. I asked him what he admired in Hemingway. He replied that he admired Hemingway's courage, the way he liked to get out and do things, the way he said what he thought and not what everybody else thought—sort of the way he wrote. "I like the way he says things," he declared. I reminded him that he didn't like the book we were reading. He said that was because of the depressing things that happened in it; he knew about a lot of depressing things and didn't feel he needed any more of them on his mind. He'd seen some depressing things on the race track and felt it was best not to think about them too much.

It is clear he admired the public image of Hemingway's personality and life style. Can this image be called style in a literary context? That seems to be a matter of definition. It is certainly a stance, a generalization in the broad sense noted earlier. If an infant at birth were given an opportunity to choose a life style modeled on the public image of either Ernest Hemingway or Oscar Wilde, he'd know he had a real choice.

The racing driver's coupling of the public image to the literary style, the way Hemingway says things, complicates the

matter. It is complicated still further and more interestingly
by his rejection of Hemingway's book. Perhaps the coupling
of man and style was only our culture's ritual tribute to the
Comte de Buffon's saying that style is the man himself. But it
may have been more than that. This racing driver was neither
stupid nor insensitive. Everyone is familiar with instances of a
reader's being captivated by an author's style, sometimes an author about whose personal life he knows nothing at all. We all
revere Homer. In any event, as we talked that morning two
things became clear. One was that whatever the relationship in
my visitor's mind between the author's public image and the
style of the book, the style of the book represented for him something real and desirable in human experience. He was able to
approximate an abstract statement of the meaning the style
had for him. This meaning, however, was so close to the quality
of felt experience that the moment I start thinking about it now
I feel myself struggling with the difference between the idea
of meaning and the idea of experience. Here was an instance of
a generalization's being held close to experience and in this
way limited.

The second fact that became clear to me was that I still
hadn't learned to be wary enough about discussions of what a
book means. Had my visitor come in with the usual abstractions about the Hemingway code I would have thought of the
content of the book; I would have thought of Jake's stoicism
and of Brett's breaking off her affair with the young bullfighter
Romero in order not to ruin him. The racing driver's "stylistic"
approach to the book as a whole put abstractions about these
matters into a different light. I doubt that he was much im-
pressed by Brett's generosity in giving up Romero. I have since
learned from *Reader's Digest* that racing drivers have lots of
girls.[92]

Irony

An important contribution made by the New Criticism to classroom practice is the special concept of irony it developed. This
concept is usually, and properly, associated with Cleanth
Brooks, and I will seek an example from his writing.

Brooks's idea of irony stands about midway between a literal definition (an intended meaning which is opposite the surface meaning) and Romantic irony. Romantic irony, which takes many forms, is concerned essentially with the feeling that the human self both is and is not a part of the world in which it exists. Further, Romantic irony is concerned with the feeling that art is designed both to absorb the observer or reader completely and at the same time to create in him a wariness or skepticism about the art object.[93]

If I understand Brooks correctly, he thinks of an ironic literary work as one in which every part reflects a necessary awareness of the meaning and implications of every other part of the work and in which every statement is qualified or limited in whatever ways are necessary to keep it within the bounds of intelligent and informed judgment. This concept has encouraged close examination of how any given aspect of a work is both limited and strengthened by other aspects.

Our interest at the moment will be in irony as a limitation of meaning. It is rather generally agreed now that in the New Criticism the idea of irony was pushed too far, but that should not be allowed to obscure what is useful in it.

To illustrate his concept of irony, Brooks turns to the closing stanza of Matthew Arnold's "Dover Beach." This stanza reads as follows:

> Ah, love, let us be true
> To one another! for the world, which seems
> To lie before us like a land of dreams,
> So various, so beautiful, so new,
> Hath really neither joy, nor love, nor light,
> Nor certitude, nor peace, nor help for pain;
> And we are here as on a darkling plain
> Swept with confused alarms of struggle and flight,
> Where ignorant armies clash by night.[94]

From this stanza Brooks singles out for comment the statement that the world "which seems / To lie before us like a land of dreams . . . Hath really neither joy, nor love, nor light." He thinks some readers might consider this statement a truism, while others might consider it false or at least questionable. He declares that the statement is to be justified in terms of the

context—that is, in terms of its relationships to other parts of
the poem. In the quotation which follows, where Brooks pursues his idea about the statement he singled out, I have itali-
cized what seem to me the key passages.

> *How is the statement to be validated?* We shall prob-
> ably not be able to do better than to apply T. S. Eliot's
> test: *does the statement seem to be that which the mind
> of the reader can accept as coherent, mature, and found-
> ed on the facts of experience?* But when we raise such a
> question, we are driven to consider the poem *as drama.*
> We raise such further questions as these: Does the speak-
> er seem carried away with his own emotions? *Does he
> seem to oversimplify the situation?* Or does he, on the
> other hand, seem to have won to a kind of detachment
> and objectivity? In other words, we are forced to raise
> the question as to whether the statement grows properly
> out of a context; whether it acknowledges the pressures
> of the context; whether it is *"ironical"*—or merely *cal-
> low*, glib, and sentimental.[95]

With the one exception of the reference to drama, the thesis in
Brooks's comment appears to lie in such key phrases as "validation," "coherent," "mature," "facts of experience," "detachment and objectivity," "pressures of the context," and of course
at the end "ironical." I will venture to say that through these
"ironic" qualities in a work Brooks feels the abstract meanings
are held adequately close to experience. I think he himself
would prefer to say abstractions are not permitted to develop.

In commenting on this passage, I will discuss Brooks's statement about validation, his introduction of the idea of drama,
and finally the possibility of describing the poem in the terms I
myself have been using.

The point of commenting on validation, however, is only to
avoid a misunderstanding. In the practical world of the classroom, I don't believe the statement in Arnold's poem is validated in the way Brooks implies. With the single exception of
the reference to drama, Brooks centers his attention upon qualities which are found in much good poetry, although not all,

but which in themselves can hardly make a poem good.[96] The qualities he selects are coherence, maturity, and the poem's being founded on experience. I am reminded of an occasion on which I heard Yvor Winters read a paper about the many excellent qualities of some eighteenth-century poem I've now forgotten. Afterward I asked a number of the others present what they thought of the paper. The consensus was that the paper was fine but the poem itself quite dull. The same kind of situation develops in every literary classroom. Proof that a poem has an ironic context is no guarantee it will fly. Oddly enough, Brooks never does say whether he thinks the statement he singled out is actually validated. What he means by validated is also left unclear.

The reference to drama, which appears around the middle of the passage by Brooks, opens up a whole new set of possibilities. The fact is, when the passage quoted from Brooks is looked at as a whole, we see that it is concerned with two different subjects. One is the relationship of the parts of the poem to one another and the "maturity" of their total content. The other is drama, which, I presume, refers to the purpose controlling the relationship of the parts. Brooks's name for both these subjects is context (or irony).

The reference to drama stands out as an exception to the content of all the rest of the passage. After introducing the idea of drama, Brooks returns at once to the kinds of problems noted at the outset: maturity (the poem should not be callow) and coherence (the pressures of the context should be acknowledged). Nothing more about drama. Nevertheless, his point is a good one, and I believe its value is made clearer when it is thought about in terms that have become familiar in this discussion: element, semblance, purpose, generalization, and assent. Since our subject is now the application of these terms to the passage from "Dover Beach," I will conclude my remarks on irony as a means of limiting generalizations by briefly pondering the stanza from the poem.

The statement singled out by Brooks for comment comes near the end of the poem, where the speaker is summing up his view to his companion. The poem is a dramatic monolog; the presence of a woman the speaker loves is indicated. Taken at

face value, the generalization expressed by the speaker is false.
Here it is again.

> . . . the world, which seems
> To lie before us like a land of dreams, . . .
> Hath really neither joy, nor love, nor light, . . .

The agony of human experience is sometimes inexpressible, let
us agree, yet it is not true there is no joy or love in the world.
The speaker's statement is false.

In the terminology we've been using, on the other hand, the
statement presents an easily articulated technical problem:
does the statement function as an element in a semblance?

To answer the question, we ponder the author's purpose. I
don't want to become involved in a detailed analysis of "Dover
Beach," but one possible answer to the question deserves attention. Suppose the author's purpose was to create a semblance
centered upon the experience of a man so emotionally oppressed
by his spiritual situation that to vent his feelings he makes
exaggerated statements. I've always been a little puzzled over
the speaker's telling the woman he loves that the world has no
love. I assume she loves him too, however, and tolerantly understands he's thinking about big, important problems and did not
mean to insult her. His exaggeration is a natural human habit.
Everybody does it. A mature reader may be a little amused by
what the speaker says to his lover, but still sympathetic. The
reader perceives the speaker as a character in a drama; the
exaggeration is the speaker's, not the author's. In this way, the
potential offensiveness of the exaggeration is muted. To say that
the generalization is limited is only to express the same idea in
different terms.

As a last step we might think a moment about the author's
intended meaning. Does Arnold want us to believe the speaker's
agitation is justified by the state the world is in? Or is this poem
to be understood as only a psychological drama, with attention
focused not upon the state of the world but upon the state of the
speaker? Surely the former of these two possibilities is the correct one. It is, moreover, one the reader can probably accept as
a mature judgment. We must not pass it by, however, without

recognizing that this judgment that the world is in bad condition, which I am attributing to Arnold, is an unrestricted universal, in contrast to the speaker's statement on which we have been concentrating. I don't believe the introduction of this unrestricted universal makes Brooks's concept of irony inapplicable to the poem. It is a judgment which can reasonably be called mature and objective and which thus conforms to Brooks's concept. Perceiving the author's intention as the expression of concern over the waning of religious faith, the reader grants his intellectual assent. At least a lot of readers have done so.

In doing so, they have acted out the essence of what Brooks means by irony, as I understand it. They have recognized the poem as drama, precisely in keeping with Brooks's suggestion. They have comprehended the relationship between the speaker's agitation and the truly oppressive conditions in the spiritual life of the western world, and they have given their assent to the speaker's concern. They have acknowledged that Arnold was successful in transforming the material of the speaker's exaggerated generalization into an element in the semblance of life on an evening by the sea in Victorian England.

In summary, irony is a concept which is useful in helping us comprehend how generalizations are limited through their contextual relationships, to use Brooks's term, or through their relationship to semblance and intention, to use my terms. The concept of irony can also accommodate unrestricted universals, as just observed, but that is not our primary subject at the moment.

Self-limiting Generalizations

Having got this far, it is only natural to wonder what a completely and perfectly ironic work would be like. Brooks regards as the ideal form of irony a statement which acknowledges the pressures of the context. With this in mind, it follows that the most elegant form of irony would be a generalization which established pressures on itself not to become either simplistic or exaggerated. Although such an idea appears rather paradoxical, examples can be found. I came across one in the form of a story told by a Zen master, in Abraham Kaplan's *The New World of Philosophy*.[97] I'll tell it in my own words.

Two monks were journeying together. One was a Zen monk, the other an orthodox Buddhist. Presently they came to a river. The water was high and swift, and a young woman was standing helplessly on the bank, fearful of trying to cross. The Zen monk picked her up, made his way through the water to the other bank, and put her down. After the two monks had continued in silence for several miles the Buddhist monk suddenly burst out, "I don't understand how you could do that! You know perfectly well we priests are not even supposed to touch a woman, and yet you picked that woman up and held her in your arms!"

"I put her down back there by the river," the Zen monk replied. "Are you still carrying her?"

This story gives pleasure, but the pleasure is hardly the sole point of its existence. The Zen people wanted to embody some meaning in it, in their own antimeaningful way. It seems to be about a rule. The rule as understood by the Buddhist monk is, "Thou shalt not touch a woman." But as understood by the Zen monk the rule apparently is something like, "Thou shalt not touch a woman except . . ." The rule as seen by the Buddhist monk is a universal; as seen by the Zen monk, it is a self-limiting generalization. In my own formulation of the two versions of the rule, the self-limitation appears in the word "except." In the story, the limitation is more diffuse: it appears in the Zen monk's decision to carry the woman and again in his implicit denial of guilt for having carried her. He does not deny that the rule exists.

What words would logically follow "except" in my formulation of the Zen monk's version of the rule? An infinity of words, all the conceivable exceptions to the rule, a verbal equivalent of an irrational number. Faced with this endless, irrational multiplication of specific exceptions the story gives us instead an example.

One last, amusing problem now appears. The story as a whole could itself be read as an unrestricted universal. That is, it could be interpreted as meaning, "There is at least one exception to every rule." This is a universal. But should it be interpreted instead as meaning, "There is at least one exception to every rule, including the rule that there is at least one exception to every rule"? Perhaps stories told by Zen masters are incurably abstract.

A large-scale example of irony in the form of a self-limiting generalization can be seen in James Gould Cozzens's long novel *By Love Possessed*. The universal with which the book begins might be formulated as follows: "To be a good man you must be honest, open, and law-abiding." As the story goes along, the "except" is added.

A Series As a Limited Generalization

As a last example of a limited generalization I will return to the subject of a series. Earlier, I asserted that a planned series can in effect become a generalization. Now I will try to illustrate how this kind of generalization can be limited. The illustration can be quite brief.

I have before me a tattered, secondhand copy of Shakespeare's plays, opened to the last page of *Hamlet*. At the bottom of the page are the following notes, apparently written in some long-forgotten classroom: "quick, thorough action of Hamlet shows he would necessarily have been a good king: gets revenge, instructs Horatio, forgives Laertes, Gertrude, bids goodbye to Horatio, prevents Horatio's suicide." It's a good summary. The generalization is one there's little doubt Renaissance theater audiences apprehended at once: Hamlet would have made a good king. Like a good Renaissance man, even at the point of death Hamlet is concerned about kingmanship.[98] He has obviously thought over the potential in young Fortinbras and now instructs Horatio to make it known it's Fortinbras he'd vote for.

The generalization, expressed in the play only in the form of a series of actions, heavily dependent upon cultural background, is limited. It says only "Hamlet would have made a good king," not "All kings should be like Hamlet." Fortinbras seems unlike Hamlet, with his conquest and his warlike salute to the ambassadors from England. A great deal of literature is concerned with just such generalizations. To avoid misunderstanding, I should add I am not suggesting that this limited generalization is the thesis of the play.

Summary

We have looked at evidences of how generalizations are limited through style, irony, self-limitation, and a planned series. A couple of summary comments are in order.

The first is that upon reflection the idea of style as a means of limiting the import of a literary work may appear so broad, so close to the psychologist's concept of perceptual orientation, as to be virtually pointless. Philosophically this conclusion can probably in certain ways be justified, but I don't believe it is justified for the purposes of the classroom. Practically, style enters into the experience of individual members of a group in the form of significance—as defined earlier. It is sometimes quite a wrench for an individual to open himself to the temperament implied by a style. Yet it seems to me that one of the important functions of a literary classroom is to provide exactly this confrontation, together with a frank recognition of all it means. In Part Three I will explore this idea.

The second summary comment is that probably the most useful of the examples presented is Brooks's idea of irony, along with its somewhat whimsical corollary of the self-limiting generalization. The notion of testing the integrity of a work by examining the relationships of its parts and the maturity of its generalizations, which seems to me the heart of the concept of irony, is surely a fundamental procedure in any classroom.

Looking back over these examples of ways of limiting generalizations, however, I myself am inclined to prefer Max Delbrück's Principle of Limited Sloppiness. This principle asserts that "in carrying out an experiment one must be sloppy enough that unexpected things will be discovered (penicillin, for example), but not so sloppy that the procedures can't be repeated."[99] In literary terms, I presume this would mean being sloppy enough about generalizations to leave room for other opinions, so nobody would believe you were claiming to have discovered the Final Word, but clear enough that people could understand what you meant and make use of your ideas if they wanted to.

After all this attention to the limitation of generalizations, it is time to give some thought to the advantages of explicit indications of the author's intention in a work. Such indications may be given by the author himself, either as part of the work or elsewhere. In a classroom, they may also be given about the work by a member of the group. One of the pleasanter experiences of a teacher's life occurs when, after he has "explained" a work which baffled everyone, the group responds, in effect, with a collective, relieved, "Oh, I see!" This is the teacher's equivalent of the writer's recognition scene.

In this chapter I will discuss what effect the assertion of an intention by an author has on the dramatic or concrete quality of a work. As we have seen several times already, an author's intention need not appear in the form of an explicit generalization; it may only be implied by a pattern within the work. On the other hand, if an author has a clear intention it can usually be expressed in the form of a generalization regardless of how he has presented it. My concern will be with the advantages in the classroom of deliberately focusing attention upon the relationship between the abstract, generalized, intentional aspect of a work and the dramatic or felt aspect of it.[100]

One brief comment on terminology. Dramatic literature always appears in the form of a semblance, but a semblance is not necessarily very dramatic. It is at least theoretically possible to conceive of an illusion of human life which though strong is not very interesting. What we will be concerned with is specifically that kind of semblance which is dramatically interesting. It is for this reason that the word "drama" appears in the title of this chapter, rather than the word "semblance." I will begin with the concept of a recognition scene, which is virtually an epitome of my subject, and will then experiment with the effects of taking intention out of, and adding intention to, literary materials.

The Recognition Scene

The great source of the idea of a recognition scene is Aristotle's *Poetics*. Aristotle says recognition is "a change from ignorance to knowledge of a bond of love or hate," but he adds that this change can assume many forms. In *The Essence of Tragedy*, Maxwell Anderson discusses the idea from a writer's point of view. He reports that in a survey he made of great tragedies, he found one of the few common elements in the structure of these plays to be a recognition scene. His way of articulating the meaning of the term will serve our purpose somewhat more conveniently than Aristotle's.

> A play should lead up to and away from a central crisis, and this crisis should consist in a discovery by the leading character which has an indelible effect on his thought and emotion and completely alters his course of action. The leading character, let me say again, must make the discovery; it must affect him emotionally; and it must alter his direction in the play.[101]

The concept of a recognition scene is so familiar it needs no particular explanation, but perhaps a brief illustration would ensure understanding of my own intention. *King Lear* will do. At the beginning of the play Lear is arrogant, feeling himself superior to other men—possibly reflecting the old concept that kings are divinely set apart. When Lear is abusing his one honest daughter, Cordelia, and the good courtier Kent attempts to take her side, Lear says, "Come not between the dragon and his wrath." The discovery Lear makes during the course of the play is that he is no dragon but a man like others, susceptible to human folly. Turned out into a bitter storm by his two dishonest daughters, Lear speaks one of the great passages of the play:

> Poor naked wretches, whereso'er you are,
> That bide the pelting of this pitiless storm,
> How shall your houseless heads and unfed sides,
> Your loop'd and window'd raggedness defend you
> From seasons such as these? O, I have ta'en
> Too little care of this! Take physic, pomp;
> Expose thyself to feel what wretches feel.[102]

The idea of a recognition scene is a relatively simple and effective way of discerning an author's intention, but in the classroom it does present two practical difficulties. One is that sometimes nothing deserving to be called a recognition scene can be found. The other is that once you begin looking, you begin to see them everywhere. For instance, Pamela perceives she can trust Lord B——, and it seems to be a recognition scene; she soon discovers she can't trust him, and it seems to be another. Later she marries him. What now? In spite of such inescapable ambiguity, it is better to have the concept of a recognition scene than not to have it. No great harm is done if it is overworked, and a reader who fails to grasp the import of a genuine, major recognition scene is certain to be confused. Awareness of the concept may help him perceive what he otherwise would never notice.

The Subtraction of Meaning

In principle, the literature least likely to contain a general clarifying indication of intention, apart from surrealistic works, is probably imagistic poetry; that is, any poetry which appears —on the surface, at least—to offer the reader's mind nothing to take hold of but sense impressions. It is in such poetry that the very idea of meaning becomes most elusive. My objective will be to explore the way in which the author's intention is recognized in imagist poetry and to consider the advantages the classroom can find in explicit discussion of the intention.

As an example I have chosen Pound's "translation"[103] of the Chinese poem "The Jewel Stairs' Grievance." My reason for this choice is not only that it is a good representation of imagistic poetry but also that Pound himself attached a note to it explaining its meaning. Poem and note follow:

THE JEWEL STAIRS' GRIEVANCE

The jeweled steps are already quite white with dew,
It is so late that the dew soaks my gauze stockings,
And I let down the crystal curtain
And watch the moon through the clear autumn.
                              By Rihaku

NOTE: Jewel stairs, therefore a palace. Grievance, therefore there is something to complain of. Gauze stockings, therefore a court lady, not a servant who complains. Clear autumn, therefore he has no excuse on account of the weather. Also, she has come early, for the dew has not merely whitened the stairs, but has soaked her stockings. The poem is especially prized because she utters no direct reproach.[104]

It's a beautiful poem—and would be beautiful without any note or even without any title. To tell the truth, I rather prefer it without note and title, but perhaps that's because of its familiarity. The words "grievance," "so late," and "already" aggressively demand the note, the effort to tease out a meaning. In these words a miniature drama is created.

For curiosity's sake, let's try the poem without these drama-creating words.

THE JEWEL STAIRS

The jeweled steps are quite white with dew,
The dew soaks my gauze stockings,
I let down the crystal curtain
And watch the moon through the clear autumn.

If a woman we knew and loved had written these lines would they not seem beautiful? We would have no need of a dramatic situation to arouse our interest but would enjoy the lines because of their power to give us a shared moment of life and because the woman had gone to this trouble to invite us to participate in the moment with her. But as I write these words I feel the first faint stirrings of apprehension. Suppose this kind woman prepared a whole book of such poems? Wouldn't it become paralyzingly dull? The question is worth some thought. Virtually without drama, the shortened version of Pound's poem is little more than sense impressions; the only remaining hint of drama lies in the orientation toward elegant objects.

In a way, the vividness of the shortened version resembles that of the you-fight-'im-'e-cry example presented earlier (p. 109). But this latter rhetorical figure comes embodied in its own miniature dramatic situation, as it must to be effective. "Supper-silent highway," in contrast, is a lively element requiring no supporting drama. It presents directly to our senses the image of a deserted highway at the hour of the evening meal. In principle, the shortened version of Pound's poem seems closer to the lively element than to the story of the savage and

the piano. And it is difficult to imagine anyone's preparing, for
the reader's pleasure, a whole book of such mere lively elements. The closest approximation is probably the bright-say-
ings-of-children book. Such books of bright remarks by children,
however, are concerned precisely with the you-fight-'im-'e-cry
kind of miniature drama, each remark having its own setting.
It seems unlikely anyone would ever care to read a book of lively elements not provided with settings. Of course the idea of
these supporting miniature dramas must include the kind of
background that gives meaning to Williams's "Between Walls,"
which we considered earlier.

The shortened version of the Pound poem is not a drama.
This fact is indeed the exact point of its difference from the
original version. The reason it is not drama is that the meaning has been taken out.

What does the original version mean? We can examine
Pound's note, which contains a couple of odd proposals. Pound
indicates that a woman has come early for a meeting with a
man. Perhaps so, but I don't understand why Pound says
"early." The poem says, "It is so late . . ." The poem seems to
say it's so late there's a lot of dew, which of course accumulates
with the chill of evening. Perhaps the woman came on time
and after a long wait realized her stockings had become soaked
with dew. Or had she walked through dew-soaked grass? A
strange thought; I don't know. Pound speaks of a man, too, but
none is mentioned in the poem.

Nevertheless, we can certainly accept Pound's view that the
poem does have meaning, and I believe there is meaning on
which we can agree. To begin with: a noble woman who can
adjust the crystal curtain in a building to which a jeweled stair
is attached has a grievance and dew-soaked gauze stockings on
a clear autumn evening through which she begins watching
the moon. To these facts we must add another: the title invites
the reader to guess what the grievance is. Pound's guess that the
woman had been stood up by a man fits the facts as well as any
other I can think of, although it must be pronounced only a
guess.

With these facts before us, we can ponder the author's probable intention, which appears to be much concerned with elegance and servants. The stairs are jeweled; the curtain is crys-

tal; the woman is elegantly dressed. And, as Pound points out, the woman offers no direct reproach: her manners are as elegant as her dress, the stairs, and the lines she writes. Pound says the poem is especially prized because she utters no direct reproach. But by whom is this elegance especially prized? By Georg Lukács? By Karl Marx? By the servant who keeps the crystal curtain clean? Pound indicates that servants complain.

The direct reproach is actually uttered by the author, in his use of "grievance" in the title. He expresses this idea directly, whereas the woman never mentions it. The author's intention is apparently to display an aristocratic life style in miniature: the elegance, the code, the stoicism. And it seems to me he succeeds in his intention. It's really a superb poem (with one possible exception). Its integrity passes the test of Brooks's irony; perhaps its beauty coupled with its implication of a social code almost passes the test of Lukács's concept of totality (which we need not examine here). A weakness in any idea that the poem achieves a total grasp of its tiny situation, however, is that the servants' view of the matter is left out. Where there are aristocrats there must be servants, as Pound himself perceives, but the poem reveals no interest in the feelings or opinions of servants. The character of the servants' role in the poem, and a recognition to which the poem (including the title) finally leads, can perhaps be expressed by stating the recognition in the following negative form: "In this poignant moment, how admirable is the woman's nonservantlike life style."

However, this abstraction is so dreary, it so obviously would be detested by both Pound and Rihaku, that I believe I should reconsider. The statement doesn't exactly appear to be wrong, only unacceptable. Perhaps, therefore, the concepts of significance and assent will come to our aid.

Clearly, two different kinds of significance may be found in the poem. To an aristocratic reader, the presentation of the aristocratic values would seem natural and laudable. He would indeed prize them. For such a reader, the recognition should perhaps run something as follows: "In this poignant moment, what a flawless gesture is seen in the woman's turning silently to contemplate the moon, no longer watching for the coming of her lover." To an aristocratic reader, the significance of such a statement would be wholly acceptable. To a Marxist, the significance of the same statement might be at least in part objectionable. It is to the Marxist, then, that the question of assent must be put. Even while objecting to aristocratic values, can he sufficiently assent to their vitality to enter into the experience of the poem? No doubt some Marxists could, some couldn't. For those who could, the second version of the recognition presented above might seem to express the writer's intention; the first version, with its implied contempt of servants, might seem to articulate the significance they felt in this intention.

Our fundamental subject is the effect of intention on the dramatic or concrete quality of a work. What we have just observed is an explicit, generalized assertion of an intention which was presented indirectly in "The Jewel Stairs' Grievance." The key to perception of the intention in the poem lies in the difference between Pound's own version of the poem and the shortened version. The shortened version offers pleasant, perhaps lively, sense impressions, but that is about all that can be said for it apart from the possibility of some kind of personal association or background. To increase the power of these lines, we can add the meaning-laden words of the original version; and when these meaning-laden words have been added we discover that drama has been added also.

It is true that restoring the words of the original version does not in itself introduce any clarifying generalization, with the rather vague exception of "grievance." Nevertheless, it is when these words are restored that we can generalize about the poem, as Pound exemplified in his note. In such circumstances, as remarked earlier, the question of whether the work contains a clarifying generalization is best relegated to second place anyhow, in favor of the broader question: what was the author's probable intention? (See page 135 for further comment on the relationship between drama or semblance and intention and page 190 for further comment on the relationship between meaning and the author's probable intention.)

The Addition of Meaning

Contemplating the fact that the restoration of meaning to the poem restored drama too, we are compelled to wonder about the

chances of reversing the process. If we introduced meaning into
a literary work originally made up only of sense impressions,
would we discover we had simultaneously introduced drama?
The answer appears to be a qualified yes. Meaning creates
drama, within certain limits. It is in this answer that the practical importance of explicit generalizations in the classroom
becomes evident.

In the example just considered we began with the poem containing a dramatic situation and took the meaning, the recognitions, out. What we had left was virtually nothing but sense
impressions. Now we need an example in which we can see
what happens when we introduce meaning into what at the
outset are merely sense impressions. Will drama be created?
For this purpose, I have made up, or partly made up, the clearest example I could think of.

Suppose that by magic we are suddenly put down beside a
prize-fight ring in which two men are battling. Perhaps this
magic was accomplished through our influence with the shade
of Hazlitt, the great essayist, who was a prize-fight buff. As we
watch the two men in the ring, both strangers to us, one of
them fouls the other—hits a low blow. The man who was fouled
doubles over in agony. The referee is about to stop the fight
and, as the rules require, award the victory to the man who was
fouled, but the latter straightens up and objects. The referee is
puzzled. The fighter continues to object, even though he appears to be in pain; he insists there was no foul and demands
to go on with the fight. Finally the referee signals the men to
resume. They do so. A moment later the bell rings, ending the
round.

At the beginning of the next round the two fighters come out
of their corners as usual and begin sparring. The one who was
fouled still appears to be in pain. After a few punches have been
exchanged, the man who was fouled hits the other a hard, low
blow, a deliberate foul. The second fighter now doubles over
in agony in his turn. Unlike the first, however, he makes no
effort to resume the fight. The foul was obvious, and the referee
awards the victory to the second man. The first man to be
fouled leaves the ring in defeat.

As we observe these events in our imagination, we find ourselves confronting a kind of question that was noted in the in-

troduction to this chapter. The events undoubtedly constitute a semblance, but are they of any special interest? Are they dramatic? In some measure the answer must be yes. What has happened is so extraordinary that the observer feels himself in the presence of drama even if he doesn't know exactly what the drama is. And yet, if he never learned anything beyond what has already been said, the observer's response might well be no more than a frustrated and diminishing interest mixed with disgust at two dirty fighters. The kind of deficiency which, in principle, is found in what has so far been presented to our imagination concerning these fighters is indicated in Erich Auerbach's comment on fifteenth-century French realism as a genre:

> This realism is poor in ideas; it lacks constructive princi-
> ples and even the will to attain them. It drains the reality
> of that which exists and, in its very existence, falls to
> decay; it drains it to the dregs, so that the senses, and
> the emotions aroused by them, get the flavor of immedi-
> ate life; and having done that, it seeks nothing further.[105]

In effect, we are confronting the same problem that was encountered in the shortened version of Pound's poem. In the former case, the lines are so brief and the action so slight that to speak of what we perceived as mere sense impressions seemed appropriate. The more complex events of the prize-fight story are less amenable to this term. On the other hand, to refer to the events of the prize-fight story as a drama would surely be to go too far in the other direction.

To decide whether meaning can create drama, then, we can proceed by adding a small measure of information to the events described above. The information to be added will be this: each of the two fighters had made a secret commitment to throw the fight. Each was involved in a scheme whereby he would profit through losing. A sure way to lose was—or at first seemed to be—to commit a foul. The fighter who technically lost the fight thus was the one who actually succeeded in his purpose.

Does this bit of information about motives, about the meaning of the actions, create some drama? I would say it does, but everyone will have to decide for himself.

Now we can add another small measure. Let's assume that

one fighter was aging. For some years he had been, and still was, champion of the welterweight class. But before this fight was arranged he realized his ability was declining and foresaw the end of his earning power. He needed money for the support of his family and decided to get it by betting heavily against himself. This fighter was the one who succeeded in losing the fight and thus winning his bet.

It is difficult to say whether this further information heightens the drama. If it does, it is no doubt because of the somewhat humanizing effect of the man's concern about his family.

But we can add still another small measure. To win a large enough sum of money on which to retire, the aging fighter had to make a secret arrangement with professional gamblers. The fighter gave them his word he would go through with the deal. In losing, the fighter thus both won his bet and kept his word. He did so at the cost of enduring intense pain.

This last addition of information makes a considerable change in the nature of the drama, for two reasons. First, it indicates the fighter's awareness of and concern about personal honor. Second, it raises a question about the meaning of honor. That is, what should we think of a man who at one and the same time throws a fight and endures pain for the purpose—at least in part—of keeping his word? Here is a question that is likely to reveal marked differences in the significance the story has had among a group of readers.

Finally, we might look briefly at these events from a fiction writer's point of view. The writer who undertook to transform such materials into fiction would have a wide range of possible treatments from which to choose: sentimental ("poor old fighter"), brutal ("sock it to him!"), comic ("oof!"), and others. Indeed, the writer's first problem would be simply to decide whether these materials were adaptable to any intention with which he cared to work. We can choose an intention for ourselves. Let us choose the depiction of a man who, although he had lived a hard life among devious people, had great courage and a strong sense of honor that was suited to his circumstances. With such a statement, we have reached the most abstract of our additions to the events originally described.

The story I've recounted is of course essentially Hemingway's "Fifty Grand." The interpretation I've given is Philip Young's.

Whether Young's interpretation is correct doesn't matter, since even if it is not correct a good story could be written in conformity with his views (which can be found in his book *Ernest Hemingway*). I believe his interpretation is correct.

Now we can review the events, the additions of information, and our terminology and see if we come out with any practical advantage.

1. We began with the bare events as seen by a stranger.

2. The first addition of information was that both fighters wanted to throw the fight.

3. The next addition was the fact that one fighter was aging and wanted to retire and enjoy his family with the money he won betting against himself. Both the first and the second additions create motives; the second humanizes a little, but only a little. When a fighter begins to age he is still only in his thirties, and it would be hard to feel deep sympathy for a man merely because he could not retire to a life of leisure at that age. Nevertheless, there can be little doubt that this much meaning is sufficient to create an intense drama.

4. The third addition of information to the bare events of the prize-fight story was the fighter's highly individualistic sense of personal honor. The point of interest was his willingness to deceive a great many people by throwing the fight while at the same time scrupulously honoring his word to the gamblers. This particular addition introduces an entirely new dimension. It either creates or calls attention to the distance between reader and character. If we assume that reasonably mature readers commonly identify completely and thoughtlessly with a protagonist, then this addition invites such readers to abandon complete identification and take a somewhat detached look at the character. If, on the other hand, we assume that reasonably mature readers are simultaneously involved and detached, then this addition gives form and meaning to the detachment. I myself prefer the latter view, for reasons I explained in Part One.

At any rate, in so openly placing deceit and honor side by side, the author is directly suggesting to the reader that he stand back and ponder the fighter's code of conduct. Apparently many readers find drama heightened by such a play of meaning through it, as indicated by the popularity of the Hemingway code, to which "Fifty Grand" contributed. T. S. Eliot endorses this relationship between meaning and drama in some lines in "The Dry Salvages":

> We had the experience but missed the meaning,
> And approach to the meaning restores the experience
> In a different form, . . .[106]

5. The last addition was the articulation of meaning in terms of the author's probable intention (i.e., the fighter had courage and his own sense of honor). This addition does not differ in principle from the previous one but merely states it in its most abstract form. Of course my stating the author's intention in an abstract form does not necessarily mean that he himself conceived it so abstractly.

An unacknowledged but no doubt noticeable problem throughout this discussion has been the choice between the words "meaning" and "information." The idea that bits of information were being added to the story as the discussion proceeded is surely not objectionable, but it does appear to be inadequate, since our primary concern is not with information but with meaning. Yet to refer to the additions as meaning creates a difficulty. The difficulty becomes immediately apparent when we use the word "mean" in such a question as the following: "What does the story 'Fifty Grand' mean?" No acceptable answer seems possible. We feel simultaneously that the story is meaningful and that we cannot form a sentence which says what the meaning is. This problem has for a long time been a source of much uncertainty and controversy about procedure in the classroom, but it can be resolved quite easily in a practical way through attention to the concepts of meaning and intention. The key lies in the fact that the word "meaning" has more than one meaning.

As a preliminary, let us briefly review a bit of reasoning leading into the familiar tangle concerning the idea that a literary work cannot have meaning. To simplify this review we can substitute for a literary work a quantitative formula—say Einstein's famous equation $E = mc^2$. What is the meaning of this equation? Our natural impulse is to reply that it means energy is equal to mass times the square of the velocity of light. But this is only what the equation *says*; we have merely paraphrased it. In doing so, moreover, we have lost the economy and elegance of the original form. Perhaps, then, we might say the equation means that a certain quantity of mass is equivalent to a certain quantity of energy. This is a true statement. But, again, it is merely a different way of expressing the equation with which we started; it is what the equation says. And there was never any doubt as to what the equation says. Our question was about what the equation means. We seem forced to conclude that it is wrong to ask what an equation means. Apparently we can ask only what it says. Equations must therefore not have meaning. Perhaps we should say about an equation what Archibald MacLeish said about a poem: it should not mean but be.

Obviously, something is wrong. Such reasoning doesn't make good sense. Without trying to untangle the verbal snarl we have got into, let's see what happens if we ask our question in a different form. Suppose we ask what Einstein's intention was in writing the equation $E = mc^2$. This question is easily answered: he was presenting some observations he had made about physical reality. And suppose we next ask what Hemingway's intention was in writing the story "Fifty Grand." This question can be answered in the same way: he was presenting some observations he had made about human experience. The words "presenting" and "observations" do not mean exactly the same thing in Einstein's case as in Hemingway's, however.

Now let us return to the word "meaning." Like most things, meanings come in different varieties. One kind of meaning is prescriptive. What does a red traffic light mean? "Thou shalt stop." Another kind of meaning is descriptive. Considered from a descriptive rather than a prescriptive point of view, a red traffic light means that information is being communicated to drivers about the traffic flow. Sometimes a driver disregards this information. It can be, and has been, argued that all description is in the end prescriptive, but this is an issue to which we can return in a moment.

The meaning of the equation $E = mc^2$ is descriptive. It is not a command. The equation describes certain circumstances in physical reality. Einstein's intention was to describe these circumstances. Similarly, the meaning of "Fifty Grand" is descriptive. Hemingway's intention was to describe certain circumstances in human experience. The elements involved in

Hemingway's description are of course somewhat different from those in Einstein's. Or we might say that what these two writers present creates different effects. Einstein's elegance creates an intransitive rapt attention, Hemingway's a semblance. But both present meaning, too—descriptive meaning. Some literary works, on the other hand, contain prescriptive meaning. For example, in *The Scarlet Letter* Hawthorne commands his reader to "be true!" At the present time, however, readers have a distaste for such commands. It seems likely that the existence of such prescriptive meanings in some literary works has resulted in an overreaction. People have tended to assume that because some meanings in literature are prescriptive all meanings, or abstractions, in literature are prescriptive, and some people have consequently denied the appropriateness of meaning to literature at all.

A last point to be noted in this brief review is that a description can also be prescriptive in certain situations and that the moral implications everyone feels in descriptive literature are in part derived from this fact. For example, $E = mc^2$ is merely descriptive for an armchair reader, but in the performance of certain experiments this equation prescribes part of what must be done. Similarly, the observation presented in "Fifty Grand" may be felt as prescriptive in certain situations in real life. The prescriptive power of literature is always limited, however, by the problem of the logical gap that was discussed in Chapter 8.

Some Conclusions

On the evidence provided by the illustrations considered, finally, the following conclusions appear to be warranted.

First, meaning and drama, or intention and drama, or abstraction and semblance are inextricably interwoven. As Abraham Kaplan and Ernst Kris have argued, emotions in art are contained in complex structures, and the process of experiencing them requires active intellectual participation. An instructor, or a reviewer in a periodical, should not feel that in discussing the meaning of a literary work he is somehow guilty of distorting it. He *can* distort it in this way, but only if he fails to keep the importance of semblance well in mind. There is prob-

ably as much danger that some members of the group will fail
to enjoy the illusion of a work because they didn't grasp the
meaning as that a discussion of the meaning will destroy the
illusion. Either of these undesirable results can occur; one of
an instructor's functions is to help people avoid them both.
An advantage of explicit generalizations in the classroom, then,
is simply that they are a way of enhancing the enjoyment of
literature.

A second conclusion is that through explicit generalizations a
literary work is related to the real social community inhabited
by the reader. For example, through a group discussion of the
code of conduct in the prize-fight story just considered, an individual who is unaccustomed to thinking about principles of conduct may find himself drawn into doing so—by direct peer pressure if nothing else. This approach to the illusion and the meaning of literature, which appears to be a fundamental element
in the social function of the classroom, will be discussed in Part
Three.

Finally, I would like to make a suggestion about the role of
instructors in discussing the meaning or intention of a work.
Sometimes it is desirable to present a reader with a thorough
account of what a work is all about before he begins to read. Let
him have some of the genuine experience of the recognition
scene before he even begins. An example of this kind of presentation is Mary McCarthy's eight-page review of Solzhenit-
syn's *August 1914* in the *Saturday Review*, September 17, 1972.
(For the classroom, some of McCarthy's adverse criticism would
be held back until later, to give the work its own chance.)

There are two reasons for my mentioning this idea. The first
is that a difficult work can easily become a hated work, especially for people who are under such tension as described by Barrett
Mandel in the essay from which I quoted earlier. Faced with
this possibility, why not give all the help possible? An objection, of course, is that such help may spoil the story and bias
the reader's judgment. Perhaps; quite so. But I will say frankly
that I was grateful for McCarthy's help with *August 1914*.

The second reason goes a little deeper. Sometimes people have
a profound psychological need for direction, for support. I remember once talking with a brilliant young woman who not
long before had experienced a severe emotional crisis. I asked

her if she had found the reading of literature a help during this time and she said no, she had not because it seemed too ambiguous. She told me that sometimes in her desperate need she would walk along the rows of shelves in a library hoping that by mere chance she would come upon some book containing an assurance that would let her sleep. Finally she began to read existential philosophy, and for some reason it provided what she had been looking for. Later, having—as she said—a set of meanings to which to relate things, she returned to the reading of literature.

It is not the purpose of the literary classroom to discern such desperate needs as this and provide for them. Nevertheless, among all the individuals who for a time occupy a place in the classroom there will be some whose needs, if not so great, are at least similar in kind to that of the young woman just mentioned.[107] Keats's "negative capability," the capacity for uncertainty and ambiguity, is a fine thing but it is not well suited as a program for everyone at all times. On occasion clarity, definiteness, order, and explicit generalizations do prove a welcome introduction to a complex and intense work of art.

What I would stress most of all in these comments on the need for explicit generalizations in the classroom is that abstractions, universals, generalizations are a perfectly natural part of literature. Indeed, they are an almost indispensable part. It is meaning that makes available the semblance of great works of literature—surely one of the most treasured of all human experiences. An instructor should never hesitate to talk about meaning. Understandable as it is, the current fear that a discussion of meaning is an act of aggression against the hearer is quite mistaken, in my opinion. Granted a reasonable courtesy and considerateness, human relationships must not become so delicate that one person cannot speak out his mind to another without feeling guilty of an imposition. Friendship and love, themselves probably forms of semblance, are made possible only through the meaning of structured communication, imperceptible as that structure may become to one who is sheltered by it.

Before this discussion of abstractions is brought to an end one additional general topic calls for attention. Despite the evident role of abstractions in literature, a significant portion of modern literature reflects what can loosely be called nonrationalism. Nonrational behavior has been an important subject in literature from the beginning, of course. Historically, however, literature dealing with nonrational subject matter has tended to be itself structured and intentionally meaningful, although a considerable exception is needed for myths and folktales. In the modern world, on the other hand, there is a body of literature which deliberately attempts to mirror the inferred formlessness of its subject matter with a formlessness of its own. The problem of the relationship of abstractions to such literature is the primary subject of this chapter.

A secondary subject, even though not a less important one in itself, is the question of the relationship of virtually all literature to the unconscious mind. What I am thinking of here is illustrated in a recent remark by David Littlejohn: "To me [Faulkner] seemed an author who had virtually free access to unconscious materials of an unparalleled richness and intensity —unparalleled since Dostoevsky—materials he was sometimes able to convert to supreme artistic use."[108] It is in this latter context that we can ponder the meaning of a question already encountered several times: what does it really mean to say that an author intended a given series or pattern?

Confronted with the nonrational in both subject matter and form, the instructor's obligation is thus twofold. First, he must deal as best he can with the presentation of nonrationality as subject matter wherever he encounters it. Second, when concerned with modern works which are nonrational in form he must have something to say about why anyone would choose such a form. At first glance the best way to satisfy both needs might appear to lie in a judicious use of psychology, as recommended in recent works by Frederick Crews and Norman Holland. As far as nonrationality in subject matter is concerned, I myself know of nothing better to recommend. Depth psychology is an invaluable source of insights into human behavior; it is only necessary to remember that the project of turning these insights into a rigorous science has not yet been accomplished, and probably—as Crews remarks[109]—never can be accomplished.

To turn to psychology for ideas about why literature that is deliberately nonrational in form appeared in the modern world is less inviting. Psychology is fundamentally an attempt to organize kinds of insights that have been apparent in literature, and elsewhere, throughout history. What is new about psychology is therefore not so much its subject matter as the notion of treating its subject matter scientifically.

The problems that spring up all around as these ideas are contemplated are formidable and far too great in scope to be attacked here. Yet there remains the practical need of the classroom. What are the surrealists, to take the most obvious example, trying to tell us by choosing a nonrational form for their work? When we look into their works and into what they say about their works, what we find is the idea that the world is not rational. But, for our practical needs, the question we need an answer to is: what does it mean to say that the world is not rational?

It can mean at least two things. One is that in some ways the structure of the physical universe appears to be nonrational. The other is that there are nonrational processes of thought in which we find delight and wisdom. Reflecting these two possibilities, the principal topics in the following discussion will be, first, some ideas about the relationships between modern physics and literature; second, intuition regarded as both a rational and a nonrational process; and, last, the concept of the unconscious as a source of strength and purification.

Relationships between Physics and Literature

My purpose in taking up the familiar story of modern physics[110] is not to claim that here may be found the origins of nonrational form in literature. It is instead to claim that here is an easily available and helpful way in which to perceive one important force among the several primary forces underlying nonrational literature. I do not know which had the greater influence on the other, nonrational art or modern physics. Their development is roughly parallel in time, beginning at approximately the turn of the century. They both encouraged a view of reality captured in the currently popular term "discontinuous."

Physics is an easily available source in which to examine this idea because it presents concentrated examples; it is helpful because it is somewhat (but only somewhat) less subjective than corresponding literary materials.

As my concentrated example from modern physics I will choose the idea of complementarity. This idea, first presented in a paper by Niels Bohr at a meeting of physicists in September 1927, was originally concerned with the now familiar paradox that light appears to be both a wave motion and a motion of particles. Later, Bohr expanded the concept into other areas.

From a literary man's point of view the idea of complementarity presents three very curious features. One appears in the fact that this concept is the physicists' response to the first professional encounter they ever had with what outside of science is an age-old problem.[111] This problem is the paradox of basic irreconcilables: good and evil, justice and love, the one and the many. At least Niels Bohr himself came to believe that the principle of complementarity he had derived from physical phenomena was the same that was required in these other areas. A second curiosity lies in the bizarre physical phenomena themselves, some of which I will briefly review. The third lies in the fact that from their encounter with irreconcilables the physicists have turned, in effect, to the Republic of Letters, as will become apparent later.

The particular basic irreconcilability the physicists met up with is that electromagnetic radiation and elementary material particles behave like both waves and particles. The common sense which sees only six horses in a field that actually contains only six horses says this is impossible. Nevertheless, in some experiments light (a form of electromagnetic radiation) clearly behaves like waves, while in others it clearly behaves like tiny particles. The principle of complementarity asserts that light is a more complex phenomenon than can be comprehended in our common-sense notions of either waves or particles; it asserts that these two notions must complement one another if we are to approach a true understanding of the nature of light.[112] That is, both notions must be regarded as true, but neither as adequate for a complete explanation of the phenomenon.

We can examine an instance of the kind of experimental result requiring the principle of complementarity. My account, which will be highly simplified and idealized, will be based on discussions by J. M. Jauch and Gerald Holton.[113]

We begin our experiment by providing ourselves with a very weak source of light, so weak it will emit only one photon—or particle—of light at a time. We place this light source in front of a screen. In this screen, which is impenetrable to light, we pierce two small holes. Behind this screen we place a second screen which is coated with a sensitive material that will darken wherever a photon strikes it. Therefore, if any photons pass through either of the two holes in the first screen this fact will be evidenced by a darkening of the appropriate areas on the second screen.

Next we cover one of the two holes in the first screen and turn on our light source. Photons begin passing through the hole that was left open, as shown by darkening of the sensitized material on the second screen. The darkened area is in line with the hole and the light source; its size is determined by the amount of scattering that occurs after the photons have passed through the hole. The effect is somewhat as if we fired a number of shots at a target from a rifle held in a vise. The bullets would not all strike the target in precisely the same place but rather would form a small cluster.

Now we cover the hole through which the photons have been passing and uncover the second hole. A second darkened area appears on the sensitized material on the second screen. This darkened area is in line with the hole just uncovered in the first screen.

Finally we uncover both holes and at the same time replace the sensitized screen with a fresh, unmarked one. As the photons leave the light source one at a time they can pass through either one of the two holes. Since the two holes are close together, we would expect to find some overlapping of the darkened areas on the sensitized screen. And the darkened areas do overlap. But now something startling appears. The darkening in the overlapping area is not merely an increased darkening: it is in the form of alternating lighter and darker bands. Patterning of this sort occurs only when waves originating in different sources collide or interfere with one another, alternately reinforcing one another and canceling one another out. For such a pattern to appear as we now see on the sensitized screen, light must be entering both holes simultaneously, with interference occurring as the light from the two holes passes to the sensitized screen. Yet we know that only one photon at a time is reaching the first screen. So we are faced with a seemingly impossible conclusion: one photon is passing through two holes simultaneously and interfering with itself. We are forced to recognize that each one of the photons which had at first seemed to pass through a hole as if it were a tiny bullet is also a wave which can encounter two holes simultaneously and diffract into interference patterns.[114]

Judged by common sense, a universe in which a photon behaves both like a particle and like a wave is either chaotic or structured in a way the human mind cannot comprehend. Physicists have responded to these amazing results in two ways: by withdrawing into a mathematical system not bound to a common-sense concept of waves and particles and by developing the principle of complementarity.

Mathematically, Heisenberg says, physicists have achieved an unambiguous correlation with the experimental evidence.[115] The mathematical system appears to be isomorphic with the "reality" being examined. But physicists are not mathematics; they are only human beings who use mathematics. Like everyone else, the images they can form in their minds must be created out of the materials their senses can handle; their world, like everybody else's, is one in which a particle cannot be a wave. Therefore, as the physicists Weidner and Sells put it:

> Any energy-transport phenomenon, whether or not remote from our direct observation or experience, must be described in terms of waves or of particles. If the phenomenon is to be visualized at all, if we are to have some sort of *picture* of what goes on in interactions that are inaccessible to direct and immediate observation, it must be in terms of a wave behavior or a particle behavior. There is no alternative.[116] [Italics in original.]

In view of all these considerations, some refinement is desirable in the assertion that the universe may be structured in a way incomprehensible to the human mind. A distinction is needed in the meaning of "comprehend." The fact is that to an effective degree physicists *have* comprehended the behavior of photons—mathematically. On the other hand, as Weidner and Sells indicate, physicists have not comprehended the behavior of photons in the sensuous, imagistic way in which everybody grasps the law of momentum when he hits a baseball with a bat. Whether he can express the law of momentum mathematically or not, the batter can describe the event in plain language. And as Heisenberg says, "Even for the physicist the description in plain language will be a criterion of the degree of understanding that has been reached."[117] By "understanding" I believe he means something like the import of my adjectives "sensuous" and "imagistic" or simply of the phrase "common sense." A word the physicists use a good deal is "classical," meaning in the language of Newton's physics, which is closer to common-sense experience than is the language of atomic physics. The behavior of photons has not been understood in sensuous, imagistic, common-sense, or classical language. It should be remembered, however, that through long experience a physicist may become able to respond sensuously to a good deal of the content of the world of atomic physics.

I must also add an important qualification. I have not meant to imply that I believe the structure of the universe can be comprehended by the human mind even mathematically. What, I wonder, would structure mean in so vast a project? Strictly speaking, I don't believe a thoughtful physicist would want to swear that his mathematical system is truly isomorphic with the behavior of photons either, as I casually said it was. There is always the possibility that new discoveries, or even new points of view, will reveal an incompleteness in the system where least anticipated. Indeed, Eugene Wigner goes further, saying that by definition science is incomplete, because its foundations lie partly outside of science.[118] That is, an attempt to define science as a complete, formalized, airtight system would reduce it to meaningless signs. His point is similar to Eddington's in the story about the elephant. If you try to reduce the elephant to nothing but numbers, the elephant disappears.

Besides responding to bizarre experimental results by creating a successful mathematical system, physicists responded also with the idea of complementarity. As noted earlier, the principle of complementarity asserts that the concepts of wave motion and of particle motion must complement one another if we are to approach an understanding of the behavior of photons or of electromagnetic radiation and elementary particles generally.

From the point of view of a literary man, the principle of complementarity appears to be a literary idea, for three reasons.

First, it is a textual commentary, not a primary text. The primary text is the mathematical system, which, we are told, gives an unambiguous account. The idea of complementarity functions like a commentary on a difficult poem written in a language we do not understand very well. The more we struggle with text and commentary, the more we are forced to realize that although the commentary is helpful in giving us a general idea of the poem, the commentary is not the poem. As we begin to catch glimmerings of the force of the poem, we see that in attempting to simplify it the commentary has itself become ambiguous. Complementarity, Heisenberg declares, encourages the use of an ambiguous language.[119]

Second, complementarity is a fiction, a necessary fiction. It is not isomorphic with the physical reality it describes and therefore it is fictional; yet it is necessary if the human imagination is to approach this reality in a sensuous, imagistic way. Bohr's own conviction of the necessity is clearly evident in a remark he made while defending his principle: "The aim of our argumentation is to emphasize that all experience, whether in science, philosophy, or art, which may be helpful to mankind, must be capable of being communicated by human means of expression."[120] Complementarity, of course, provides such a human means of expression. The mathematical system is not "human" in the same way, since it lies in part beyond the power of the sensuous imagination.

A third reason for thinking of complementarity as literary is, then, that it represents an attempt to achieve the characteristic literary fusion of abstraction and virtual life. One factor that makes this entire situation so fascinating is that here, in the mathematical system of quantum mechanics, we finally confront a pure abstraction. With one important exception, this system is apparently devoid of sensuous content. The exception is that when the system is viewed as a human creation or a human act, persons competent to judge do pronounce it beautiful, elegant. Clearly, they regard it with intransitive rapt attention. Abstraction can be beautiful. But the desire among physicists themselves to bring this pure abstraction closer to experience—through the fiction of complementarity—seems to indicate that the human mind can't live with abstractions alone, no matter how beautiful.

Perhaps in referring to the virtual life sought in complementarity, as I did a moment ago, I am going too far. Certainly I am violating in some measure the distinction I made earlier between semblance (i.e., virtual life) and intransitive rapt attention. There, I limited semblance to dramas involving human actions. It still seems a proper way of distinguishing between the two terms. Nevertheless, I feel myself constantly pressed to extend the concept of virtual life, as I indicated on page 79. The more we become aware of the degree to which the world around us is invested with our own feelings and even created by our own meanings, the more difficult it is to draw a line between the human and the nonhuman or between what is generally called the concrete and the abstract. The difficulty is captured in what seems to me an elegant definition of light, by Gerald Holton:

> When you ask, "What is light?" the answer is: the observer, his various pieces and types of equipment, his experiments, his theories and models of interpretation, *and* whatever it may be that fills an otherwise empty room when the lightbulb is allowed to keep on burning. All this, together, is light.[121]

In sympathy with the tenor of Holton's comment, I believe I will again abandon my earlier distinction and think of complementarity as a fiction vested with virtual life.

The relationship of complementarity to the idea of a discontinuous universe is somewhat obscured by the fact that in popular usage the term "complementarity" has acquired two quite different meanings. Only one of these meanings was intended by Bohr, who strongly resisted any tendency to employ the concept in a looser way. Bohr limited the idea of complementarity to a situation involving elements that were mutually exclusive. I'm afraid he suffered some lapses from this intention, but that is not important. His original intention was to deal with the fact that a photon viewed as a particle cannot simultaneously be viewed as a wave. Human senses can conceive of photons only in the one mode or the other. Complementarity is therefore a recognition of the fact that the two modes are mutually exclusive, but that both must be retained and must literally complement one another. The principle of mutual exclusion is clearly stated in Bohr's paper of 1927,[122] and his later extensions of complementarity to humanistic areas retained this principle.

In popular usage, however, complementarity came to be associated with the quite different idea that two apparently contradictory views could be resolved in some higher or broader concept. For example, in a recent book on the subject of human consciousness the author tells the familiar story of the elephant which was examined by blindfolded men—one, feeling its leg, claiming it to be cylindrical and solid; a second, feeling its trunk, claiming it to be a flexible tube which emitted air; etc. This story is used to illustrate the principle that from "higher perspective[s] . . . views which might otherwise seem opposite can be seen as complementary."[123]

Bohr's principle was not called forth by such easy problems. The bizarre universe into which he was looking confronted him with stark irreconcilabilities, as it still confronts us now. Consequently, when he extended the idea of complementarity into the field of human relationships he was careful to preserve the principle of exclusion. His ideas about this extended application, which finally constituted an important part of his intellectual life, can be illustrated with the concepts of love and justice. As he saw them, these concepts are necessary parts of human life; they are often mutually exclusive and, when they are exclusive, they should be complementary.

In 1947, upon being awarded the Danish Order of the Elephant, Bohr was required to design a coat of arms to be placed in Frederiksborg Castle. He chose a design representing complementarity. Above the symbol for Yin and Yang, he inscribed the legend "Contraria sunt complementa."[124] Perhaps as we contemplate Bohr's Order of the Elephant, remembering meanwhile that other elephant—Sir Arthur Eddington's—we may infer a generalization. Perhaps elephants of all sorts represent our hope, and even our conviction, that the most bizarre circumstances can somehow be domesticated by the human imagination.

In summary, the literary aspect of Bohr's response to the strange world of atomic physics is profoundly interesting because of its recognition of a need to keep the generalizations of science close to human experience. Nevertheless, I feel he was only partly right in telling Werner Heisenberg that Kronberg Castle represents our need to make a home for Hamlet here on earth. As Bohr himself observed, it was Hamlet who imparted meaning to the castle, not the other way around. From a literary point of view, Hamlet and complementarity play much the same role: each constitutes a fiction enabling our imaginations to domesticate certain of the bizarre circumstances of our lives. Still, Bohr's instinct was surely right. Only to the degree that we perceive Hamlet as a living man who needs a home can we feel he matters. The powerful virtual life of the play and, I presume, our assent to it arise out of a fusion of all the materials represented by Kronberg Castle as a part of human experience, on the one hand, and the meaning of the questions Hamlet asked, on the other.

An important difference between Bohr's concept of complementarity and Shakespeare's *Hamlet*, however, is that Bohr's interest in the idea of complementarity was first made necessary by a world Shakespeare never knew. Let us look now at a literary work that reflects Bohr's world. The following poem is by Genevieve Anderson.

THE SUN ROMPS IN THE MORNING

Dark dogs lick the fingers
of white daisies.
Tigers lurk behind the ears of
children to eat them
with careful nibbles.
Nothing can keep the blue iris
from marching smartly
across wide dining tables
covered with wet hair and
happy voices
singing singing
never never never.[125]

Like much apparently surrealistic poetry, this poem demands an initial choice between alternatives. Is it based on obscure private symbols and allusions, like Samuel Beckett's "Whoroscope," which can be reduced to coherent discourse by employment of the proper keys? Or is it instead essentially a profusion of images, issuing uninhibitedly from the author's mind, which presumably cluster around some focal point of attention? Because of the calculated control exerted by the author in the first of these alternatives, the resulting work could not be called surrealistic. Having found no key to "The Sun Romps in the Morning," however, I must presume it represents the second alternative, a genuine surrealism. It is true that the title, coupled with the smartly marching blue iris and the happy voices, invites the reader to contemplate the exuberance of early morning, but this invitation does not by any means lend a ready significance to all the lines of the poem. Even if a meaning were puzzled out for such a phrase as "across wide dining tables covered with wet hair," the primary point of these lines would still appear to be a rejection of meaning. This poem cannot be said to create a useful fiction in any sense comparable to what I earlier claimed for *Hamlet* and for complementarity. It bears more resemblance to the behavior of photons themselves than to complementarity.

Nevertheless, many people have found something intensely appealing in such poetry. An example may be seen in the following passage from an essay by Robert Bly in *The Fifties*, the journal he himself edits (with a new title for each decade).

> Beginning with Baudelaire, French poetry went through a dark valley, a valley filled with black pools, lions, jungles, turbid rivers, dead men hanging from trees, wolves eating the feathers of birds, thunder hanging over doors, images of seas, sailors, drunken boats, maggots eating a corpse with the sound of a sower sowing grain, endless voyages, vast black skies, huge birds, continual rain. This immersion has given French poetry its strength, its rich soil, whereas our soil is thin and rocky.[126]

The similarity of the surrealistic quality of such imagery to that of "The Sun Romps in the Morning" is obvious, but Bly's reference to this imagery as representing the rich soil of French poetry introduces something new. The discontinuity and randomness revealed by modern science and, as scholars generally agree, reflected in modern art are somehow transformed by Bly into a source of strength and delight.

The kind of imagery Bly describes is often associated with Freud's concept of the unconscious, a concept developed more or less simultaneously with the emergence of modern physics. To use a term I employed earlier, as finality drifted ever farther away from an anthropomorphic God, until even the structure of the physical universe appeared alien to the human mind, people began to turn inward to the unconscious mind Freud had assured them they would find.[127] Bly, for example, insists that poetry must establish its foundations on imagery derived somehow from the unconscious. The surrealists in general were fascinated by the idea of the unconscious. In short, psychoanalytical theory and modern physics combine to encourage literature that is nonrational in form.

Intuition as Rational Thought

Accordingly, we should give some attention to the role of the unconscious mind in literature and to the question of how this role is related to abstractions. My first topic in this area will be intuition as rational thought. In other words, I will consider some evidences of thinking that is not done in the conscious mind but that is nevertheless the kind of thought we associate with the conscious mind.

The most interesting example I have come across of rational intuition is not from psychoanalytic histories but from an account of the remarkable abilities of Alexander Craig Aitken, for many years professor of mathematics at the University of Edinburgh. Aitken performed almost incredible feats of mental calculation. He could, for example, square a three-digit number almost instantly. His account of his subjective experience while performing such a feat introduces a strange bit of evidence concerning rational intuition. Aitken writes:

> . . . mostly it is as if [the numbers] were hidden under some medium, though being moved about with decisive exactness in regard to order and ranging; I am aware in particular that redundant zeros, at the beginning or at the end of numbers, never occur intermediately. But I think that it is neither seeing nor hearing; it is a compound faculty of which I have nowhere seen an adequate

description; though for that matter neither musical mem-
orization nor musical composition in the mental sense
[has] been adequately described either. I have noticed
also at times that the mind has anticipated the will; I
have had an answer before I even wished to do the calculation; I have checked it, and am always surprised to
find that it is correct.[128]

In this remarkable account, the most astonishing element of all
is no doubt Aitken's statement about having an answer to a
problem before he had even decided he wanted to perform the
calculation. The implications concerning the role of the will are
most puzzling.

I once encountered this puzzling problem in a direct and personal way in a classroom. Many years ago I chanced to read an
account of some medical observations made by a surgeon during the First World War while he was treating a soldier who
had a head wound inflicted by shrapnel. A small part of the
skull had been cut away and the gray matter of the brain exposed, but the soldier was conscious and not in great pain. As
the surgeon was cleaning the wound the soldier moved his arm
and then moved it again—and the surgeon suddenly wondered
if his touching the exposed brain tissue was somehow related
to the movement. He experimented a little and discovered that
touching a particular area of the exposed brain tissue with his
scalpel was invariably followed by a movement of the arm. So
he asked the soldier why he moved his arm, and the soldier,
seeming a bit surprised, replied that of course he moved it because he wanted to.

Long after I read this account I mentioned these observations
by the surgeon to a class I was talking to—and immediately an
arm was raised in the back of the room. It was that of a com-
bat veteran. What he had to say was that he himself had undergone the same experience as this other soldier. The surgeon
who cared for his wound had talked with him about the phenomenon. Naturally, everyone in the classroom immediately
demanded to know how it had felt. The young man replied that,
well, it only felt as if he wanted to move his arm.

In principle, this kind of experience is no longer a novelty,
because of the widely publicized results of experiments in electrical stimulation of the brain. So I had better explain my rea-

son for telling this story at all. The point of the stories about
both the soldiers is obviously, I presume, that the relationship
of an individual to his own will is extremely complex. The
point of joining the stories of the two soldiers to the account
given by Professor Aitken of his experience with mental arithmetic is to suggest that the relationship of an individual's conscious mind to both his will and his power of analytical thought
is also extremely complex. There can be no doubt that something at least resembling Freud's notion of the unconscious is
involved in these activities. In this context, then, the idea of intuitive knowledge is still mysterious enough, but it is a mystery
that is contained within our own heads, one which we can begin to relate to ordinary experiences—both literary and other.

In fact, there is an example of an intuitive ability fully comparable to Professor Aitken's that is so familiar it is surprising.
This ability is everybody's power to produce sentences. In a
conversation we talk along without planning out our grammar.
Where do the sentences come from? Sometimes we speak before
thinking, too—and are sorry later. Aitken was only making
sentences with numbers. His ability is surprising merely because the gift for handling numbers in this way is so much rarer
than the gift for handling words. The gift for handling numbers is no more complex than that for handling words; indeed
it is probably less complex. Other gifts come to mind as well:
a composer's ability to create a melody, a painter's ability to
create a graphic form, an engineer's ability to conceive a mechanism. All these gifts are ultimately as mysterious as Aitken's.

Still more dramatic and puzzling, and yet as much a part of
natural human experience, are those occasions on which a surprising idea appears in a dream, in what Yeats called a light
trance, or in the first moments upon awakening from sleep.
Poincaré awoke with the solution to a difficult mathematical
problem he'd been puzzling over; Knut Hamsun with a passage
for a novel he was working on. Kekulé conceived the benzene
ring in a dream. Faulkner saw one of the novels in the Snopes
trilogy in a sudden vision. Kafka wrote a story he didn't understand until he read it aloud to his fiancée.

Because of their fame, these achievements seem remote and
untouchable, but I feel sure anyone can have similar experiences, on a more modest scale, if only he watches for them. I
can speak on this point from experience. A few days ago, for

example, when I was still only half-awake before getting out of bed in the morning, I saw clearly in my mind's eye some printed words—apparently suspended in space. The words, which would have been totally nonsensical to anyone else, were the following, punctuation included:

Wordsworticle: a punk particle

They were only a joke. Their source, I presume, lay in the fact that on the previous afternoon I'd been reading an analysis of some of Wordsworth's poetry and in the evening an essay on nuclear particles. Wort, of course, means plant. Punk is a soft, woody, or plantlike material. When I was a boy I used smoldering sticks of punk to light fireworks. I have often thought about what seems to me a similarity between words and nuclear particles, how words combine with one another as mysteriously as nuclear particles do. But words seem softer, more organic, more punky. Punk means not much good, too. I must admit I have mixed feelings about Wordsworth, whose name was evidently being punned on. Some of his poetry is magnificent, but he did offer to the public certain pieces that seem to have suffered from overexposure to the moist climate of the Lake Country. Why my unconscious mind put these things together into such a wretched pun I don't know, but at least it is a simple illustration of the fact that the activity of the unconscious mind is a perfectly natural part of human experience; its effects need only be watched for to be observed. A reference to intention, as we try to interpret a text, may clearly involve either the author's conscious or unconscious mind or both.

As far as our problem of abstractions is concerned, the principle which emerges from all the examples just considered is that a literary work drawn from an author's unconscious mind may still have pattern and meaning in it, even as explicit a pattern as a series.

The Logic of Emotion

We have considered some relationships between nonrational elements in physics and literature and have observed examples of rational intuition or of the rational operations of the uncon-

scious mind. A related but different area is found in what is
commonly spoken of as nonrational logic, or alogical logic, or
poetic logic, or the logic of emotion. I will use the last of these
terms.

An unfortunate element in all these terms is again that they
suggest a mystery where really there is none. There is no lack
of mystery in human experience, as we've already noted, but
as far as our present interests are concerned there need be no
mysteries in the idea of alogical logic or the logic of emotion.
That this is true becomes evident if we consider the matter in
terms of the difference between logic and understanding.

To begin with, emotional "logic" is merely a sequence of
feelings having relationships to one another that are experienced as compelling. Here is a made-up example. Somebody in-
sults a friend or acquaintance at a cocktail party. Having done
so he crosses the room and joins another group. He gives the
appearance of attending to the conversation but is actually preoccupied in examining his feelings. He is experiencing a strong
satisfaction at having told off the other person, but he is also
beginning to feel remorse. He had spoken in anger and now
begins to wonder if he was really justified. After a half-hour or
so of examining his feelings and thinking about the circumstances, he apologizes to the person he'd insulted. Logical? No,
if the word "logical" is used to refer to the entire series of events.
If it was logical to apologize, then presumably it was illogical
to insult. Or vice versa. But the entire episode is certainly understandable. As interested observers our goal is, again, Verstehen.

It is true we often fail to understand someone else's sequence
of emotions, and occasionally we don't even understand our
own. Studies in psychology have provided some insights into
this problem. The psychologist Charles Osgood uses the term
"psycho-logic" or "cognitive congruity." Erich Fromm attacks
the problem by distinguishing between rational and irrational
emotion. He defines a rational emotion as one which strength-
ens an individual's psychic structure and an irrational emotion
as one which weakens it. He says, for example, that an irrational love is one which increases an individual's dependency,
resulting in anxiety and hostility.

If we leave literature and examine the nonverbal arts we may
come to something closer to a pure logic of the emotions. A

melody, for instance, clearly has form; it is orderly, and in that sense it is logical. Perhaps its logic is somehow emotional. This notion has appealed to people who, like Wallace Stevens, were interested in the possibility of "pure poetry" and hoped to create poetry as free of abstractions as a melody. Stevens became convinced, however, that poetry could not exist without ideas.[129]

With these thoughts in mind, let us now take a look at a couple of examples of the logic of emotion. The first example I have chosen, for a very particular reason, is John Donne's "The Canonization." In his distinguished book *The New Apologists for Poetry*, Murray Krieger selected this poem to exemplify fundamental theoretical issues he proposed to analyze. Prominent among these issues was the significance of what Krieger termed poetic as opposed to logical development.

Krieger's explication of the poem is, in my opinion, quite persuasive. Like Krieger, who professedly based his own interpretation on Cleanth Brooks's analysis in *The Well Wrought Urn*, I have no desire to try to establish a new interpretation. Like his, my interest is centered not in the poem for its own sake but in the principles it exemplifies. I will therefore, although in my own words, follow his and Brooks's interpretation closely. The use in my own comments of the rather inelegant term "series," however, is my own. My objective will be to show that although the sequence of emotions in Donne's poem is not logical, it is readily understandable.

THE CANONIZATION

> For God's sake hold your tongue, and let me love,
>   Or chide my palsy, or my gout,
> My five gray hairs, or ruined fortune, flout,
>   With wealth your state, your mind with arts improve,
>   Take you a course, get you a place,
>   Observe His Honor, or His Grace,
>   Or the King's real, or his stamped face
>   Contemplate; what you will, approve,
>   So you will let me love.
>
> Alas, alas, who's injured by my love?
>   What merchant's ships have my sighs drowned?
> Who says my tears have overflowed his ground?

When did my colds a forward spring remove?
    When did the heats which my veins fill
    Add one man to the plaguy bill?
Soldiers find wars, and lawyers find out still
    Litigious men, which quarrels move,
    Though she and I do love.

Call us what you will, we are made such by love;
    Call her one, me another fly,
We're tapers too, and at our own cost die,
    And we in us find the eagle and the dove.
        The phoenix riddle hath more wit
        By us: we two being one, are it.
So, to one neutral thing both sexes fit.
    We die and rise the same, and prove
    Mysterious by this love.

We can die by it, if not live by love,
    And if unfit for tombs and hearse
Our legend be, it will be fit for verse;
    And if no piece of chronicle we prove,
        We'll build in sonnets pretty rooms;
        As well a well-wrought urn becomes
The greatest ashes, as half-acre tombs,
    And by these hymns, all shall approve
    Us canonized for love:

And thus invoke us: You whom reverend love
    Made one another's hermitage;
You, to whom love was peace, that now is rage;
    Who did the whole world's soul contract, and drove
        Into the glasses of your eyes
        (So made such mirrors, and such spies,
That they did all to you epitomize)
    Countries, towns, courts: Beg from above
    A pattern of your love![130]

Of the five stanzas in the poem, the first two are made up of pleas by the lovers to be left alone. The third notes what the world thinks of the lovers, then suggests substitute ways in which they themselves believe they should be regarded. The fourth stanza asserts that when their love is properly comprehended the world will approve their canonization. The last stanza is a prayer made to the canonized lovers by the rest of the world. The crucial stanza is the third: here the speaker transforms the image of the lovers, through the logic of emotion.

I will now summarize in a little more detail the content of each stanza.

STANZA ONE. The speaker begs to be left alone, to love.

STANZA TWO. The speaker declares his love has no effect upon the rest of the world.

STANZA THREE. A crucially important series of images appears in this stanza: flies, taper, eagle and dove, phoenix, die, and mysterious. Perhaps the last two items do not qualify as images, but let's consider. Before examining the individual items in the series, we should note two primary themes: sexuality, which is present throughout with the possible exception of the word "mysterious," and a developing religious implication. The first two images, flies and taper, represent the world's view of the lovers. Both images are common Renaissance representations of sexuality. But the lovers substitute for the flies the eagle and the dove, winged creatures of greater nobility and representative of idealized masculinity and femininity. Then the lovers introduce the phoenix, which is winged like flies, eagles, and doves and burns itself up like a taper. The phoenix is a fabled bird, of neither sex and of both, that consumes itself by fire once every five hundred years and is then reborn from the ashes. When the two lovers become one, both sexes are combined, as in the phoenix; and being one they are, also like the phoenix, sexually neutral. Die means to die and also—in the Renaissance—a sexual climax. In this pun the religious and the sexual themes are combined, since from this death the lovers, like the phoenix, are resurrected ("rise the same"), and because of this resurrection they become mysterious or—in terms of Christian mystery—saintly.

STANZA FOUR. The stanza begins with the punning die. Then a series of three items is developed: verse, sonnets, and hymns. This series is placed within a contrasting context of the ostentatious memorials desired by worldly people: chronicles, half-acre tombs. The series progresses from simple verse to sonnets (love poems) and then, by quite a leap, to hymns—appropriate for religious love—and to sainthood. And thus the lovers achieve canonization.

STANZA FIVE. This stanza, following the words "And thus invoke us," is spoken to the canonized lovers by the rest of the world. The lovers, who at the beginning are begging to be left alone to the peacefulness of their love, are now paradoxically said to have concentrated the entire world in one another. Looking into one another's eyes, they see the world mirrored there, or epitomized, through the power of their saintly love. And the rest of the world, desiring to learn how to emulate them, prays for a pattern of their love.

Looking at the poem as a whole, now, I will comment on the three aspects of it that are of special interest in the present context: the logic of emotion, or poetic development; the generalized meaning; and the author's intention.

Neither of the two principal series is logical in development. That of the third stanza, which contains the most items, begins with flies and terminates with mysterious. It is not by the power of reason that "we are flies" is transformed into the religious "we are mysterious," but by the lovers' repeated attempts to find an image that will impart how they feel about themselves. The progression is from wantonness to holiness. Similarly, the progression in the other series is from the modestly secular verses to the religious feeling of hymns. In neither series is the progression logical. But in both, it seems to me, the progression is easily understandable.[131] That is, holding in mind the combined sexual and religious implications of the terms in the series, we find it natural enough to go from flies to taper to eagle and dove, to phoenix, to die, and to mysterious. And, again, from verse to sonnets to hymns. And this is the evidence we have been seeking of the understandable quality of the logic of emotion.

But how abstract is the meaning of understandable? Is the series from flies to mysterious an abstraction in the same sense as the series from the numeral 1 to the numeral 10? From mysterious we look back at flies and wonder how we got from there to here. Pondering the gap, we perceive we are confronting the issue of generalized meaning in the poem. The reader cannot believe he is supposed to think that sexual intercourse, symbolized by flies, leads to canonization, symbolized by mysterious.

Clearly, he is not supposed to think anything of the kind. As Krieger points out, the ambiguities in the relationship between sexuality and holiness in the poem have deliberately been

made too obvious to miss. The punning on the idea of dying
and resurrection, for example, unmistakably warns the reader
that an exercise in wit is going on. And yet everyone seems to
agree this is a poem of such power that the reader is swept effortlessly along, assenting to the canonization at the end as if
everything had been logically proved. Surely this effect is no less
a deliberate part of the poem than is the wit. For the moment,
we can only conclude that the poem jokes about any possibility
of a serious relationship between sexual and divine love and
the poem seriously asserts a close affinity between sexual and
divine love.

If I have understood Krieger's discussion of the poem, the
conclusion just stated is one he would share, with the possible
exception that he might think it too explicit. Here is what he
says:

> The ambiguities prove that the reader was not meant
> only or merely to be fooled all the way [i.e., fooled into
> thinking the poem was only a sober argument in favor
> of what I have called the affinity between sexual and di-
> vine love]. On the other hand, neither is he to look upon
> the poem merely as a faulty argument or as a joke. For
> in one sense—through the operation of its language—it
> *has* proved its case.
>
> I believe no more precise statement can be made about
> what the poem is saying. All I can do is point to the com-
> plex of internal relations . . . and say that the meaning
> of the poem is somehow there.[132]

I would go a little farther. But my circumstances are different
from Krieger's, who was engaged in a difficult theoretical analysis. His orientation toward his problem is, I believe, captured
in these sentences: "I find that when I am reading well the
poetic context controls my experience and the meanings I see
in it. To allow the poem to function referentially is to break the
context."[133] My problem, in contrast, is to learn how to say
something helpful to people who have completed their reading
and now want to talk about it. I disagree with Krieger about the
idea that breaking the context is necessarily harmful, however.

I would go farther than Murray Krieger simply by asking
what the author's probable intention was. Looked at from this

point of view, the poem presents no special difficulty. Donne's intention, I suppose, was to capture in artistic form the generally experienced fact that the relationships between sexual and divine love *are* ambiguous. Hymnals are filled with sexual imagery, the lyrics of love songs with references to divinity.

Given the hypothesis that Donne's intention was to assert the ambiguity of the relationships between divine and sexual love, the two series we've examined are both meaningful. The base of both is a progression from sexual to divine love. In fact, it is even possible to make a stab at replacing an item deleted from one of the series, as if we were to restore a missing numeral in the series of 1 to 10. Suppose, for instance, that the item of the eagle and dove were taken out of the series it is in. We'd have left flies, taper, . . . phoenix, die, mysterious. What we need for replacement is something winged, sexual, associated with fire, and moving away from the wantonness of flies and a taper toward the idealization of the phoenix. How about Apollo and a nymph or demigoddess? Apollo, god of the fiery sun, used to go about on a winged tripod. Logically, Apollo and a demigoddess seem to fit the slot more closely than do the eagle and the dove. At least they might have served Donne's purpose. Perhaps he thought of them and rejected them.

I am not proposing an improvement in Donne's great poem, nor am I saying that Apollo and a demigoddess would be the better choice. The value of the kind of reasoning I've been suggesting is only its disclosure that the logic of emotion is not somehow mysterious and foreign to the thoughtful mind. It is understandable, even if it is not logical in the same way that arithmetic is. Donne's intention surely was to present an ambiguity, not a process leading from sexual intercourse to canonization. In attaining one end of the series, we do not abandon the other. Perhaps we might conclude, in Geoffrey Hartman's manner of speaking, that both ends of the series are overspecified and it is somewhere in the middle that we actually live out our lives —which, I presume, was what Donne intended to say.

To achieve some balance in our view of the logic of emotion we should consider a modern as well as a Renaissance poem. Furthermore, in recognition of changes in attitudes toward meaning since the Renaissance, the poem selected should be one by a writer whose declared intention was to convey not a message but a feeling. A brief look at Donald Hall's well-known "The Man in the Dead Machine" will serve these purposes.

THE MAN IN THE DEAD MACHINE

High on a slope in New Guinea
the Grumman Hellcat
lodges among bright vines
as thick as arms. In 1942,
the clenched hand of a pilot
glided it here
where no one has ever been.

In the cockpit the helmeted
skeleton sits
upright, held
by dry sinews at neck
and shoulder, and webbing
that straps the pelvic cross
to the cracked
leather of the seat, and the breastbone
to the canvas cover
of the parachute.

Or say that the shrapnel
missed him, he flew
back to the carrier, and every
morning takes his chair, his pale
hands on the black arms, and sits
upright, held
by the firm webbing.[134]

Hall says this poem came to him as a visual image while he was driving on the New York thruway. The image he saw was one of an airplane that had come down in a jungle; there were vines around the plane and a skeleton in the cockpit.[135] Hall worked on the poem a good while and has published two different versions of it.

The first stanza of the poem establishes the situation. Hall refers to this stanza as an introduction. The second stanza presents the central image: the skeleton in the plane. Before considering the contribution made by the third stanza, however, we might ponder what we'd have if there were no third stanza, if it were only a two-stanza poem.

I believe we would agree these first two stanzas constitute an intense image. When we asked ourselves what the author's intention was in presenting this image, however, I am not sure any two people would find their responses to be the same. One conceivable response would be that here is an image of heroism and daring. The sadness of death, yes; but all life ends in death and here were a life of action, and a manly death in battle. Another conceivable response is that of unnecessary loss, of useless waste. Another is that of a life lived and lost in bondage to circumstances beyond the control of the individual. And probably there are other possibilities I haven't thought of.

With this array of conceivable responses in mind, let us consider the third stanza. Here we have an image of what is presumably a middle-aged man (pale hands, the war long over) now in civilian life (takes his chair). As a matter of fact, in the first published version the lines "his pale / hands on the black arms" did not appear; in their place were these: "every / morning takes the train, his pale / hands on the black case." Hall says he made the change because he didn't want to implicate only businessmen or commuters in the poem; he wanted to implicate everybody.

The dominant elements in the third stanza are paleness and blackness, rigidity, and constraint (the firm webbing). The question we now confront is, as in "The Canonization," by what logic of emotion do we get from the image of the skeleton to this image of the civilian? As before, the process is not really logical but it is understandable. In "The Canonization," it was understandable that Donne would associate lovers with an eagle and a dove; here, it is understandable that Hall would associate people who are, as he believes, caught in the web of technological society with a flier who in life and death was caught in the webbing which strapped him into the cockpit.

Hall himself has this to say:

> . . . poems are never *about* anything. I mean, what's "The Man in the Dead Machine" about? Is it about the middle-aged man, the Second World War? I don't know what it's about except that it embodies a feeling. . . . the spider

web is never mentioned in that poem, but the skeleton is like a fly in a web, a spider's web; webbing is mentioned, but not a spider's web.[136]

It is, of course, the meaning added in the third stanza that transforms the poem from an elaborate lively element into a semblance—or which creates an intransitive rapt attention. It is the third stanza which gives meaning to "webbing" in the second stanza and binds the two stanzas together through this word. In terms of the author's intention, we can conclude with Hall's own statement:

> I recognized that it [the vision of the downed plane] was an image of how I felt in my life, then . . . I wanted to bring him [the flier] back into the contemporary world, to say that it made no matter whether he was alive or dead.[137]

In summary, we can assert that Hall's intention of imparting his feeling of being caught in the strangling web of modern society was carried out through the emotional association of the middle-aged civilian with the strapped-in pilot. The particular kind of association presented is created principally by the meaning of webbing. I myself feel Hall's declaration that poems are never about anything is misleading. However, if we stick to the term "intention," which is clearly useful in understanding his poem, there is no need to become involved in the problem of what the poem is about.

To speak more precisely than I have so far, the logic of emotion is *usually* understandable, as in "The Canonization" and "The Man in the Dead Machine." When it does break free altogether it becomes surrealistic.

The Unconscious as a Source of Strength and Purification

I now come to my last topic in regard to abstractions, the idea that the unconscious is a source of strength and purification. Here abstractions seem to be rejected altogether. This subject is potentially vast in scope, but I intend only a brief review of one or two problems of special interest to the literary classroom.

Robert Bly will again provide a point of view from which to start. Bly is unusual in that while strongly advocating propagandist poetry, he also urges that such poetry be based on deep imagery, or imagery that emerges from the unconscious. He has written so much propagandist poetry that *Time* once (July 12, 1971) quite misleadingly categorized him as a polemical roarer. A great deal of his poetry is actually intensely personal. His dedication both to personal poetry and to deriving all poetry from sources in the unconscious is implied in a rather dramatic statement he made during an interview:

> ... when I hear poetry being discussed in the classroom, I often get this nauseous feeling in my stomach. ... when I hear an ecstatic poem being described, being discussed in these calm, clear voices, non-passionate voices in a classroom, I get a nausea.[138]

It seems likely that anyone who did not occasionally get such a nausea would not be well suited for the literary classroom. Yet Bly himself talks and writes a good deal *about* poetry. What is the real source of the nausea he describes?

I suppose the key words in Bly's statement are "ecstatic" and "passionate." What these words mean is exemplified by Bertrand Russell's account of how, on his first encounter with Blake's poem "Tyger, Tyger, Burning Bright," he was so affected he became dizzy and had to lean against a wall.[139] No doubt it is the incompatibility of such an intense experience and the idea of calm discussion that was in Bly's mind. In an ecstatic experience the individual feels overpowered, displaced from his usual self—which is what ecstatic literally means. The power seems to come from outside, at least from outside the conscious mind. For convenience, let us use Freud's term and say the power comes from the unconscious mind. In any case, what we are concerned with is the sense of a potent force transcending the normal self.

The first problem of special interest, then, is the role of the classroom concerning such experiences as Russell describes and Bly implies. The intensity of these experiences need not be so great as Russell's to deserve recognition. I suppose one thing an instructor can do in confronting this problem is simply to make evident his awareness that the idea of analyzing the structure of a poem may seem completely incompatible with the experience the poem has evoked. In my own opinion, another thing he can and should do is to indicate that no lifetime can be made up entirely of such highs as Russell describes and that to pursue them in disregard of the analytical aspect of life is to miss at least half the fun—as Russell would certainly agree. From the creative point of view Samuel Taylor Coleridge, who should know, talked about the importance of deliberate design in the poetic expression of powerful feelings that well up spontaneously in the poet.[140] Robert Ornstein has noted that one of the remarkable things about literature is its ability to work on both the intuitive and analytical (or linear, as he says) modes of the mind.[141]

A second problem of special interest is how to relate an experience like Russell's to both depth psychology's unconscious and to those ideas about altered states of awareness currently receiving so much attention. It's a practical problem, because as soon as you acknowledge the existence of a high like Russell's you invite comparison to highs of other sorts.

A first fact to consider is that in Freud's system the unconscious is literally unconscious; it is incapable of consciousness. Only its effects, Freud said, could be known. He did, in addition, identify a "preconscious" which could, when excited, reach consciousness. These two components of the psyche are clearly distinguished from one another, however.

With respect to the current idea of altered states of awareness such a clear distinction is not evident. Instead, the various states are thought of as lying along a continuum. "It must be realized that we are referring to a continuum of phenomena," asserts Timothy J. Teyler, commenting on the entire range of experience from dreams while sleeping to alert wakefulness.[142]

Within this continuum are fantasy (e.g., as studied by Jerome Singer); meditation (e.g., as practiced by Zen monks); feelings of timelessness (e.g., as reviewed by Robert Ornstein); moments of seemingly intense clarity of perception (e.g., the theme of "moments" in Virginia Woolf's fiction or in Maurice Natanson's discussion of Thomas Wolfe in *Literature, Philosophy, and the Social Sciences*); ecstatic visions (e.g., Saul on the road to Damascus); hallucinations induced by drugs, boredom, or exhaustion (e.g., as studied by Woodburn Heron); intuitions

like Alexander Craig Aitken's; intuitions like Coleridge's
"Kubla Khan"; dreams while sleeping. To this array of experiences should be added the well-known astonishing results of
experimentation with electrical stimulation of the brain and of
surgical separation of the hemispheres of the brain. There must
be still more spaces along the continuum, too, since among
those I mentioned none appears completely suited to Russell's
experience.

The relationship of these states of awareness to the concept of
the unconscious is not clear to me, although this is probably
only because of my lack of familiarity with depth psychology.
I puzzle, for example, over the relationship between Aitken's
performing a mental calculation he hadn't yet decided to attempt and the emotional problems represented by Oedipus in
Sophocles's play. Both the calculations and the emotions appear
to be manifestations of the unconscious, and yet they are so unlike one another it seems odd to link them to the same source.

Nevertheless, with the possible exceptions of fantasy, meditation, and the surgical separation of the hemispheres of the
brain, all the altered states of consciousness noted have one element in common with revelations from the unconscious. They
present the individual with something that is inside himself
but that seems outside. The dreamer—asleep or awake—is, as
we say, in a transport, or transported.

Why this experience should have the significance indicated
by Robert Bly in his denunciation of the calm discussion of
poetry is another puzzle, but many people would add their testimony to his. André Breton, for instance, writes, ". . . the goal
I pursued was no less than the objectification of the activity of
dreaming."[143] Even so, why would anyone take pleasure in
writing down such a collection of surrealistic images as seen in
the passage quoted earlier (p. 205) from Bly? Probably no one,
including Bly himself, can really answer that question. We
might speculate about it for a moment, however.

One important factor in the situation appears to be the intimate relationship of such imagery to dreams, and conceivably
there is a clue here. The act of dreaming while asleep is evidently a sheer necessity. It seems to occur during a restorative
period in which, as Ernest L. Hartmann speculates, "rich re-
connections" are being established among the neurotransmit-

ters in certain regions of the brain. At least one fairly definite physical evidence of the importance of dreaming has been observed. This evidence is found in the distinction between two kinds of sleep, one in which dreams occur, the other in which they do not. If an investigator in a laboratory persistently inhibits a sleeping person from dreaming, the electrical activity of the sleeper's brain presently reveals that dreaming is beginning to take place in the unaccustomed nondreaming part of the sleep cycle.[144] In other words, the brain is finding a new way to retain at least a part of the dreaming activity.

This observation suggests a speculative explanation of the appeal of nonrational dreamlike imagery in art. Possibly such imagery induces a satisfying feeling somewhat resembling the state of mind experienced during the nourishing, restorative act of dreaming while asleep. Hartmann points out that one of the most obvious aspects of dreams is the dreamer's lack of surprise at the occurrence of bizarre events. He concludes that "an entire faculty is shut off during the dream, a higher ego function having to do with reality testing or judgment."[145] Bly and others have argued that by approaching the unconscious mind through surrealistic literature an individual may be relieved of the aggressiveness of our culture. On the other hand, Paul Ilie, in *The Surrealist Mode in Spanish Literature*, describes surrealistic literature as "disturbing," as "projecting the forms of distortion and the emotions of alienation."[146] Hartmann's account of research into dreaming seems a little closer to Ilie's view than to Bly's. Hartmann says, for example, that "it appears that the simpler and more primitive emotions predominate in dreams, while the softer or subtler, more adult emotions seem to be lost."[147] Yet I recall an unusual incident that Lévi-Strauss describes in *Tristes Tropiques* which seems to affirm the restorative power of surrealism. Watching a surgeon removing bits of metal from a wound in a man's hand, Lévi-Strauss became absorbed with a vision of a forest, full of shapes and threats. The man had been wounded in a forest, although it isn't clear that this fact is relevant. Presently Lévi-Strauss began to draw landscapes made up of hands emerging from twisted bodies. Having made about a dozen of these sketches he felt relieved and went back to his customary observations. Possibly different people find different kinds of satisfactions in surrealism; possibly "surrealism" is too broad a concept to be very useful. We can only speculate.

I may as well confess that appreciation of surrealistic art, especially surrealistic literature, did not come easily to me. Had it not been for the example of people I respect, I might have given it up. The trick, for me, was to learn to give intense concentration to each new image as it appeared, neglecting any thought of the relationships among the images. For me, this works; I am given a pleasurable feeling. I suspect that the feeling is associated with a sense of the inexhaustible fluidity of life. Both Bly and Breton stress the importance of making the juxtaposition of images a sudden one, and they are probably right.

Apparently surrealistic literature, looked at in this way, is a close approximation to pure poetry, dependent upon imagery and with relatively little "syntax." Such surrealistic literature is, moreover, in keeping with the principles of Rimbaud, a godfather of surrealism. Rimbaud believed that poetic language is not meant for knowing but for forgetting, that it is a way of losing the conventional self and thus discovering the true self.[148] Today, people who hold such views are less inclined to speak of a true self, however.

But Poe, an even earlier spiritual ancestor of surrealism than Rimbaud, was right: poetry as we commonly think of it requires an idea. Poetry without an idea remains essentially a curiosity, as it doubtless always will, simply because language is by nature meaningful. Language seems impoverished when it is devoted to nothing more than a succession of images having no meaningful relationship to one another. Nevertheless, there has lately been some tendency to attribute the value of literature to—as a paper in one of my graduate classes put it—the concept of writing as an energy-bearing act. It will not do to question the vitality of the idea of nonrational or surrealistic art.

Writing as sheer energy is an interesting notion. Perhaps there is something in it. Observation of people who are voracious readers suggests it is indeed the act of reading, the mere stream of language, that is their primary need. Good reading is preferred, but poor reading is better than no reading at all. Words are not mere hydrocarbons, however; and the word

"language" is itself particularly complex. What is a stream of
language? Apparently we can, and to some degree must, respond that it is semblance, intransitive rapt attention, abstractions. The idea of energy is appropriate to language, but it has
a very limited usefulness.

Probably the interest in literature as energy has been taken
over from rock music, where it is somewhat more useful.

> Moving toward noise and let-loose energy is good times.
> It's good, rock audiences feel, more than think, to move
> toward entropy, toward random energy, toward "useless
> information," toward a total promiscuity where all
> modes, all styles, each diction, every voice and note are
> mixed into an overcooked stew where all discrete sys-
> tems are broke, broken, broken down, running into—
> not merely juxtaposed with—one another.[149]

Mick Jagger, of the Rolling Stones, sometimes only mumbles
the words; the words don't matter very much. On the other
hand, a good deal of rock music—Mr. Jones—has contained a
straightforward message.

In this shrinking, preempted world, I think if I were young
I'd care a good deal for rock music. I suspect it's all the old
wilderness, all the seeming promise of unrestricted freedom,
the young can have. And at any age we need a little relief from
the grimness of our homework, a little room for the unconscious to play. Even Jonathan Edwards, one of the greatest
minds America has produced, dreamed of a world in which a
good man would not have to be at the trouble of a train of reasoning. But unrestricted freedom is never more than a seeming
promise, never a fact, and the real freedom created by meaningful language cannot be equaled by mere images or mere
energy. Rock music of the kind represented by the Rolling
Stones might be added to surrealism and dada in a sympathetic
statement made by Leon Edel: "Art can flow into the chaos of
surrealism and dada and back again into a beauty more formal
and disciplined."[150]

In contemporary classrooms, a deliberately held nonrationalism seems to take the form of a devotion to primitivism, or to
the experience of highs, or to art tending toward either of the
two foregoing life styles. In any event, it is worth noting Dr.

Andrew Weil's report of his practical observation that among
people who had used drugs, "the highs of meditation are universally perceived as better than drug highs"[151]—as well as the
primitivistic D. H. Lawrence's observation: "We must all develop into mental consciousness."[152] It is my opinion, and my
own practical observation, that sense impressions are simply
not enough for a healthy and powerful literature.

The idea that art could provide an identity for the self was
for a long time highly appealing. But philosophy, natural science, and psychology incessantly eroded the possibilities of any
personal identity that could not be verified by testing, and
finally quantum physics announced that even testing had become subjective. In place of verification, people are now talking
about validation; in place of the self, they are talking of selves,
voices, fields. The results obtained in tests are no longer
claimed as true, only as apparently real within the limited
range of transient human perception. The history of modern
graphic and plastic art parallels this decline of assurance. As it
has retreated steadily from a deliberate assertion of generalized
forms or ideas, graphic and plastic art has appeared intent on
destroying itself. Morse Peckham writes brilliantly of its spiral-
ing down from abstract expressionism through pop art, op art,
mini art, funk art, earth art, and packaging art. "The message
of pop art was that pure feeling at any cultural level is redemptive," he declares. "Op art and mini art propagated the rhetoric
that pure perception is redemptive."[153] Literature, bound to
meaning by its syntax in a way not true of painting and sculp-
ture, has shown less tendency toward total discontinuity.

In spite of what appears to be a destructive purpose in the
history of modern art, however, its continuous relationship to
the inescapable human experience of compelling sequences of
emotion should be recognized. The felt power of the unconscious, the understandable sequence of emotions, and the en-
tanglement of both with the marvel of the mind's abstractions
are captured in a magnificent little poem by the great Pablo
Neruda:

REASON

The oblong reason of the bough
seems unmoved to us; yet it hears

light's sound in the sky
in a zither of leaves;
and if you lean closer to learn
how water climbs in the flower
you'll hear the moon sing
in the night of the roots.[154]

In my own opinion, what appears so destructive in art's downward spiral is more a preparation for change than outright destruction. It seems to me that people are groping toward what might be called an antigenre genre or toward what Ruth Nanda Anshen—in a remark I quoted earlier—calls not the purpose of man but the purpose in man. I will try to explain my opinion in Part Three.

Part Two, in summary, has been devoted to the idea that an effective semblance depends on meaning and that two needs for validation of a work are an effective semblance and a meaning to which readers assent. I have tried throughout to see these matters in as simple and practical a way as I could, to apply a little horse sense to the daily problems of the classroom. Folk wisdom notes a difference, nevertheless, between horse sense and a horse's sense, a distinction involved in a story told by the psychologist Erwin Straus, with which I will conclude.

The story is about a race horse named Rocky and his trainer, named Joe. By chance, Joe discovered that Rocky could talk, and the two became good friends. It happened one day, unfortunately, that Rocky lost an important race, and Joe wasn't too happy about this. Rocky said maybe the judges were wrong, but Joe said no, he had a photograph of the finish, and Rocky had lost all right. Rocky wasn't familiar with photographs, however, and he began to ask Joe some hard questions about how a piece of paper could serve as a judgment concerning what had actually taken place. Joe showed him the picture. Rocky asked what happened if he turned the photograph around and looked at the other side. Joe showed him there wasn't anything on the other side. Rocky asked how deep the picture went, then. Joe said it had no depth, that you might say it was immaterial, or even abstract. But the more Joe thought about these questions the more puzzled he himself became. Finally he said to Rocky,

> "You're right, it's amazing that this thing whose weight, size, volume, place, position, direction, and time do not count, that this fragment, this excerpt from our surroundings, serves to objectively determine the size and direction of other things in the fullness of their real existence."

As so often happens, confidence was repaid with confidence. Rocky replied,

> "Joe, I must tell you something. I can't see any picture at all, no matter whether you turn it this way or

that. This side is all white; the other one is a bit brighter here, a bit darker there."

[To which Joe responded,]

"Don't give it a second thought! That probably happens because your eyes are situated more to the side. Thereby, you have a better eye for things that approach you, even from behind—things you shy away from. You are always in a sort of contact with things—always poised and ready. A picture, on the other hand, demands a certain distance from things, a suspending of their actuality. For you, it is difficult to find the right posture to put yourself at a distance from things. In this, you are like all other horses. That probably is the reason, too, why horses usually do not speak."[155]

No doubt there is, as the saying goes, a semblance of truth in Joe's remarks.

Part Three.

Validation

The last major division of our subject is the concept of the validation of literature. We will be returning for a last consideration of both semblance and abstraction, joined now in the presence of the unique and often astonishingly different individuals who make up any classroom.

The association of the idea of validation with individuals, with a classroom, and with particular literary works immediately suggests two basic questions. First, how is a literary work validated? Second, how is a literary classroom validated as an educational experience? The purpose of this part of the book is to try to answer these two questions.

They may seem impossibly ambitious questions, appearing at first to be only other versions of those ancient conundrums, "Is literature true?" and "Is literature socially valuable?" Two elements in the questions themselves drastically limit the scope of our problem, however. One is the concept of validation, as distinguished from truth. The other is the restriction of the discussion to the practical needs of the classroom, as distinguished from a theoretical approach. The limiting effect of relating the discussion to the practical needs of the classroom will be apparent throughout, but the idea of validation needs to be clarified. Before attempting such a clarification directly, I must relate the word "validation" more clearly to the two basic questions noted above.

Part of an answer to the question of how a literary work is validated in the classroom has already been suggested. Literary works are validated through a reader's experience of the power of their semblance and through his willingness to grant them intellectual assent. This answer will need to be amplified in only one respect: the role of the concept of genre will need to be accounted for in relation to the idea of assent.

The question of how a literary classroom is validated as an educational experience can be broken down into five distinct problems, as listed below. Of these five, however, only the last two will need consideration here. To be validated as an educational experience, the classroom must

    1. provide individuals with literary works which create an intense semblance, or intransitive rapt attention,

    2. clear up misunderstandings of the text,

3. provide necessary background information,
4. reveal the source of irreconcilable disagreements about the text, and
5. relate the concept of mediation to irreconcilable disagreements.

The first of these problems, semblance, was discussed in Part One. The second, clearing up misunderstandings, requires selection among all the many critical and linguistic methodologies available. As explained previously,[1] with the single large exception of the fundamental concept of abstraction no effort will be made in this book to comment on these methodologies. This omission implies no lack of respect for them. The third problem, providing background information, was commented on in both Part One and Part Two. In one sense the term "background information" becomes misleading in the present context, however. The content of literary works is directly educational concerning our cultural heritage, even when no special help is needed from a teacher to illuminate this content. I do not want to slight the great importance of the study of literature from this perspective. My concern in this book begins at the point at which this content, through failure of semblance or assent, is not self-justifying.

The fourth problem mentioned, irreconcilable disagreements about a text, has not yet been discussed. The chief interest this problem affords is not the disagreements themselves but the insight such disagreements yield into the nature of literary genres. Similarly, the concept of mediation—the fifth and last problem—is concerned not so much with settling disputes as with apprehending the fundamental idea of order in a way appropriate to the cultural and educational role of the classroom.

As indicated, the fourth and fifth of these problems—irreconcilable disagreements and the concept of mediation—will be taken up directly in considering how the literary classroom is validated as an educational experience.

Now we must review the idea of validation itself. My impression is that use of this word is currently fashionable—and probably for a good reason. In classical rhetoric a distinction is made between truth and validity. Truth is concerned with the subject matter of an argument, but validity only with the form or logic of the argument. Consequently, it is possible to have an argument which is valid but not true. For example: everybody in Cornwall loves corn; *A* is from Cornwall; therefore *A* loves corn. This syllogism is valid and false. It is false because its major premise is untrue. With this distinction in mind, I speculate that people are finding it easier these days to say that an idea is validated than that it is true. When finality becomes remote, comfort may be sought in small things. Moreover, the meanings attributed to validation in current usage are remarkably interesting. "To validate" may mean anything from "to prove" to something curiously even more complex than "to establish as a belief or conviction." Among the following examples, the words in brackets are my own inferences as to the particular meaning actually intended by the author.

> The objective precision of operant conditioning methodology validates [proves] the power of hypnosis to induce alterations in time perception.[2]

> Humanistic and existential therapists try to validate the patient's view of the world [try to make the patient's own view of the world seem true or reasonable to him] by entering into it with him, thereby counteracting the patient's sense of alienation and meaninglessness.[3]

> How does an author validate the setting of a novel [make the setting of a novel seem appropriate], that is, how does he induce his reader to accept a given locale as the necessary showplace for a sequence of action?[4]

> This analysis requires questioning the fundamental assumption that empathy and self-projection are necessarily enhanced by the use of the set of first person terms I, me, my, and the like. In theory, these terms acquire in the reader's mind the force of his own ego so that when the narrator or protagonist says "I," the reader assumes the identity and responsibility of the personal pronoun, thus validating [experiencing a powerful semblance and granting assent to] the text in a way impossible with other modes.[5]

The last of these usages is the most curious and interesting of them all. The reader is said to perform a positive act through predominantly passive means. He validates by having an experience.

What is going on here becomes clearer if a simpler experience is substituted for the experience of reading a literary work. How, for instance, is an apple pie validated? By eating it, of course. But nobody ever asks if an apple pie is *valid*; they ask if it is *good*. The goodness of a pie is determined by the subjective experience of eating it. Similarly, people don't ask their friends if a novel is valid, they ask if it is good. Application of the idea of validity to a subjective experience like eating, or enjoying a novel, is incongruous.

Nevertheless, as the passages quoted demonstrate, there is something about the idea of validity in literature that is strongly appealing. Perhaps, to paraphrase Brett Ashley, validation is what we have instead of a finality like Saint Paul's.

If we turn to the dictionary rather than to classical rhetoric, we are told that to be valid is to conform not only to logic but to the law, the facts. There is a reassuring ring of objectivity in the sound of validation, even if validation falls short of proof. Nevertheless, the last of the passages quoted finds the source of validation not in objectivity but paradoxically in the subjectivity of the reader's identifying with a narrator.[6]

We may conclude that validation is a useful term for the discussion of literature from the restricted point of view with which we are concerned, provided a good deal of caution is employed.

On the positive side validation, though falling short of proof, or truth, stands beyond mere subjectivity. It allows for the subjectivity of semblance but demands intellectual assent. It welcomes illusion but rejects total substitution of illusion for the daily world shared by mature and rational people. In what follows, I will try to use the term with these connotations.

On the side of caution, the principal hazard is the possibility of imagining that through this brief consideration of validation we have attained an understanding of what literature is. For example, if we replace the predicate "validate" with the adjective "valid" we make an unnerving discovery. Consider the following sentence: the circumstances in which a reader feels a literary work to be a valid ———— are the following. The slot can be filled with generic terms such as tragedy, entertainment, sonnet, pornographic thriller, or detective story. When we try to go beyond these terms to the fundamental concept of literature or art, however, we find ourselves in difficulties. We confront the fact that nobody has ever come up with a definition of literature which is both useful and universally acceptable. Recent attempts to find a linguistic solution to this problem look very promising, but it isn't clear yet whether these attempts will prove successful. Robert Scholes makes an eloquent plea on their behalf in *Structuralism in Literature.*

Without pressing further into the linguistic and logical problems involved, we can conclude that we must not be misled by our loose, practical definition of validation. In saying that validation is the experience of a powerful semblance (or intransitive rapt attention), plus the granting of intellectual assent, we have established a useful idea but have not defined literature. We are, in fact, only assuming that we know what literature is, and we are talking about our relationship to this assumption. For philosophy this would never do, but for the literary classroom it works very well. When we refer to "literature" in the classroom, we have a good working understanding of what we are talking about. Part of this understanding is an awareness that there are no definite boundaries between belles lettres and other kinds of writing.

The following discussion is divided into seven chapters. The first three (Chaps. 16 to 18) are devoted to consideration of those circumstances in the classroom in which a need for intellectual assent develops. Chapters 19 and 20 are concerned with certain elements in the idea of literary order—order in some sense being a prerequisite of validation. It is in these chapters that validation of the classroom as an educational experience will be considered. Chapter 21 is devoted to the human, individual component. The closing chapter is an attempt to bring together the foregoing ideas.

16. FORCED DECISIONS & THE CULTURAL ROLE OF THE CLASSROOM

Introduction

One consequence of bringing people together for discussion of a literary work is that they force decisions upon each other. This forcing is usually not unwelcome; in fact, it is eagerly sought. As Wolfgang Iser says, people talk about books because they feel a need to do so. They seek a heightened understanding of what they experienced during their solitary reading.[7] Quite unexpected decisions are nevertheless forced upon the participants.

The result of these forced decisions is a compelling recognition that a semblance may function as what the psychologist Sigmund Koch calls a perceptual display. A further and more extreme result may be the transformation of an abstraction into a perceptual display. In other words, abstract meaning can be turned into experience by the necessity of making a responsible decision about it. Deliberate employment of the process of perceptual display is evidently one of the primary cultural functions of the literary classroom. Besides the ideas of a perceptual display and of forced decisions, in this chapter I will comment on the exploration of multiple hypotheses as a part of the total process.

Perceptual Display

A perceptual display is only the show part of show-and-tell. Teaching a child to tie a shoelace is a process of perceptual display. To teach this skill through verbal explanation alone, arms folded, is practically unimaginable. The idea of perceptual display as related to semblance and to abstractions is merely a refinement of the daily experience of communicating by showing.

The character of the refinement involved becomes apparent in the context of Sigmund Koch's remarks about the use of perceptual display. As seen in the following statement, his own concern is fundamentally with the process of definition.

> . . . if we want to pinpoint with a term any reasonably subtle, embedded, or delicately "contoured" relation or property, we must often, if using verbal means of defini-

tion, build up our defining expression from words that are *just as*, or even more "rarefied" (remote from the presumptive definition base) as the one at issue. Moreover, for defining abstract or subtle concepts based on "new" discriminations, we will have to go outside language and relate the term to a carefully controlled "perceptual display" (as it were) far more often than any logical positivist, especially of an older day, would care to admit.[8] [Italics in original.]

In offering an example of such a need for perceptual display as he has indicated, Koch discusses the problem of identifying "contours" in physical objects. If two objects have different shapes but nevertheless seem to resemble each other, how is the resemblance defined? He suggests that a skilled artist might approximate a definition by drawing the contours that are shared, in essence, by the two objects.[9] Elsewhere, Koch provides an illustration closer to our own interests. He points out that the subtleties of the art of clinical psychology can be acquired only through prolonged experience in working with one of its acknowledged masters.[10] In other words, through perception of what the master actually does, the apprentice refines his own skills.

In applying Koch's ideas about perceptual display to the literary classroom, however, we encounter a special problem. Koch speaks of going outside of language to a perceptual display. Is it possible, or natural, to seek a perceptual display outside of language as a help in understanding a literary work, a work whose medium *is* language? The answer to this question entails such complex theoretical problems, as well as such passionate convictions, that instead of attempting to answer it directly I will explore a typical classroom situation to try to understand what happens in practice.

Decisions

What we need now is an example of a perceptual display. I have chosen John Steinbeck's *Tortilla Flat* as an appropriate source, for three reasons. One reason is that here is a book

which charms almost everybody. The second is that whenever
I have assigned this novel to a class, the result has invariably
been a tremendous debate; decisions were forced. The third
reason is that *Tortilla Flat* embodies a kind of problem in the
concept of order that will finally have to be thought about.

Tortilla Flat is described by Steinbeck as an area on the out-
skirts of Monterey, California, high above the bay, where the
city meets the forest. Its inhabitants are paisanos. What is a
paisano?

> He is a mixture of Spanish, Indian, Mexican and assorted
> Caucasian bloods. His ancestors have lived in California
> for a hundred or two years. He speaks English with a
> paisano accent and Spanish with a paisano accent. When
> questioned concerning his race, he indignantly claims
> pure Spanish blood and rolls up his sleeve to show that
> the soft inside of his arm is nearly white. His color, like
> that of a well-browned meerschaum pipe, he ascribes to
> sunburn.[11]

The paisanos Steinbeck writes about work only when the mood
strikes them, which is not very often. They sleep where they
can and look to providence for sex, wine, and food. One of them,
Danny, inherited two houses from his grandfather and there-
upon invited his friend Pilon to live in one of them with him.
Pilon accepted.

> While Danny went to Monterey to have the water turned
> on, Pilon wandered into the weed-tangled back yard.
> Fruit trees were there, bony and black with age, and
> gnarled and broken from neglect. A few tent-like chicken
> coops lay among the weeds, a pile of rusty barrel hoops,
> a heap of ashes, and a sodden mattress. Pilon looked over
> the fence into Mrs. Morales' chicken yard, and after a
> moment of consideration he opened a few small holes in
> the fence for the hens. "They will like to make nests in
> the tall weeds," he thought kindly. He considered how
> he could make a figure-four trap in case the roosters
> came in too and bothered the hens. "We will live hap-
> pily," he thought again.[12]

In a foreword to the 1937 Modern Library edition, Steinbeck

asserted his affection and admiration for the paisanos of Tortilla Flat. I will quote his words, because they always become deeply involved in the debates this book provokes.

> I wrote these stories because they were true stories and because I liked them. But literary slummers have taken these people up with the vulgarity of duchesses who are amused and sorry for a peasantry. These stories are out, and I cannot recall them. But I shall never again subject to the vulgar touch of the *decent* these good people of laughter and kindness, of honest lusts and direct eyes, of courtesy beyond politeness.[13] [Italics in original.]

The trouble develops over Steinbeck's statement that the stories in *Tortilla Flat* were true. Exactly what Steinbeck meant by true I do not know, but whatever he meant the word has been repeatedly both challenged and defended. The issue over which the arguments usually develop is basically simple. Is this book in essence a true account of the lives of real people, or is it only a fantasy about unreal people in a place that never was?

In my classes, acceptance of Steinbeck's assertion that the stories in *Tortilla Flat* are true is not unusual. I don't think anyone has believed them to be literally true, but the conviction that they are true to the spirit of people and place has been quite common. The following is a fairly representative comment from a paper written in class.

> *Tortilla Flat* is told from the omniscient viewpoint with the recording of the story line being a generally objective one. Steinbeck withholds his critical judgment within the context of the novel, leaving the reader to judge for himself. But, although Steinbeck does not make moral judgments per se about Danny, Pilon, and friends, it is quite inescapable that his view is sympathetic toward their way of life as opposed to life in Monterey.

Another paper in the same class stated that "Steinbeck seems to be saying, with the use of the characters in *Tortilla Flat*, that the generalized laws and moral codes of our society do not apply to everyone and offenders of either of these codes are not necessarily evil people." Through the second of these comments, especially, the idea of a perceptual display becomes evident:

"Steinbeck seems to be saying, with the use of the characters . . ."

The thought of an author's deliberately using a character for a perceptual display is of course repugnant to every prominent critical theory in the modern western world. And yet people will persist in speaking in this way. Apparently here is only another version of the familiar conundrum of the abstract and the concrete, but it is a version that will reappear several times in this discussion. Meanwhile, it will be helpful to pause for contemplation of the frankly offensive qualities in the notion of art as a perceptual display and for consideration of what usefulness the term may have in spite of this offensiveness.[14]

Three things are seemingly wrong with the idea of a perceptual display for literary purposes: it reduces art to the function of providing concrete examples of abstract concepts, it overemphasizes mere visualization, and it transforms aesthetic experience into a problem-solving activity. It fact, however, the offensiveness of these perfectly natural objections disappears when the needs of our practical situation are examined.

First of all, our subject is not art itself but the discussion of art. It would certainly be a mistake for a reader to concentrate continuously on the idea of a perceptual display as he tried to enjoy a novel. Use of this term is not intended to modify in any way the initial, fundamental aesthetic experience. Second, it would be a mistake to think of perception, in this context, as mere visualization. Rather, I will be using the term perceptual display as synonymous with semblance, except for one difference. A semblance is an illusion of human life, together with the feeling evoked in a normal person by such an illusion; a semblance is experienced effortlessly, sometimes almost helplessly. In contrast, a perceptual display—as I will use the term—is deliberately willed by the person who experiences it. When thinking explicitly of the literary classroom, I will mean by perceptual display a deliberately willed semblance derived from a given text. On other occasions I will sometimes mean by perceptual display a semblance deliberately willed in the context of daily life. One of the principal bonds between the classroom and the life of the community is of course the fact that semblances are a natural part of daily life as well as an essential part of literary experience.

The third objection to the idea of a perceptual display is that it transforms aesthetic experience into a problem-solving activity. This last objection will be easier to talk about in the next chapter, where the notion of multiple hypotheses will be explored. For the moment, it is only necessary to remember that in a discussion of a literary work (which is our subject) people often discover they have perceived a given episode in quite different ways. When this happens, these people have a problem to solve: is one perception preferable to the other, or others? What was the author's intention?

In the context of our subject, then, the idea of a perceptual display is valuable because it encourages recognition of the process at work when people compare different readings of a given literary composition. It clarifies the cultural role of the classroom. Like almost any such idea, however, it can be pushed too far, in which case the objections mentioned earlier become substantial.

A closer approach to the way in which a perceptual display is related to the cultural role of the classroom can be made if we now contemplate a forced decision involving *Tortilla Flat*. The people who wrote the comments about this book quoted above were sincere and spontaneous in their responses to it, I feel sure, but—as usual—they were headed for trouble. I recall, for example, a day in class when such views were challenged by a young Chicano woman. Her argument was simple and direct. The Tortilla Flats in this country, she said, were not the way Steinbeck said they were. They were sordid and brutal. Go to a slum, she said, and see for yourself. The others replied that, in principle, Monterey wasn't so wonderful either. She agreed enthusiastically but said that didn't make Tortilla Flat any better.

Her view of the matter is reflected in a comment my wife once brought to me from a most unexpected source: a sober descriptive bibliography entitled *Materials Relating to the Education of Spanish Speaking People in the United States*. In this bibliography *Tortilla Flat* had been given a routine listing, with the following annotation by the bibliographer.

> Danny, the central character, returns from World War I
> and leads a carefree and unmoral life with his friends
> after he inherits two houses in Tortilla Flat. The Flat was

a tumble-down section of Monterey, California, inhabited by a mixture of Spanish, Mexican, Indian and Anglo
people. Fairly accurate, but told in a patronizing, un-
sympathetic manner.[15]

For those readers who, like myself, have been charmed by *Tortilla Flat* such a comment comes as a shock. What had been at
one moment only a playful, affectionate, mildly ironic bit of fiction (but "true" fiction) becomes a problem demanding a harsh
decision. Is *Tortilla Flat* a meretricious book, lulling middle-
class readers into acceptance of and even admiration for what is
in fact a brutalizing slum?

The Chicano woman who made the charge in my class was
not alienated. She was well liked by the others. But she demanded a decision. One of the passages that became particularly involved in the discussion that followed was the scene of the beating of Big Joe Portagee. Big Joe stole a bag of money which had
been accumulated a quarter at a time by a simple-minded character called the Pirate. Through a complicated chain of circumstances Danny and his friends, including Big Joe, had become
the guardians of the Pirate's money. After Big Joe stole the bag
of money, the others beat him until he confessed where he had
hidden it. Then they beat him some more.

The scene of the beating begins with the friends' waiting for
the guilty Big Joe to return to the house in which they all lived.
Danny found a heavy pine stick, Jesus Maria a broken pick handle, Pablo a can opener. Danny sat in a chair waiting, and his
body "weaved a little, like a rattlesnake aiming to strike." Finally Big Joe entered the house.

> "Hello," said Danny. He stood up and stretched lazily.
> He did not look at Big Joe; he did not walk directly
> toward him but at an angle, as though to pass him. When
> he was abreast, he struck with the speed of a striking
> snake. Fair on the back of Big Joe's head the stick
> crashed, and Big Joe went down completely out.
>
> Danny thoughtfully took a string of rawhide from his
> pocket and tied the Portagee's thumbs together. "Now
> water," he said.
>
> Pablo threw a bucket of water in Big Joe's face. He
> turned his head and stretched his neck, like a chicken,

and then he opened his eyes and looked dazedly at his
friends. They did not speak to him at all. Danny meas-
ured his distance carefully, like a golfer addressing the
ball. His stick smashed on Big Joe's shoulder; then the
friends went about the business in a cold and methodical
manner. Jesus Maria took the legs, Danny the shoulders
and chest. Big Joe howled and rolled on the floor. They
covered his body from the neck down. Each blow found
a new place and welted it. The shrieks were deafening.
The Pirate stood helplessly by.[16]

There is more to the scene, but this is enough for our purpose.
When it is all over Danny says, "I think he will be honest now."

What attitude should we take toward this episode? There appear to be two basic possibilities—and the Chicano woman in
my class was demanding a decision between them.

One possibility is that the reader is witnessing the cohesiveness among the group of friends. The reader is being given a perceptual display of a moral bond. These are men accustomed to
deceit and trickery; they do not trust one another very far. On
the other hand they have a code of their own, and it is this code
which holds them together. The beating is a perceptual display
of the bond which unites them. Big Joe is made "honest," and
once he has been made honest he is welcomed back into full
comradeship with the group. The friends solicitously care for his
hurts.

The second possibility is very different. Here, the reader is
witness to a sordid episode. Big Joe, presumably an alcoholic, a
wino, in the compulsion of his need steals money and buys wine.
When he enters the house he has the jug of wine in his hand. He
is given a savage beating. We see here a group of men among
whom there is a social bond of sorts, but it is always perilously
close to sheer brutality. These men are light-years away from
grasping the concept of alcoholism as a compulsion.

The Chicano woman demanded a choice between two perceptual displays, and with this demand in mind we can pursue one
step further the two ways of regarding the beating of Big Joe.
The question now becomes: what do we actually see?

We see a man being beaten by other men, but upon reflection we may well decide there is more than one way, fundamen-

tally, to perform this act of imaginary seeing. The problem of distance arises. I am reminded of a review I once read of a violent movie. I've forgotten where I read it and what the movie was, but I remember a point the reviewer made. He said the movie he was writing about was sickeningly brutal; in contrast, he said, *For a Fistful of Dollars* was like only a dream of violence. I believe he meant that in *For a Fistful of Dollars* there was more distance.

I am reminded, too, of Martin Buber's account of what happened when he learned during the World War I years that his friend Gustav Landauer had been brutally assassinated. Having been told the details of what happened, Buber says he was compelled to go through these details, one by one, in his imagination, with almost intolerable agony.[17] And, again, I am reminded of Richard Henry Dana's description of the flogging of a sailor on shipboard in *Two Years Before the Mast*. Dana, who found himself unable to watch what was happening, reported that the man never seemed to recover psychologically from the experience.

The Chicano woman was forcing upon the attention of those who disagreed with her a perceptual display of such an experience as those I've just mentioned. She was demanding a vivid perception of a confused and bloodied man who was in great pain. Steinbeck's description of the beating, which includes a passage I didn't quote about how Pablo used the can opener on Big Joe's back, fully supports such a perception. But in my experience it is rare to find a reader who has responded to the description in this way. Usually the reader is comfortably distanced from the whole episode.

Conceiving of semblance as an instrument of the human intellect, how should we use it in reading *Tortilla Flat*? What should we permit ourselves, or require ourselves, to see? The Chicano woman was taking Steinbeck literally: Tortilla Flat was a real place, and Big Joe was a real and suffering man. She demanded a decision: are you going to read the story as if it is true, or aren't you? She transformed Steinbeck's abstraction "they were true stories" into a perceptual display and made a number of us quite uncomfortable. I believe she precipitated an educational experience that was valid in the most profound sense: she incited her peers to use their powers of semblance to make a discovery. What they discovered was that they were not going to have a real Tortilla Flat without having real pain and misery too. Should this Chicano woman someday happen to read these words I trust she will forgive me for saying again, as I said then, that I think she was only partly right in her view of the novel. Before explaining in what sense I feel she was not right, however, I would like to take the next couple of chapters to follow up the idea of the use of semblance as an educational experience. I will return to *Tortilla Flat* in Chapter 19.

17. MULTIPLE HYPOTHESES

Introduction

If a semblance can function as a perceptual display, as I just claimed it can, then it can also function as a hypothesis. In this possibility, we confront a similarity between the study of literature and the bases of western scientific thought. As Daniel Bell has pointed out, one of the criteria of the scientific habit of mind is the tendency to attack problems in terms of hypotheses.

The idea of a perceptual hypothesis is actually simple and familiar. A friend comes by and says, "How would you like to go sailing this afternoon?" We consider. The wind is good; we have visual and kinetic images of the boat heeling over, the spray flying. On the illusional projection screen of our mind we form the hypothesis, in images, that today would be a fine day for sailing.

As far as the social, educational function of the literary classroom is concerned, we merely replace the idea of *a* hypothesis with the idea of *multiple* hypotheses. Again, a simple example will make the point clear. The example will not be concerned with hypotheses in the form of semblances of human experience but will lead to consideration of such hypotheses.

I have a friend who is director of a group of scientists in a physics and engineering research organization. These people design and construct extremely complex mechanisms. My friend told me one time that when a young person has just been added to the staff and has been given his first design problem, he invariably comes back with an idea for a single design. My friend then says to him, "This looks pretty good, but please go back and think up three other, different, possible designs and then we'll talk over all four of them and decide what seems most promising." In short, the first idea may not be the best idea or the first hypothesis the best hypothesis.

In the area of human experience, Hannah Arendt had in mind that same principle when she wrote in her recent book *On Violence* that the trouble with the brain trusters in the military-industrial complex is not that they are "cold-blooded enough to 'think the unthinkable,' but that they do not think!"[18] What does she mean by think?

In order to respond reasonably one must first of all be

"moved," and the opposite of emotional is not "rational," whatever that may mean, but either the inability to be moved, usually a pathological phenomenon, or sentimentality, which is a perversion of feeling.[19]

In regarding semblance as a hypothesis, we are of course concerned with an individual's ability to be moved emotionally as well as his ability to visualize. Semblance is an illusion of human life, not merely a spectacle. In other words, the Chicano woman in the previous chapter was asking the rest of us to perform a vivid act of the imagination as a hypothesis. She wanted us to enter deliberately into the world of the book *Tortilla Flat* in two different ways. One way gave relatively little weight to pain and fear, the other a good deal more. We were to report back which of these hypotheses won our assent as being true. Some people might prefer to say that the question was which hypothesis was isomorphic with human experience, others which hypothesis was validated. "True" was Steinbeck's word.

These different ways of putting the question reveal an ambiguity, however. Are we to form multiple perceptual hypotheses concerning Steinbeck's intention, or concerning the validity of his depiction of human experience, or both? Conceivably Steinbeck meant the beating scene to be distanced, not very realistic. In fact, my own opinion is that he did indeed consciously intend the scene to be distanced. The Chicano woman, in contrast, refused to read the scene as distanced. Paradoxically, she considered the book to be unrealistic, whereas her opponents thought it fairly true to life.

In thinking about the educational value of multiple perceptual hypotheses, therefore, we must keep in mind two quite different procedures. One procedure is to form several hypotheses regarding the author's intention; our objective in this case is to choose the reading most probably representing his intention. The other procedure is to form hypotheses not only about the author's intention but about the probable real-life nature of the events he is describing; our objective here is to decide whether the author's work conforms with human experience. As a practical matter, there should be full awareness that abstractions are involved in these procedures. The proposition "Life in Tortilla Flat is better than life in Monterey" is an abstraction. The decision concerning whether this proposition is correct, however, is one we tend to derive from perceptual displays.

In pursuing further the idea of the educational value of perceptual hypotheses in the literary classroom I will offer a couple of examples of such hypotheses from outside literature. The opinion I will be presenting is that discussion of literature in a classroom provides an unequaled opportunity for acquiring the socially indispensable skill of forming multiple perceptual hypotheses. For this purpose, the particular role of literature can best be seen by comparing it with other disciplines.

Perceptual Hypotheses and Social Problems

My first example of a perceptual hypothesis from outside literature is found in Riessman's *The Culturally Deprived Child*. The passage that follows, which is a description of a particular episode in a clinic, is part of a discussion of the effect of social situations on children's performance on tests.

> A few years ago a birthday party for a member of the staff at a well-known psychological clinic played a novel role in the test performance of a Negro child. Prior to the party this boy, whom we shall call James, had been described on the psychological record as "sullen, surly, slow, unresponsive, apathetic, unimaginative, lacking in inner life." This description was based on his behavior in the clinic interviews and on his performance on a number of psychological measures including an intelligence test and a personality test. His was not an unusual record; many culturally deprived children are similarly portrayed.
>
> On the day of the birthday party, James was seated in an adjoining room waiting to go into the clinician's office. It was just after the lunch hour and James had the first afternoon appointment. The conclusion of the lunch break on this particular day was used by the staff to present a surprise birthday cake to one of the clinicians who happened to be a Negro. The beautifully decorated cake

was brought in and handed to the recipient by James' clinician who was white, as were all the other members of the staff. The Negro woman was deeply moved by the cake—and the entire surprise. In a moment of great feeling, she warmly embraced the giver of the cake. James inadvertently perceived all this from his vantage point in the outer office. That afternoon he showed amazing alacrity in taking the tests and responding in the interview. He was no longer sullen and dull. On the contrary, he seemed alive, enthusiastic, and he answered questions readily. His psychologist was astonished at the change and in the course of the next few weeks retested James on the tests on which he had done so poorly. He now showed marked improvement, and she quickly revised not only the test appraisal of him on the clinical record card, but her general personality description of him as well.[20]

Apparently James's hypothesis concerning his psychologist, and perhaps concerning the clinic, was changed by what he observed. Indeed, he himself later said his attitude had been changed by what he saw.

But this apparent fact suggests a curious thought. Is it possible the psychologist's hypothesis about James was somehow affected by what happened during the giving of the cake? Did she approach her interview with James that day in an unusually buoyant and generous spirit? Was the apparent change in James actually in some degree a change in the psychologist's perception of him? In a way this is a mean and suspicious thought, but it calls to mind the ironic "moral alchemy formula" proposed by the distinguished sociologist Robert Merton. This formula reads that a given behavior must be differently evaluated according to the person who exhibits it. Presumably none of us is innocent of the occasional application of this formula, and the question I am raising is whether the white psychologist's evaluation of the black child James might have been somewhat affected by a suddenly heightened empathy with him because of the warm reception of her gift of the cake to the black woman. James evidently formed two successive perceptual hypotheses about the psychologist, so it is at least conceivable that she might have formed

two about him. In fact, I am confident both Riessman and
James's psychologist herself would accept this as a possibility.

In any event, Merton's explanation of his formula, which he
presents from a negative point of view, will serve as my second
example of the concept of multiple hypotheses from an area outside literature.

> . . . the very same behavior undergoes a complete change
> of evaluation in its transition from the in-group Abe Lin-
> coln to the out-group Abe Cohen or Abe Kurokawa. We
> proceed systematically. Did Lincoln work far into the
> night? This testifies that he was industrious, resolute,
> perseverant, and eager to realize his capacities to the full.
> Do the out-group Jews or Japanese keep these same
> hours? This only bears witness to their sweatshop mental-
> ity, their ruthless undercutting of American standards,
> their unfair competitive practices. Is the in-group hero
> frugal, thrifty, and sparing? Then the out-group villain
> is stingy, miserly, and penny-pinching. All honor is due
> the in-group Abe for his having been smart, shrewd, and
> intelligent and, by the same token, all contempt is owing
> the out-group Abes for their being sharp, cunning, crafty,
> and too clever by far . . . Was the resolute Lincoln un-
> willing to limit his standards to those of his provincial
> community? That is what we should expect of a man of
> vision. And if the out-groupers criticize the vulnerable
> areas in our society, then send 'em back where they came
> from.[21]

In Merton's terms, then, it is conceivable that the psychologist's
perception of, or hypothesis about, James was shifted a little
from an out-group to an in-group status by the incident of the
cake. The implications of this possibility can be considered further when we come, in a moment, to Robert Rosenthal.

The passage quoted from Riessman doesn't tell us much about
James, and of course Merton offers no detailed examples at all.
Where should we look for a semblance relevant to Merton's
forcefully expressed formula? To Malamud's *The Fixer*? Sol-
zhenitsyn's *Gulag Archipelago*? Ellison's *Invisible Man*? The

brilliant opening section of Ellison's novel comes vividly to mind. In this section, a black boy is treated with excruciating psychological and physical humiliation in a "ceremony" he had expected to be the occasion of honor for his achievements. Merton's formula takes on almost intolerable life in this scene, a life it does not have in his own book, although I feel sure some such vivid perception must have been present in Merton's mind as he wrote.

Will the opening section of Ellison's novel result in multiple hypotheses for a white person brought up in a segregated society? Naturally, it depends. I have no doubt it is possible to read Ellison's story with the same easy comfort experienced by most of the people in my classes when reading about the beating of Big Joe. But given a sensitive reader brought up in a segregated society and now confronting the equivalent of the Chicano woman in a good-will discussion of the opening section of *Invisible Man*—what then? I don't know; I have no predictions. Yet I have seen people accept new ideas and new attitudes in the classroom: doubtfully, usually; uneasily and defensively. That's the way things happen. For a wonderfully understanding and perceptive account of such an occasion see Benjamin DeMott's story of his experience in a Mississippi classroom.[22]

Having given attention to other disciplines, I must now emphasize that an essential element in the idea of the educational value of perceptual hypotheses in a literary classroom is the presence of a text, together with the assumption that the author's most probable intention can be discerned. The literary classroom is not, or at least in my opinion should not be, an encounter group. Our concern is not directly with the response of one personality to another but with a comparison of responses to a text. The forcing of decisions has nothing directly to do with the nature of the personal relationships among members of the group, beyond the expression of different opinions about a text. This way of putting the matter is of course idealistic: personal relationships are inevitably involved in very complex ways, as well as all those aspects of fusion that were considered earlier, in Part One. Nevertheless, there is a vast difference between the personal interaction encouraged in an institution like Esalen and a discussion structured around a passage in a literary text. To clarify this difference, we need to explore a little further the objective of forced decisions, and hence of multiple perceptual hypotheses, in a classroom.

The first step in the process of creating forced decisions is the selection of the material the group is to discuss. We look for the richest presentation of human experience available to us in a crystallized or objective form, a form that can be examined at leisure. This form is a literary masterwork. In a sense, a great literary work has the potential of making geniuses of us all. It presents to our view that rich, abundant comprehension of human experience which is presumably characteristic of the intellectual and emotional life of the greatest geniuses. Someone who had known Isaac Newton, I recall, wrote that he felt Newton's great power lay in his ability to hold a problem steadily before his mind in prolonged contemplation of all its details and implications. Malcolm Cowley, quite properly, said the same thing about William Faulkner.[23] This holding up of a subject for contemplation is a service a literary masterpiece can provide for us. We can go back to reconsider, and go back to reconsider again, while the work stands steadily before us in all its complexity and elegance. The objective of forced decisions in a classroom is best understood in this context. The objective is not to confront one ego with another but to make it possible for people to compare their individual responses to the richest environment available in a contemplative mode: that is, to the environment constituted by a great literary work.

Let us pause to think about the term "great literary work" as I am using it here. Obviously, I have in mind that kind of work which could be called ironic in the very best sense of our earlier consideration of irony: mature, aware, concerned, intense. Where are such works to be found? I myself would reply that they are usually found between the covers of books. They can also be found in the form of staged drama and of movies, but with these forms we encounter a difficulty as far as the idea of forced decisions is concerned. You can't ask the actors to go back and run through a scene again to clarify your understanding. Of course you can see a play a second time, or a fifth time; nevertheless, staged plays and movies are at a disadvantage for the purpose of forced decisions. They have their own special advantages too, but that isn't the subject just now.

I would also reply that great literary works can be found in conversations. I am still thinking of the creation of a rich environment in the contemplative or distanced mode. In a sustained, thoughtful conversation among concerned people, about a single well-defined problem in human experience, when all the imaginative and intellectual powers of the participants are being exerted and when different perceptual hypotheses are being explored, what I am now calling a great literary work may come into being. It is not the same *kind* of great literary work as *Hamlet*; it is not the same genre. But surely such an occasion deserves recognition as a literary form in our present context, which is devoted to the multiple-hypothesis aspect of the classroom experience.

The classroom itself, looked at in this way, is always potentially an art form.[24] A free-form art form, you might say. And this must be true of any classroom, not just those in which the subject matter is literature. As I listen to what people say about courses they have enjoyed in departments all over the campus I often detect that indication of "semblanced" excitement which is characteristic of the literary experience. We would be unwise to think ourselves, as literary people, somehow different from other people. We would be equally misled, however, not to recognize that the literary classroom can do some things more effectively than other kinds of classrooms. I have never taken part in, or even heard of, a spontaneous conversation providing as rich an environment as, say, *War and Peace*; and *War and Peace* is in effect the unique property of the literary classroom. It is no doubt a thirst for the kind of environment represented by *War and Peace* that leads so many philosophers to write novels. Indeed, the most moving representation I've seen of the bond between philosophy and literature is the philosopher-novelist William Gass's beautiful tribute to Ludwig Wittgenstein, where he compares Wittgenstein's agonized searching for articulation to Valéry's.[25]

It would seem, then, that the abundant virtual life of a great literary work and the potentialities of discussion within the classroom itself present a continuing invitation to multiple perceptual hypotheses. And yet, among all the people to whom Robert Merton's formula of moral alchemy might apply, probably no group should be more apprehensive than teachers.

The Pygmalion Effect

I am not thinking now just about teachers of literature but about
all teachers. And I am not thinking only of racial prejudice, although it is an ever-present hazard. What I have in mind is the
alchemy the academic world was startled to discover might take
place on a purely individual basis between a teacher and a person in his class. I am thinking of the "formula" of *Pygmalion in
the Classroom*, to use the title of Rosenthal and Jacobson's famous book. What these researchers asserted was that when a
teacher (or a supervisor on a job) expected an individual to do
well, the individual actually tended to live up to this expectation.
Children who were believed by their teachers to be bright actually tended to improve significantly in their performance on
IQ tests, even though there was no basis for the teachers' belief.
Men training to be auto mechanics or welders whose supervisors
had been led to believe, falsely, that these particular men were
gifted did excel in their work. Their superior performance appeared inexplicable, except in terms of the Pygmalion effect.
But a subsequent finding relates more directly, and more sadly,
to Merton's formula. When children who were *not* regarded by
their teachers as "bloomers" did happen to increase in IQ, the
teachers' attitude tended to be negative. The more such children
improved, the "*less* well-adjusted, interesting and affectionate
the teachers thought them."[26]
  Evidently teachers are not immune to what Merton calls
moral alchemy. A teacher may respond enthusiastically to
achievement by one individual and with displeasure to the very
same achievement by another. The factors determining the
teacher's attitudes apparently include far more subtle elements
than racial or social prejudice, although these prejudices were
unmistakably among the elements that might be involved.
  Do those of us in the academic world have the moral, emotional, and imaginative capacity to learn to form multiple perceptual hypotheses concerning the human beings in our classrooms? When our initial perception of an individual begins to
lose its correspondence to his actual performance, can we recognize the need for a new hypothesis? I don't know, but I sincerely
believe we can, despite Rosenthal's dismaying report of the

moral alchemy he sometimes observed in the classroom. Of course no profession ever fully achieves its objectives; I am not talking about perfection. But I believe most people who enter the teaching profession are strongly committed to their important cultural role. Rosenthal remarks that when evidence of their bias was pointed out to teachers they "reacted with surprise and insight."[27]

Nevertheless, acquaintance with Rosenthal's research is not in itself enough. Much as I admire the literary perceptiveness of Cleanth Brooks, I feel Brooks was careless about the implications of his terse comment that "a formula can be learned and applied."[28] The application of formulas is often a difficult and perplexing process. Learning the formula of moral alchemy or of the Pygmalion effect is no guarantee that the necessary perceptual hypothesis will follow. We all need practice. Such practice is, however, a routine element in the best classrooms I know, even when it is not formally conceptualized. Perhaps the art of multiple perceptual hypotheses is an art that can be learned only through certain kinds of experience. Experience in the classroom is what we have been talking about.

Two last comments about perceptual displays, or hypotheses, are needed.

First, it must be remembered that multiple perceptual displays are not themselves any assurance that wisdom and understanding will prevail in responses to a text. The weakness of perceptual displays is that they may not reflect reality, as any study of the literature concerning attempts to found utopias quickly confirms. The weakness of "facts," on the other hand, is that they do not adequately present the quality of felt experience. It is this weakness in the usual idea of facts that Hannah Arendt had in mind. Thinkers in the area of human relations, as well as in many other areas, who do not employ perceptual displays are not good thinkers. The use of multiple perceptual displays, or semblances, is only a skill, however; it is no guarantee of valid decisions. The relationship of validation to semblance is, again, a subject for the next chapter.

Finally, the idea of significance discussed earlier should be mentioned once more. There is no special problem here, only a need to recognize that when more than one perceptual display is derived from a given passage, the question of significance almost inevitably arises. What seems at first the best perception may be only that one which has a special personal import. The usual care must be taken to discriminate between meaning and significance.

18. THE DISCRIMINATION POOL

Introduction

If a perceptual display is to be used in making a definition, as Sigmund Koch suggests it can be, then the display itself must be meaningful. The value of a display for such a purpose, however, is dependent on many different factors. Most obviously, it is dependent on the ability of the observer to understand what he is seeing. To understand a display of highly complex materials, Koch declares, it is therefore necessary to develop a group of highly trained people. These people, he remarks, might be thought of as a discrimination pool or a language community.[29] He points out that even within a given field of science subgroups have difficulty understanding one another's technical discussions. Naturally, they also have difficulty understanding perceptual displays involving one another's equipment and materials. A discrimination pool is, then, a group of people capable of unusually subtle and precise discriminations in some area of knowledge. An example is the Eskimos' legendary ability to identify and name a great many different varieties of snow.

As my example indicates, discrimination pools are not limited to science. I am not talking about a social elite. In fact, the idea is a commonplace. It is recognized even in the art of burgling, where it is said it takes a thief to catch a thief. Evidently two elements are necessary for the creation of a discrimination pool. One is people with the necessary aptitudes. For thievery, it is easy to see, a considerable recklessness, moral defiance, and manual dexterity would be essential. The other necessary element is a methodology. Safe-crackers, a subgroup, have a high technology. In the humanities, the idea of methodology in defining discrimination pools is even more critical than in science and technology because of the lack of ways of testing results. Indeed, as we continue to examine the idea of a discrimination pool in relationship to the humanities, and especially in relationship to the literary classroom, the role of methodology or discipline will become increasingly important. An example from historiography will indicate both why this is so and why we need to be cautious about carrying such an idea too far. Sometimes people become so enthusiastic about a methodology that they begin to trust it to make its own decisions.

The Problem of the Idea of Autonomy

My example of what seems to me an overemphasis on methodology will be taken from an analysis by Leon J. Goldstein of the validation of historical writing. In his analysis, Goldstein discusses the idea of history as an autonomous discipline. If I have understood his intention correctly, what he means by autonomous discipline is something like the following. News stories often refer to the great achievements of the medical profession, yet they also sometimes describe cases in which an individual physician has made a serious professional mistake. We have a good deal of confidence in the profession as a whole, but we can't rule out the possibility that in a given instance any physician might commit an error. Therefore, it could be argued that our greatest confidence is given not to individual physicians but to the methodology or discipline of the profession as a whole.

Similarly, but even more emphatically, Goldstein declares that history as a discipline depends on shared meanings and values. Although an individual historian may make an erroneous judgment, the discipline as a whole, he believes, tends to detect and correct the judgment.

> [Historians] have an organized structure of historical research. We have widely-shared techniques and generally-agreed-to results. We have, in sum, an inter-subjective discipline, and while it is carried on by individuals, they are committed to a common enterprise *having determinate features*. The claim, then, that history is autonomous need only be made with reference to that discipline. History is autonomous in a way historians may well not be. It is, then, the autonomous discipline of history which controls and has the final say about historical evidence.[30] [Italics in original.]

Goldstein's view seems on the whole quite sensible, but it does contain a problem in logic which appeared in our earlier consideration of interpretation and which we need to be careful about in the present context. The problem lies essentially in the words "determinate" and "autonomous." I'm not sure what Goldstein means in saying history is an autonomous discipline.

The meaning in my dictionary closest to what he apparently has in mind is "without outside control." Perhaps I have misunderstood him, but he seems to be describing history as a discipline, or methodology, which is complete within itself. As we will see in a moment, the idea that any discipline can be complete has been severely challenged, as no doubt Goldstein is aware. He says further, however, that the techniques of historical research are widely shared and the results generally agreed to.

A logical difficulty arises from assuming that a shared methodology can ensure a valid result. Astrologers come to mind; according to my understanding, these people have a shared methodology which doesn't work. The results historians achieve are of course far superior in quality to the results obtained by astrologers. And the successes of historians are admittedly heavily dependent on their having acquired a subtle and complex methodology of research and formulation. My only reservation about what Goldstein says is that while the methodology is necessary, it is not self-sufficient or determinate. Logically, it is conceivable that an entire generation of historians might appear who were foolish and who would systematically employ the best methodology with only foolish results. I do not expect this to happen. Brilliant and dedicated men and women will continue to produce intelligent results in historical research and writing. These men and women, not an autonomous discipline, will have the final say about historical evidence.

Although I can't agree with the logical implications of his assertion, therefore, I do think the practical import of Goldstein's remarks is entirely sensible. We can place a great deal of confidence in the group of people who are known as historians. We can do this because, like any discrimination pool, they combine intelligence with methodology, and their methodology is sophisticated and effective even if it isn't autonomous.

The Incompleteness of Any Formal Discourse

No complex methodology is autonomous, or capable of ensuring valid results without the active participation of the intelligences of the persons who make up the discrimination pool. Since we will soon be confronting once more the idea of logical order as

it relates to the concept of the classroom we should give renewed
attention to this proposition.

I would, for this reason, like to quote at length from a lucid
and relevant statement made by Michael Polanyi during a discussion with the nuclear physicist Eugene Wigner. The key term
in Polanyi's remarks is "incompleteness." What he means, if I
understand correctly, is essentially that no methodology for seeking knowledge can ever function by itself; it will always be incomplete without the addition of an active intelligence. In his
comment on ostensive definitions, incidentally, we encounter another version of the notion of perceptual display. Polanyi's statement follows.

> What we have heard [from Professor Wigner] was that
> the formal structure of physics is incomplete and has to
> be supplemented. Now, I think that such incompleteness
> has been mentioned often in quite different contexts. For
> example, it is very common among philosophers to say
> that reflection on ourselves is necessarily incomplete
> because there is always something which is still reflect-
> ing at the last moment which has not been reflected upon.
> In metamathematics, to talk of another kind of reflection,
> there is also an incompleteness; metamathematics is in-
> trinsically incomplete in so far as it remains unformal-
> ized, because that which reflects *on* the formalisms of
> mathematics cannot itself be formalized to the same ex-
> tent as its own subject matter. Another very common and
> perfectly correct statement, also often made by philoso-
> phers, is that all the definitions of classes or external ob-
> jects must end up with reference to an undefined form of
> ostensive definition, which is very much like the kind of
> personal participation which people describe in the mat-
> ter of the ultimate link of observation. That is, if you
> have a syllogism, you cannot really conclude anything
> since all you have before you is a conditional statement;
> you still have to detach the consequent, and nobody au-
> thorizes you to do that except your own common sense.
> This reminds me, of course, of the Gödelian theorem of
> the incompleteness of axiomatic systems of a certain rich-
> ness (as represented perhaps by arithmetic). Moreover,

there is an incompleteness of any mathematical theory of experience (I have tried to define that myself), in so far as it is meaningless unless it is supplemented by a process by which it will bear on experience. It always has to be in a kind of tacit relation to something on which it bears. In mathematics we have tried to become more formal than has been usual by completely transposing it into symbols and the operation of symbols. Then it turns out that this only leads to an uninterpreted mathematical or, generally speaking, deductive system which doesn't say anything about anything. And as soon as you interpret a deductive system, you introduce an unformalized procedure. There might be, therefore (I would like to hope that there *could* be), a general theory of incompleteness, a general theory of the incompleteness of formal discourse of any kind.[31] [Italics in original.]

At the conclusion of Polanyi's statement, Wigner expressed agreement with what he had said.

The import of the line of thought we've been following all along is that methodologies of any sort, powerful as they may be, are no more than tools in the hands of those trained to use them. In this sense, all methodologies are incomplete. Our ultimate resource is a discrimination pool, which is a group of people reinforcing one another in their struggle with subtle distinctions.

So we come to a fundamental question. What kind of discrimination pool should the literary classroom, as a cultural institution, seek to create? This is a question to which there is surely no single, final answer. Still, some useful things can be said in response to it. The next two chapters will approach this question from the point of view of genre, which is one of the principal means of discrimination in literature, and from the point of view of the concept of order itself. Subsequent chapters will relate the concepts of genre and order to human relationships in the classroom and finally to the idea of validation.

Introduction

Genre is, in English, an awkward substitute for "kind of literature," but to talk of kinds of literature is even more awkward than to talk of genres. The word "genre" is most commonly used in calling attention to a discrimination. The gross discriminations are easy: novel, poem, play. As the discriminations become progressively finer, disagreements arise. No one doubts that the concept of genres is valid, but agreement on a general system of classification of literary works into finely subdivided genres is unlikely. The practical value of the term lies chiefly in its power to define rather than to classify.

A familiar example of the defining role of genre is seen in the treatment of Petrarchan and Shakespearian sonnets. The special defining character of the Shakespearian sonnet is of course the concluding couplet, which puts a demand on the poet for a sharp, emphatic closure. The Petrarchan moves more slowly at the end. In choosing between these two subgenres, the poet thus to some degree chooses the effect he will create. The existence of literary genres is said therefore both to give the writer a wide freedom of choice and to lock him into a form once he has made a choice. The idea of being locked in requires one qualification, however. In addition to providing a basic form, one of the values of a genre is that it makes possible the principle of deviation. Within the general range of the reader's expectation, the author can pleasurably alter the form he is employing. When the Shakespearian sonnet first appeared, part of the fun was that although it was a sonnet it was not a Petrarchan sonnet. Whether an author adheres strictly to a genre or deviates from it, his intention is expressed to some degree in his basic choice of genre.

The great value of the idea of genre lies in its power to provide a commanding view of an entire work, thereby presenting a means of relating the individual parts to one another as well as to the controlling intention. Looked at from one point of view, the concept of genre is a way of objectifying the concept of intention. Looked at from the opposite point of view, genre is the structure without which intention would have no means of manifesting itself or perhaps even of coming into existence. Nevertheless, the natural tendency to begin substituting the word "structure" for genre indicates a need for taking thought. There are literary structures which are not commonly regarded as genres. Do these other structures have the power of relating parts to one another and to the work as a whole? Apparently some do. Let us note just one example—very briefly, since genre, not other structures, is the subject with which we will be concerned.

Style will serve as the example. Not so long ago it would have seemed odd to speak of style as structure, but the structuralists have eliminated that concern. The first sentences in Crane's "The Open Boat" will do as an instance of the relevant quality of style: "None of them knew the colour of the sky. Their eyes glanced level, and were fastened upon the waves that swept toward them."[32] Without attempting to analyze the sources of the effect these sentences create, we can agree that they establish certain kinds of expectations just as strongly as does the announcement that a given literary work belongs to the genre "short story." The style of the sentences tells us, in some degree, where we are going, what the structure of the coming experience will be. And when we have completed our reading we look back upon the style of the story as a whole and perceive that it has structured our vision in certain ways, both enabling us to see and limiting what we see. The concept of genre, then, is not the only structural aspect of literature which might serve our purposes.

On the other hand, it is the most useful. There are two reasons for this usefulness. One is that the idea of genre, broadly conceived, is relatively easy to grasp and to talk about. The other is that, although it has the advantage of being quite objective in many ways, genre can be—and has been—effectively related to the personal, subjective aspect of literature. This relationship has been formalized in the concept of intrinsic genre.

Genre and Intrinsic Genre

E. D. Hirsch defines intrinsic genre in this way:

> *[An intrinsic genre] is that sense of the whole by which an interpreter can correctly understand any part in its de-*

> *terminacy*. Since the interpreter can do this before he
> knows the precise sequence of words in the utterance as
> a whole, and since more than one sequence of words can
> fulfill his generic expectations without altering his un-
> derstanding of the parts he has understood, it follows that
> this determining sense of the whole is not identical with
> the particular meaning of the utterance. That particular
> meaning arises when the generic expectations have been
> fulfilled in a particular way by a particular sequence of
> words.[33] [Italics in original.]

That is to say, if a man falls from a high building he perceives
at once that he is involved in the genre "falling." Genre means
a kind; falling is a kind of experience. Let us pursue the analogy
a little. Obvious clues the man has that he is indeed falling are
reports by his internal organs and various visual observations.
Perhaps he bounces off some lower rooftops and projections on
the way down. The character of the particular rooftops and projections he encounters is in one sense unimportant; they could
be changed without affecting the genre. On the other hand, the
character of the rooftops and projections will certainly participate to some degree in the particular conclusion he comes to.
They will help determine whether the falling man reaches the
end of his generic experience dead or only bruised. In either
case, it's the same genre. Still another consideration appears,
however. If a falling man encountered a rooftop without having
noticed he was falling, he would be vastly puzzled. It's the generic expectation that gives meaning to such an encounter. For
the same reason if, halfway down, the falling man stopped falling and levitated, he would no doubt feel bemused. His situation
would resemble that of a reader of *Catch-22*, which seems so different a novel at the end from what it was at the outset. In contrast, Iris Murdoch is said by some to have been successful in a
similar attempt at shifting from the comic to the serious in *A
Fairly Honourable Defeat. Catch-22* is a good book for all that;
control of genre isn't everything.
    Finally, it should be emphasized that immediately after the
start of the fall the man is able to predict the kind of experience
he is about to have. He anticipates encounters. The precise character of the encounters can be learned only by waiting until

they occur, but the sense of falling assures him that encounters there will be. This quality of predictability, limited though it must remain, is the factor noted earlier of the mind's strange power to give proper emphasis to the words in a sentence never before read. As Hirsch indicates, genre—whether in the form of sentences, or novels, or falls—is that sense of the whole by means of which we grasp the meaning of the parts.

Actually, what Hirsch has in mind in his definition, and what I myself referred to at the beginning, is not genre but intrinsic genre. I've been sliding over the distinction between the two terms, but the distinction is really at the focus of my concern. We are interested in being able to make much finer definitions than merely those of Petrarchan and Shakespearian sonnets. What we would like to know is how it is possible to grasp the relationships among the particular parts of a sonnet never before read. Hirsch says, in effect, that this is made possible by our perception of the intrinsic genre as a whole. Hirsch's intrinsic genre is designed to address the same problem as Dewey's enveloping quality (see p. 47). That is, how does the mind intuit the nature of a whole with which it is still largely unacquainted? Hirsch relies more strongly on the formal concept of type than Dewey does.

The idea of an intrinsic genre thus represents a narrowing of the concept of genre as a whole. Or, looking at it from the opposite point of view, we might say intrinsic genre is a slight depersonalizing and broadening of the author's intention.[34] As Hirsch says, to understand the first lines of *Paradise Lost* we need to grasp the type of epic it is in a more specific way than any label could indicate. It helps, but it is not sufficient for us to know its genre is that of a Christian-humanistic epic. We need to grasp its intrinsic genre or quality in the same more intimate way we grasp the quality of a sentence as we start to read it.

The concept of an intrinsic genre therefore provides a helpful insight into one of the elements we want our discrimination pool to learn to perceive, as I will try to illustrate further in a moment. But I must in honesty pause to say I feel this concept is ultimately ambiguous.[35] Without going into detail here, I will remark only that it seems to me to involve the following difficulties. In its reliance on the concept of type, it appears to transgress upon that old and stubborn fact that the human mind can create a new type almost at will—and is a new, unique type a type? How is a new type of meaning, seen in one instance only, to be distinguished from a particular meaning? Second, in the narrowing of the concept of genre to intrinsic genre there is an implication that an intrinsic genre is somehow snuggling up to a particular; but nobody understands how the mind relates universals, or genres, to particulars, as the unsettled question of real-vs.-nominal univerals demonstrates. And, last, although the idea of intrinsic genres does seem to represent a narrowing of genre it also, paradoxically, involves an opening out to accommodate the areas of vocabulary, syntax, common backgrounds of experience, and other elements of socialization. In these comments I am not saying anything, as far as I am aware, that Hirsch would not say too, only putting it more emphatically.

Because of these perplexities, I would prefer to say that even though such concepts as intrinsic genre and enveloping quality imply a kind of perception people can and should learn to make, nobody can explain how the act is done. And this difficulty is intensified if to our present considerations we add, as we must, the principle of fusion discussed earlier. In fact, if we simply drop from Hirsch's definition the words intrinsic genre, with their implication of the problem of universals versus particulars, the statement left is exactly what we need for our practical purposes. What we want our discrimination pool to learn to perceive is "that sense of the whole by which an interpreter can correctly understand any part in its determinacy."

In spite of all these misgivings about the concept of intrinsic genre, it is a concept and a term I will continue to use. Its practical value may be limited by its ambiguity, but it is not destroyed. The concept of intrinsic genre reminds us continuously of the fact that genres do exist and that whatever conclusions we draw about an author's intention must be consonant with this fact. The concept of intrinsic genre prepares us for the discovery that disagreements which at first seem to spring from nothing more than personal prejudice may have their origin in the existence of mutually exclusive structures.

Consideration of the intrinsic genre of a work has the practical value, finally, of being adaptable to virtually any critical methodology. Fundamentally, the idea of literary kinds is a key opening a door to many different interpretative techniques. It is not, however, a panacea; it is merely an instrument.

Intrinsic Genre and Tortilla Flat

The ideas just discussed can be illustrated by returning to *Tortilla Flat*. Previously, I described an incident in one of my classes in which a Chicano woman challenged the assumption made by others that this novel presented Tortilla Flat as a better place to live in than Monterey. She pointed to the scene of the beating of Big Joe and reminded us that Steinbeck had called these stories true. With this episode in my class in mind we might consider the genre and the intrinsic genre, respectively, of *Tortilla Flat*. Our ultimate objective is to establish relationships among the concepts of forced decisions, perceptual display, and the kind of discrimination the literary classroom can develop.

Everyone agrees *Tortilla Flat* is a mock epic. Danny and his friends are explicitly compared to King Arthur and his knights. "Mock" means only something like "pretend," however. Steinbeck does not make fun of the Arthurian legend. This novel is not a parody. Nor does it, like Barthelme's *Snow White*, belong to that genre which makes fun of genre.

Unthinkingly, I said it is a novel, but it's very loose in construction: much like the picaresque novel in form, which is at the very edge of noveldom. Steinbeck called it stories.

It is humorous, gently ironic (in the popular sense); the only irascibility found in it is directed at capitalism: "The paisanos are clean of commercialism, free of the complicated systems of American business, and, having nothing that can be stolen, exploited or mortgaged, that system has not attacked them very vigorously."[36]

In a general sense, it is primitivistic. Perhaps it is best thought of as an attempt to write a pastoral; if so, it is a technically unsuccessful attempt.[37]

To what genre does this book belong, then? Its genre is that of mock epic ↔ picaresque novel ↔ humor ↔ unmalicious irony ↔ primitivism ↔ and/or pastoralism. And Steinbeck said it was true, and the bibliographer that it was patronizing.

With this information before us, the concept of intrinsic genre, or even of enveloping quality, becomes attractive because the question of how best to regard the scene of the beating of Big Joe is not clearly answered by information about possible genres.[38] The concepts of mock epic, of the picaresque, of primitiv-

ism, of true stories, and of patronizing stories can all comfortably accommodate our regarding the beating scene either as a
display of forthright brutality or as an incident so distanced that
it doesn't have much emotional effect. Therefore, the concept of
genre doesn't help decide between the Chicano woman's interpretation and that of the others. At first thought, the idea of unmalicious irony as a genre might seem to exclude brutality and
thus determine the meaning of the beating scene, but the author's open irascibility toward capitalism makes this possibility
doubtful. Steinbeck is ready enough to be brutal about capitalism. Here is another instance of such irascibility, as Steinbeck describes what was happening in the streets of Monterey one afternoon: "Through the streets of the town, fat ladies, in whose eyes
lay the weariness and the wisdom one sees so often in the eyes of
pigs, were trundled in overpowered cars toward tea and gin
fizzes at the Hotel Del Monte."[39] This is irony, but it is an irony
fully capable of appearing in the company of brutality; there is,
in fact, a similar passage in Chapter 15 of *The Grapes of Wrath*.
Moreover, the reasoning that excludes irony, as a genre concept, from a determining role in the interpretation of the beating scene also excludes humor from this purpose. The question
of how to regard the beating scene is not answered by exploring
the genre of the book.

The idea of the *intrinsic* genre of *Tortilla Flat* can be approached through the details of the beating scene. After the beating Big Joe finally comes to and groans, but:

> The paisanos paid no attention to him until at last Jesus
> Maria, that prey to the humanities, untied Big Joe's
> thumbs and gave him a jar of wine. "Even the enemies
> of our Saviour gave him a little comfort," he excused
> himself.
>
> That action broke up the punishment. The friends
> gathered tenderly about Big Joe. They laid him on Dan-
> ny's bed and washed the salt out of his wounds [which
> Pilon and Pablo had put there]. They put cold cloths on
> his head and kept his jar full of wine. Big Joe moaned
> whenever they touched him. His morals were probably
> untouched, but it would have been safe to prophesy that

never again would he steal from the paisanos of Danny's house.[40]

As far as the question of how we should perceive this scene is concerned, two elements reveal Steinbeck's probable intention: the author's description of Jesus Maria as a prey to the humanities and the author's remark that Big Joe's morals were probably untouched. Both elements create distance between the reader and Big Joe's suffering. This scene is not to be regarded in the same way as Dana's description of the sailor who was changed by the flogging he received.

Such a discrimination is a first step toward what might be called recognition of the intrinsic genre of the book. The discrimination could have been made much earlier, and by experienced readers it is routinely so made. For the facts are that the beating scene is only one item in a series and more broadly one item in a pattern. The series is comprised of thefts by Big Joe, and punishments. He is introduced with an account first of his enlistment in the army while drunk, and later of his experience in the infantry, where he stole two gallons of cooked beans and the major's horse and was sent to prison. The second occurrence of stealing, like the third, was a theft from Danny's house. Big Joe stole one of Danny's blankets and traded it for wine. Pilon, who discovered the theft, took the thief by the throat to shake him, but Big Joe was so big that Pilon succeeded only in shaking himself. As punishment, Pilon then made Big Joe do all the digging on a treasure hunt. Big Joe was afraid of Pilon when Pilon was armed with a righteous cause. The third theft was the Pirate's money; and so, to echo Hugh Kenner, with three we eliminate chance. Perhaps one additional incident deserves mention, however. On an evening not long before the day of the beating, Big Joe went to sleep while a woman was trying to get him to make love to her. She became so angry she began hitting him with her fists. To protect himself from this punishment, he held the woman tightly in his arms, and as he did so love finally came to Big Joe.

Big Joe's monumental insensitivity distances him from the reader, and this distance is a principal factor in shielding the reader from the perception of real pain in the beating scene. The other characters, in other ways, are similarly distanced and the whole book is wrought into a delightfully unreal, irresponsible realm. It is a realm which is nevertheless given point and its own seeming reality through contrast to the relentless presence of the irrational and savage Monterey. Offered a choice between that Tortilla Flat and that Monterey which appear *within the book*, who would not choose Tortilla Flat?

Our first discrimination, then, is the simple choice of the book's Tortilla Flat as opposed to the book's Monterey. Our second discrimination is an awareness of how this choice is related to the intrinsic genre of the book. As Hirsch says, an intrinsic genre cannot be given a label; it's a sense of the character of the whole. But elements contributing to the intrinsic genre can be analyzed out, as just observed with respect to the beating scene, and perceptions can be sharpened through this means. Having grasped the intrinsic genre of *Tortilla Flat*, any reader will be slow to let it serve as a basis for judgments about the real Tortilla Flat. Such caution does not in any way imply what the final judgment should be about the relative merits of Tortilla Flat and Monterey; it is only a recognition that the author's intention concerning the materials he was working with may or may not have corresponded to a reality mature readers could assent to.

Intrinsic Genre and the Author's Intention

Two other discriminations concerning *Tortilla Flat* will conclude this exploration of its intrinsic genre. The first is concerned with the bibliographer's view of the book, the second with the author's. The second will constitute a further consideration of the idea of the author's intention first taken up in Part Two (see pp. 12 ff.).

Searching for the truth about Latin America, the bibliographer has failed to grasp the intrinsic genre of the book. Perhaps the bibliographer's view can be safely filed away under the heading of "significance" only. If he has not completely misinterpreted the book, perhaps he has at least made the common mistake of confusing significance and meaning.

As evidence of what Steinbeck intended, we might think fur-

ther about a couple of sentences quoted earlier with reference
to the distancing in the book: "Big Joe moaned whenever they
touched him. His morals were probably untouched, but it would
have been safe to prophesy that never again would he steal from
the paisanos of Danny's house." Apart from the distancing, what
was Steinbeck's probable intention in writing "His morals were
probably untouched"? Or, to put it another way, what perceptual hypotheses can be formed with respect to this sentence?
This last question may seem odd. But let's consider.

The question is odd in the sense that Steinbeck's statement
about Big Joe's morals is an abstract proposition. Looked at in
this way, nothing perceptual appears to be involved. Yet the
statement does have a perceptual dimension, if we keep in mind
the fact that perceptual does not necessarily mean visual. The
statement is a judgment by one person (the implied author)
about another. The reader becomes aware of an "affective" relationship; he perceives the implied author's attitude toward Big
Joe. He forms a perceptual hypothesis concerning the implied
author's emotional posture. I presume everyone would agree this
posture is patronizing. The word "patronizing," however, is a
signifier for a complex emotional state. Steinbeck insisted, almost in anger, that these are true stories, and I cannot believe
he consciously meant to be patronizing.

What, then, could he possibly have meant by "true"? Two
hypotheses immediately suggest themselves if we merely reconsider where to place the emphasis in reading his words. Did he
mean *true* stories or true *stories*? My own intuition is the latter.

When Steinbeck's word "true" is examined in relationship to
the idea of intrinsic genre, the meaning the word initially assumes is, I believe, something like authentic, coherent, internal-
ly consistent. Surely Steinbeck would have made these claims
for his stories. But true implies more than this. It implies that
if you hold them up alongside the real Tortilla Flat you will
find that everything in these stories corresponds to something
in the real community. As noted earlier, this implication of true
is made insistent by Steinbeck's deliberate and favorable contrasting of Tortilla Flat to the real Monterey and the value system Monterey represents.

Perhaps in some degree this implication is valid, as the bibliographer himself indicated it to be. That is, if we examined the

book part by part and compared each part to a real Tortilla Flat, or barrio, we might discover that in spirit and in principle each episode bears a strong resemblance to elements in the life of the real community. It is my opinion that this is indeed what we would discover, although I have no great authority for holding such a view. We would certainly agree, however, that in these stories there are also both exaggeration and incompleteness. Danny's prowess as a lover, for instance, is wildly exaggerated in the account of the party at the end of the book. On the other hand, much has obviously been left out of these stories about Tortilla Flat: the misery, the hopelessness, the lack of self-esteem. And here, I should imagine, is the source of the bibliographer's complaint, as it unquestionably was of the Chicano woman's complaint. From their point of view, the account of the beating of Big Joe is incomplete, patronizing.

The moment these stories are assessed, through perceptual hypotheses, against the full range of human experience they appear greatly limited and incomplete. They are deliberately limited at the very beginning by their assignment to a mock, a let's-pretend genre. We may conclude that if Steinbeck could have remade the world in any image he desired he would have created an Edenic garden of Tortilla Flats in which pain was only a minor discomfort and right living was maintained through the menace of a Monterey just beyond the wall. A penalty he paid for his vision was the necessity of patronizing it. A mature mind can assent to and delight in *Tortilla Flat* as representative of a special, limited genre, but it cannot assent to the vision apart from the genre, and it is disturbed by a feeling that the author was not thoroughly self-conscious in his employment of the genre. It is the implication of a lack of self-awareness that is so disturbing in Steinbeck's "true." The situation can be contrasted to Tolkien's *The Hobbit*, with its similar, although more restrained, irascibility and its similar condescension. The contrast lies in the fact that, as far as I know, Tolkien never said "true."

Tortilla Flat is admittedly a simple example, but I do not believe its simplicity affects the inferences drawn from it. Although many works of art are far richer than *Tortilla Flat* and approach closer to Cleanth Brooks's ideal of the ironic work, no work of art is a complete vision of human experience. What would the events of *Beowulf* look like from Grendel's point of view? John Gardner's recent novel *Grendel* explores this question. Stoppard's *Rosencrantz and Guildenstern Are Dead* explores the opinion these luckless courtiers might have of events in *Hamlet*. Nowhere in *Hamlet* does Shakespeare provide adequately, at least in Stoppard's judgment, for the kind of view these men might hold. As Jacques Lacan remarks, "In simple terms . . . in a universe of discourse nothing contains everything."[41] Since works of art are always incomplete, there is always a possibility of disagreement about them.

Thus the intrinsic genre of *Tortilla Flat* must be formulated in such a way as to provide for an intention that was affectionate, true (in principle), humorous, ironic (in the popular sense), patronizing, and incomplete as far as a realistic presentation of life in Tortilla Flat is concerned. We could describe the author's intention itself in the same terms but with a crucial exception. Were the author's intention our primary concern, these terms would begin to seem excessively abstract. We would want to pursue them into the details of the handling of specific elements.

In any case, we still have the problem of the bibliographer's opinion to settle.

20. MEDIATION & THE CONCEPT OF ORDER

Introduction

The bibliographer is more of a problem than he seemed at first. It has become clear that in what a psychologist would call operant terms the views of Steinbeck and the bibliographer are actually not in conflict. The bibliographer said the novel is patronizing, and we have seen that in the novel Steinbeck did indeed patronize. The two men are therefore clearly in agreement in the operant sense, and yet at the same time it is surely all wrong to suppose they could feel themselves to be agreeing in spirit.

As so often happens, the idea of semblance throws a ray of light on this conundrum. If pressed hard, Steinbeck might declare that what he intended was not an insult but a genre. He might argue that the patronizing was only an element in a semblance and that the semblance in turn was controlled by a particular genre, or more exactly by a particular intrinsic genre. You can't tell an Irish joke without having an Irishman in it; and I've known some Irishmen who could relish an Irish joke. The "patronizing" isn't necessarily all that much of an insult. I feel sure Steinbeck meant no more than the equivalent of a good-natured Irish joke. In fact, my guess is he meant less, that he wasn't thinking about jokes in the Irish-joke sense at all. He'd be more inclined to make deliberate Irish jokes about the establishment in Monterey than about Tortilla Flat. The entire body of his work bears out such a conclusion.

Is the bibliographer sympathetically smiling? I doubt it. Humor is a tricky business, and there is humor in *Tortilla Flat*. It is one thing for people to share in humor directed at themselves, even-handed all around, or for a prosperous middle-class Irishman to enjoy an Irish joke; it is a very different thing when the humor, the joke, comes from both outside and above, from a middle-class Anglo joking about a slumdweller of another ethnic group. And this is the point the bibliographer saw, looking at the book from his special perspective. He might therefore quite understandably declare that his feeling about Steinbeck's intention is somewhat different from Steinbeck's feeling about his own intention. Accordingly, we are compelled to move the bibliographer's view of the book over into the significance category. Steinbeck's meaning, which the bibliographer correctly understands, has for the bibliographer a distasteful significance.

But, still, what right have we to say that the meaning the book has for the bibliographer is only significance and not really meaning at all? What facts are changed by these words?

This question is the most fundamental we can ask concerning intention, significance, forced decisions, and—ultimately—validation. It is a question which in one form or another has been encountered throughout our discussion.

Suppose *Tortilla Flat* is lying open on a table. On one side of the table Steinbeck is standing, on the other side the bibliographer. These are intelligent, perceptive men. They talk, and they understand one another sympathetically. Steinbeck talks about genres and intentions. He explains he meant no harm. The bibliographer understands and believes him. The bibliographer in his turn points out that sometimes, in certain situations, it is hard to be made the subject of a joke, to be patronized. Steinbeck replies that he realizes what the bibliographer says is true and that he had no intention of patronizing. He assumed, he declares, that the distancing involved in the genre was thorough protection against any personal injury. The bibliographer admits the logic of this assumption. Complete and sympathetic comprehension has been reached on both sides of the table. The bibliographer is convinced Steinbeck had no deliberate intention of implying an arrogance toward the people of the real Tortilla Flat. Only one difficulty remains: the book is still there, open on the table between the two men. The book will not go away. Knowing what Steinbeck's intention was does not render the book inoffensive to all readers. The men fall silent—or at least I should think they would.

The only way to eliminate the problem represented by the difference in view between these two men would be to eliminate the *possibility* of a difference. If we lived in a society without slums and without social classes the potential sting of the patronizing in *Tortilla Flat* would be greatly diminished. There would remain only the implied *willingness* to patronize. As long as slums persist, however, nothing can prevent the unintended arrogance from bursting out of the genre of *Tortilla Flat* whenever a susceptible or even a particularly thoughtful and sensitive reader takes up the book. Steinbeck's protestation of good intentions could not hold it back. The arrogance is always there, unintended though it may have been and unnoticed by many readers though it may be.

Gladly as we would receive news of the elimination of slums, such a change would not in principle solve our literary problem. Basically, our literary problem is not slums—bad as they are—but the principle of difference itself, of incompleteness. It is incompleteness that is keeping the book open on the table, a transparent but impermeable wall between two people. Were *Tortilla Flat* a "complete" work, no one would complain about it. Readers would become as serene as if in the presence of God. But *Tortilla Flat* is not a complete vision.[42] No work of art is.

Works of art come to us in the limited form of genres, as they must. We can build only with the materials we have. There can be no literary work that is not a kind of literary work. No work can be simultaneously a sonnet and a novel. Nor can any literary work escape its own intrinsic genre.

Most abstractly, now, our subject is incompleteness. Our subject is the proposition that literary works always appear in the form of genres, and also of intrinsic genres, and that both a genre and an intrinsic genre are by definition incomplete presentations of human experience. If a new genre appears it may in its novelty seem to have escaped the limitation of being only another literary kind; but as time passes the character of the kind it is begins to emerge. We are groping toward, although we won't achieve, that theory of the incompleteness of all formal discourse Polanyi declared we need.[43]

The ultimate value of the idea of intrinsic genres does not lie in its usefulness in identifying such transparent walls as we have just observed. That is only a step toward realization of its value. Ultimately, its importance lies in its power of calling attention to structure as a basic principle. Once we are accustomed to thinking in terms of structure, a confrontation may not be necessary to alert us to the fact that we are locked into one.

Nevertheless, encounters with transparent walls are common. Below are half-a-dozen examples from my own classroom experience. One caution is needed, however. Protagonists on either side of a wall are likely at first to declare there is no wall at all, that the trouble lies entirely in their opponents' prejudice. The art of the classroom, of course, is to reveal the wall. But classrooms do become confused and insist there is a wall where there is really only misunderstanding. All I can say is that the experiences noted below seemed to me to represent genuine walls. By my first choice in what follows, I stress the difficulties I've just been describing.

One side: In "A Slumber Did My Spirit Seal" Lucy is as lifeless as stones and trees.

The other side: Lucy shares in the life of trees and stones.

One side: In *An American Tragedy*, Clyde Griffiths's case is sad, but his execution is society's way of protecting itself. What keeps the deer healthy? The wolves destroy the unfit.

The other side: Clyde Griffiths was made into what he was by a wolfish society.

One side: In *The Scarlet Letter*, Hester Prynne's return to Massachusetts Bay represents her final psychological capitulation to the somber view of life held by the Puritans ("Young Goodman Brown" cited as supporting evidence).

The other side: Hester's return represents her final recognition of the value of community as a principle.

One side: Eldridge Cleaver's *Soul on Ice* is a primitivistic rationalization of the relationship between blacks and whites.

The other side: Soul on Ice employs the primitivistic myth to symbolize the true relationship between blacks and whites.

One side: In *The Red Badge of Courage*, Henry is a mere mechanism, made courageous by the stimulus of the initial mistaken respect of his comrades. Crane patronizes him.

The other side: Henry is a youth who achieves maturity through an act of personal courage. Crane admires him.

Choose-ups: Richard B. Hovey refers with disapproval

to a freshman who told him Thoreau's attack on ma-
terialism was a rationalization of his own failure.
("Freshman Illiteracy and Professorial Jeopardy,"
AAUP Bulletin 44, no. 2 [June 1958]: 438)

Perry Miller says the secret of Thoreau's success was
that he was a failure. (Henry David Thoreau, *Con-
sciousness in Concord: The Text of Thoreau's Hitherto
"Lost Journal" [1840–1841] Together with Notes and a
Commentary by Perry Miller* [Boston: Houghton-
Mifflin, 1958], pp. 4–5)

". . . we may even suspect that he meant what he said.
And what he said was that he went to the woods in order
to live deliberately." (R. W. B. Lewis, *The American
Adam* [Chicago: University of Chicago Press, 1955],
p. 27)

The impulsive jocularity of my heading "Choose-ups" reveals a difficulty, however. Are the differences of opinion revealed in these examples, taking the group as a whole, actually
indicative of structural problems? Or are they little more than
casual personal responses? What does structural mean?

Let us ponder the idea of structure. For our purposes, probably the most important element in the idea is wholeness—that
is, a relationship among parts which is not merely random but
rather organized according to some principle. Jean Piaget adds
two other elements. "The notion of structure," he says, "is comprised of three key ideas: the idea of wholeness, the idea of
transformation, and the idea of self-regulation."[44] "Transformation" is a term with which Piaget approaches the problem
of how one structure is related to another out of which it appears to have emerged or developed. To go from water to ice
requires a transformation, and this transformation is governed
by law. The idea can be applied to literature in various ways.
For example, the concept of a recognition scene involves a
transformation, a "change of state." Or, as noted earlier, the
creation of a semblance requires a transformation of materials.
Concerning his third term, "self-regulation," Piaget suggests
we think of the principle of feedback. A structure tends to
maintain itself. If a humorous passage in the style of Mark
Twain were inserted into *Tortilla Flat*, for instance, we would

find it incongruous. The "structure" of *Tortilla Flat* would reject it. But the felt need for quotation marks around structure is a warning that we are approaching the limits of the meaning of this term.

At some point of attenuation the idea of structure seems to pass over into the idea of quality, of something involving a judgment which has become no more than an intuition. And this possibility is forced upon our attention in confronting such an idea as that of defining the kinds of humor. Distinctions between subtly differentiated forms of humor appear to lie beyond the analytical power of the concept of structure. It is at such a point that Cleanth Brooks's objection to abstraction takes on force, and it is at such a point that linguistics has so far failed to relate form and meaning.[45] It does not follow that either literature or language comes to us without abstractions or form.

The ideas of wholeness, transformation, and self-regulation do clarify the concept of structure with reference to the examples of transparent walls noted above. The structure of *Tortilla Flat* does "reject" the broadly different humor of Mark Twain. It is only necessary to remember, then, that the concept of structure has its own limitations, that at some point it tends to dissolve into mere intuition. In fact, it has become evident that the deliberate attenuation of the concept of genre (a kind of structure) into intrinsic genre is necessary precisely to acknowledge this tendency.

We should now attempt to devise a test for the presence of structure as a crucial element in the examples being considered. This attempt could quickly become overwhelmingly complex, but our need is only to establish a simple test that will work reasonably well in the course of a classroom discussion. Such a test can be made by deleting from a text, in imagination, the entire element represented by the point at issue and observing whether the text is significantly changed by the deletion. For example, the point at issue in *The Scarlet Letter* is the character of Hester's relationship to the Puritan community. When we think of deleting this element throughout the novel, it is at once apparent that we are dealing with a fundamental structural element. *The Scarlet Letter* would be vastly changed by such a deletion. On the other hand, I cannot see that the question of whether Thoreau was a failure is a structural question. What is of interest in Thoreau's story is the values which may be found in a particular life style. If the values he reports to have experienced are indeed mere rationalizations, they could have been mere rationalizations for many reasons besides some kind of failure. (I myself am persuaded by what he says. I do not think he was rationalizing—at least not in any sense this side of the complexities of depth psychology.)

The Red Badge of Courage, to take a third and last example, presents a special problem. No doubt everyone would agree that the issue of whether Henry was brave is structural, but beyond that agreement lies a considerable uncertainty. The problem is that evidence on both sides of the question is so unavoidably obvious. As John Berryman remarked, Crane is simultaneously on the side of and making war upon his protagonist. In short, transformation has in this novel become an end in itself. Bravery is transformed into mere stimulus and response and back again into genuine bravery. Henry is made as unstable a figure, in this respect, as Wittgenstein's duck-rabbit, but without harm to the novel. We are forced to conclude that a transparent wall may itself be primarily what an author intends. In fact much modern fiction, like Nabokov's *Pale Fire*, is devoted to exploiting exactly this possibility. We see now from this point of view, now from that; now from this side of the wall, now from the other. The shifting point of view itself becomes a structural element. Inevitably, the effect is hortatory: do not let yourself be trapped by a transparent wall, the writer urges; see how I can make and unmake transparent walls before your very eyes; see how we are all threatened by incompleteness.

It is time to recognize, however, that the either/or choice implied by the figure of the transparent wall is not the only kind of choice which can be traced to a structural or generic source. Sometimes a choice must be made among several possibilities. For example, in *The Mirror and the Lamp*, Meyer Abrams reviews a wide variety of opinions about the role of Satan in *Paradise Lost*, and there can be no doubt that at least several of these opinions can be related to structural sources. Consequently, it is evident that instead of a single transparent wall something like a cluster of transparent-walled booths is needed. The fundamental principle is mutual exclusion among choices: Satan cannot simultaneously be a Puritan villain, a Romantic hero, and a modern ambiguity—unless, as we shall see, the choice is approached in a mediational mode. Like all analogies, the figure of a transparent wall can be pushed too far; but the principle of mutual exclusion it represents is not an analogy and retains its force even when a choice is to be made among several possibilities.

Two other aspects of the subject of incompleteness become especially relevant, at this point, to the question of what kinds of discriminations should be sought in the literary classroom. The first is a further exploration of the kind of barriers or walls we have just been examining. The second is the possibility of mediation between people caught in such a predicament as Steinbeck's and the bibliographer's. In the course of discussing the latter we can return to the question of significance and the bibliographer's opinion about *Tortilla Flat*.

The Transparent Wall

"Transparent wall" seems an unnecessarily ornate term. I haven't been able to think of any better way, however, to express the sense of frustration characteristic of an irreconcilable disagreement which is sympathetically understood by both sides.

If the problem of transparent walls indeed arises fundamentally from difference or incompleteness, as I claimed, it should be observable in areas outside of literature too. Examination of a couple of examples will reveal its presence in social structures and in physics, respectively. These examples will also demonstrate how the ability to apprehend literary genres is related to experience in other areas of life. The bases of the practical cultural role of the classroom will thus begin to take shape.

As the social structures to be considered I have chosen two communes: our founding fathers' Plymouth Colony and Twin Oaks, a community established in Virginia in 1967. Before discussing them specifically, however, a perspective on our subject can be borrowed from Kenelm Burridge's recent anthropological study, *Encountering Aborigines*. In his introductory chapter, Burridge makes a curious observation. Noting that the

Australian Aborigines' traditional culture has been among the most exhaustively studied in the world, he considers what the results will look like to the Aborigines' descendants a few generations hence. Quite possibly, he says, these descendants will take it for granted that their culture should have been studied. He declares that an act of the imagination will likely be required for them to realize that if strange peoples other than Europeans had come to Australia, their culture would probably have gone unrecorded and been lost. Only within the European tradition and its derivatives, he asserts, do we find that systematic approach to the study of social institutions we call anthropology.[46]

However this may be, it is my impression that an anthropological habit of mind is now widely held among educated people sharing the European tradition. I suspect that in America a kind of critical mass was reached with the publication of Ruth Benedict's famous *Patterns of Culture* in 1934.

An anthropological habit of mind creates a self-consciousness about a given social structure, revealing it as no more than one kind, or genre, among many possibilities. This idea is embodied with dramatic force in a comment by Burridge:

> Every field anthropologist knows the moment when, his own intellectual and cultural props slipping away, but not yet able to lean on the understandings of the other culture, he is utterly alone and wants either to run home or "go bush" . . .[47]

As seen in Kathleen Kinkade's account of her experience at Twin Oaks, this commune clearly bears the marks of the anthropological habit of mind and even more strongly the marks of another western tradition: behavioristic psychology. It was modeled on B. F. Skinner's *Walden Two*. The habit of thinking objectively about social structures is especially evident in Kinkade's cool appraisal of the commune's policy concerning sexuality. A commune must choose, she says, between dealing with either sin or jealousy.[48] Granted unrestricted freedom, there will be jealousy. Given rules, there will be sin. Twin Oaks chose freedom—and jealousy. Examples are described by Kinkade. With the approval of the community, Brian and Carrie decided to have a child. It was understood the child would be-

long to the community. In the fifth month of Carrie's preg-
nancy Brian became interested in another woman, Marjorie.
Carrie objected. Brian offered to spend alternate days with the
two women, and they accepted. Marjorie was finally driven
from the commune, by not being voted a permanent member,
but Brian formed other liaisons. After the baby was born Carrie
left, taking the child with her.

According to the commune's policy Brian was within his
rights. There was objection to his behavior but there was objection to Carrie's too. Kathleen Kinkade, who voted not to give
Marjorie permanent membership, says she later felt embar-
rassed by her vote. Without knowing how they really felt, we
can with good reason imagine that Brian and Carrie, as in our
imaginary confrontation between Steinbeck and the bibliographer, perceived one another's position with at least a degree of
sympathy and yet found this perception to be without the
power of altering their situation. Carrie was obviously helpless,
and Brian was following the code accepted by the commune as
a whole.

In one respect, Plymouth also chose freedom and jealousy; in
other respects it chose sin. The choice of freedom lay in the
initial economic arrangement. All were to work, and all were
to share alike in what was produced. There were no complex
rules about property. The result was jealousy. The form the
jealousy took was dissatisfaction on the part of the stronger
members of the community over the weaker members' receiving as great a share of the produce as they themselves did.
Single men grumbled about helping to support other men's
wives. There was also, in Governor Bradford's opinion, an increase in social friction with the weakening of the traditional
status system associated with property. So this arrangement
was abandoned.

Everybody knows about sin in New England. Virtually
everything in the life of the members of Plymouth was scruti-
nized and judged. Sin became crime; swearing was legally
punishable. The motto of the colony was love and watchful-
ness: love of one another and exposure of one another's sins for
the salvation of one another's soul. Governor Bradford thought
it proper that "every Lord's day some are appointed to visit
suspected places,"[49] a view that persisted in Monterey, accord-

ing to *Tortilla Flat*. In contrast, Kathleen Kinkade says she really can't give much of an account of sexuality at Twin Oaks, because what other people did was their own business and she doesn't know much about it.

Had Brian and Carrie been living in Plymouth, or in a commune modeled on Plymouth, Brian's situation would have been very different from what it was. His behavior might not have been so different as would at first be expected, although any sexual transgressions would have been conducted secretly. The point is that unless he was a very unusual personality he would have been tormented by far more intense guilt feelings than it is conceivable he experienced at Twin Oaks. Even an unfulfilled desire for sex could be a source of guilt. From an anthropological point of view, such is the power of genre.

As jealousy was the foundation on which a transparent wall arose in the genre of Twin Oaks, sin was the foundation of a similar wall in the colonies. The most striking evidence is the synod of 1637, the first convening of the ministers of New England for the purpose of settling disagreements over what was and what was not sin. It turned out they could not reach a definitive settlement. Eighty-two points of dispute were considered. The sincerity of the disputants in their unsuccessful efforts to settle their problems in a spirit of love and sympathetic understanding cannot, on the whole, be doubted. Herbert Schneider has written a splendid sentence on this point: "Mr. Cotton's case proved the most difficult, for though he desired to be orthodox, he found himself able to hold his own in argument against the great majority of his brethren."[50]

There is a good reason for describing the synod as striking evidence that the concept of sin was the source of transparent walls in the colonies. The colonists hated synods. They had suffered much from them in England. But, alas, the synod of 1637 proved to be only the first of many. It was adjourned in a spirit of seeming harmony, but soon another synod had to be called. And, as Schneider says, each new synod was a symptom of differences.[51] Differences is our subject.

The most obvious contrast between Plymouth and Twin Oaks is perhaps the presence in one and the absence in the other of the anthropological view. Kathleen Kinkade asserted in full consciousness that Twin Oaks's policy on sexuality could either be structured in such a way as to deal openly with sin or structured in such a way as to deal openly with jealousy. Governor Bradford, in contrast, asserted that the economic structure ultimately adopted by Plymouth was derived from the finality of God's will. He explicitly rejected the possibility that the failure of the initial economic system arose from faults in the people rather than from faults in the system. He said the system did not reflect God's plan. Here, from *Of Plimmoth Plantation*, is the conclusion of his comments on the abandonment of the initial communal arrangement.

> Upon the poynte all being to have alike, and all to doe alike, they thought them selves in the like condition, and one as good as another; and so if it did not cut of those relations that God set amongst men, yet it did at least much diminish and take of the mutuall respects that should be preserved amongst them. And would have bene worse if they had been men of another condition. Let none objecte this is men's corruption, and nothing to the course it selfe. I answer, seeing all men have this corruption in them, God in his wisdome saw another course fiter for them.[52]

Perhaps Bradford was locked into his genre to about the same degree Steinbeck was when the latter spoke of *Tortilla Flat* as true. Had Steinbeck been more self-conscious about genre, I believe he would have avoided the dangerous word "true" and spoken directly about genre instead. Whether he later had second thoughts about what he said I don't know, but likely enough he did. Some of the colonists had second thoughts. Samuel Sewall regretted his part in hanging witches. On the other hand Roger Williams took a somewhat anthropological view of the Indians and in certain ways of the colonists themselves. But Williams was banished from Massachusetts Bay Colony.

In brief, the choice of a genre, in social structure as in literature, imposes an incompleteness. This incompleteness is the cause of difference. Since there was no official sinfulness in Brian's conduct, Carrie couldn't keep him. And since there was no official freedom from sinfulness in New England, the ministers could not agree to disagree. To do so would have been sinful. There would have been no need for synods were theology, a genre, complete. It might be objected, with reason, that since jealousy was thought objectionable at Twin Oaks, being jealous was a sin. Sin is surely too strong a word, however. There was apparently no feeling that being jealous was an affront to finality, to God's will; it was, rather, a distressing circumstance the commune thought it could learn to cope with.[53]

Finally, these social parallels suggest that since neither *Tortilla Flat* nor any other literary structure can be both what it is and what it is not, what it is not must always be accepted as a potential source of difference of opinion. Incompleteness is not the only cause of disagreements, of course; it is merely the particular cause which at the moment we are trying to analyze.

Physics reveals the same situation as the social structure just examined, but with a remarkable addition. Until recently, the physicist chose both anthropological thinking and sin. An example of the physicist's position is seen in the implications of the uncertainty principle, or principles. The most famous uncertainty principle is Werner Heisenberg's; it can be expressed in a simple way by saying that the position and the velocity of a particle cannot both be known at the same time. As information concerning one of these factors becomes more precise, information concerning the other becomes less precise. A second uncertainty principle, formulated by Polanyi and Wigner, asserts that the energy and the lifetime of a particle cannot be known simultaneously—with one odd qualification. The energy of a particle could be known with complete precision granted the qualification that the particle remain in existence for an infinite period of time.[54] This looks like some sort of finality, as if a genre had been made complete, infinite; we are evidently standing at the boundary between physics and philosophy.

It is possible to question the validity of the concept of uncertainty, to regard it as only one theory among others yet to be formulated. The physicist P. A. M. Dirac, for example, has expressed doubt that it will survive in the physics of the future. Thought of in this manner, the uncertainty principle may begin to seem only one way of looking at reality, as *Tortilla Flat* is one way of looking at Tortilla Flat. Remembering Gombrich's remark that painters tend to see what they paint rather than paint what they see, we might go even farther. We might speculate that quantum physics is what the theory of quantum physics says it is. Possibly physicists see what they paint too. The concept of uncertainty is part of quantum physics. Of course no one denies that the concept of uncertainty bears a demonstrable relationship to observed facts. Paintings, too, possess a relationship with "reality." Nevertheless, the history of both science and painting contains many examples of theories and styles which were once generally approved only to be regarded later as superficial or, in science, even wrong.

This line of thought is familiar to physicists. As Stephen G. Brush has recently pointed out, it can be observed in an exchange of letters between Heisenberg and Einstein in 1926.[55] Heisenberg asked Einstein if he didn't believe theories should be developed in accord with observed facts, remarking that Einstein had stressed this idea in the development of his theory of relativity. Heisenberg says Einstein replied as follows.

> "Possibly I did use this kind of reasoning, but it is nonsense all the same. Perhaps I could put it more diplomatically by saying that it may be heuristically useful to keep in mind what one has observed. But in principle, it is quite wrong to try founding a theory on observable magnitudes alone. In reality the very opposite happens. It is the theory which decides what we can observe."[56]

When he later developed his uncertainty principle, Heisenberg reflected on what Einstein had said. He understood that his own theory, or principle, prescribed what could be seen, but he also perceived an additional limitation. Since he had deduced the uncertainty principle from the laws of quantum mechanics and since any experiment concerned with the uncertainty principle must be devised in keeping with the laws of quantum mechanics, it was most unlikely any way could ever be found to disprove his principle.[57]

It is thus conceivable that the uncertainty principle may somehow be defective. Physicists are locked into that view of physical phenomena afforded by the uncertainty principle, and indeed are grateful to have it, but like the people at Twin Oaks they keep remembering it's a structure they built with their own hands. Yet until the advent of quantum physics they were like Puritans, too, in that they could sin. Their structures were presumed to manifest finality in the form of aspects of physical reality. For physicists who did, and those who still do, share this faith it would be sinful to deny the uncertainty principle without having had a more compelling revelation. In *The Structure of Scientific Revolutions* Thomas Kuhn describes a scientist's changing of allegiance from one fundamental theory to a different, competing theory as a conversion experience.[58] To abandon years of commitment to a particular view of physical reality can be a traumatic experience.

Were a bold new theory to begin forcefully challenging the uncertainty principle, transparent walls would unquestionably go up. Scientists who thoroughly and sympathetically understood one another's reasoning would find themselves on opposite sides of the wall. Indeed, I presume it can be said that such a wall arose between Einstein and Bohr when the statistical methods of quantum physics, including complementarity and uncertainty, first made their appearance.[59]

Of course the walls are not always transparent. Perhaps they seldom are. Kuhn shows convincingly how easy it is for scientists wrestling with a common problem to talk past each other. Literary critics talk past each other too. Our concern, however, is not with mere misunderstandings. It is with those kinds of discriminations we should learn to make when, with no misunderstandings, there is a transparent wall.

A final illustration, and a return to literature, can be found in a passage from Wayne Booth's recent book on irony that is surely destined to become famous. Booth says:

> I once had a student who wrote a paper about the joys of deer hunting, including a vivid description of the thrill that "coursed through" his veins as he cut the deer's throat and watched the life dying in those "beautiful, child-like eyes." It was evident to me that he was satirizing blood sport. But I found, in what seems now to have been one of the most ineffectual conferences I have ever had with a student, that my ironic reading was to him plain crazy. I made a mistake of lingering over his bloodthirsty phrases, trying to explain to him why I had thought them ironic. But he was simply baffled, as well

he might be; to read irony into any one of his statements was to misunderstand his entire perception of
what his life and the deer's were all about. Wrestling
with irony, he and I were not talking only about "verbal" matters; we were driven into debate about how a
man should live.[60]

In the next section I will take up the question of whether debate about how a man or a woman should live can dissolve a
transparent wall. But first something more needs to be said
about the basic problem, stated at the beginning of Part Three,
of how the literary classroom is validated as an educational
experience. This problem was subdivided into five parts. The
first three proved to be irrelevant to our concerns in this book.
Of the remaining two, one was the problem of irreconcilable
differences (later called the problem of transparent walls); the
other was the need for mediation. Presumably the problem of
irreconcilable disagreements has, for our purposes, now been
sufficiently discussed. That is, its sources in genre, in the kinds
of literature, in the categories in which we perforce think and
perceive, have been examined. Consequently, a discrimination
has been made between misunderstandings and truly irreconcilable disagreements. This is one of the kinds of discrimination
that evidently should be practiced in the classroom.
    The next step to be taken has to do with the other subdivision
of the general problem of validating the classroom, that is, with
the need for mediation, for whatever solutions can be found
when a transparent wall is encountered.

The Pragmatics of Mediation

After reviewing some mutually exclusive interpretations of
Wuthering Heights, Frank Kermode remarks that as a reader
becomes aware of these conflicting possibilities he will find a
mediation among them in his own response to the text or in the
role of one or another of the characters.[61] The novel is not destroyed by the incompatibility of elements in it. Contemplating
this really very profound observation, I fell to wondering about
the same kind of problem in other novels. For example, in

Huckleberry Finn does Huck mediate between slavery and antislavery views? In a way he does, and in a way he doesn't. The trouble with the notion of Huck's mediating comes when he decides not to turn Jim over to the officers of the law. Prior to this decision, Huck does seem to embody both pro and anti views of slavery. Capable of humbling himself to Jim with a forthright apology, he is also capable of feeling it is not only a crime but a sin to help a slave escape. But Huck is finally forced by circumstances into a decision. Once he has made his decision, no proslavery resident of the Old South would accept him as an embodiment of mediation. Huck's decision is the equivalent of a vote cast in a real-life political contest.

It appears desirable, therefore, to find some concept of the mediation of irreconcilable differences concerning the interpretation of a literary work that can stand exposure to forced decisions. Otherwise, literary devices that seem at first to be effectively mediating transparent walls may in the end lose their power to compel our assent. In saying this I am, of course, putting myself in opposition to some truly elegant theories concerning art as a closed system. On the other hand, equally elegant theories indicate that no formal symbol system can be assumed to have a wholly consistent internal structure. The most famous of such theories is Kurt Gödel's, in mathematics.

For our purposes, jurisprudence is especially inviting as a source of ideas concerning the possibility of mediation between mutually exclusive positions. At first it might seem unnecessary to turn from anthropology to jurisprudence, but anthropology possesses one serious handicap for our practical purpose. To the degree to which it approaches being a true science, it is tied to particular theories. In jurisprudence, as it happens, we will find a system in which this kind of limitation does not appear. We will not find it, however, in our own legal system.

Our legal system prides itself on being a government of laws and not of men, as John Adams indicated in the Massachusetts Constitution. Yet, like all formal systems, our body of law has disadvantages as well as advantages, and some thinkers have had a great distaste for it. An obvious potential—and actual—source of trouble is the abstractness of our law. It tends to be rigid, to have too little of literature's gift for self-limiting generalizations. Tom Wicker, for example, has recently severely

attacked our legal system in his *New York Times* column for
what he considers its insensitive handling of George Jackson's
crime of stealing seventy dollars when he was nineteen years
old. Curiously, this unfortunate rigidity in our law springs from
the same source out of which come its marvelous intellectual
flexibility and power for change and reform. This source is the
reduction of unique, individual human beings to a universal:
man. In the eyes of our law, all men are the same. Therefore,
an individual man is in effect reduced to a symbol which can
then be employed in a general law.

The reduction of real human beings to man makes it possible
to write complex laws which can be applied to the actions of
any specific person in the same way a law of physics is applied
to any specific problem in the realm of physical forces. It is this
possibility which gives our law its intellectual flexibility. A
powerful influence toward modification of this abstractness did
appear in the pragmatic theory of Justices Holmes and Brandeis
and their followers, but without altering the essential nature of
our law.

Gandhi is representative of a different legal view. While in
South Africa he experienced a strong revulsion against western
law in general and committed himself instead to the eastern
tradition of intuitive, mediational law. In this tradition there
are no written laws and, in its most extreme form, no judges.
Contending parties, with the help of a mediator, seek a solution
acceptable to both sides. "That action alone is just," said Gandhi, "which does not harm either party to a dispute."[62] A practical instance can be seen in T. E. Lawrence's description of
Feisal's mediating among the desert Arabs during the First
World War. "He never gave a partial decision," Lawrence
wrote, "nor a decision so impracticably just that it must lead to
disorder."[63] Here the system has been slightly modified, since
Feisal's role as mediator has begun to take on the power of
judging. An instance in which the act of judging was explicitly
excluded from the mediator's role is described by F. S. C.
Northrop.

> In Buddhist Bangkok in 1950 I found the Chief Justice
> of its Supreme Court and a former Chief Justice of its
> next highest court, the Court of Appeals, who ostensibly

were applying that most abstract of Western law, the French Continental Code, assuring me that they refused often to hear the case and urged the disputants, if Thais, to settle their differences in the approved Buddhist manner. In one instance after two such refusals and two failures of the disputants to reach agreement by themselves, the judges declined a third time to proceed in the Western manner, with the result that the intuitive mediational way succeeded.

Note its distinguishing characteristic: Not only is there no resort to a legal rule, there is also no judge. Even the mediator refuses to give a decision. Instead, the dispute is properly settled when the disputants, using the mediator merely as an emissary, come to mutual agreement in the light of all the existential circumstances, past, present, and future.[64]

A mediational system in its pure form is thus a government not of laws but of men. No interest is taken in the abstract concept of universal man or of abstract law. The principle on which the system operates is the assumption that each human being is unique and that justice cannot be achieved through application of a universal law to this uniqueness.[65] Justice can be assured only by direct, personal contact in which all the relevant considerations on both sides are explored. Such a system is philosophically akin to that spirit in aesthetics which deplores abstractions. It also suffers from the same disadvantage: relationships become precarious when extended beyond immediate perceptions to larger wholes. Mediation is effective in a patriarchal family, or a village. Its opponents declare that it breaks down for larger groups, that it cannot serve a modern nation.

Thus mediational law replaces the "right or wrong," the "guilty or not guilty," of our law with a continuum. Within this continuum contending parties seek a moral and social point of balance. From an Aristotelian perspective mediational law appears disorderly, since it has no rules. Yet order is the essence of its existence. Within limits, it works. It seems to represent the possibility of disorderly order. Mediational law somewhat resembles quantum mechanics, where certain questions are answered only in terms of probabilities.[66]

We can now ask whether the idea of mediational law can be applied to the problem of irreconcilable differences. The answer appears to be yes, within limits.

First, it should be remembered that mediational law, like quantum mechanics, is limited to microstructures.[67] Quantum mechanics is not used for analysis of solar orbits, and—as far as I know—mediational law is not used to govern any modern, industrialized nation. This limitation is of no consequence to the literary classroom, which is itself a microstructure and which deals primarily with problems of microstructures. The literary classroom does not address itself to the problem of governing the nation. Micro of course means small; it does not mean unimportant.

Having established a preliminary limit, we come to a second point. The disorderly order of mediational law raises a question about the necessity of an either/or position with respect to any microstructure.[68] Why not have Steinbeck and the bibliographer mediate their differences, instead of insisting that the view of either one or the other represents the true meaning of *Tortilla Flat*?

To answer this question we must consider what mediate could mean in these circumstances. Clearly, it cannot mean that the difference between the views of the two men is caused to vanish. The bibliographer cannot avoid reasserting the truth that the book is patronizing, and Steinbeck, I assume, cannot avoid reasserting that what he intended was not an insult but a genre. We thus encounter a second limit to the possibility of applying the idea of mediational law to an irreconcilable difference. A transparent wall is by definition a wall that can be destroyed only by destroying an entire genre, or structure. And, since we cannot do without genres, there will always be transparent walls of one sort or another. Difference, incompleteness, is a fundamental fact of human existence, and this fact cannot be changed by mediation.

Mediate could mean something else, however. In abandoning western law's either/or concept of order, we create a previously lacking potential for communication and reconciliation. We more easily recognize that we are dealing with living intelligences, not merely with abstract forms. Mediational law, based on a belief in the power of intelligence to permit differ-

ences to live together without harm, is as great an antithesis to
a genre- or rule-bound view of human experience as a practical
social order can provide. The concept of mediation invites
Steinbeck and the bibliographer to solve the problem of the
transparent wall in every way their intelligence permits. The
process is suggested in a poetic passage by Lévi-Strauss concerning his tracing of the line of division, in Languedoc, between two geologic zones. After describing how he followed the
division between them through the countryside, he writes of
how they were at last joined in human consciousness.

> When the miracle occurs, as it sometimes does; when,
> on one side and the other of the hidden crack, there are
> suddenly to be found cheek-by-jowl two green plants of
> different species, each of which has chosen the most
> favourable soil; and when at the same time, two am-
> monites with unevenly intricate involutions can be
> glimpsed in the rock, thus testifying in their own way to
> a gap of several tens of thousands of years, suddenly
> space and time become one: the living diversity of the
> moment juxtaposes and perpetuates the ages. Thought
> and emotion move into a new dimension. . . . I feel my-
> self to be steeped in a more dense intelligibility, within
> which centuries and distances answer each other and
> speak at last with one and the same voice.[69]

Although the transparent wall between Steinbeck and the
bibliographer cannot be removed, intelligence permits it to be
walked around, with one exception to be noted later. Both men
can occupy the same side of the wall at the same time, if they
wish. Whichever side they are on, both are aware they can
move to the other side at will. They can do this because both
have come to understand that the source of their difference is
genre. Once having recognized this fact, both can freely choose
either to look at *Tortilla Flat* from within its intrinsic genre or
from without. Looked at from within, it is a charming literary
work. Looked at from without, it patronizes the paisanos of
Tortilla Flat. The fact that the book exists in the real world, a
world in which there are Tortilla Flats, creates a wall between
the two men. Yet because these two men on opposite sides of the
wall can sympathetically understand one another's feelings the

wall is transparent. And once they have traced the origin of
the wall to a genre they can go from one side of the wall to the
other at will.

More abstractly and more precisely, it is possible for each
man to hold mutually exclusive perceptual hypotheses in mind
at the same time, although he may be unable to look at both at
the same time. While looking at one, he does not forget the
other is there. And most important of all, if he is granted a
mediational frame of mind he does not have to make a permanent choice between the two perceptions or interpretations.
From the mediational point of view, and within the limits of a
literary classroom or its equivalent, there is no need to make a
rule that *Tortilla Flat* must be seen exclusively either from
Steinbeck's view or from the bibliographer's.

Most abstractly considered, this solution to the dilemma of
Steinbeck and the bibliographer results from the application of
what in game theory is called the principle of metalogic. This
principle states that when a paradox is encountered a solution
should be attempted by enlarging, in successive steps, the
framework within which the paradox is perceived.[70] It was
through such an enlargement, for example, that Zeno's paradox
of Achilles and the tortoise was solved. In the concept of a convergent series a generalization was achieved which embraced
both of the hitherto incompatible elements of the paradox. The
dilemma of Steinbeck and the bibliographer is solved in the
same way. Their point of view is enlarged sufficiently to enable
them to see the structure of their problem from the outside, so
to speak. Mediational law employs the same principle; through
the presence of the mediator it compels disputants to enlarge
their perception of their personal relationship to include the
relationship both of them have to their entire community.

When such an enlargement is linked to some form of finality
lying outside the community, however, a very different situation can develop. In contrast to Steinbeck and the bibliographer, for example, the Puritans' trouble was that their wall
extended all the way to the finality of God's will and they were
unable to get around it. Their wall was unquestionably transparent in many instances. They could sympathetically understand one another's reasoning. But when one Puritan (like John
Cotton) believed he would go to hell if he acted on the prompt-

ing of his own heart rather than on what the elders said, and another (like Roger Williams) believed he'd go to hell if he did *not* act on the prompting on his own heart, they had an insoluble problem. The finality of hell made the wall an impassable barrier.

The problem of Twin Oaks, though less desperate, was similar in kind to the Puritans' problem. Once they had made their anthropological choice of a social structure at Twin Oaks, they were both sheltered by it and trapped in it. Confronted with the transparent wall of a severe case of jealousy they had two possible solutions: to destroy their structure and try a different structure in its place or to learn not to feel jealousy. They chose the latter. As one means of learning not to feel jealousy they organized encounter groups. In other words, they elected to try to make a change in themselves rather than in their social structure. Perhaps their dream of becoming immune to jealousy is realizable, but I am most dubious. The Puritans' comparable dream was to learn not to sin.

A moment ago I remarked there was one exception to the ability of Steinbeck and the bibliographer to walk around their transparent wall and completely resolve the differences between them. In considering this exception, I can both conclude and summarize these ideas about mediation.

The exception arises when the interpretation of *Tortilla Flat* is linked to a decision in real life involving as serious a problem as the jealousy Carrie felt about Brian at Twin Oaks. Suppose, for example, a group of people become so enamored of the structure of Steinbeck's imaginary community of Tortilla Flat as to set up a commune modeled upon it. They might be encouraged to do so by the precedent of Twin Oaks, which was modeled on the imaginary community in Skinner's novel *Walden Two*. And suppose the people in the Tortilla Flat commune insisted that the bibliographer become a member. They would no doubt find they had a problem on their hands. My guess is that the bibliographer could be enrolled as a member only by physical force—which is another way of saying that the transparent wall between Steinbeck and the bibliographer would become an impassable barrier as soon as it was linked to so serious a problem in real life.

Of what use, then, is the concept of mediation? In my opinion, the ideas which have been considered yield two simple but profoundly important answers. Each of these answers can be expressed in both social and literary terms.

In social terms, the first answer is that mature, reasonable people who have looked deeply into the concepts of genre and order and mediation would never think of enrolling anybody in their commune by force. They would be too keenly aware of the fact that their commitment was to a man-made structure. They would be unable to entertain the kind of desperate emotional conviction necessary for violence on behalf of their structure. No witches have been hanged at Twin Oaks. Anthropological thinking does have at least this one clear advantage. Were the world inhabited only by mature, reasonable people with an anthropological habit of mind, perhaps no more would need to be said in the way of a social answer.

In literary terms, this first answer appears as the concept of learning to apprehend genres and intrinsic genres and to discriminate between misunderstandings and irreconcilable differences. In the unique richness of both the feeling and thought provided by literature, people can learn through decisions forced by direct confrontation how transparent walls come into being and how such walls can be got around. Practice in making these discriminations would seem to be a fundamental cultural obligation of the literary classroom.

The second social answer is that the mature and reasonable people we have in mind would attempt in every way possible to develop a social structure in which the intellectual flexibility of western law was so combined with the personal concern of mediational law as to produce an absolute minimum of transparent walls. The bibliographer would probably stand in line to join. But like so many second answers, this one is overcast with sadness. Probably no social structure can ever be devised that will eliminate both jealousy and sin or, in fact, that will eliminate either one of them. And of course this pair of problems only epitomizes the multitude of issues which incessantly create impassable barriers in human life. In Pogo's immortal words, we have met the enemy and it is us. Nevertheless, as the intention embodied by Walt Kelly in Pogo's words appears to say, understanding can reduce tension. Recognizing the hazards inherent in the structures in which we live, we can antici-

pate and avoid some of the impassable barriers we might otherwise encounter. And by recognizing the hazards inherent in
the structures which we ourselves are, as Norman Holland
would have us see, perhaps we might avoid some additional
barriers. From the social point of view, a primary function of
the literary classroom is to afford the individual an opportunity
to apprehend and, in imagination, to manipulate social and
even personal structures in a mode which is both intensely perceptual and distanced.

Translated into literary terms, the second social answer takes
the form of a literary theory concerned more with definitions
and discriminations than with rules about which single interpretation is correct. It is a theory which welcomes a disorderly
order. It is a theory which feels no need of patronizing the
bibliographer by informing him that his interpretation of
Tortilla Flat is merely significance. It is, finally, a kind of theory toward which I feel art has been struggling, one in which
aesthetic finality is conceived in the form of unique but socialized minds and spirits rather than in the form of either omnis-
cience or a set of rules.

I may seem to be contradicting the statement I made in Part
One that a correct interpretation of a text is a fundamental goal
of the literary classroom. I may also seem to be disregarding
my previous emphasis on the value of the idea of significance.
It is not my intention either to contradict or disregard, however. In my opinion, a correct interpretation of *Tortilla Flat*
includes both the idea that the book is patronizing and the idea
that the book is not patronizing, together with the reasons for
these mutually exclusive views. There are probably additional
interpretations I haven't thought of which are correct and
should be included. Naturally, there are also false interpretations. The possibility of more than one correct interpretation
does not exclude the possibility of false interpretations. The objective of the classroom is correctness. And who is to be the
judge? As in any art or science, we simply have to rely on interested and informed people who talk things over and come to
the best conclusions they can. It is not unreasonable to hope for
discrimination pools which are wise, although not omniscient.

The bibliographer's interpretation of *Tortilla Flat* surely deserves to be called meaning, not merely significance. But even if his interpretation is not *merely* significance it nevertheless is significance; and here we have a practical problem in terminology which demands attention. To solve this problem, however, we must first agree on the concept of the author's intention.

As noted earlier, there are difficulties involved in the concept of the author's intention, and perhaps this problem should be briefly reviewed once more (see p. 121). Its principal elements are the following: with the passing of time and the changing of circumstances our ability to perceive an author's intention diminishes; the meaning the author intended may cease to be the most important meaning of a text; the author's intention may have been confused; attending to the author's intention may diminish the power of the semblance; and, last, the concept of the author's intention may seem to grant him a greater degree of willed control over his work than he actually could have had.

Despite these difficulties, in my experience the concept of the author's *most probable* intention is useful in the classroom. Moreover, from a mediational point of view there is no need to pretend that difficulties do not exist while making use of the concept. Its practical values begin with the utterly simple advantage of providing a reference point. If we are to allow the bibliographer the dignity of having his interpretation called meaningful, we need a way of discriminating between this meaning and Steinbeck's generic meaning; the latter can be identified as the author's intention. A second value in the idea of the author's intention is its potential help in clarifying a text which, without such help, is ambiguous. I do not mean to suggest that all ambiguities can be resolved in this way. Finally, the concept of the author's intention fulfills a perfectly natural psychological need. It may be true, as some have said, that myths seem to come out of nowhere, and perhaps we can grant orally transmitted myths the status of authorless stories. But the readers in our classrooms usually know perfectly well where the art works they study come from. They recognize them as, and feel them to be, presentations from a unique individual directed to other unique individuals. It will surely prove as impossible to turn literature into an autonomous, complete, symbol system as it has been to turn physics or mathematics into such a system.

Granted the concept of the author's intention, then, we may for our purposes properly call the bibliographer's interpretation of *Tortilla Flat* significance rather than meaning. But granted also the concept of mediation, we can call his interpretation both significance *and* meaning.

We have been pondering the advantages of mediational law as a model for the interpretation of literary works. Although we haven't pressed very far into the philosophical complexities of the idea of mediation, we have observed that it affords appreciable help in our problems. According to this model, the disorderliness of simultaneously holding mutually exclusive interpretations of a work is not necessarily a cause for alarm. It is only needful to keep in mind the power of human intelligence to recognize in the necessary incompleteness of genre the source of what I have called transparent walls. When confined to literature, a transparent wall can in effect be walked around, but when such a wall is involved in decisions in the real world it is likely to become an impassable barrier, as in Plymouth and Twin Oaks. Forced decisions arising from confrontations in the literary classroom provide an exceptionally rich opportunity for developing an awareness of how transparent walls come into being, and a link is thus formed between the classroom and the cultural and educational needs of the community. An interpretation which may properly be called significance takes on the status of meaning when associated with a transparent wall.

These ideas, together with the many implications which cannot be recognized in a mere summary, provide a useful vantage point from which to view a literary classroom. But these ideas now need to be supplemented by recognition of the social actualities found in classrooms.

Among the many kinds of bonds that hold people together in groups or in pairs, one of the most powerful is what has often been called the relationship of the significant other. Through a brief exploration of this concept we can observe some of the principal social forces at work in the literary classroom and relate them to the discriminations with which we are concerned. My discussion of this subject will be frankly sketchy. To omit it would be to distort much of what I've said; to treat it thoroughly would require another volume. Despite their sketchiness, those ideas which can be considered here are of practical value with respect to several common problems.

One meaning given the concept of the significant other by Harry Stack Sullivan, with whose name the term is particularly associated, is love—or what he calls the end state of love. He writes, "When the satisfaction or the security of another person becomes as significant to one as is one's own satisfaction or security, then the state of love exists."[71] Sullivan also relates the concept to the forces binding a group together, but Daniel Bell offers a more dramatic statement of this notion than does Sullivan. Bell writes, "The idea of reality, sociologically, is a fairly simple one. Reality is confirmation by 'significant others.' "[72] In addition to love, Bell is thinking of respect and admiration. He cites as examples of confirmation various rites of passage such as a graduation or initiation ceremony. Confirmation need not be a ceremony, on the other hand, but only a recognition. Tacit acceptance of a boy into a gang is an effective confirmation by significant others. Those familiar with Walker Percy's *The Moviegoer* will recall with amusement that his notion of certification represents still another version of confirmation. For example, Percy describes how a dispirited pair of honeymooners is certified, and given a day promising romance and excitement, when movie star Bill Holden asks them for a light for his cigarette on Royal Street in New Orleans. "It is their peculiar reality," the narrator says of movie stars in general, "which astounds me."

Robert Merton suggests three alternative terms: reference group, reference individual, and role model. A reference group is illustrated by the gang a boy wants to belong to. A reference individual is one whose entire set of roles is considered worthy of emulation. In contrast, a role model is an individual among whose roles (e.g., businessman, fisherman, scout leader) only one is selected for emulation.[73] Merton has thus refined the more general concept of significant other. He himself uses the term "significant other" to mean reference individual.[74]

The discrimination Merton has made can be quite helpful in thinking about classrooms, but in the discussion that follows I will not try to maintain it. I will use the term significant other, and except when I note otherwise I will have in mind the meaning given this term by both Bell and Merton. I will be concerned with application of this term to the role of the teacher, to the literature being discussed, and to members of the group in the classroom. Finally, I will comment on the problems created by the great variety of "others" who may be significant.

It seems obvious that a teacher should be a significant other in the eyes of the class. I will not try to examine all the many questions this thought brings to mind, but instead will single out just one which offers a possible solution to a particularly difficult situation often arising in the classroom.

Let us take the case of a young man who resists in every way possible having anything to do with poetry. Without pondering the sources of his resistance, let us further assume that his distaste for poetry is genuine. The idea I have in mind, already apparent, is that if any change in his attitude is to occur it will probably have to be through an awakening interest in a pleasure clearly enjoyed by a significant other. Evidence that such changes do occur will be considered in a moment. The implication that a teacher has an obligation to try to fulfill the role of significant other for everyone in a classroom is admittedly daunting and certainly a matter of individual judgment.

Of course the teacher is only one of the factors in the situation. Another is the literature itself. Here, a reversal occurs. Instead of regarding sociological reality as recognition *by* significant others, we discover that in the reader-text relationship such reality is recognition *of* significant others. An example can be seen in the experience of Peter Abrahams, a black writer who left Johannesburg at the age of twenty after being educated in a white suburb there. Shortly after leaving he read the work of the black writers W. E. B. Du Bois and James Weldon

Johnson for the first time. Abrahams wrote, "These poems and stories were written by Negroes! Something burst deep inside me. The world could never again belong to white people only! Never again!"[75] In a less extreme form, such discoveries are common. With a tremendous sense of release and elation, readers come upon works articulating for the first time ideas and feelings which have been pent up inside them.

It is hard to say how relevant the idea of literature as recognition of significant others may be to the problem of a person having a strong distaste for literature. Yet I have often learned that someone who was resisting everything I offered in class was avidly reading other things. Perhaps had I chosen more perceptively I would have had more success.

One of the strongest forces at work in the classroom is the relationships among the members of the group. These relationships assume two subtly different forms: the relationship among individuals and the relationship of individuals to the group as a whole. When fortune smiles the group becomes, in Merton's terms, a reference group, a "frame of significant reference." I suspect an academic class seldom becomes significant in this group sense to more than a limited degree; the element of competition is too strong, the feeling of a common purpose too insubstantial, and the prestige bestowed by membership not great enough. Still, everyone is aware of the occasional class that feels itself very special and close-knit.

Relationships among individuals in a class involve three aspects of the idea of significant others: social relationships, value systems, and psychological differences.

Stuart Levine has conducted interesting research on social relationships, centering his investigations on people enrolled in elective courses serving as introductions to various arts, including literature. His results indicate that the role of the significant other is highly important in the decision to take such courses. To the question of why they had enrolled in a particular class, he reports, people's responses were almost uniformly of this sort: "I've met some interesting people who are deeply involved in the arts. I like them and want to associate with them and so assume that the thing to do is to get to know about whatever they like."[76]

This motive did not preclude a direct interest in learning to appreciate art for its own sake; Levine found that most of the people questioned did in fact learn to enjoy the art they were studying and began to give this art a regular place in their lives. Neverthelesss, their primary reason for entering an art class was the social one initially identified.

These results seem to tell us something about the relationship of a teacher to his class—or a critic to his audience. The content the audience is looking for in the message is probably quite personal. "Do *you* get pleasure out of this thing, and if so how do you go about doing it?" In my opinion this is a discovery a great many teachers of science need to make, especially in courses required of nonscience majors. I'll never forget a course in botany I had as a freshman, taught on the assumption that it was good for me to memorize the names of the phylum, class, order, family, genus, and species of many plants. The possibility that the teacher was actually enjoying the study of botany did not occur to me. Perhaps he wasn't. Now, though—as I write— I perceive that in his class I was the equivalent of the young man who dislikes poetry.

Of course the kind of teacher-class relationship we infer from Levine's work to be most desirable may seem irrelevant to a class which is highly professional in spirit and purpose. Such a class is more difficult to find just now than it used to be, but that will change.

The research of Lawrence Kohlberg and his associates reveals another dimension of the problem of significant others. Although their theoretical model is controversial, the empirical observations reported by this group do appear to reinforce the idea of the potential for change inherent in an individual's participation in a group. Kohlberg has for years been studying changes in the kinds of moral evaluations children make as they mature. One phase of his study has consisted of following the development of the moral thinking of seventy-five boys. At the beginning of the study these boys were ten to sixteen years old. They are now in their twenties and thirties.

Kohlberg believes the development of moral evaluations is a process which passes through six distinct stages.[77] Furthermore, his research indicates that within certain limits passage from one stage to another can be achieved through group discussion, in the classroom, of moral problems. It is the potential for change that is primarily of interest to us in Kohlberg's study.

The stages of moral evaluation Kohlberg identifies range from a simple punishment-and-obedience orientation through a doing-one's-duty-for-law-and-order orientation to a final orientation based on respect for the individual. Kohlberg presents participants in discussions with problems in the form of what I earlier called minidramas. For example, a man's wife is sick and will die unless he can procure a certain drug for her. The only source of the drug is in the hands of someone who is seeking exorbitant profits from it, and the man whose wife is sick doesn't have enough money to buy it. Could he be justified in stealing the drug? Kohlberg offers six possible justifications, each corresponding to one of six stages of moral judgment, and asks for evaluation of them. Partly because of their evident similarity to forced decisions often encountered in discussions of literature, it will be worth our while to examine the justifications Kohlberg offers for evaluation in this case.

"God would punish me if I let her die. I'd go to Hell." (Stage 1: obedience and punishment avoidance.)

"I have a right to the services of my wife, and naturally I regard this as more important than whatever rights the druggist may claim. No one is going to look out for my interests, or my wife's, unless I do." (Stage 2: instrumental relativism.)

"I regard myself as a tender and loving husband, and as such I'm going to do what any half-decent husband would do—save his family and carry out his protective function." (Stage 3: personal concordance with stereotyped role models.)

"When we entered into the state of holy matrimony, my wife and I submitted ourselves to a higher law, the institution of marriage. The fabric of our society is held together by this institution. I know my lawful duty when I see it." (Stage 4: law and order. Authority-maintaining orientation.)

"My wife and I promised to love and help each other, whatever the circumstances. We chose to make that commitment, and in our daily life together it is constantly renewed. I am therefore committed to saving her."

(Stage 5: social-contract orientation to shared values.)
"The principles at stake here include the love of my
wife and me for each other, the value of a human life,
and the threat to this life caused by exploitive commer-
cial relationships. No contract, law, obligation, private
gain or fear of punishment should impede me from saving her, or impede any man from saving those he loves.
I will steal the drug, especially for her, but also for all
those who might suffer in similar situations. I will do it
publicly so that this society may cease to sacrifice human
relationships to the profit motive." (Stage 6: conscience
and principle orientation.) [78]

To bring Kohlberg's illustration closer to our own immediate
interests, let us consider a comparable literary example. In *The
Scarlet Letter* Hester Prynne asserts that her adultery with
Arthur Dimmesdale had a "consecration of its own." In my
experience, some readers invariably accept this statement as
true, and a good deal of analysis of Hawthorne's intention is
necessary to show them it is not true, at least not true in any
sense Hawthorne himself would finally accept. It is unusual,
however, to find anyone who does not in the end willingly
agree that there is distance between Hawthorne and Hester in
the moment of her assertion of the consecration of the adultery.
Hester might be described as symbolic of Hawthorne's awareness that the concept of sin was the source of a transparent wall
in Massachusetts Bay Colony. Hester's assertion was an attack
on the Puritan concept of sin, and there can be no doubt it was
an attack in which Hawthorne was, at least unconsciously,
deeply involved. Her point of view was not one, however, which
Hawthorne would have related to Kohlberg's sixth stage of
moral judgment.

It isn't clear to me whether the changes in moral thinking
that Kohlberg has observed taking place through group discussion of such problems are accompanied by changes in behavior.
Nor have I any evidence that changes in behavior follow a
heightened ability to make the discriminations necessary for
understanding how Hester Prynne's statement relates to the intrinsic genre of *The Scarlet Letter*.[79] Perhaps these uncertainties
are to be regretted, but they are not catastrophic. The classroom

is not a substitute for a good home, or a stable community, or a meaningful church. It has its own unique but not commanding cultural role to play. It can be culturally effective by enhancing awareness of such elements as perceptual hypotheses, forced decisions, and the sources of transparent walls. Through such awareness, the classroom enlarges the possibility of wisdom in social conduct. Awareness is never commanding, it is only enabling.

Some group discussions do not have good results in any sense. Occasionally the others who are significant only exacerbate problems. Sullivan points out that a group may form because of a shared paranoia.[80] Such groups are hardly to be expected in a classroom, but some notice should be taken of the problem of individual differences they illustrate.

Obviously the theories of the various schools of psychotherapy should be taken into account in considering such problems, but here I will not attempt to discuss such theories. Instead I will comment on just two specific factors: verbal ability and affect. Both of these factors can easily be observed by any thoughtful person; they are not merely theoretical. Both are of great importance in the classroom.

One of my colleagues and I once spent some time gathering information about the scores of several thousand college freshmen on their entrance examination. What we were looking for was all those freshmen who had scored on the 80th percentile or above on either the verbal or the quantitative part of the examination and on the 20th percentile or below on the other part. We found approximately twenty freshmen in each category: twenty who were above the 80th percentile on the verbal and below the 20th on the quantitative, and another twenty who were above the 80th percentile on the quantitative part and below the 20th on the verbal. I don't have exact figures because our records were later accidentally destroyed.[81]

In any event, we didn't know what conclusions to draw from our records, except for one broad implication. That is, being rather stupid about either language or mathematics doesn't mean a person is stupid about everything. This is a fact which I'm afraid is sometimes forgotten by teachers working happily in their own medium of either words or numbers. I feel quite sure that here, too, is a dimension C. P. Snow overlooked in his

Two Cultures. As he illustrates in his own person, being gifted with either words or numbers does not preclude being gifted with the other also. But not everyone is as lucky as Sir Charles, and it is probable that the respective natures of the two cultures—the sciences and the humanities—represent deeply individual as well as cultural sources. But even here there is a mystery. Are the sources of such individual differences hereditary, or environmental, or both? Nobody knows, as far as I am aware.

If the young man who dislikes poetry is a low verbal, what do you do? Do you excuse him from poetry class, on the grounds that making him take it will only increase his distaste and resentment? The American Society for Engineering Education once suggested that perhaps engineers should be given courses in music or the plastic or graphic arts rather than literature.[82] Although they were no doubt speaking with the voice of experience, I think it would be a serious mistake to follow their advice—provided the special needs of those not verbally gifted, or not emotionally receptive to literature, can be sympathetically recognized. One of the perplexities of the situation is that the average engineer *is* verbally gifted—or was among the group we investigated. On the other hand, he is more gifted quantitatively than verbally. I write with great uncertainty about this entire subject of aptitudes, much aware of my own ignorance and my own bias. All I feel sure of is that the importance of the subject in the teaching of literature has not been generally understood.

My second and last topic is affect. The word "affect" has a complex technical meaning for psychiatrists and a rather ambiguous popular meaning. I'll disregard the technical meaning. One sense of the popular meaning is something like "an ability to feel emotion." The other, which is the usage I'll employ, is "an ability to feel concern about someone else's emotion." For example, "[Jim's] characteristics are essentially cold logic, hypersensitivity, and lack of affectivity."

The words just quoted were written by one Nobel prizewinner, André Lwoff, while in the process of both scolding at and sorrowing over another Nobel prizewinner, James Watson. The occasion was Lwoff's review of Watson's book *The Double Helix*.[83] In this book Watson describes in vivid, personal detail

the events leading up to the discovery of the double-helix form
of DNA by Francis Crick and himself. Watson and Crick shared
a Nobel prize for this discovery. Lwoff continues his comment
on the youthful Watson's lack of affect with such statements as
these: "Jim appears to be ignorant of the fact that the naked
truth can be a deadly weapon. . . . He seems completely unaware of the injuries he inflicts, completely unaware of the
harm he can do his friends." In addition to Watson's lack of
affect, Lwoff comments on his hypersensitivity, his ability to
analyze personal relationships with the skill of a novelist. The
individuality of those described, Lwoff says, emerges with
"unusual intensity."

Lack of affect is no prerogative of scientists. It is common
among humanists and may be encountered in any classroom.
In a literary classroom, its consequences can be devastating. But
here again a problem develops. Does a lack of affect imply an
inability to respond to the emotional aspect of literature, or a
disinclination to do so? I do not know the answer to this question. In fact, I suspect that to deserve a serious answer the question would have to be formulated in a much more complex
way.

We come now to a question I've been leading up to, and a
conclusion. What happens if chance sprinkles a discussion group
with high-quantitative low-verbals who are low in affect? This
question is, of course, only an epitome of a very general problem. What is the relationship between literary theory and human individuality?

This general question leads into largely unexplored territory.[84] It is a poor research area, in the practical sense, because
of the particular departmental structure of our universities. And
yet in almost every required course in literature it presents itself in a demanding form. How far should an instructor go in
requiring evidences of an ability to make the discriminations
we have been discussing in previous chapters? I don't know the
answer, but I have an intuition on at least one point: such difficulties as a low verbal ability, or a low quantitative ability, or
a low affect are all characteristics which can be changed—not
instantaneously, but over a period of time. Martin Buber made a
relevant point in a remarkable dialog he had with Carl Rogers
concerning a psychotherapist's relation to his patient. In a lit-

erary classroom we are not concerned with the relief of emotional disturbances, but I believe what Buber said is related to the problems we do have.

Rogers remarked, during this spontaneous, taped dialog: "It seems to me that the moment where persons are most likely to change, or I even think of it as the moments in which people *do* change, are the moments in which perhaps the relationship is experienced the same on both sides."[85] That is to say, the therapist enters wholly and sympathetically into the patient's world and the patient meets him there with complete trust that there is no reservation or arrogance on the therapist's part. They meet as equals.

Buber replied, "A man *helped* cannot think, cannot imagine helping another. How could he? . . . You see, you give him something in order to make him equal to you."[86] Buber's point is that when you look at the situation as a whole you are forced to the realization that the person being helped could hardly consider his role as equal to that of the person doing the helping. And yet, Buber went on to insist, the person being helped must somehow be assured that his worth as a human being is not less than that of the other. Indeed, such assurance is essential if change is to occur. Therefore, Buber concludes, the person doing the helping must simultaneously convince the other that in his worth and dignity as a human being he is an equal, yet make clear to him the possibility and desirability of change. To this process, which is clearly far more complex than anything Daniel Bell had in mind in his definition of sociological reality, Buber applied the same term used by Bell: confirmation.[87] It looks like an interesting, if difficult, ideal for a classroom.

In fact, I suppose it's the only possible cultural ideal (as distinguished from personal ideal) for any literary classroom which is not devoted merely to the transfer of information from one head to another. As I have throughout this book, I use the word "cultural" to refer to the socializing, communal function of the classroom, not forgetting that the classroom also serves the personal objective of showing people how to enjoy literature. The cultural goals of the literary classroom which have been assumed throughout are direct acquaintance with our literary heritage, correctness in the apprehension of the purpose embodied in semblance,[88] and correctness in apprehension of the author's probable intention as embodied in meaning and structure. The last of these goals involves an understanding of the process of mediation. Perhaps the development of affect is necessarily a part of these goals; perhaps it is an additional goal, only incidentally related to these others. Whatever the case may be, we can probably agree that the objectives of the classroom should include all these elements.

Everything I myself have learned through experience or through the reports of others indicates that the combination of abilities required for an individual's attainment of these goals is likely to appear only when it is nurtured for a prolonged period in an appropriate environment. Such an environment is one in which pleasure is taken in learning, as well as one in which sensitivity to and concern about other people's feelings are encouraged. Presumably one of the ways, although not the only way, by which a teacher constitutes himself a significant other is through creation of such an environment.

22. VALIDATION

Two topics remain to be discussed. The first is a summary of the idea of validating a literary work. The second is the corollary idea of validating a literary classroom. A good deal has already been said indirectly about this second topic, but it has not yet been taken up directly.

A reader feels a literary work to be valid when it creates for him a powerful semblance, or intransitive rapt attention, and when it also compels his intellectual assent. Both of these elements in the process of validation depend on a complex variety of factors. I will briefly review what has been said about both and will then turn to the subject of the validation of the classroom.

The power of semblance is a function of maturity, again in a complex way. Probably the intensity of semblance is greatest in childhood; on the other hand, works gripping to the imagination of a mature reader may be powerless to interest children. In all cases a fusion is involved, the joining together of what the work contains and what the reader contains. It is, however, possible for a reader to be temporarily enthralled by a work he finds intellectually distasteful.

Assent to a work appears to involve judgments about the emotional quality of the work, its intellectual force and coherence, its conformity to acceptable models, and its genre.

Judgments about the aesthetic quality of a work are, in my opinion, basically intuitive. An illuminating comparison is the situation of a mathematician who pronounces a certain mathematical proof logically sound but not elegant. Without knowing how to make the proof beautiful, he may nevertheless feel it could be done. Assent to a literary work requires the same sort of judgment, a judgment complexly involving both emotional and intellectual factors.

Assent also requires respect for the abstract intellectual quality of the work. The work must seem to make sense, even when its intention is antirational. Its point of view need not be one the reader shares. But there are clearly limits to this tolerance.

The work must fall within the limits of standards acceptable to the reader. These standards, however, are constantly changing. Each generation rejects the standards of its parents and then, as the years pass, is astonished by the bad taste of the young. Still, there are limits to this lack of tolerance too. Half-blinded by genre though the human mind may be, it is also characterized by the potential of mediational and anthropological thinking; it can surmount its familiar models and accept a new model, or an old one.

A deep sensitivity to genre and intrinsic genre enhances tolerance. Knowing what a thing is, we forgive it for not being something else. Assent may depend on such understanding. *The Sound and the Fury* is a magnificent example.

Faulkner himself described *The Sound and the Fury* as the same story told four times. Each of the tellings is different in kind. It is curious to imagine what our opinion of Jason's savage section would be if it were the only work Faulkner had ever published. Could any analysis of the probable intention in this one piece of work win our assent? No doubt readers are exhilarated by the unrestrained malice in it; the semblance is powerful. There is, on the other hand, abundant rhetorical evidence of distance between author and protagonist. Nevertheless the end result, were Jason's section all we had from Faulkner's hand, would probably be a fascinated horror, as at a moral antinomy. Why, we would wonder, this compulsive interest in so repulsive a character? In fact, everything is clarified when Jason's section is seen not as compulsive but as a literary kind taking its place among the other kinds making up the novel as a whole. The mind conceiving Jason's malice, we realize, is also conceiving the compassion shown by Dilsey and Caddy. The intrinsic genre to which Jason's section belongs, we then perceive, can be understood only as an element in the larger design. The deliberateness of Faulkner's choice of the intrinsic genre in Jason's section thus becomes clear. An author's choice of both genre and intrinsic genre, in summary, must always be taken into account as part of his intention.

One other element in the generic aspect of *The Sound and the Fury* deserves notice in these summary comments on the validation of literature. In any normal sense, comprehension of such books as *The Sound and the Fury*, *Ulysses*, and *Gravity's Rainbow* lies beyond the power of the solitary reader. One of the functions these books are designed for is to serve as the focal point of discussions. I suspect a thoughtful analysis of their cultural role would indicate that these books, and others like them, are in part responses to a cultural vacuum. They seem to be offering themselves to us as a key permitting discussion of matters we have no other means of articulating. This notion may, however, be too fanciful.

Finally, literary works are validated through the judgments of significant others. In a superficial sense, this means only that books are certified by prominent intellectuals in the same way the honeymooners' day was certified by Bill Holden in *The Moviegoer*. But what I am thinking of just now is a little different. I have in mind the fact that in many areas of our lives finality is social. As George Herbert Mead said, we must become socialized to become ourselves. Without language, which is a property of society, we would not really be human. As the implication of these thoughts is explored, it becomes clear it's meaningless to speak of the validation of a work as if validation represented a final, absolute transformation involving nothing but the book and the reader. Rather, the relationship of book and reader is a part of, and is affected by, an inconceivably intricate network of relationships within an entire culture. Parts of this network are of course more significant in respect to any given reader-book relationship than other parts, and validation is particularly dependent on a perception of the book as having a meaningful relationship to these especially significant elements. I have had, for instance, more than one slightly eerie conversation with people of other nationalities in which we discovered disagreements about which American authors are the greatest. The sensed power of the backing given such conflicting opinions by entire societies produces a strange uneasiness. We return with relief to our own significances.

In conclusion, a few comments about the validation of a literary classroom.

For people with a highly authoritarian orientation, the classroom may be satisfyingly validated in a strictly institutional way. Take this course, do these required things, and in return certain benefits of money, personal satisfaction, and prestige will follow. For many people the situation is less simple. While granting its institutional role, many people clearly desire the classroom to offer them something meaningful which they themselves somehow have a hand in determining. At the present time a relatively heavy emphasis is falling upon this kind of personal demand because of the disorganization of our cultural value system. It therefore becomes important to recognize that there are things the classroom can't do, as well as things it can.

Expectations which are occasionally associated with the idea of a literary classroom, but which actually lie beyond its scope, are easily discerned. The literary classroom cannot directly serve a religious purpose, or a psychotherapeutic purpose, or a political purpose. It could more readily serve philosophical or sociological or historical or anthropological purposes. Anthropology, says anthropologist Kenelm Burridge, is still a literary genre.[89] Classrooms in these other disciplines could themselves directly serve a literary purpose too, if they wished, and in fact there is a good deal of overlapping in all directions. University departmental structures distortingly emphasize the distinctions and obscure the relationships. Nevertheless, there are differences between the study of anthropology or history and the study of literature and it would be awkward and confusing to assume that the literary classroom could effectively serve these other purposes.

In contrast to what it cannot do, or cannot do well, the literary classroom is ideally suited to offer certain personal and cultural benefits. One such benefit is learning to enjoy elitist literature, with the social benefits accompanying this skill. It is difficult to write about this topic without appearing to condescend, but I do not mean to condescend. Particularly for people from what we now call a disadvantaged background (e.g., John Stuart Mill), the experience of initiation into the world of art and literature can be profoundly moving. Classrooms designed for this purpose can be large, provided the lecturer is capable of projecting a public image of enjoying the works he discusses, as well as of being lucid in what he says.

In the end, however, such personal benefits may not save the literary classroom, as an institution, from seeming trivial. Jack London's *Martin Eden*, a poor novel in many ways, contains a moving account of just such a disillusionment. It is worth pondering. The trouble arises when personal benefits, won at the cost of great effort, no longer seem related to those broader social and cultural values that had at first seemed inseparable from them. In *In Bluebeard's Castle*, George Steiner has vividly described the powerlessness of art to assure humane behavior. Some of the most barbarous Nazis, as he points out, were dedicated to the arts.

On the other hand, there is a vast difference between causality and possibility. The study of literature can force no one to be humane, but apparently the study of literature can make it possible to be more humane than would otherwise be the case. This aspect of the role of the literary classroom seems to me located primarily in the discussion of literature by a small group, the focus of my concern throughout this book. The literary classroom becomes validated in a more than personal sense when it is felt to be structurally integrated into the culture which supports it.

In our culture, the conviction that such an integration has come into being is found, according to my own observations, when forced decisions about real human problems are made in the environment provided by the illusional power and the abstract complexity of a work of art. Through such experience we discover that the questions we ask, and the ideas we propose, take on perceptual life only when—as with Niels Bohr at Elsinore—we have made them incomplete by providing them with castles to dwell in.

NOTES

1. Robert K. Merton, *The Sociology of Science*, ed. Norman W. Storer (Chicago: University of Chicago Press, 1973), pp. 343 ff.
2. Thomas S. Kuhn, *The Structure of Scientific Revolutions* (Chicago: University of Chicago Press, 1962), pp. 155–157.
3. Roland Barthes, "The Death of the Author," trans. Richard Howard, in *The Discontinuous Universe: Selected Writings in Contemporary Consciousness*, ed. Sallie Sears and Georgianna W. Lord (New York: Basic Books, 1972), pp. 7–12. Barthes seems to make a distinction between the relationship of a reader to a text and the relationship of a critic to a text. With explicit reference to a critic, he asks, "How could we believe, in fact, that the work is an object exterior to the psyche and history of the man who interrogates it . . . ?" (*Critical Essays*, trans. Richard Howard [Evanston: Northwestern University Press, 1972], p. 257).
4. Stanley Fish, "Literature in the Reader: Affective Stylistics," *New Literary History* 2, no. 1 (Autumn 1970): 145–146.
5. Claude Lévi-Strauss, *Tristes Tropiques*, trans. John Weightman and Doreen Weightman (New York: Atheneum, 1974), p. 11.

Part One. Semblance

1. Georg Wilhelm Friedrich Hegel, *The Introduction to Hegel's Philosophy of Fine Art*, trans. from the German with notes and prefatory essay by Bernard Bosanquet (London: Kegan Paul, Trench, 1886), p. 72. Like Bosanquet, F. T. B. Osmaston in his translation of Hegel's *The Philosophy of Fine Art* translates "Schein" as "semblance."
2. Susanne K. Langer, *Feeling and Form* (New York: Charles Scribner's Sons, 1953), p. 84. Langer attributes her use of "semblance" to Jung and Bosanquet. See her *Mind: An Essay on Human Feeling* (Baltimore: Johns Hopkins University Press, 1967), 1:111.
3. Ernest Hemingway, *A Farewell to Arms* (New York: Charles Scribner's Sons, 1949), p. 234.
4. Albert Camus, *The Fall*, trans. Justin O'Brien (New York: Alfred A. Knopf, 1956), pp. 37–38.
5. Frank Kermode, *The Sense of an Ending: Studies in the Theory of Fiction* (New York: Oxford University Press, 1966), p. 149.
6. Emily Dickinson, *The Complete Poems of Emily Dickinson*, ed.

Thomas H. Johnson (Cambridge: Belknap Press, 1955), p. 757.

7. Robert Frost, *The Poetry of Robert Frost*, ed. Edward Connery Lathem (New York: Holt, Rinehart & Winston, 1969), p. 225.

8. Horatio Alger, *The Young Acrobat* (Chicago: M. A. Donahoe, n.d.), p. 152.

9. Saul Bellow, *Mr. Sammler's Planet* (New York: Viking Press, 1970), p. 73.

10. A curious example of how this technical problem in fiction passes over into the problem of the relationship between the affective and the abstract in philosophy can be seen in the following remark by Maurice Alexander Natanson: "The phenomenological approach endeavours to remain true to the texture of human reality. Paradoxically, a method that brackets causal analysis is utilized to describe causation as a structure of the *Lebenswelt*" (*Literature, Philosophy, and the Social Sciences: Essays in Existentialism and Phenomenology* [The Hague: Martinus Nijhoff, 1962], p. 208).

11. Henry James, *The Wings of the Dove*, Modern Library ed. (New York: Random House, 1937), p. 177.

12. Charles Rossman, "Stephen Dedalus and the Spiritual-Heroic Refrigerating Apparatus: Art and Life in Joyce's *Portrait*," in *Forms of Modern British Fiction*, ed. Alan Warren Friedman (Austin: University of Texas Press, 1975), pp. 101–131.

SEMBLANCE & PURPOSE

13. Robert Motherwell, quoted in *Theories of Modern Art: A Source Book by Artists and Critics*, ed. Herschel B. Chipp, California Studies in the History of Art, no. 11 (Berkeley & Los Angeles: University of California Press, 1968), p. 563.

14. John Dewey, *Art as Experience* (New York: G. P. Putnam's Sons, 1958), p. 276.

15. Langer, *Feeling and Form*, p. 67.

16. Victor Erlich, *Russian Formalism: History–Doctrine*, 3d ed. (The Hague: Mouton, 1969), p. 199.

17. Claudio Guillén, *Literature as System: Essays toward the Theory of Literary History* (Princeton: Princeton University Press, 1971), p. 492.

18. Fredric Jameson, *The Prison-House of Language: A Critical Account of Structuralism and Russian Formalism*, Princeton Essays in Literature (Princeton: Princeton University Press, 1972), p. 82.

19. See ibid., p. 84, for an example of the process. In Jameson's example the idea of purpose is in effect attributed to "voice."

20. A problem that bothers everybody who accepts the importance of

purpose in art, however, is what becomes of the idea of purpose in respect to the beauty of natural objects. Murray Krieger offers a pithy summary of the situation: "If it is a natural object to which [the observer] responds aesthetically, then either it has been given a form which can so control him or he, thanks perhaps to the habits acquired in his commerce with art, projects such a form upon it and becomes an artist himself. Which of these two is the more likely possibility I leave for metaphysicians to dispute" (*The New Apologists for Poetry* [Minneapolis: University of Minnesota Press, 1956], p. 130). The same comment would apply to such items as ready-mades and found art, although in these instances the assignment of a title may complicate the situation.

21. John Cage, *Silence: Lectures and Writings* (Middletown: Wesleyan University Press, 1961), p. 17.

22. Ibid., p. 10.

23. Cindy Nemser, "An Interview with Stephen Kaltenbach," *Artforum* 9, no. 3 (November 1970): 49.

24. James, *Wings of the Dove*, p. v.

25. Ibid., p. xxii.

26. In *The Teller in the Tale* (Seattle: University of Washington Press, 1967), Louis D. Rubin, Jr., has presented what seems to me a compelling argument on behalf of the importance, in principle, of this kind of authorial presence. He discusses James at length. Perhaps he could have given more attention to an author's deliberate use of a conventional mask, especially in satire.

27. Patrick McCaughey, "Thomas Eakins and the Power of Seeing," *Artforum* 9, no. 4 (December 1970): 58.

28. Natanson, *Literature, Philosophy, and the Social Sciences*, p. 152.

29. Jonathan D. Culler, *Structuralist Poetics: Structuralism, Linguistics, and the Study of Literature* (Ithaca: Cornell University Press, 1975), p. 196.

30. Ibid., p. 193.

31. Ibid., p. 190.

32. A review by John Skow, *Time*, July 3, 1972, p. 63.

33. A closely similar but not identical idea is discussed by Wayne C. Booth at the end of Pt. Two of *The Rhetoric of Fiction* (Chicago: University of Chicago Press, 1961).

34. Virginia Woolf, *A Room of One's Own* (New York: Harcourt, Brace, 1929), pp. 119–121.

35. The following are three representative statements Langer makes about the theoretical dilemma of not being able to enjoy a work until the reading has been finished:

> [Elements] take their expressive character from their functions in the perceptual whole. (*Mind*, 1:84)

In a work that requires an appreciable length of time for complete physical perception, such as a novel . . . the author's first task is to imply, at the very outset, the scope and vital import of the whole. (*Feeling and Form*, p. 397)

The import of an art symbol [i.e., an entire work of art] cannot be built up like the meaning of a discourse, but must be seen *in toto* first; that is, the "understanding" of a work of art begins with an intuition of the whole presented feeling. (*Feeling and Form*, p. 379)

36. Dewey, *Art as Experience*, p. 192.

37. See Paul A. Kolers, "Experiments in Reading," *Scientific American*, July 1972, pp. 84–91.

38. See E. D. Hirsch, Jr., *Validity in Interpretation* (New Haven: Yale University Press, 1967), pp. 78 ff., and Noam Chomsky, *Syntactic Structures* (The Hague: Mouton, 1963), pp. 21 ff.

39. Susanne Langer comments on the concept of quality and her concept of semblance in *Feeling and Form*, p. 50: "The semblance of a thing . . . is its direct aesthetic quality. According to several eminent critics, this is what the artist tries to reveal for its own sake. But the emphasis on quality, or essence, is really only a stage in artistic conception. It is the making of a rarified element that serves, in its turn, for the making of something else—the imaginal art work itself. And this form is the non-discursive but articulate symbol of feeling." Cf. *Mind*, 1:209. I have not introduced Langer's idea of art as a symbol of feeling and therefore have not used the term "semblance" in quite the way she sometimes does. Also, I will not enter into consideration of differences between Dewey and Langer concerning how art is distinguished from ordinary experience.

40. Dewey, *Art as Experience*, p. 192. Dewey's concept of fusion is a special application of the belief generally held in pragmatic philosophy that the character of any given perception is to a considerable degree determined by the accumulated experience of the perceiver.

41. Ibid., p. 274. For a structuralist version of the fusion that occurs on a second reading, see Robert Scholes, *Structuralism in Literature: An Introduction* (New Haven: Yale University Press, 1974), p. 153. James R. Squire reports, however, that in a study of fifteen-year-old readers he found a marked absence of personal association with what was read (*The Responses of Adolescents While Reading Four Short Stories*, National Council of Teachers of English Research Report, no. 2 [Urbana: National Council of Teachers of English, 1964], p. 45).

42. Stephen C. Pepper, *The Work of Art* (Bloomington: Indiana University Press, 1955), p. 168. The character of Dewey's reasoning about the

relationship of a part to the whole in experience in general may be seen in his *Experience and Nature* (New York: W. W. Norton, 1929), p. 144. It should be remembered that we are concerned in the present discussion, however, not with meaning but with what a scholar like Hirsch would call response. See Hirsch, *Validity*, p. 38.

43. See Werner Heisenberg, *Physics and Beyond: Encounters and Conversations*, ed. Ruth Nanda Anshen, trans. Arnold J. Pomerans (New York: Harper & Row, 1971), pp. 244–245.

44. Wolfgang Iser, *The Implied Reader: Patterns of Communication in Prose Fiction from Bunyan to Beckett* (Baltimore: Johns Hopkins University Press, 1974), p. 283.

45. In these remarks, I do not intend any reference to the concept of fusion, as used by Hans-Georg Gadamer, e.g., in the theory of textual interpretation. Dewey's instrumental concept of elements leads to a different picture.

46. Langer, *Feeling and Form*, p. 318. The implied criticism of audience participation would not be shared by all. For a defense of audience-participation drama see Richard Schechner, *Public Domain: Essays on the Theater* (Indianapolis: Bobbs-Merrill, 1969), pp. 148 passim. In *New Reformation: Notes of a Neolithic Conservative* (New York: Random House, 1971), Paul Goodman associates the desire for audience participation with a religious impulse. For a discussion of how audiences are transformed into "constituencies" see Bennett M. Berger, "Audiences, Art, and Power," *Transaction* 8, no. 7 (May 1971): 29. For a discussion of the contrasting characteristics of a traditional "privileged" audience, see Erwin W. M. Straus, "Born to See, Bound to Behold," in *The Philosophy of the Body*, ed. Stuart F. Spicker (Chicago: Quadrangle Books, 1970), p. 358. The act of reading literature resembles the act of witnessing a traditional drama more closely than it does an audience-participation drama. Actually, the latter type of drama should be called traditional, since it no doubt appeared first, chronologically.

SEMBLANCE & THE READER'S MATURITY

47. J. H. Plumb, "Perspective," *Saturday Review*, March 28, 1970, p. 28.

48. Ian Watt, *The Rise of the Novel: Studies in Defoe, Richardson, and Fielding* (London: Chatto & Windus, 1957), p. 290.

49. The similarity (but not identity) between memory and semblance is nicely expressed by a comment Emerson makes in "The American Scholar": "The actions and events of our childhood and youth are now matters of calmest observation. They lie like fair pictures in the air. Not so with our recent actions,—with the business which we now have in

hand" (*The Literature of the United States: An Anthology and History from the Colonial Period through the American Renaissance*, ed. Walter Blair et al., 3 vols., 3d ed. [Chicago: Scott, Foresman, 1966], 1:1074).

50. Kester Svendsen, "Formalist Criticism and the Teaching of Shakespeare," *College English* 27, no. 1 (October 1965): 23–27. Langer reviews her concern about the possibility of an erroneous intuition of the import of a work and illustrates the remedy of structural analysis in Chap. 13 of *Feeling and Form*. The best account of the history of the formalist paradox is given in Krieger, *New Apologists*.

51. E.g., "individual works are too diverse and too complex to make it possible for anyone to keep detachment and emotion in more than a momentary equilibrium on a few occasions" (Paul Weiss, *The World of Art* [Carbondale: Southern Illinois University Press, 1961], p. 4).

52. Walter Kerr, *New York Times* News Service, July 21, 1968.

53. Walter J. Slatoff, *With Respect to Readers: Dimensions of Literary Response* (Ithaca: Cornell University Press, 1970), pp. 46–47. Cf. Norman N. Holland, *The Dynamics of Literary Response* (New York: Oxford University Press, 1968), p. 83.

54. Quoted in Claude Lévi-Strauss, *The Savage Mind*, Nature of Human Society series (Chicago: University of Chicago Press, 1966), p. 38.

55. Ibid.

56. Andrew Weil, *The Natural Mind: A New Way of Looking at Drugs and the Higher Consciousness* (Boston: Houghton Mifflin, 1972), p. 33.

57. *Psychology Today* 7, no. 6 (November 1973): 14.

58. Rollo May, *Psychology and the Human Dilemma* (Princeton: D. Van Nostrand, 1967), p. 8.

59. Samuel Taylor Coleridge, *Selected Poetry and Prose*, ed. with an intro. and notes by Elisabeth Schneider, 2d ed. (San Francisco: Rinehart Press, 1971), p. 120.

60. Ernst Kris, *Psychoanalytic Explorations in Art* (New York: International Universities Press, 1952), p. 48.

61. Jerome L. Singer, *Daydreaming: An Introduction to the Experimental Study of Inner Experience* (New York: Random House, 1966), Chap. 5. In his highly interesting study of ninth and tenth graders, James R. Squire reports that among these adolescents there was a strong positive correlation between degree of emotional involvement in fiction and analytical thinking about the elements in the fiction which created the involvement. He also reports a noticeable, but not exclusive, tendency toward concentration of the analytical thinking in the period following the reading of the work rather than during the reading. Comparable studies of more mature groups would be valuable. See Squire, *Responses of Adolescents*, p. 22.

62. Kris, *Psychoanalytic Explorations*, p. 42.

63. George P. Elliott, "Never Nothing," *Harper's*, September 1970, p. 93.

64. Kris, *Psychoanalytic Explorations*, p. 41.

65. Ibid., p. 42.

THREE SPECIAL PROBLEMS

66. Edward Bullough, " 'Psychical Distance' as a Factor in Art and an Aesthetic Principle," in *Art and Philosophy: Reading in Aesthetics*, ed. W. E. Kennick (New York: St. Martin's Press, 1964). See Holland, *Dynamics*, p. 89, for a criticism of the terms.

67. See Slatoff, *With Respect to Readers*, Chap. 2.

68. Ibid., p. 50. Cf. Georges Poulet's words: "Whatever I think is part of *my* mental world. And yet here I am thinking a thought which manifestly belongs to another mental world, which is being thought in me just as though I did not exist. Already the notion is inconceivable and seems even more so if I reflect that since every thought must have a subject to think it, this *thought* which is alien to me and yet in me, must also have in me a *subject* which is alien to me" ("Phenomenology of Reading," *New Literary History* 1, no. 1 [October 1969]: 56).

69. Some striking evidence in support of this idea can be found in Holland, *Dynamics*, pp. 94–95.

70. Slatoff, *With Respect to Readers*, Chap. 2. Cf. Pepper, *Work of Art*, p. 21.

71. Dewey, *Art as Experience*, pp. 144–146.

72. Slatoff, *With Respect to Readers*, pp. 53–54.

73. See Chap. 4 in Robert A. Durr's *Poetic Vision and the Psychedelic Experience* (Syracuse: Syracuse University Press, 1970). Cf. Robert E. Ornstein, *The Psychology of Consciousness* (New York: Viking Press, 1973), p. 89.

74. See Durr, *Poetic Vision*, pp. 82–83.

75. Michael Polanyi, *Personal Knowledge: Towards a Post-Critical Philosophy* (Chicago: University of Chicago Press, 1958), p. 133. Cf. Kuhn, *Structure of Scientific Revolutions*, pp. 154 ff.

76. Polanyi, *Personal Knowledge*, pp. 10–11.

77. Martin Deutsch, "Evidence and Inference in Nuclear Research," in *Evidence and Inference*, ed. Daniel Lerner (New York: Free Press, 1959), p. 96. As might be expected, however, it is also possible to find examples of just the opposite of the tendency Deutsch describes. That is, a person may become so absorbed in abstract concepts that the abstractions begin

to intrude strangely into his imaginative perceptions of, or relationships with, the physical phenomena themselves. The results of this latter tendency are probably often unfortunate, as can be seen in the last sentence of the passage below, written by a distinguished physicist. (The word "isospin" is a contraction of the somewhat more informative phrase "isotopic spin.")

> A second difficulty is the oversimplified picture of isospin, often propagated in introductory expositions of the concept, in which isospin is regarded as being completely analogous to ordinary spin and to arise of necessity from the symmetric nature of nuclear forces. Although this approach is essentially correct, it unfortunately suggests that isospin is a fundamental entity and that a proper understanding of the concept will lead by itself to an unlocking of the secrets of nuclei. This is not the function of isospin in nuclei. (D. Robson, "Isospin in Nuclei," *Science*, January 12, 1973, p. 133.)

Granted that it is often difficult in nuclear physics to distinguish between theory and observation, the fact that the concluding sentence is careless about this distinction becomes apparent with the realization that what Professor Robson should have written—as presumably he would agree—is, "This is not the function of the concept of isospin in nuclei." In fairness, I should add that of course the kind of imagery Deutsch describes can also lead to unfortunate results. When thinking, one does what one can.

78. Theodore Taylor, quoted in John McPhee, *The Curve of Binding Energy* (New York: Farrar, Straus & Giroux, 1974), p. 10.

79. Heisenberg, *Physics and Beyond*, p. 61.

80. Lewis Thomas, "Notes of a Biology-Watcher: Natural Science," *New England Journal of Medicine*, February 8, 1973, pp. 307–308.

81. For further discussion of this general concept see D. G. James, *Scepticism and Poetry* (London: George Allen & Unwin, 1937).

82. Evidence that this does happen is found in James R. Wilson, *Responses of College Freshmen to Three Novels*, National Council of Teachers of English Research Report, no. 7 (Champaign: National Council of Teachers of English, 1966).

83. Anshen, in Heisenberg, *Physics and Beyond*, p. x.

84. Morse Peckham, *Man's Rage for Chaos* (Philadelphia: Chilton Books, 1965), p. 68.

85. A summary of the view that what can be perceived depends to an important degree on the perceiver's attitudes can be found in John M. Ellis, *The Theory of Literary Criticism: A Logical Analysis* (Berkeley and Los Angeles: University of California Press, 1974), pp. 191 ff.

SUMMARY OF PART ONE

86. Lucien Goldmann, in a discussion in *The Languages of Criticism and the Sciences of Man: The Structuralist Controversy*, ed. Richard Macksey and Eugenio Donato (Baltimore: Johns Hopkins University Press, 1970), p. 270.

Part Two. Abstractions

INTRODUCTION TO PART TWO

1. "Real universal" implies the existence of something in the objects symbolized to which the universal refers. A "nominal universal" refers only to the unique, particular individuals comprising its class; it does not participate in them as a property.
2. Cf. the following complaint by a French sociologist: "Sociology reduces a phenomenon to the restrictive level of industrial (or post-industrial) society, circumscribes the concrete particular in descriptive monographs, and simply eliminates the event, as such, altogether" (Edgar Morin, *Rumour in Orleans*, trans. Peter Green [London: Anthony Blond, 1971], p. 267).
3. Cleanth Brooks, *A Shaping Joy: Studies in the Writer's Craft* (New York: Harcourt, Brace, 1971), p. 6.
4. Cleanth Brooks, "Irony as a Principle of Structure," in *Literary Opinion in America: Essays Illustrating the Status, Methods, and Problems of Criticism in the United States in the Twentieth Century*, ed. Morton Dauwen Zabel, 2 vols., 3d ed. (New York: Harper & Row, 1962), 2:731, 740.

HISTORICAL CONTEXT

5. Meyer H. Abrams, *The Mirror and the Lamp: Romantic Theory and the Critical Tradition* (New York: Oxford University Press, 1953), p. 335.
6. Albert Einstein, *Essays in Science* (New York: Philosophical Library, 1934), p. 4. A few sentences later Einstein comments on what I have called the logical gap: ". . . there is no logical bridge between phenomena and their theoretical principles."
7. Lévi-Strauss, *Savage Mind*, Chap. 1 and p. 172.
8. For further discussion of this point see Gerald Graff, *Poetic State-*

ment and Critical Dogma (Evanston: Northwestern University Press, 1970), pp. 147 passim.

9. Einstein, *Essays*, p. 4.

10. See Niels Bohr, "Discussion with Einstein on Epistemological Problems in Atomic Physics," in *Albert Einstein: Philosopher-Scientist*, ed. Paul Arthur Schilpp (Evanston: Library of Living Philosophers, 1949), p. 228.

11. Henry Adams, *The Education of Henry Adams*, Modern Library ed. (New York: Random House, 1931), p. 382.

12. For a general review of Adams's position on this subject see William H. Jordy, *Henry Adams: Scientific Historian* (New Haven: Yale University Press, 1952).

13. Charles A. Beard, *The Nature of the Social Sciences in Relation to Objectives of Instruction*, report of the Commission on the Social Studies, American Historical Association, pt. 7 (New York: Charles Scribner's Sons, 1934), p. 57.

14. Ibid., p. 58.

15. Ibid., p. 50.

16. Gertrude Stein, *The Geographical History of America* (New York: Random House, 1936), p. 199.

17. Ernest Hemingway, *Death in the Afternoon* (New York: Charles Scribner's Sons, 1932), p. 2.

18. Ernest Hemingway, *In Our Time* (New York: Charles Scribner's Sons, 1958), p. 184.

19. Philip Young, *Ernest Hemingway* (New York: Rinehart, 1952), pp. 150–151.

20. Ford Madox Hueffer, *Collected Poems of Ford Madox Hueffer* (London: Martin Secker, 1916), p. 135.

21. Hugh Kenner, *The Pound Era* (Berkeley and Los Angeles: University of California Press, 1971), p. 181.

22. T. S. Eliot, *Selected Essays 1917–1932* (New York: Harcourt, Brace, 1932), p. 115.

23. St. John Perse, *Anabasis*, trans. and preface by T. S. Eliot (New York: Harcourt, Brace, 1949), p. 10.

24. William Carlos Williams, "How to Write," in *The Poems of William Carlos Williams: A Critical Study*, by Linda Welshimer Wagner (Middletown: Wesleyan University Press, 1964), p. 145.

25. William Carlos Williams, *Selected Essays* (New York: Random House, 1954), p. 257. I found these two quotations from Williams juxtaposed in J. Hillis Miller, *Poets of Reality: Six Twentieth-Century Writers* (Cambridge: Harvard University Press, 1965).

26. Williams, *Selected Essays*, p. 256. He also said (p. xiii), "If the emotions do not control the poem, what in Heaven's name does? The an-

swer is the mind." I am indebted to Joseph Slate for this reference.

27. Brooks, "Irony," p. 729.

28. Morse Peckham discusses the relationship of directive-state and transactional theories of perception to literature in *Man's Rage for Chaos*, pp. 307 ff.

29. Jacques Derrida, in a discussion in *Languages of Criticism*, ed. Macksey and Donato, p. 272.

30. A detailed and interesting analysis of the concept of reality in literature is found in Chap. 2 of Käte Hamburger, *The Logic of Literature*, trans. Marilynn J. Rose, 2d rev. ed. (Bloomington: Indiana University Press, 1973).

MEANING, SIGNIFICANCE, & THE AUTHOR'S INTENTION

31. Hirsch, *Validity*, p. 31.

32. Ibid., p. 49.

33. E. D. Hirsch, Jr., "Three Dimensions of Hermeneutics," *New Literary History* 3, no. 2 (Winter 1972): 250. In this same issue, in a discussion, Quentin Skinner discriminates among three related uses of "meaning."

34. Michael Polanyi, "Life's Irreducible Structures," *Science*, June 21, 1968, p. 1311. Eliseo Vivas makes the same point when he says we see *through* language to an object. He also notes, however, that in a literary work the meaning is *in* the language to a degree not true of the language of science or practical communication. Presumably it is this quality in the language which, in combination with abstract meaning, enables a poem to evoke an intransitive rapt attention even in the absence of an illusion of life (see p. 24 above). For Vivas's comment, see his *Creation and Discovery: Essays in Criticism and Aesthetics* (New York: Noonday Press, 1955), p. 80.

35. Hirsch defines it as follows: "Significance . . . names a relationship between a meaning and a person, or a conception, or a situation, or indeed anything imaginable" (*Validity*, p. 8).

36. Frost, *Poetry*, p. 307.

37. Hirsch, *Validity*, pp. 164 ff.

38. As a combination of structure and tone, the poem presents in miniature the problem Ronald S. Crane analyzes in his essay on *Tom Jones*. See his *Critics and Criticism: Ancient and Modern* (Chicago: University of Chicago Press, 1952), pp. 631 ff. Cf. his *The Languages of Criticism and the Structure of Poetry* (Toronto: University of Toronto Press, 1953), p. 120.

39. Hilda Doolittle, *Collected Poems* (New York: New Directions,

1953), p. 81.

40. Holland, *Dynamics*, p. 25.

41. Doolittle, *Collected Poems*, p. 145. For a revelant psychoanalytic study of H.D., see Norman N. Holland, *Poems in Persons: An Introduction to the Psychoanalysis of Literature* (New York: W. W. Norton, 1973).

42. *New Republic*, October 6, 1973, p. 28.

43. Reported in Howard Gardner, *The Quest for Mind: Piaget, Lévi-Strauss, and the Structuralist Movement* (New York: Alfred A. Knopf, 1974), p. 239.

44. See Julius J. Marke, ed., *The Holmes Reader* (Dobbs Ferry: Oceana Publications, 1955), p. 67. See also Oliver Wendell Holmes, Jr., *The Common Law* (Cambridge: Harvard University Press, 1963), p. 242; for a comment on special situations in which consideration of intention is justified in the interpretation of a contract, see p. 261.

45. I suspect that, most fundamentally, an authorless text transforms one type of question about meaning into another type of question about meaning. This suspicion arises out of my admittedly debatable intuition (see p. 120) that ultimately the distinction between significance and meaning vanishes.

46. William Wordsworth, *The Poetical Works of William Wordsworth*, ed. Thomas Hutchinson (New York: Oxford University Press, 1933), p. 187.

47. For an introduction to the nature of the controversy see Monroe C. Beardsley, *The Possibility of Criticism*, Criticism Monographs series, no. 2 (Detroit: Wayne State University Press, 1970), pp. 27–29, 45–48.

48. For a comment on the relationship between the concept of intention and the concept of the intentional fallacy, see Hirsch, *Validity*, pp. 11 ff., and Marcus B. Hester, *The Meaning of Poetic Metaphor: An Analysis in the Light of Wittgenstein's Claim That Meaning Is Use* (The Hague: Mouton, 1967), pp. 147 passim.

49. Conrad H. Waddington, *Behind Appearance: A Study of the Relations between Painting and the Natural Sciences in This Century* (Cambridge: MIT Press, 1970), p. 116.

50. Hirsch, *Validity*, p. 207.

51. Quoted in Wayne Shumaker, *An Approach to Poetry* (Englewood Cliffs: Prentice-Hall, 1965), p. 54.

52. Ibid.

53. William Carlos Williams, *Selected Poems*, intro. by Randall Jarrell (New York: New Directions, 1963), p. 57.

54. Miller, *Poets of Reality*, p. 346.

55. The concept of the author's intention can also be subdivided further and in other ways. E.g., in a dramatic or ironic work additional steps may be introduced between the literal intention of an assertion and the au-

thor's real intention. See Hirsch, *Validity*, pp. 243–244. A distinction can also be made between an author's intention to write a literary work and to write a particular kind of literary work. See Roland Barthes's discussion of literary signs in *Writing Degree Zero*, trans. Annette Lavers and Colin Smith, preface by Susan Sontag (New York: Hill & Wang, 1968).

56. A similar idea is expressed in dialectical terms by Merle E. Brown: "It is poetry if its essence is poetic, and its essence is poetic if the subjective moment of the dialectic dominates over the objective and the synthetic moments of its experience" (*Neo-Idealistic Aesthetics: Croce-Gentile-Collingwood* [Detroit: Wayne State University Press, 1966], p. 163).

57. For an analysis of Bremond's view and a comparison to some other adherents of the concept of pure poetry, see Hester, *Meaning*, pp. 87 passim.

58. Edgar Allan Poe, *The Complete Works of Edgar Allan Poe*, intro. by Charles F. Richardson (New York: G. P. Putnam's Sons, 1902), p. 163.

59. There is currently a good deal of opposition among structuralists to the idea that the author's intention is a useful analytical concept. A characteristic statement of position is Barthes's ". . . the author is the only man, by definition, to lose his own structure and that of the world in the structure of language" (*Critical Essays*, p. 145). An especially interesting argument against the importance of the author's intention is found in Michel Foucault's discussion of the enunciative function in his *The Archaeology of Knowledge*, trans. A. M. Sheridan Smith (New York: Pantheon Books, 1972), pp. 88–105. Foucault believes discourses should be treated as "practices that systematically form the objects of which they speak" (p. 49) and as a "set of anonymous rules" (p. 210). Jonathan Culler asserts that "linguistics is the surest guide to the complex dialectic of subject and object that structuralism inevitably encounters" and continues that "any account of the system [i.e., linguistics] must be evaluated by its ability to account for our judgments about meaning and ambiguity" (*Structuralist Poetics*, pp. 30–31). Culler adds that linguistics cannot be applied automatically: the results must be checked. In this somewhat paradoxical joining together of a methodology which can account for human judgments and the need for a "discrimination pool" (to check results), Culler quite forthrightly indicates a basic problem in structuralism. If emphasis on the concept of structure is to be carried to the point of denying the significance of the author's intention, what counterargument will be found against that powerful current in contemporary thought which asserts that no methodology is autonomous, that language and mathematics are themselves fundamentally, as systems, ambiguous? (See p. 262 above.) A rich source of argumentation over the role of the author's intention, on both sides, is found in Mack-

sey and Donato, eds., *Languages of Criticism*; from this source I will quote a few examples of *support* of the importance of the author's intention. Lucien Goldmann takes a position quite unlike Culler's; Goldmann writes, "If applied to the meaning or content of a work, linguistic studies will surely fail to grasp the form of meaning" (pp. 108–109). He further asserts, "We sociologists and historians have been saying . . . that . . . there is still an *I* who *becomes*" (p. 148). Georges Poulet writes, ". . . it is not a question of going from the work to the psychology of the author, but of going back, within the sphere of the work, from the objective elements systematically arranged, to a certain power or organization inherent in the work itself, as if the latter showed itself to be an intentional consciousness" (p. 71). Neville Dyson-Hudson writes, ". . . we need a concept of the *individual* . . . as a sentient being with definable *interests*" (p. 238; italics in original). Charles Morazé says, "The author supplies a certain energy. . . . It is precisely on the way that this energy fixes itself to ideas, signs, and images in order to direct them toward the creation of new ideas, signs, and images that I want to insist" (pp. 28–29). Later, in the discussion following his paper, Morazé responds to a comment by Jacques Lacan with these words: "You said, 'what is the [kind of] energy which draws one's interest? What is this energy . . .?' I would say to you, 'Define for me what you mean by "interest" and you can immediately get from that my definition of "energy"!' " (p. 46). Morazé's concept of energy is related to the ideas of purpose and intention I myself have been using. Concerning the problem of intention, see Hayden V. White, "Historicism, History, and the Figurative Imagination," *History and Theory* 14, no. 4, supplement 14, pp. 48–67. Working from Jakobson's concept of metaphor and metonymy, White demonstrates the presence of "poetry" in a passage of historical writing; the role of intention in this passage, although not identified as such, becomes evident in the discussion on p. 57. Also see John R. Searle, "The Logical Status of Fictional Discourse," *New Literary History* 6, no. 2 (Winter 1975): 319–332. See especially p. 327. See several items in *New Literary History* 7, no. 1 (Autumn 1975), especially Alastair Fowler, "The Selection of Literary Constructs," pp. 39–55; Quentin Skinner, "Hermeneutics and the Role of History" (a discussion), pp. 209–239 (see particularly pp. 211–215); and Göran Hermerén, "Intention, Communication, and Interpretation," pp. 57–82 (see, however, Skinner's criticisms on pp. 211 and 214).

60. Joyce Carol Oates, *New Heaven, New Earth: The Visionary Experience in Literature* (New York: Vanguard Press, 1974), pp. 120–121.

61. Ibid.

62. Barrett John Mandel, "The University Context for the Teaching

of English," *CEA Critic* 33, no. 4 (May 1971): 11. This essay was reprinted in a longer version in the *AAUP Bulletin* 57, no. 3 (Autumn 1971): 334–340.

63. Sylvia Plath, *Crossing the Water* (New York: Harper & Row, 1971), p. 26.

64. In deference to phenomenological thought, it should be remembered that we are not discussing Plath's relationship to her own soliloquy but to signs or "indications" that she has presented to the natural world.

SERIES & PROBABILITY

65. Paul Goodman, *The Structure of Literature* (Chicago: University of Chicago Press, 1954). Quoted in James L. Kinneavy, *A Theory of Discourse* (Englewood Cliffs: Prentice-Hall, 1971), p. 347.

66. Kenner, *Pound Era*, p. 201.

67. My attention was called to the role of probability in literature many years ago by Archibald A. Hill. A lucid example of its application can be seen in his "Imagery and Meaning: A Passage from Milton, and from Blake," *Texas Studies in Literature and Language* 11, no. 3 (Fall 1969): 1093–1105.

68. *Time*, August 6, 1973, p. 70.

69. Both quotations are from "Mandelbaum on Historical Narrative: A Discussion," *History and Theory* 8, no. 2 (1969). The first is by Rolf Gruner, p. 283; the second by William Dray, p. 288.

70. Edgar Lee Masters, *Spoon River Anthology* (New York: Macmillan, 1916), p. 17.

71. Percy Bysshe Shelley, "Ode to the West Wind," in *The Norton Anthology of English Literature*, ed. Meyer H. Abrams et al., 2 vols., rev. ed. (New York: W. W. Norton, 1968), 2:417.

72. See J. D. O'Hara, "No Catcher in the Rye," *Modern Fiction Studies* 9 (Winter 1963–1964): 370–376; and Warren French, "Holden's Fall," *Modern Fiction Studies* 10 (Winter 1964–1965): 389. I am indebted to James Ellis for these citations.

73. Jerome D. Salinger, *The Catcher in the Rye* (Boston: Little, Brown, 1951), pp. 273–274.

74. Ezra Pound, *Literary Essays of Ezra Pound*, ed. with an intro. by T. S. Eliot (London: Faber & Faber, 1954), pp. 4–5.

75. Northrop Frye, *Anatomy of Criticism* (Princeton: Princeton University Press, 1957), p. 158.

76. Ezra Pound, *Gaudier-Brzeska: A Memoir* (New York: New Directions, 1970), p. 92.

77. Norwood Russell Hanson, *Patterns of Discovery: An Enquiry into the Conceptual Foundations of Science* (New York: Cambridge University Press, 1961), pp. 145–146.

78. William Stafford, "Existences," *Southern Review* 9, no. 1, n.s. (Winter 1973): 163.

79. Kenner, *Pound Era*, p. 403.

80. Culler, *Structuralist Poetics*, p. 174.

81. Kenelm Burridge, *Encountering Aborigines, a Case Study: Anthropology and the Australian Aboriginal*, Pergamon Frontiers of Anthropology series, no. 1 (New York: Pergamon Press, 1973), p. 223.

82. Andrew Marvell, *The Poems and Letters of Andrew Marvell*, ed. H. M. Margoliouth, 2 vols. (Oxford: Clarendon Press, 1967), 1:27.

83. Hester, *Meaning*, p. 24.

84. Clifford Collins, "Theme and Convention in *Wuthering Heights*," in *Wuthering Heights*, by Emily Brontë, ed. William M. Sale, Jr., Norton Critical ed. (New York: W. W. Norton, 1972), p. 315.

85. Michael Polanyi, "From Perception to Metaphor," a lecture given at the University of Texas at Austin in the spring of 1969.

LIMITED GENERALIZATIONS

86. Dylan Thomas, *The Collected Poems of Dylan Thomas* (New York: New Directions, 1953), p. 112.

87. Richard T. Weidner and Robert L. Sells, *Elementary Modern Physics*, 2d ed. (Boston: Allyn & Bacon, 1968), p. 3.

88. Two relevant concepts that I will not take space for but which deserve mention in passing are concrete universals and—from science—the principle of correspondence. Concerning the idea of a concrete universal, I feel compelled to agree with Geoffrey H. Hartman's observation, in *Beyond Formalism: Literary Essays, Nineteen Fifty-Eight to Nineteen Seventy* (New Haven: Yale University Press, 1972), p. 338, that calling art a concrete universal does not resolve an antinomy but merely restates it. In the classroom, I have found it impossible to discuss concrete universals without turning them into ordinary discursive universals. One of the more appealing ideas I have come across on this subject is that of the South African philosopher Errol Harris, who says the concrete universal is mind.

The principle of correspondence asserts that it must always be possible to reduce a new law to any earlier, more restricted law that it supersedes. Thus quantum physics can be reduced to classical physics, but classical physics cannot be expanded to quantum physics. The reduction of the broader law may be impractical, however. Examples of this difficulty are given in Alvin M. Weinberg, "The Axiology of Science," *American Scientist* 58, no. 6 (November–December 1970): 614. An approximation of what Weinberg's point would look like in literary terms is given in Richard Palmer Blackmur's well-known essay, "A Critic's Job of Work" (in *The Double Agent: Essays in Craft and Elucidation,* Arrow ed. [Gloucester: P. Smith, 1935], pp. 269–302). Blackmur argues that Van Wyck Brooks's theme of the private tragedy of the unsuccessful artist, taken over from Henry James, is so broad that application of it to concrete cases is meaningless.

89. Hartman, *Beyond Formalism,* p. 267.

90. Emile Zola, quoted in Ernst H. Gombrich, *Art and Illusion: A Study in the Psychology of Pictorial Representation* (New York: Pantheon Books, 1960), p. 64.

91. It seems unnecessary here to enter into the problem of defining style. An excellent survey of definitions appears in Kinneavy, *Theory of Discourse,* pp. 375 ff.

92. *Reader's Digest,* November 1973, p. 296.

93. See, e.g., William K. Wimsatt, Jr., and Cleanth Brooks, *Literary Criticism: A Short History* (New York: Alfred A. Knopf, 1957), pp. 378–380 passim. For a comparison to Russian formalism, see Jameson, *Prison-House of Language,* pp. 79 ff.

94. Matthew Arnold, *The Poetical Works of Matthew Arnold,* ed. C. B. Tinker and H. F. Lowry (New York: Thomas Y. Crowell, 1897), p. 213.

95. Brooks, "Irony," p. 732.

96. For further discussion of this kind of problem in Brooks's thought see Krieger, *New Apologists,* pp. 126 ff.

97. Abraham Kaplan, *The New World of Philosophy* (New York: Random House, 1961).

98. See Francis Fergusson, *The Idea of a Theater, a Study of Ten Plays: The Art of Drama in Changing Perspective* (Princeton: Princeton University Press, 1949), pp. 110 ff.

99. Max Delbrück, in George W. Beadle, "An Introduction to Science," in *Listen to Leaders in Science,* ed. Albert Love and James Saxon Childers (Atlanta: Tupper & Love, 1965), pp. 9–10.

DRAMA & INTENTION

100. For a general comment on the relationship between intention and feeling see p. 135.

101. Maxwell Anderson, *Essence of Tragedy and Other Footnotes and Papers* (New York: Russell & Russell, 1970), p. 7.

102. William Shakespeare, *King Lear,* act 3, sc. 4, lines 28–34.

103. For an account of the use Pound made of the original material in such "translations" as this, see Kenner, *Pound Era.*

104. Ezra Pound, *Selected Poems*, ed. with an intro. by T. S. Eliot (London: Faber & Faber, 1968), p. 131. In addition to the evidence of this note, Pound's recognition of the natural role of abstract meaning in poetry is indicated in such a passage as the following, from his *Literary Essays*, p. 51: "You wish to communicate an idea and its concomitant emotions, or an emotion and its concomitant ideas, or a sensation and its derivative emotions, or an impression that is emotive, etc. etc. etc."

105. Erich Auerbach, *Mimesis: The Representation of Reality in Western Literature*, trans. Willard Trask (Garden City: Doubleday, 1957), p. 227.

106. T. S. Eliot, *Collected Poems 1909–1962* (New York: Harcourt, Brace, 1963), p. 194.

107. See Squire, *Responses of Adolescents*, p. 47.

THE NONRATIONAL

108. David Littlejohn, "How Not to Write a Biography," *New Republic*, March 23, 1974, p. 25.

109. Frederick Crews et al., *Psychoanalysis and Literary Process* (Cambridge: Winthrop, 1970), p. 16.

110. Two interesting studies of the relationship between modern science and art are Wylie Sypher, *Loss of the Self in Modern Literature and Art* (New York: Random House, 1962), and Waddington, *Behind Appearance.*

111. Of course paradoxes had been encountered in physics before, but as far as I know none which gave so much evidence of being permanently irreconcilable, rather than being merely two elements in what would later prove to be a higher unity.

112. The principle of complementarity has sometimes, even by distinguished scholars, been confused with the different principle of correspondence. The latter was discussed in note 88, above. For further information a convenient source is Weidner and Sells, *Elementary Modern Physics.* Perhaps I should mention here, as I did not before, that the principle of correspondence is somewhat controversial. An attack upon certain uses of it can be found in Hanson, *Patterns of Discovery*, pp. 149 ff.

113. Josef M. Jauch, *Are Quanta Real? A Galilean Dialogue* (Bloomington: Indiana University Press, 1973), pp. 72–73. Jauch also provides a schematic sketch of equipment used in a related experiment (p. 80). See also Gerald Holton, "The Roots of Complementarity," *Daedalus* 99, no. 4

(Fall 1970): 1024–1026. Another account of this parallel slit experiment, together with some mathematical presentation, is found in Weidner and Sells, *Elementary Modern Physics*, pp. 187–188. Werner Heisenberg's *Physics and Philosophy: The Revolution in Modern Science* (New York: Harper & Bros., 1958), to which I will refer several times, has an account on pp. 51–52.

114. More precisely, the diffraction pattern found when both slits are open is more complex than can be accounted for by the superimposition of one single-slit diffraction pattern upon another.

115. Heisenberg, *Physics and Philosophy*, p. 179.

116. Weidner and Sells, *Elementary Modern Physics*, p. 181.

117. Heisenberg, *Physics and Philosophy*, p. 168. Cf. Niels Bohr: ". . . the exploration of the world of atoms was, as we have seen, to reveal inherent limitations in the mode of description embodied in common language developed for the orientation in our surroundings and the account of events of daily life" (*Essays, 1958–1962, on Atomic Physics and Human Knowledge* [New York: Interscience, 1963], p. 59).

118. Eugene Wigner, "Epistemology of Quantum Mechanics—Its Appraisal and Demands," *Psychological Issues* 6, no. 2, monograph 22 (1969): 34, 47.

119. Heisenberg, *Physics and Philosophy*, p. 179.

120. Bohr, *Essays, 1958–1962*, p. 14.

121. Holton, "Roots of Complementarity," p. 1019.

122. Niels Bohr, *Atomic Theory and the Description of Nature* (Cambridge: At the University Press, 1962), pp. 56–57. See also his *Essays, 1958–1962*, p. 61.

123. Ornstein, *Psychology of Consciousness*, p. 174. Cf. p. 178.

124. A reproduction can be seen in Holton, "Roots of Complementarity," p. 1021.

125. Genevieve Anderson, "The Sun Romps in the Morning."

126. Robert Bly, "Some Thoughts on Lorca and René Clair," *Fifties*, 3d issue (1959): 8.

127. An exception should be made to the idea that the "discontinuity" in the physical universe is alien to the human mind. Discontinuity may be a source of pleasure, as well as of apprehension. This possibility is interestingly explored by Alfred M. Bork in his "Randomness in the Twentieth Century," *Antioch Review* 27, no. 1 (Spring 1967): 40–61.

128. Alexander Craig Aitken, "The Art of Mental Calculation; with Demonstrations," Society of Engineers (London) *Journal and Transactions* 45, no. 4 (October–December 1954): 302.

129. See Frank Doggett, "The Transition from *Harmonium*: Factors in the Development of Stevens' Later Poetry," *PMLA* 88, no. 1 (January 1973): 122–131.

130. John Donne, "The Canonization," quoted in Krieger, *New Apologists*, pp. 12–13.

131. An excellent analysis from a psychoanalytic point of view of what I am calling the logic of emotion can be found in Holland's discussion of the "Tomorrow and tomorrow and tomorrow" speech from *Macbeth* in *Dynamics*, pp. 107–114.

132. Krieger, *New Apologists*, pp. 17–18.

133. Ibid., p. 20.

134. Donald Hall, "The Man in the Dead Machine," *Falcon* 4, no. 7 (Winter 1973): 6. Reprinted in Hall, *The Alligator Bride: Poems New and Selected* (New York: Harper & Row, 1969).

135. Gregory FitzGerald and Rodney Parshall, "An Interview with Donald Hall," *Falcon* 4, no. 7 (Winter 1973): 6.

136. Ibid., p. 7.

137. Ibid., p. 6.

138. Jay Bail and Geoffrey Cook, "With Robert Bly," *San Francisco Book Review*, no. 19 (April 1971), n.p. For this reference and for other suggestions concerning Bly, I am indebted to Frances Sage.

139. Bertrand Russell, *The Autobiography of Bertrand Russell* (Boston: Little, Brown, 1967), p. 77.

140. Samuel Taylor Coleridge, *Biographia Literaria*, ed. with his Aesthetical Essays by John Shawcross, 2 vols. (London: Oxford University Press, 1907), 2: 49–50.

141. Ornstein, *Psychology of Consciousness*, p. 171.

142. Timothy J. Teyler, preface to *Readings from Scientific American: Altered States of Awareness* (San Francisco: W. H. Freeman, n.d.), n.p. Cf. Weil, *Natural Mind*, p. 33: "I want to underline the idea that these [altered states of consciousness] form a continuum beginning in familiar territory."

143. André Breton, "Crises of the Object," in *Surrealists on Art*, ed. Lucy R. Lippard (Englewood Cliffs: Prentice-Hall, 1970), p. 53.

144. Ernest L. Hartmann, *The Functions of Sleep* (New Haven: Yale University Press, 1973), pp. 49–51.

145. Ibid., pp. 137–138.

146. Paul Ilie, *The Surrealist Mode in Spanish Literature* (Ann Arbor: University of Michigan Press, 1968), p. 5. Bly also recognizes the potential of surrealistic imagery for being disturbing, but feels that in a harmonious, integrated culture this element is controlled, in contrast to our own culture.

147. Hartmann, *Functions of Sleep*, p. 136.

148. For an analysis of Rimbaud's views see Wallace Fowlie, *Rimbaud* (Chicago: University of Chicago Press, 1965).

149. W. T. Lhamon, Jr., "On Rock," *New Republic*, March 2, 1974, p. 29.

150. Leon Edel, *The Psychological Novel 1900–1950* (New York: J. B. Lippincott, 1955), p. 214.

151. Weil, *Natural Mind*, p. 71.

152. D. H. Lawrence, quoted in Durr, *Poetic Vision*, p. 136.

153. Morse Peckham, "The Arts and the Centers of Power," *Proceedings of the Conference of College Teachers of English of Texas* 37 (September 1972): 16.

154. Pablo Neruda, *New Poems (1968–1970)*, ed., trans., and with an intro. by Ben Belitt (New York: Random House, 1972), p. 97.

SUMMARY OF PART TWO

155. Erwin W. M. Straus, *Phenomenological Psychology*, trans. Erling Eng (New York: Basic Books, 1966), p. 132.

Part Three. Validation

INTRODUCTION TO PART THREE

1. See pp. 122–123.

2. Philip G. Zimbardo, Gary Marshall, and Greg White, "Objective Assessment of Hypnotically Induced Time Distortion," *Science*, July 20, 1973, p. 282.

3. Jerome Frank, "Stimulus/Response: The Demoralized Mind," *Psychology Today* 7, no. 1 (April 1973): 31.

4. Alexander Gelley, "Setting and a Sense of World in the Novel," *Yale Review* 62, no. 2 (Winter 1973): 186.

5. Bruce Morrissette, "The Alienated 'I' in Fiction," *Southern Review* 10, no. 1 (Winter 1974): 17.

6. I realize Morrissette is describing a theory he rejects. I am not endorsing the theory, only noting the meaning given to the word "validating."

FORCED DECISIONS & THE CULTURAL ROLE OF THE CLASSROOM

7. Iser, *Implied Reader*, p. 290. A discussion of ways in which imaginative literature forces decisions upon the solitary reader is found in

Liane Norman, "Risk and Redundancy," *PMLA* 90, no. 2 (March 1975): 285–291.

8. Sigmund Koch, "Psychology and Emerging Conceptions of Knowledge as Unitary," in *Behaviorism and Phenomenology: Contrasting Bases for Modern Psychology*, ed. T. W. Wann (Chicago: University of Chicago Press, 1965), p. 26.

9. Sigmund Koch, "Value Properties: Their Significance for Psychology, Axiology, and Science," *Psychological Issues* 6, no. 2, monograph 22 (1969): 266.

10. Koch, "Psychology," p. 27.

11. John Steinbeck, *Tortilla Flat*, Modern Library ed. (New York: Random House, 1937), p. 11.

12. Ibid., p. 29.

13. Ibid., foreword. Cf. Elaine Steinbeck and Robert Wallsten, eds., *Steinbeck: A Life in Letters* (New York: Viking, 1975), pp. 88, 91.

14. It is helpful to compare the concept of perceptual display with Wittgenstein's concept of "seeing as," which he illustrates by reference to a drawing which can be seen as either a duck or a rabbit. He would no doubt object to the term perceptual display, since he quite reasonably asserts that seeing as is an act of will, whereas ordinary seeing or perception is unwilled. Basically, however, he believes that seeing as involves learning a technique, which is exactly the idea with which I am concerned. In continuing to use the term perceptual display for this learned technique I do not mean to question the validity of his distinction between perception and seeing as. See Ludwig Wittgenstein, *Philosophical Investigations*, trans. G. E. M. Anscombe (New York: Macmillan, 1958), pp. 193 ff.

15. George I. Sánchez and Howard Putnam, eds., *Materials Relating to the Education of Spanish Speaking People in the United States*, Texas Institute of Latin American Studies, no. 17 (Austin: University of Texas, 1959), p. 15. The particular bibliographer quoted is unidentified. He was one of a group of people working on the project. I would consider it a pleasure to hear from him.

16. Steinbeck, *Tortilla Flat*, pp. 201–202.

17. Martin Buber, *The Knowledge of Man: Selected Essays*, ed. Maurice Friedman, trans. Ronald Smith (New York: Harper & Row, 1965), p. 168.

MULTIPLE HYPOTHESES

18. Hannah Arendt, *On Violence* (New York: Harcourt, Brace, 1970), p. 6.

19. Ibid., p. 64.

20. Frank Riessman, *The Culturally Deprived Child* (New York: Harper & Row, 1962), pp. 49–50.

21. Robert K. Merton, *Social Theory and Social Structure*, enlarged ed. (New York: Free Press, 1968), pp. 482–483.

22. Benjamin DeMott, *Supergrow: Essays and Reports on Imagination in America* (New York: E. P. Dutton, 1969), pp. 61–71.

23. Malcolm Cowley, *The Faulkner-Cowley File: Letters and Memories* (New York: Viking Press, 1966), p. 40.

24. A commentary on the classroom as a model of the critical process and even of the existence of literary works can be found in Brown, *Neo-Idealistic Aesthetics*, pp. 169–170. Brown is describing Giovanni Gentile's aesthetics. Although I disagree with Gentile's position, Brown's presentation is unusually lucid and thought-provoking.

25. William H. Gass, *Fiction and the Figures of Life* (New York: Alfred A. Knopf, 1970), pp. 247–252.

26. Robert Rosenthal, "The Pygmalion Effect Lives," *Psychology Today* 7, no. 4 (September 1973): 62. The research reported in Robert Rosenthal and Lenore Jacobson, *Pygmalion in the Classroom: Teacher Expectation and Pupils' Intellectual Development* (New York: Holt, Rinehart & Winston, 1968), is only a small part of the work done by Rosenthal in the area of the effect of the social situation on individual performance. For a general survey of work in this field, see Neil Friedman, *The Social Nature of Psychological Research: The Psychological Experiment as a Social Interaction* (New York: Basic Books, 1967). For an attack on the Rosenthal-Jacobson study, and for a reply to the attack, see Janet Dixon Elashoff and Richard E. Snow, *A Case Study in Statistical Inference: Reconsideration of the Rosenthal-Jacobson Data on Teacher Expectancy* (Educational Resources Information Center, ED046892 [Stanford: Stanford University Center for Research and Development in Teaching, December 1970]), and Robert Rosenthal and Donald B. Rubin, *Pygmalion Reaffirmed* (Educational Resources Information Center, ED059247 [Cambridge: Harvard University, July 1971]).

27. Rosenthal, "Pygmalion Effect," p. 62.

28. See p. 88.

THE DISCRIMINATION POOL

29. Sigmund Koch, "Psychology and Emerging Conceptions of Knowledge as Unitary," in *Behaviorism*, ed. Wann, pp. 28–29.

30. Leon J. Goldstein, "Collingwood's Theory of Historical Knowing," *History and Theory* 9, no. 1 (1970): 24.

31. Michael Polanyi, in a discussion in *Psychological Issues* 6, no. 2, monograph 22 (1969): 46.

THE CONCEPT OF INTRINSIC GENRE

32. Stephen Crane, *Men, Women, and Boats*, ed. with an intro. by Vincent Starrett, Modern Library ed. (New York: Boni & Liveright, 1921), p. 23.

33. Hirsch, *Validity*, p. 86.

34. See ibid., p. 94: "It is the speaker who wills the particular intrinsic genre and, having done so, is constrained by its proprieties, but the interpreter can never be completely certain what that genre is and can never completely codify its proprieties in all their complexity."

35. I like a statement made by Albert Einstein on a related problem: "The theoretical attitude here advocated is distinct from that of Kant only by the fact that we do not conceive of the 'categories' as unalterable (conditioned by the nature of the understanding) but as (in the logical sense) free conventions. They appear to be *a priori* only insofar as thinking without the positing of categories and of concepts in general would be as impossible as is breathing in a vacuum" ("Reply to Criticisms," in *Albert Einstein*, ed. Schilpp, p. 674).

36. Steinbeck, *Tortilla Flat*, p. 11.

37. For an analysis of this aspect of the book see Stanley Alexander, "The Conflict of Form in *Tortilla Flat*," *American Literature* 40, no .1 (March 1968): 58–66.

38. I do not mean to suggest that identification of genre cannot be helpful in determining the interpretation of a specific episode. E.g., the inversion of values characteristic of the picaresque is a concept illuminating many episodes in this book, such as the voluntary efforts of thieves (Danny's friends) to provide food for a woman ignored by the establishment. This is an inverted version of the structure typified by the Biblical story of Ruth. My immediate purpose is to analyze an episode which is not determined by such a familiar structure.

39. Steinbeck, *Tortilla Flat*, pp. 65–66.

40. Ibid., pp. 204–205.

41. Jacques Lacan, "Of Structure as an Inmixing of an Otherness Prerequisite to Any Subject Whatever," in *Languages of Criticism*, ed. Macksey and Donato, p. 193.

MEDIATION & THE CONCEPT OF ORDER

42. I am sympathetically aware of the problems involved in the word

"vision," as pointed out by Murray Krieger. See his "Mediation, Language, and Vision in Literature," in *Interpretation: Theory and Practice*, ed. Charles S. Singleton (Baltimore: Johns Hopkins University Press, 1969), pp. 226 ff.

43. See p. 262. Some might claim Jacques Lacan or Jacques Derrida has achieved it.

44. For Piaget's discussion of the concept of structure see the first chap. of his *Structuralism* (trans. Chaninah Maschler [New York: Harper & Row, 1971]) and the last essay in his *Six Psychological Studies* (ed. David Elkind, trans. Anita Tenzer [New York: Random House, 1968]). In the latter he considers the problem of genesis. With the addition of "semblance" to his terminology of structure, part, and transformation, the basic concepts of Pt. One of my discussion—except for the idea of purpose—could effectively be given a structuralist formulation. For a review of the origins of the concept of structure as that concept appears in the structuralist movement see Emile Benveniste, *Problems in General Linguistics*, trans. Mary E. Meek, Linguistics series, no. 8 (Coral Gables: University of Miami Press, 1971), Chap. 8.

45. See, e.g., Chomsky, *Syntactic Structures*, pp. 93–94.

46. Burridge, *Encountering Aborigines*, p. 7.

47. Ibid., p. 12.

48. Kathleen Kinkade, *A Walden Two Experiment: The First Five Years of Twin Oaks Community* (New York: Wm. Morrow, 1973), p. 168.

49. Gov. William Bradford, *Of Plimmoth Plantation. From the original manuscript. With a report of the proceedings incident to the return of the manuscript to Massachusetts. Printed under the direction of the secretary of the Commonwealth, by order of the General Court* (Boston: Wright & Potter, 1898), p. 227.

50. Herbert Schneider, *The Puritan Mind* (Ann Arbor: University of Michigan Press, 1958), p. 66.

51. Ibid., p. 67.

52. Bradford, *Of Plimmoth Plantation*, pp. 163–164.

53. See Kinkade, *Walden Two Experiment*, pp. 167–169.

54. An explanation and a mathematical statement of the uncertainty principle can be found in Weidner and Sells, *Elementary Modern Physics*, pp. 188–189. The time-energy version was presented in Michael Polanyi and Eugene Wigner, "Bildung und Zerfall von Molekülen," *Zeitschrift für Physik* 33 (June 27, 1925): 429–434. Most basically, the uncertainty principle embraces all "canonically conjugate dynamic variables of the wave packet" (Robert M. Besançon, ed., *The Encyclopedia of Physics* [New York: Van Nostrand & Reinhold, 1974]).

55. Stephen G. Brush, "Should the History of Science Be Rated X?" *Science*, March 22, 1974, pp. 1164–1172.

56. Albert Einstein, quoted in Heisenberg, *Physics and Beyond*, p. 63.

57. Ibid., p. 78. Cf. Brush, "Should the History of Science Be Rated X?" p. 1167. For a comment on a comparable situation in the interpretation of a text, see p. 115 above.

58. Kuhn, *Structure of Scientific Revolutions*, p. 150.

59. See Einstein, "Reply," pp. 665 ff.

60. Wayne C. Booth, *A Rhetoric of Irony* (Chicago: University of Chicago Press, 1974), p. 38.

61. Frank Kermode, "A Modern Way with the Classic," *New Literary History* 5, no. 3 (Spring 1974): 425.

62. Mahatma Gandhi, quoted in Erik H. Erikson, *Gandhi's Truth: On the Origins of Militant Nonviolence* (New York: W. W. Norton, 1969), p. 342.

63. T. E. Lawrence, *The Seven Pillars of Wisdom* (New York: Doubleday, 1936), p. 176.

64. F. S. C. Northrop, *The Complexity of Legal and Ethical Experience* (Boston: Little, Brown, 1959), p. 185. On pp. 184 ff. Northrop compares the mediational system to other great legal systems.

65. For illustrations of ways in which this pure mediational system was modified in practice see E. Adamson Hoebel, "Status and Contract in Primitive Law," in *Cross-Cultural Understanding: Epistemology in Anthropology*, ed. F. S. C. Northrop and Helen H. Livingston (New York: Harper & Row, 1964), pp. 284–292.

66. True in one way, this analogy is false in another. The notion of the answering of questions only by probabilities is true, but the possible implication that the replacement is arrived at simply by observing "reality" is false. As already noted, the probabilities of quantum mechanics are in part created by the theory and therefore are only in part derived from observations that appear to confirm the theory. Anthropology, with its body of theory, is also related to mediation in this limited way. For further discussion of the analogy, see Northrop, *Complexity*, Chap. 12, and also pp. 19 passim of his intro. to Heisenberg, *Physics and Philosophy*.

67. Mediation of disputes between labor and capital, or between warring nations, may appear to contradict this statement, but reflection indicates that it does not. In both these instances, only small groups of people are directly involved in the negotiations. The problem involved in the principle of mediation for large groups can be seen by imagining that the Internal Revenue Service dispensed with all rules concerning federal income taxes and proposed to mediate with everyone in the country having an income.

68. I noted earlier that in quantum mechanics either the position or the velocity of a particle could be known. For calculations made for as-

sumed finite values of both velocity and position, see Weidner and Sells, *Elementary Modern Physics*, p. 188.

69. Lévi-Strauss, *Tristes Tropiques*, pp. 56–57.

70. A lucid discussion of this idea and of its relationship to ethical problems is found in the article by the mathematician Anatol Rapoport, "Escape from Paradox," *Scientific American*, July 1967, pp. 50–56.

SIGNIFICANT OTHERS

71. Harry Stack Sullivan, *Conceptions of Modern Psychiatry* (Washington, D.C.: Wm. Alanson White Psychiatric Foun., 1947), p. 20.

72. Daniel Bell, "The Disjunction of Culture and Social Structure: Some Notes on the Meaning of Social Reality," *Daedalus* 94, no. 1 (Winter 1965): 211.

73. Merton, *Social Theory*, pp. 356 ff.

74. Ibid., p. 269.

75. Peter Abrahams, quoted in Susan Anderson, "Something in Me Died: Autobiographies of South African Writers in Exile," *Books Abroad* 44, no. 3 (Summer 1970): 399.

76. Prof. Stuart Levine has not yet published the results of his work, and I am quoting, with his kind permission, from a personal letter in which he described his research. The rationale of his work is presented in his highly interesting article "Art, Values, Institutions, and Culture: An Essay in American Studies Methodology and Relevance," *American Quarterly* 24, no. 2 (May 1972): 131–165.

77. Lawrence Kohlberg, "Stage and Sequence: The Cognitive-Developmental Approach to Socialization," in *Handbook of Socialization Theory and Research*, ed. David A. Goslin (Chicago: Rand-McNally, 1969), pp. 379–382.

78. Lawrence Kohlberg, with Phillip Whitten, "Understanding the Hidden Curriculum," *Learning* 1, no. 2 (December 1972): 12. This is a popularized presentation of concepts which appear in the essay listed in note 77.

79. Kenneth A. Feldman and Theodore M. Newcomb believe college effects little change in people. Perhaps they are right; they certainly deserve respectful attention. But the concept of change is subtle and complex and possibly there is more to be learned about the matter. See their *The Impact of College on Students*, 2 vols., Higher Education series (San Francisco: Jossey-Bass, 1969). An unusually interesting study of changes in people's interpretation of literature resulting from classroom discussion is Wilson, *Responses of College Freshmen*. See also Fehl L. Shirley, "The Influence of Reading on Concepts, Attitudes, and Behavior," Ph.D.

diss., University of Arizona, 1966. A survey of the subject of attitude changes can be found in Charles A. Kiesler, Barry E. Collins, and Norman Miller, *Attitude Change: A Critical Analysis of Theoretical Approaches* (New York: John Wiley & Sons, 1969). The authors jokingly suggest that for the section in their book entitled "Behaviors and Attitudes" they should instead have used the title "The Relationship Between Certain Kinds of Behavior, Arbitrarily Designated by Most Social Scientists as Measures of Attitude, and Other Kinds of Behavior Which, According to Theory, Should be Influenced by the Attitude in Question" (p. 23).

80. Sullivan, *Conceptions*, p. 96.

81. A more methodical study had previously been made by Ella Sanders in "The Relationship between Verbal-Quantitative Ability and Certain Personality and Metabolic Characteristics," Ph.D. diss., University of Texas at Austin, 1958. For another version of this general problem see Roman Jakobson and Morris Halle, *Fundamentals of Language*, 2d rev. ed. (The Hague: Mouton, 1971), pp. 90–96.

82. American Society for Engineering Education, *General Education in Engineering: A Report of the Humanistic-Social Research Project* (Urbana: American Society for Engineering Education, 1956), p. 16.

83. André Lwoff, *Scientific American*, July 1968, p. 136.

84. An excellent review of relevant research is presented in Alan C. Purves and Richard Beach, *Literature and the Reader: Research in Response to Literature, Reading Interests, and the Teaching of Literature* (Urbana: National Council of Teachers of English, 1972). See also David Bleich, *Readings and Feelings: An Introduction to Subjective Criticism* (Urbana: National Council of Teachers of English, 1975).

85. Buber, *Knowledge*, p. 175.

86. Ibid., pp. 176–177.

87. Ibid., pp. 28–31.

88. This concept is discussed on pp. 54–55.

VALIDATION

89. Burridge, *Encountering Aborigines*, p. 151.

INDEX

Abrahams, Peter, 304–305
Abrams, Meyer: *The Mirror and the Lamp*, 91, 282
Abstraction(s)
 Cleanth Brooks's objection to, 88, 172, 281
 difficulty in distinguishing from concrete, 202
 in Hemingway's work, 101
 historical sources of opposition to, 91
 meanings of, 103–110
 and nonrational literature, 195–227
 and perceptual displays, 249–250
 and perceptual hypothesis, in *Tortilla Flat*, 273
 pure, 201
 relation to concrete, 107, 109
 relation to directive-state theory of perception, 108
 vs. spontaneity in creation of poetry, 105
 transformation into elements, 28
 value of, in literature, 146, 149
Abstractness of American law, 292
Abstract reasoning, a fictional character's as an element in a semblance, 70
Adams, Henry, 94
 History of the United States during the Administrations of Thomas Jefferson and James Madison, 99
 scientific historian, 97–99
 theory of writing compared to Hemingway's, 101
Aesthetic emotion, and mathematics, 74
Aesthetic experience as source of transcendence of ego, 73
Aesthetic judgments, 314
Affect
 consequences of lack in classroom, 311
 meaning of, 310–311
 relationship to cultural goals of classroom, 313
Aitken, Alexander Craig, 206–208, 222
Alexander, Stanley, 342 n. 37
Alger, Horatio, 29, 31, 34
 The Young Acrobat, 26, 27
Ambiguity, 194

of author's intention, i, 137
American Society for Engineering Education, 310
An American Tragedy (Dreiser), 53, 279
Anabasis (Perse), 105
Anderson, Genevieve: "The Sun Romps in the Morning," 204–205
Anderson, Maxwell: *The Essence of Tragedy*, 180
Andre, Carl: *Joint*, 40
Anshen, Ruth Nanda, 80, 227
Anthropology
 as a habit of mind, 284, 286, 287, 288, 292, 299
 as a science, 292
Antiintellectualism, 141
Arendt, Hannah, 257
 On Violence, 248
Aristotelian concept of purpose, 37–38
Aristotelian dichotomy, substitution of alternatives for in theoretical physics, 52
Aristotle, 33, 47
 Poetics, 23, 179
Arithmetic, mental, compared to production of sentences, 208
Armstrong, Edward, 162
Arnold, Matthew: "Dover Beach," 171–175
Art
 as anything before which individual adopts aesthetic attitude, 80
 and retreat from generalizations, 226
Assent, intellectual, 185
 and "Dover Beach," 175
 emotional factors in, 314
 to a literary work, 167
Auerbach, Erich, 187
Authorless text, 123–127
 advantages and disadvantages of concept, 124–127
 types of, 123–124
Autonomous discipline, 260–261
 history as, 261
Autonomy vs. the referential in poetry, 61, 65
Awareness, states of, 221–222